CW01096045

DIVINE

ABOUT THE AUTHOR

Anthon St Maarten is an international spiritual advisor, intuitive consultant and destiny coach. He is also a sought-after inspirational speaker, metaphysical teacher and spiritual author.

Anthon has been consulting as a professional psychic medium since 2004 and in his home country he has established himself as a trusted advisor to many, including prominent business leaders, celebrities and politicians. He is the owner of a leading-edge metaphysical consulting service aimed at individual and organizational transformation, and his services are offered on-site, in-person or by phone, as well as online via video conferencing. He offers a variety of psychic and mediumship readings, as well as teaching, consulting and coaching services.

He is the author of a popular spirituality blog titled *The S Word* and he is also the content editor for *PsychicBloggers.com*. Anthon has appeared as guest on various radio and television shows, and he was one of the original producers and co-hosts for *The Psychic View* on Psychic Access Talk Radio. Anthon is currently the only psychic medium on the African continent listed on Bob Olson's *Best Psychic Directory*.

Anthon is a hereditary psychic empath and clairvoyant medium. He was born with the psychic legacy of his Celtic ancestors, which he inherited from his paternal grandmother. He holds a BA degree in Psychology from the University of Pretoria (UP), with post-graduate studies completed at the University of South Africa (UNISA). Anthon currently lives in Gauteng, South Africa.

For further information visit www.anthonstmaarten.com.

DIVINE LIVING

The Essential Guide To Your True Destiny

ANTHON ST MAARTEN

INDIGO | HOUSE

Published by Indigo House, South Africa. If you wish to contact the author or would like more information about this book, please submit enquiries via the author's website at www.anthonstmaarten.com.

ISBN: 978-0-9870441-0-5 (Paperback)
ISBN: 978-0-9870441-1-2 (Hardcover)
ISBN: 978-0-9870441-2-9 (Kindle Edition)
BISAC: OCC014000 Body, Mind & Spirit / New Thought

Dedicated to those Indigo Souls
of my generation who may have lost their way
May you find the wisdom to know your path
and the courage to spread your wings

In memory of
Hilet de Klerk,
Jamey Rodemeyer
and Amy Winehouse

If we were talking to you on your first day of physical life experience, we would say to you, "Welcome to Planet Earth. There is nothing that you cannot be, or do, or have. You are a magnificent creator. And you are here by your powerful and deliberate wanting to be here. Go forth, giving thought to what you are wanting, attracting life experience to help you decide what you want and once you have decided, giving thought only unto that."

~ Esther-Abraham Hicks ~

CONTENTS

ACKNOWLEDGMENTS

Yarden יַרְדֵי for your guidance, protection and wisdom
May we continue to strive for the highest good
and be of service to humanity.

Clients, students and contemporaries for encouraging
me to write this book, and for all your feedback,
successes and suggestions I now share with the world.
May this book serve to guide and inspire you on your
continued journey towards enlightenment.

Family and friends for unconditionally supporting me
even when you do not always understand
exactly what it is I do for a living.

Jacques for sharing my enthusiasm and
for all the late night cups of coffee.

Chaka, Boom-Boom and Slippers for tirelessly
fetching the ball when I needed to take a break.

Those peers and custodians who in my youth
excluded me, thus preventing me from growing up
mediocre. Thank you for always making me feel
different. You have no idea how right you were.

To all the crazy ones, misfits, rebels, troublemakers;
the round pegs in the square holes, the ones who see
things differently. Thank you for pushing the human
race forward and for changing things.

PREFACE

Are you truly happy? It's quite normal and perfectly understand-able if you are not. These days many people feel their lives leave much to be desired. Discontent truly is the disease of our time, and at times it feels as if our world is increasingly spinning out of control.

Many of us are wandering aimlessly through our lives. Not only do we have to deal with our personal issues and the demands of our hectic modern lives, but we also face the challenges of an increasingly cynical and violent society, as well as a planetary environment that appears to be in serious jeopardy. To find true peace, joy and purpose amid all this havoc seems like an impos-sible dream.

Many of us also abandon dogmatic religion, because it leaves us disappointed and disillusioned; it no longer provides the direction or comfort we so desperately seek. To add insult to injury, main-stream science keeps telling us that there is no special meaning or purpose to our lives. The majority of scientists and academics proclaim that we are nothing more than 'highly evolved animals', and that there is nothing more to our daily reality than that which can be physically observed using the classic five senses (unless it is some abstract formula or piece of lab equipment).

Most members of the scientific community also maintain that the Universe is entirely random, and that mankind's silly belief in the existence of a Spiritual Realm, God or the Afterlife is utter superstitious madness. And suggesting that the Cosmos may in some way be 'conscious' is to them nothing more than ignorant insanity and scientific heresy. They disregard the spiritual beliefs and paranormal experiences of millions of people all around the globe, writing it off as mere "figments of the imagination", or they simply attribute it to the mental delusions of the more unsophisticated and uneducated among us.

For some this post-modern lack of meaning and purpose is more troubling than for others, especially if you have a constant 'inner knowing' that you were meant to do something significant with your life, but you just cannot figure out exactly what. It really does become a frustrating struggle when there is this voice within calling you forward, but you just don't know where you should be going, or what you should be doing.

Is your life also such a worst case scenario? Well, if that is the case, rest assured that you are in extremely good company. I am no stranger to a miserable, meaningless existence. There was a long period in my own life when I had no passion for living, and I had exhausted all options to find a cure for my growing desperation. The prognosis was really grim at the time. I had absolutely no hope for the future, and in my self-absorbed despair the last thing on my mind was consideration for my fellow man, or the future well-being of our planet.

I spent many years chasing academic achievement, career success, material status and romantic fulfillment. Despite a decent level of success, both personally and professionally, my early adult life increasingly became a really wretched affair. I felt I was drifting aimlessly in the dark ocean of a futile existence.

In those days I had the growing desire to break free from the restrictions of my lackluster, superficial existence. All the things I thought would make me happy, when I was younger, meant nothing to me anymore. I was yearning for a true purpose, seeking a meaningful reason to live.

Sure, there were times when I felt I had some sense of direction, but none of my pursuits ever delivered the lasting joy, peace or contentment I was seeking. Like many people, I was chasing 'fool's gold' - the material trappings of the *mirage* we call 'post-modern living'. I felt lost and my life wasn't going anywhere.

So, I know all too well what it feels like to be that restless, adrift and deeply unhappy. Trust me, I know.

Looking back I realize now that my predicament should not have come as a surprise. I understand now that the Universe first sent me a tiny pebble, then I was struck by a rock, and eventually, because I still didn't get the message, I ended up under a ton of bricks! I should have seen the signs and followed the clues.

The tale of my own spiritual awakening and finding my true life purpose is a profound example of how disconnected one can become from your spiritual origins. It took a series of traumatic, life-changing events to ultimately lead me back to my spiritual path, which finally empowered me to embrace my natural psychic abilities and accept my true calling in life.

There were many signs and synchronicities over the years, of which some were quite exceptional, but I only managed to connect all the dots much later in my life. My Divine Self was reaching out to me constantly, but I did not heed the call. My bruised Ego had taken over at a very young age due to a traumatic childhood, and ever since it had been making all the decisions in my life. I was oblivious to the voice of Divine Providence that was trying its utmost to steer me towards my true destiny.

As a gifted, unusual child, growing up in the chauvinistic, prejudiced society that was South Africa under Apartheid, my youth was traumatic, painful and confusing. I guess you could say I am one of those individuals who somehow succeeded despite my background. Mark Twain's famous words, "I have never let my schooling interfere with my education" is probably the most apt way to describe the complete disaster that was my formal education. From an academic perspective I did well, especially in high school, but in terms of my emotional, psychological and spiritual well-being it was a colossal disaster.

My school environment was shaped by a government policy known at the time as "Christelike Nasionale Opvoeding" (Christian National Education). This restrictive policy was geared towards social engineering and allowed very little religious or ideological freedom. Even the Catholic faith was considered suspicious. We were expected to embrace the Calvinistic and highly chauvinistic values that were forced upon us. We were also programmed not to question authority, and to comply with the prescribed cultural expectations of the community. In this environment I was misunderstood, excluded and bullied, to the extent that I soon began to view my psychic heritage as a shameful secret, as some kind of personal disability. I fervently began to resist my extra sensory experiences and my fascination with all things metaphysical. Later, in my teenage years and early adulthood, I sadly succeeded in blocking most of my psychic awareness from my consciousness, although I could never really suppress it entirely. It became the curse I had to endure, my "cross I had to bear".

During my early adulthood I went through a long-drawn-out Dark Night of the Soul, from which I was finally released by a profound spiritual awakening less than a decade ago. During those difficult years I often thought how fantastic it would be if someone could write a book that would help someone like me find comfort, purpose and meaning in their life. None of the inspirational self-help books I read at the time truly provided the answers I was seeking. Or maybe they did, but I just was not ready for the message? Little did I know that I would someday write exactly such a book myself, and that all the challenges and obstacles I was facing in my life would one day serve as a template of insight to serve others.

Today, my diverse life experiences empower me daily in my work with people all over the world. It enables me to support others in their pursuit of spiritual connection, happiness, joy, peace, healing, and forgiveness, as well as their quest to manifest true abundance, and achieve their goals and dreams. Everything I have learned from working with my clients and students, as well as from my own life experiences and the many mistakes I made, ultimately became the foundation for this book.

The contents of *Divine Living: The Essential Guide To Your True Destiny* developed over several years and came from three major sources of inspiration: my own spiritual journey; the numerous success stories and experiences of my clients; and the channeled metaphysical guidance I received through extra sensory perception, dreamwork, daily meditation and intuitive mindful living.

The information you will encounter on these pages goes beyond New Thought Philosophy and Esoteric Mysticism, because this manuscript also grew out of the real life insights, the tried-and-tested methods and the practical techniques I have been applying for several years with great success in my practice as spiritual advisor, intuitive consultant and destiny coach.

The more I learned from my work with so many diverse people from different cultures and religious backgrounds, the larger the body of information became that I felt a need to share with new clients and students. In recent years I increasingly began to realize that my new clients would benefit much from some kind of 'guide-book' or 'manual' that contains all the essential information I know they will need on their path towards personal transformation and spiritual growth. I often do not have enough time to share everything with them that I feel they need to succeed in the long-term. This need to share more with them inspired the genesis of this book.

My quest with all my writings is also to liberate others from dogma, prejudice and skepticism. My early life experiences compel me to search for deeper answers, and continue to inspire me to research, teach and write. The confusion and frustration I had to endure as a child, often due to the ignorance, fear and intolerance of others, made me vow to learn and share as much as I could about alternative spirituality, psychic phenomena, mediumship, parapsychology, divination and metaphysics.

If I can spare just one sensitive child unnecessary trauma, or inspire just one adult to come out of the 'spiritual closet', or save just one Indigo soul's life from ending in tragedy, then the bewilderment I had suffered as a child will be worth it. It is my hope and wish that this book will do exactly that.

May the energy of the Divine Self inspire you and the Light of the Soul direct you. Namaste.

Anthon St Maarten
Gauteng, South Africa
May 2012

HOW TO USE THIS BOOK

Divine Living is not a religion or a belief system. Neither is it a method, a process, or a set of universal laws, rules or dogmatic principles. It is not something you can attain through regular practice or study. It does not demand some form of deep devotion or sacrifice. It is not the beginning of anything, or a means to an end. The capacity for Divine Living is not something you must acquire or become, it is simply who you already are. To live the Divine Life you originally intended is your very reason for being, in this life and the next.

The only reason why so many of us are not living the Divine Life is because we have forgotten who we really are. We have lost touch with our spiritual roots; we cannot recall with clarity why we came here in the first place. Many of us have yet to remember our true origins and our innate spiritual heritage. Awakening to our Divine nature is the missing puzzle piece that unlocks the floodgates for Divine Living. To live a Divine life is to have clear sense of purpose, to savor the bliss of the present moment, to experience the joyful surrender of the Ego, and to live in seamless harmony with yourself, and with others, the environment and the Laws of the Universe.

In his book *The Phenomenon of Man*, Pierre Teilhard de Chardin, a visionary French philosopher and Jesuit priest, made a profound, but simple statement: "We are not human beings having a spiritual experience; we are spiritual beings having a human experience." These words have since been paraphrased and quoted by many seekers, teachers and gurus. Its inherent truth and wisdom is so profound that it has even been misattributed to acclaimed authors like Wayne Dyer and Stephen Covey, who among many others have both quoted it in their work. Even the most skeptical among us cannot help but pay attention when we hear or read these simple words. Even if you are a confirmed nihilist or atheist, you cannot stop yourself from contemplating the implications of this statement, even if only for a moment. It resonates with most people, because it resurrects an intuitive recognition and faint recollection of who they truly are.

The Ascended Masters, Prophets, Gurus, Philosophers, Visionaries and all of their disciples, fans and followers may have been on to something all along. Like it or not, it appears each and every one of us is required to become 'a mystic', or an 'earthbound deity' in our own way. And we do have that responsibility towards our fellow man. It is no longer only about ourselves. The time has come for us to accept that we are indeed our brother's keeper.

Divine Living: The Essential Guide To Your True Destiny aims to remind you of your true origins as a spiritual being and disclose the purpose of your spiritual mission in this lifetime. It endeavors to clarify the original intention of your current human incarnation and empower you with spiritual inspiration, metaphysical insight, scientific support and practical guidance towards understanding your Divine nature and manifesting a purposeful, fulfilling life. The ultimate goal is for you to reclaim your sacred right to a Divine Life.

You were not meant to come into this world to suffer, to endure agony, or to languish in any kind of physical or psychological torment. Neither is life on planet Earth meaningless or random. You did *not* incarnate into this time-space reality to choose self-destruction over hope, or to face a deficient, disadvantaged existence, riddled with all manner of emotional pain, loneliness, depression, disease or hardship.

Quite the contrary.

This book will guide you towards discovering the true meaning and purpose of your life. You will learn how to grab hold of the reigns of your true destiny, so that you will ultimately lead a truly charmed life and make a real difference in our world. By showing you a different perspective on reality, human life, and the world as you know it, you will be equipped with the basic tools you need to create a truly awakened and abundant Divine Life.

This book has its roots in my work as a spiritual teacher and destiny coach, and was inspired by my own spiritual awakening, as well as the many success stories and experiences of my clients over the years. You will find among these pages many practical guidelines, lifestyle tips, metaphysical tools and spiritual self-care exercises. I felt it my duty to share what I had learned thus far on my own journey, in the hope that it would open the door for many other people who may be looking for meaning and purpose in their life, or who may be going through a Dark Night of the Soul like I did. If you currently feel unable to manifest what you truly want in life; or if you believe that your life is meaningless; or if your feel that you are stuck, and that life is a constant struggle; or if you keep repeating the same old destructive patterns in your life, making the same mistakes over and over again, then read on. Your brand new life awaits you.

Part I: Awakening Your Divine Being aims to elicit a spiritual awakening, or to deepen your existing spiritual awareness. In this section you will discover that you are actually a *spiritual being having a physical experience*, not the other way around. You will be introduced to your Divine origins and you will discover why and how you became disconnected from your true spiritual nature.

Not only does this section aim to increase your consciousness and understanding of your true spiritual nature, but it also intends to reconnect you with your Divine Self and your Higher Consciousness. You will learn who and what your Divine Self is and how you can easily make contact and realign with your inner Divinity, because this is the foundation for creating a Divine Life of purpose, meaning, prosperity and joy.

Part II: Achieving Your Soul Purpose explores the Divine Life concept and examines the art of Divine Living. First you will discover the seven habits of a Divine lifestyle, as well as the seven basic truths or guidelines for conduct, known as the 'maxims' of Divine Living. These maxims will hopefully become your personal mantras to keep you on track towards fulfilling your *Life Plan*. By always being mindful of the seven habits and the seven maxims of Divine Living, you will successfully overcome and transcend many life lessons that will cross your path, and you will attract many more opportunities for soul growth, in order to achieve your *Soul Purpose*. These fundamental truths are also vital in your quest towards the ultimate accomplishment of your *Life Calling*, for it would be impossible to be truly of service to others and the environment if you did not apply these guidelines as your foundation.

This section features specific, simple practical changes you can introduce to your current lifestyle and daily routine, which will uplift and empower you as a spiritual being and create a more conducive environment for establishing a Divine Life. It also outlines exercises and techniques for transforming your *thoughts*, evolving your *emotions*, sharpening your *senses* and increasing your *intuition*. These guidelines and exercises are all designed to transcend the *Divine Disconnect* and to close the gap between the conscious and unconscious, the seen and the unseen, the rational and the intuitive, the spiritual and the physical. The aim is to empower you towards a more awakened and fulfilling life, and to ultimately enable you to achieve your Soul Purpose.

Part III: Accomplishing Your Life Calling brings together all the skills and techniques you have acquired in the previous section for the purpose of *deliberately creating*, *attracting* and *manifesting* the abundance and prosperity you need to lead a joyous and fulfilling life and to find your true mission and purpose in this lifetime.

The first chapter is aimed at retraining you in some of the 'superhero powers' you lost touch with when you gave up magical thinking in your childhood to enter the Divine Disconnect. In order to master physical survival in this time-space reality, and to gather data for your future Life Calling, you had to relinquish your awareness of your innate metaphysical ability. Once the data gathering process is complete and you are ready to embark on the next stage in your physical life experience, it becomes time for you to reclaim this sacred birthright. If applied intelligently and for the greater good it will enable you to lead a truly charmed and prosperous life. You were born to be a powerful co-creator within this time-space reality and you can be, do or have anything you wish or desire. The chapter on the art of manifesting shows you how to achieve that.

The second part chapter looks at practical guidelines for you to identify, pursue, manifest and accomplish your true *Life Calling*. You did not come into this lifetime to do a meaningless or mundane job, or to follow a career that is not your true heart's desire. Divine Living demands that we stay true to our original Life Plan and this includes accomplishing your intended Life Calling or Life Purpose. You came here to perform a particular task, to leave behind a certain legacy or to make a specific contribution to the evolution of humanity and the betterment of the planet, as well as the expansion of the Conscious Universe. This final section aims to guide you back to what it is you should be doing with the rest your life.

Part IV: The New Age of Conscious Evolution establishes the scientific and cultural context in which we find ourselves at this juncture in human history. If you are somewhat doubtful of your spiritual origins, or if you struggle to fully embrace concepts like 'manifesting' or the 'Conscious Universe', or if you simply have a questioning mind, I suggest you delve into this section of the book first, before you read the preceding three sections.

There is growing need for a *paradigm shift* that will help us rise above the limitations of our current worldview. Several scientific discoveries and new concepts about reality and consciousness support the need for a new approach to how we see ourselves and life in general. We have created many false beliefs based on a limited, concrete view of our world, and now we are beginning to discover through an emerging New Science that many of the most ancient wisdom traditions may hold more truths and insights than we ever realized. It is no longer a good idea to rely on outdated, answers and stale solutions to our modern day questions and future problems. Neither is it sensible in this day and age to blindly follow general public opinion, the mass media and main-stream scientific research funded by big business.

This section provides you with an alternative worldview, free from the false beliefs and fear-based propaganda of the 'old system'. We are currently experiencing a global spiritual awaken-ing that many believe will ultimately change life as we know it. The fact that you are reading this book is very likely due to your own growing awareness of this change or 'shift', and it will help you gain a deeper understanding of what this universal awakening of mankind really means.

As a species we have shifted into a new era where we are increasingly becoming conscious of our own evolution and that we are able to direct or control our own destiny. Until mainstream thinking catches up to the growing New Thought or New Age movement, which has gradually been emerging over the past century, it may be in our best interest as individuals to follow our own inner guidance in how we choose to live our lives for the greater good. To do this with greater confidence it is important that we gain some basic level of understanding of the global context in which we find ourselves, and that we become familiar with the most prominent philosophical concepts and scientific findings that support our quest for an alternative outlook and a more spiritually purposeful lifestyle.

Please note, however, that this book is a metaphysical self-help book that aims to inspire and uplift. It does not pretend to offer conclusive scientific evidence for any theory or philosophy; neither does this book pretend to be an academic work. I do not consider myself a scientist and I have not made any particular effort to analyze in-depth or discuss in detail the vast body of research data represented. I have also not provided annotations as one would in an academic work. This book provides sufficient information to enable the truly curious or academic reader to do additional research on the theories and studies mentioned, should they desire to do so. A list of sources and reference for suggested further reading is also provided at the end.

The aim in this work is also not to prove anything from a scientific perspective. Instead the information in this book aims to inform and enlighten with regards unconventional views and perspectives of the physical world, in the hope that increased awareness of alternative scientific information and different ways of thinking will support the reader in shaping a liberated new perspective of reality.

In the process of changing the way we live, knowledge is indeed power. Due to the manner in which we are conditioned from a young age, to adopt the generally accepted worldview of our time, many of us find it difficult to identify false beliefs we may currently hold, or to adopt unorthodox views that contradict what we have been taught or what we are expected to believe. As spiritual pioneers we simply can no longer afford to remain ignorant on these matters. We can no longer allow others to think for us.

Throughout other parts of this book you will also find brief references to scientific findings and philosophical concepts that support the premise of Divine Living, which I hope will inspire you to a new way of life and a new perspective on the world. The more knowledgeable and informed we are, the more we are able to withstand the pressure of popular culture and public opinion. This is vital during this time of our transition as a global community towards a new worldview.

Remember however that there is no need for you to try and use the information in this book to convince or recruit anyone else into your way of thinking, or living. Coercing and influencing others against their will is the old way of doing things. In the new age your first priority is to *change your own way of being,* in order to change your own energetic vibration. Become the change you wish to see in the world. If you raise your own vibration to a more positive and constructive frequency, it will automatically influence those around you for the better.

INTRODUCTION

If you knew your potential to live a life of joy, purpose and contentment, you would never again spend another moment living any other way. If you recognized your inherent ability to conceive and achieve an awakened and abundant life, beyond your wildest expectations, you would not waste another minute holding on to the second best 'reality coma' that constitutes your post-modern existence. Within you looms the potential for authentic happiness so infinitely beyond everyday measure, or common human understanding, that you will never again be willing to settle for anything less.

To unbolt this astonishing, 'superhuman' potential within you, you won't require any special tools, or elite training, or secret knowledge. It is not a talent or skill you need to develop, based on hours of hard work, sacrifice and self-discipline. It is not an ability you can acquire through some secret covert method or peculiar procedure. Neither is it a quality that you can attain after years of selfless sacrifice and religious devotion, or by spending large sums of money to learn from experts, mystics and gurus.

In fact, quite the opposite is true.

This magnificent power within you is who and what you already are as a unique Soul and incarnated Spiritual Being. Each and every one of us has this innate Creative Power and Source of love, joy and purpose within. It is known as the *Divine Self*. It is your Celestial Inner Beingness, your Eternal Consciousness, and it is at your disposal right now - ready and waiting.

Your Divine Self has always been there; geared up to be put to very good use. All you have to do is to unleash this incredible Spiritual Force that is the 'original, real you', and the rest will follow. Author Sanaya Roman captures it perfectly when she writes that joy is an all-encompassing attitude.

You are meant to live a joyful life. You are here to create your dreams; you can create a heaven on earth for your-self. You deserve to have the best life you can imagine. Do what you love and follow your heart in every area of your life, for as you do, you are aligning with the Higher Will.

This is in essence what *Divine Living* is about; it is a self-help manual for reconnecting with your Divine Self, and for reclaiming your birthright to enjoy a truly Divine Life. These pages aim to empower and inspire you to finally start living the connected and blissfully abundant life you had always intended for yourself, since long before you were born.

This book is also a 'survival guide' to help you successfully navigate the dawning of a new age in human consciousness. It is an instruction manual for effectively managing the growing pains associated with the current evolution of our species, and the imminent paradigm shift it will require. Some call it The Shift, or Ascension, or the Great Awakening. Barbara Marx Hubbard calls it The Age of Conscious Evolution, which is the term I prefer, for the next stage in our evolution is what defines the New Age.

This book will help you to move one step ahead in this global wave of change and stay on top of the inevitable transformation of our species, and our world. The coming evolutionary leap will touch the lives of everyone in some profound way. Hopefully this book will inspire you to be a pioneer and a true leader in these trying times, instead of merely being a passive follower, or a powerless wallflower.

A New System Of Seamanship

Before we continue this voyage into your new Divine Life, I wish to make it clear that this book is not about any dogmatic belief system or alternative religion. It is not my aim to get you to accept or believe anything. It is instead my aim to revive that which you already are, by reminding you of your *true potential as a spiritual being*. If it was merely my goal to change your religious convic-tions, I would be contradicting my own belief that diversity is a driving force behind true spiritual awareness and the key to our future conscious evolution as a species.

There are many names by which people worship or embrace that which is Divine. In Zoroastrianism, for example, God has a long list of 101 different names, starting with *Yazad* (Worthy of Worship) and ending with *Frash-Gar* (Refresher of the Soul with Progress). Apart from the one billion non-religious people in the world today, including agnostics and atheists, the rest of us all pray to the Divinity, or God, or Deities of our personal choosing. We worship in different ways and there is in essence nothing wrong with that. We must each believe and worship as we feel guided, while also respecting the beliefs of others.

If at any point you encounter anything in this book that may cause you to consider a 'burning at the stake', or at the very least the need to make a concerned phone call to your pastor, rabbi, priest or imam, rest assured that it is not my intention to question, confront or devalue anyone's belief system or religion.

As you progress through these pages you will see that being true to oneself is an essential component of the art of Divine Living. In fact, *individuation* is an essential pre-requisite for Divine Living. We are not supposed to all be the same, feel the same, think the same, or believe the same. The key to continued expansion of our Universe lies in *diversity*, not in conformity or coercion. It is therefore not my intention to change anyone's religious views or personal convictions, no matter what their beliefs may be.

Deepak Chopra writes in *Why Is God Laughing? The Path to Joy and Spiritual Optimism,* "God descends to earth like fresh spring rain, and at every level his grace is received differently. For some it feels like love, for others like salvation. It feels like safety and warmth at one level, like coming home at another."

If you are a true seeker you will probably find the contents of this book to be compatible with most, if not all religious persuasions and spiritual traditions. If anything, this book should ideally persuade you to appreciate your own religion of choice all the more and hopefully see its teachings in a newer, broader and more meaningful perspective. In fact, if your current belief system can support you in any way to create a better life for yourself using some of all of the content in this book, I certainly would encourage it. It should be relatively easy to use the information and tools in this book to embrace your religious convictions with even greater zeal.

However, if your existing religious persuasion requires or encourages you to be biased, rigid, bigoted, authoritarian, narrow-minded, prejudiced, dictatorial, intolerant, dogmatic, blinkered or cruel, then you may find some of the content in this book some-what challenging. If this is the case, I hope you will muster the courage and tolerance to approach the message with an open mind, because we really do need all hands on deck as we venture into our collective future.

In *The Story of Mankind,* Hendrik van Loon wrote that "this world is in dreadful need of men who will assume the new leadership - who will have the courage of their own visions and who will recognise clearly that we are only at the beginning of the voyage, and have to learn an entirely new system of seamanship".

If you currently do not subscribe to any religion or belief sys-tem, or you have completely given up on the faith you used to follow, it is my hope that these pages will be a source of inspira-tion for you to once again believe in something uplifting and affirmative. The content of this book aims to remind you of who you really are, namely a being of *spiritual origins.* It will hopefully awaken you to reconnect with the omnipresent Stream of Pure Well-being, the Positive Creative Energy that is the Supreme Source of Everything, and therefore also your true nature and sacred heritage. In fact, you are right now a complete miniature replica of this Cosmic Holograph of Divine Oneness that we call the Universe. This beingness within is your Higher Self, your Divine Self.

In my opinion, this Divine connection we have with God, or the Divine, is what should be driving all religions, no matter whom or what you choose to worship. Ralph Waldo Emerson captured this fundamental religious need very aptly in the Harvard Divinity School Address he delivered on July 15th, 1838, before a gradu-ating senior class.

> Meantime, whilst the doors of the temple stand open, night and day, before every man, and the oracles of this truth cease never, it is guarded by one stern condition; this, namely; it is an intuition. It cannot be received at second hand. Truly speaking, it is not instruction, but provocation, that I can receive from another soul. What he announces, I must find true in me, or reject... The absence of this primary faith is the presence of degradation... Then falls the church, the state, art, letters, life. The doctrine of the divine nature being forgotten, a sickness infects and

> *dwarfs the constitution... And because the indwelling Supreme Spirit cannot wholly be got rid of, the doctrine of it suffers this perversion, that the divine nature is attributed to one or two persons, and denied to all the rest.*

Like many teachers and thinkers of our time, Emerson clearly also sensed how lost we have become as spiritual beings. Shockingly, he spoke these words almost 200 years ago. Clearly very few listened then and very few are listening now.

We all have open access to our inner Divinity or Divine Self, but so many of us do not recognize it from our typical human perspective, because in order to return to a state of true spiritual awareness and reconnection, we must rely on our *intuition*, or our inner, spontaneous knowing of this universal fact. We cannot be taught by anyone to be spiritual, or forced to believe in anything, neither can we be convinced to feel a connection with a God or a Divine Source. We can only be "provoked" or reminded by what others say, and do, and believe.

But within that provocation we must find our own truth, or we must reject it. Should we reject the existence of our basic spiritual nature, everything else in our lives and our society suffers, including the environment, politics, the arts and sciences. By forgetting our Divine Nature we become "sick" as individuals and as a society. We become diminished or weaker versions of our original design and true self.

This book aims to awaken within you that innate knowing, that intuitive understanding of your original Divine nature and your everlasting connection to the Divine Source, no matter what you believe, or who, how or where you choose to worship or devote yourself to spiritual practice.

Divine Discontent

Divine Living is a very real lifestyle choice for millions of enlightened Souls all over the world. It is the lifestyle of the future Earth, and the key to the next stage in the conscious evolution and ultimate survival of our species. It is my hope and prayer that this book will be your one way ticket to a brand new life and a much happier, spiritually enriched existence.

Divine Living is your sacred birthright and this book aims to empower you to share in this 'secret' that some believers have known for centuries. You are the heir to a heavenly fortune, the beneficiary of an abundant spiritual inheritance that is beyond all measure, and defies all human comprehension. Many lost souls sit right on top of this proverbial goldmine of sacred abundance their whole life, but remain none the wiser. For them their rightful inheritance of a Divine Life remains unclaimed and beyond their reach. They choose to stay ignorant of their true legacy.

Did you know you actually chose to incarnate on this planet at this particular moment in human history? And before you came here, you custom-designed the entire experience for yourself. You designed a detailed *Life Plan* that was to be your blueprint or road map for this amazing journey. You also understood your *Soul Purpose*, as well as your *Life Purpose* (they are not the same thing). And you had full awareness of your true destiny and the milestones and obstacles you were to expect along the way. And in your original, non-physical form you looked forward to the thrill of this physical, human adventure with much anticipation!

But somewhere, somehow, between the moment you were born and the present day, it is very likely that you lost your way. Maybe you feel side-tracked and uncertain, or even confused and completely disillusioned.

Maybe you already know that you had somehow 'lost the plot'. You suspect you many have forgotten your original mission and ever since you have been looking for answers, or a sense of direction. Maybe your life until now has not been an easy ride, or maybe it has even been a 'living hell'. Either way, you probably don't feel as connected to your own Earthly existence as you would like to. Maybe you were doing fine at one stage, but due to unforeseen circumstances your most recent life experiences left much to be desired. That would not be unusual, as many spiritual seekers all over the world currently feel this way.

And if you are in denial, like I used to be, you may also be telling yourself that life is so unfair, that you have had a lot of 'bad luck' and 'raw deals' you really don't deserve. Or you may even believe that you have been cursed in some way, causing true happiness to elude you forever. Maybe you feel like the 'frog prince' or the 'sleeping princess' in a very tragic fairytale.

Maybe you had an abusive childhood, or you lost someone very dear to you at a vulnerable age, and you never really recovered from the pain or feelings of abandonment.

Perhaps you have been single all your life, still searching for that someone special, or perhaps you may have had so many failed relationships that you have lost count, or maybe you are deeply in love with someone who no longer loves you in return, or never did to begin with.

Maybe you were recently diagnosed with depression or bi-polar disorder, or a serious condition like cancer, HIV-infection or multiple sclerosis that now threatens to change your life forever.

Perhaps you already own the perfect house, the luxury car, the two-and-a-half children, the pedigree pets, the latest hairstyle and fashion accessories, and the shiny white picket fence, yet you still question the meaning and substance of your life.

Oh, if only you were a little richer, or a little skinnier. If only you were more talented, attractive, popular or self-assured. If only you could be famous, or better yet, so obscenely wealthy that you would never have to work again. Maybe then you would feel happy and content?

Perhaps you have always been the black sheep of the family, the one who they all said would "never amount to anything", and you now feel you never really proved them wrong. Or maybe your family had too many high expectations of you, pressuring you to become accomplished, affluent and happily married according to a certain standard, but you never made it over the bar they had set.

Maybe you recently lost your job, or you never found a decent job to begin with, despite your talent and qualifications. Or maybe you had to declare bankruptcy due to your out-of-control spend-ing during difficult economic times. Maybe you lost your home. Maybe you are stuck in poverty stricken or politically unstable country. Maybe your life is just a dull, daily routine spent in rush hour traffic or a dead-end career. Perchance you are sitting some-where in an office right now, staring at your computer screen, wishing for the day to come to a swift end.

I actually remember such a moment in the 90's when I was doing exactly that. I was sitting at a corner desk in an open plan office, my back to my co-workers, staring vacantly at my computer. Nobody knew that tears were running silently down my cheeks. I distinctly remember how I had to resist the intense, overwhelming urge I had to stand up, grab that computer and toss it through the window. I was even imagining how liberating the sound of all that breaking glass would be and how such an impulsive action might 'set me free' from that stifling, mind-numbing place.

Like me, you may have also reached a point in your life now where you have been trying to ease the pain by searching for relief in all the wrong places; such as engaging in co-dependent, abusive relationships, or hurling yourself into manic religious experimentation. Or maybe you tried to fill the void the way I did, with obsessive academic studies, artistic expression, compulsive exercise or frenzied entertainment pursuits. Alternatively, you may have attempted to escape your predicament by overindulging your senses with addictive behavior – food, drugs, alcohol, sex, shopping, television.

Perhaps you don't even realize how miserable you really are. Like many of us, you may have wrapped yourself in so many layers of insincere friends, meaningless materialism, mindless activities and hollow status symbols, that you no longer feel the pulse of your true inner being. Perhaps your life appears to others to very busy, even glamorous, but true inner fulfillment remains beyond your reach. Perhaps you have become numb, anesthetized, and obsolete. Your life unofficially mundane and empty.

Whatever your unique situation, you probably sense there must be more to life, but you have no idea how to find your way there. If not, you would not be reading this book.

Well, you are correct! There certainly is so much more to your current life experience than mere existence, humdrum and day-to-day survival. This restless sense of dissatisfaction you are feeling is the state of *Divine Discontent*. And contrary to what you may believe, unlocking the door to a happier, more fulfilling life is not remotely as complicated as you may think. You have been sensing all along there may be more, because deep within your being you have always known that there is so, so much more.

Somewhere in the deepest recesses of your soul there is that faint memory of who you really are, and where you really came from, and why you really came here. That inner knowing is the Divine 'spark' we need to ignite within you.

Dreaming Of Inanna

I started writing this book about six years ago, but only managed to finish a couple of draft chapters. I lost my inspiration, while my other work got in the way, so this book was eventually placed on the back burner. Spirit, however, had other plans for the project.

One night about two years ago, I had a vivid dream that jump-started this book in an awe-inspiring way. It is not unusual for me to have memorable dreams, as I use dreams a lot in my work, and I therefore pay close attention in order to keep a journal for later use. But this dream was very different.

I normally experience clairvoyant or *precognitive dreams* that provide me with information about significant future events or revelations about currently unresolved matters in my own life, or in the lives of my clients. Instead, this dream was what is best described as a *prophetic dream* with an element of *visitation.* It was the first of a series of similar dreams that would shape and inform the contents of this book, along with other intuitive signs and spiritual messages I received as the contents of this book progressed.

In the initial dream I was standing on some kind of a balcony or terrace, high up on what I believe must have been a mountain or hilltop looking out over a strange, surreal world. Below me were the rooftops of what I originally thought was an ancient Egyptian or Mayan city of the future. Later my research revealed to me that the architectural features and symbols on the buildings were much more in the style of the ancient Sumerian civilization – a culture that I did not know anything about at the time of this dream. The fantastic place I saw before me was both *historic* and *futuristic* at once. It was primordial and prehistoric, yet also ultra-modern, socially advanced and highly technological.

I was not alone. I knew that my guide Yarden was with me, but I also sensed the presence of a third entity, but I did not see any-one or anything. I remember thinking how unusual it all was, and how excited I felt about being there.

Behind me I then heard a voice speak. I knew it was not Yarden. He often speaks to me in my dreams, and this was not anything like his voice. I don't recall the exact words this unfami-liar voice spoke, as I did not recognize the language; but for some reason I fully understood what was being said. My version below is a humble attempt at a literary interpretation of the words I heard.

This is the New Earth, the Future World, Atlantis resur-rected. It holds the promise of the next Golden Age of Man, the return of a time of Peace and Prosperity when the Gods shall once again dwell among men, and man shall be as the Gods. Go forth, share what you have witnessed, bring unto others the Wisdom of Inanna.

As I so often do during lucid dreams, I was not just going to accept this peculiar message at face value. I remember thinking or saying in my dream, "This is madness. What must I do? How? I don't know how? This makes no sense!" The mysterious voice replied.

Be guided by your dreams. We shall come to you in your dreams. Meditate. Observe. Witness. You shall be guided.

"But I have no idea where to start", I thought aloud. "Where do I begin?" Once again the response came without hesitation.

Inana, find Inana.

When I woke up I remembered clearly the five letters **I N A N A** written in large, black ink letters on what looked like desert sand, or possibly a rock surface or some sort of parchment. When I woke up I had no idea what those letters meant. I had never heard of this "Inana"?

I made some notes in my dream journal and for the time being forgot all about the dream. But a few days later I had almost the exact same dream, with even more vivid intensity. This time my curiosity got the better of me, because there was clearly something really unusual or extraordinary going on.

I searched the Internet for the word "Inana", which led me to discover that the more appropriate or commonly used spelling is in fact *Inanna*. Additionally, I also learned that Inanna was the principal Sumerian goddess. She was later known as Aphrodite, in ancient Greece, and as Venus, in Rome. Further information I subsequently found about her and what she represented, astounded me. I soon realized that the details of her personality and story were to become the inspirational spark for this book.

Cuneiform Clairvoyance

I love psychic dreams, because their unfamiliar content is always a clear confirmation that their meaning or message originate from an external or mystical source. It still amazes me every morning, when I open my dream journal, how intricate, complex and layered the symbols, metaphors and messages in our dreams can be. I practice dreamwork very often, for both personal and work purposes, and I also support clients on a regular basis in the analysis and interpretation of their dreams.

What made the recurring Inanna dream especially intriguing was that it contained so much *visual detail*, more than I had never experienced before in any other dream. I often have this kind of dream, but never before had any of them been so vivid and detailed. Furthermore, it was also a *visitation dream.* I have had these before also, but they are usually dreams of deceased individuals, or the loved ones of clients who are in the process of crossing over. And, of course, Yarden is present in most of my dreams, but he is hardly a visitor! The Inanna dream, however, was a profoundly *numinous* experience, meaning that I felt the clear presence of some form of Divinity or a Supreme Being.

The moment I started reading more about the goddess Inanna, the layered meanings and message hidden in my dream came together in an instant 'light bulb moment'. I immediately knew what the dream meant and that it was a sign. I know this not only because of my intuitive certainty or inner knowing, but also because of the spelling of her name in the dream. In my research I had discovered that her name is usually spelled INANNA, but when referring back to the original Sumerian cuneiform script, one finds that the original spelling is in fact broken down into symbols that represent the words or sounds INA + NA. In Akkadian, an extinct Semitic language once spoken in ancient Mesopotamia, the Assyro-Babylonians also wrote her name as INANA, although they used different cuneiform symbols.

Sumerian: "DINGIR INANA"

There was simply no way I could have known of this ancient spelling of the name beforehand. I have never studied or read anything about Inanna, or ancient Mesopotamia for that matter.

Even if I had come across her name before in modern literature, and simply forgot, it would have been written in my mind as 'Inanna', since I have never before had any interest in studying Sumerian or its cuneiform script symbols. Before I started researching this dream the script symbols would have meant nothing to me and I would probably have thought of them as some kind of Egyptian hieroglyph or ancient Mayan imprint.

Akkadian: "INANA"

Interestingly, many scholars believe ancient Sumerian was the *first written language.* There is controversy about exactly who wrote first, but what we do know is the writing of language was invented independently in more than one civilization around the same time in human history, which includes Sumer (Mesopotamia) 3200 BC, Egypt 3200 BC, China 1300 B, and Mesoamerica, (Maya) 600 BC. None of these civilizations taught each other to write, they all discovered it on their own. I found significance in the concept of 'writing in symbols' in ancient times. Symbolism is the written language of the unconscious, intuitive mind.

The Four Elements

The puzzle finally came together, sparked by the symbolism attached to the name of this long-forgotten deity. I found that the ancient Sumerian civilization conceived of the Universe as consisting of the four elements, namely Fire, Air, Earth and Water, which they believed were ruled over by the twin forces of Inanna, who is the Goddess of Love and War, and of Heaven and Earth.

These four universal elements are found throughout classical philosophy and ancient belief systems, especially in Hinduism and Buddhism. Similar lists of elements also existed in ancient China, Japan, Babylonia, Greece, and Egypt. The four classical elements were also central to medieval alchemy and in Western astrology the twelve signs of the zodiac are divided into the four elements.

The Fire signs are Aries, Leo and Sagittarius; the Earth signs are Taurus, Virgo and Capricorn; the Air signs are Gemini, Libra and Aquarius; and Water signs are Cancer, Scorpio, and Pisces. In Tarot, the Suits of Cups, Swords, Wands, and Pentacles also correspond to water, air, fire, and earth respectively.

The renowned psychologist Carl Jung equated the four elements with the functions of the human psyche, namely Thoughts (Air), Feelings (Water), Sensations (Earth) and Intuition (Fire). And in the same way the four elements are governed by Inanna's opposing powers of Creation and Destruction, Jung proposed that the psychological functions they represent are presided over in our psyche by what he termed the transcendental function, which is basically the interaction of the *Conscious* and *Unconscious.*

Jung's Transcendental Function

In Jung's model for the human psyche the goddess Inanna therefore symbolically represents the *transcendental function*. In simple terms, the concept of the transcendental function refers to our ability to regulate the *natural psychological tension* that seems to exist between our conscious and unconscious mind. It is essentially a form of *self-regulation of our psyche*, which then results in a *new attitude or outlook* we achieve towards ourselves and towards life in general.

Jung used the word 'transcendence' because it refers to a state of being, or existence, above and *beyond the normal limits* of material experience. Something is considered to be transcendent when it is beyond the ordinary range of perception, or above and beyond the material world.

The transcendent function makes possible the transition from one attitude or state of being to another; it enables us to achieve a new insight or an *enlightened perspective* or an *altered state of being.*

Jung believed that the transcendental function is the key to *individuation.* Prof Victor Daniels explains the concept of individuation as the premise that a human being is inwardly whole, but that most of us have lost touch with important parts of ourselves.

Through listening to the messages of our dreams and waking imagination, we can contact and reintegrate our different parts. The goal of life is individuation, the process of coming to know, giving expression to, and harmonizing the various components of the psyche. If we realize our uniqueness, we can undertake a process of individuation and tap into our true self. Each human being has a specific nature and calling which is uniquely his or her own, and unless these are fulfilled through a union of conscious and unconscious, the person can become sick.

Jung's theory, as inspired by Inanna, is the crux of what a Divine Life is all about. Divine Living is in essence the mindful, spiritual application of Jung's concepts of *transcendence* and *individuation*. This book is however not an academic attempt at the psychological or therapeutic interpretation of Jung's ideas. It merely serves as a guiding framework or structure inspired by the archetype of Inanna and Jung's psychological interpretation of it.

The Duality Of Inanna

Divine Living is the result and the ultimate purpose of spiritual awakening. It is the essence of our soul growth and our life purpose in this lifetime. In order for us to rise above, or *transcend* our disconnected material existence and our lack conscious post-modern lives, and bring lasting fulfillment, purpose, peace and joy into our Earth experience, we have to, like the goddess Inanna, overcome our own *duality*. We have to reclaim our innate ability to *balance* both the spiritual and material side of our human existence. Most people today are either zealously spiritual or religious, or they are completely materialistic and secular. Inanna and Jung show us the magical path to finding the perfect balance between these two extremes.

To achieve this dynamic balance in our daily existence we must strike a harmonious balance between the conscious and the unconscious, and the physical and the metaphysical. In the realm of the conscious and physical we need to transform our *thoughts* and sharpen our *senses* to better accommodate our innate spirituality, while in the realm of the unconscious and the metaphysical we must evolve our *emotions* and increase our *intuition,* to better inform the purpose, meaning and direction of our material existence.

Like Inanna we must abandon the false temple of our Ego and descend into the 'underworld' of the collective unconscious to awaken our true Spiritual Beingness within, and upon our return we must resolve the resulting tension that it will bring with our rational conscious mind and the external world. To achieve this we need integrate the right brain with the left brain, the spirit with the mind, the unseen with the seen, the physical with the metaphysical, the secular with heavenly, the conscious with the unconscious. To achieve a Divine Life of Heaven on Earth we must aim to bring our spirituality and humanity back into balance and harmony.

The tension we are feeling daily between the conscious and unconscious, and the rational and the intuitive, stems from our innate spiritual nature increasingly being in conflict with our conditioned *Material Self* or *Ego*, as well as the pressures of a post-modern, materialistic society shaped by rationalism and Newtonian science. Spiritually and subconsciously we are struggling with the demands of our current global reality and the materialistic expectations, and greed of our society. Many humans have also lost all faith in the 'unseen', due to the demands of the currently dominant scientific paradigm.

We seem to have created our own modern monster. The discord and dissonance between the spiritual (or inner being), and the physical (or external being), is the fundamental cause for the dissatisfaction, frustration, nihilism, anger, misery and depression that millions of people increasingly experience all over the world. This schism or separation between the conscious and unconscious, the spiritual and the material is the state of *Divine Disconnect* and it is the cause of our global state of *Divine Discontent.*

The twin forces of Love and War, Creation and Destruction, over which Inanna ruled, have become profoundly unbalanced in our world. We have become creatures driven by war and destructtion, and we have forgotten our natural powers of unconditional love and creation. We have become the victims of our innate spiritual need for expansion, for instead of creating and expanding in love and peace, we are destroying ourselves with our own science and technology.

We have an inner know that all is not well in our world. Our species is increasingly being trapped in an uncomfortable co-created time-space reality. We are stuck in the growing clash between the Ego (Material Self) and the Divine Self (Higher Self), and the result of this fracas is our intensifying state of global Divine Discontent. It is also the cause for our prolonged Divine Disconnection from our spiritual heritage from a very young age.

Spiritual Awakening

Our future as a species seems uncertain, even bleak should we not harness the wisdom of the goddess Inanna and transcend to a different way of life through conscious evolution. But how do we achieve this balancing power?

Well, first we must *awaken* that which is unseen, unconscious, ethereal, and eternal within us. We must access the Book of Life, or the Akashic Records, and tap into the Oneness of Being that is the Collective Unconscious, the Great I Am, the Supreme Source. This will bring about a reconnection with our Evolving Soul, our Higher Consciousness, our Divine Self. We must tap into the collective unconscious in order to reconnect and realign with this Divine Self.

To create a Divine Life we must rediscover our Divine origins; we must have a spiritual awakening. The 'light switch must be flipped on' that will bring into the spotlight of our lives the profound realization and acceptance that we are in fact *spiritual beings having a physical experience* – not the other way around!

Once the blinding spell of the Divine Disconnect has been broken and we have awoken spiritually from our 'reality coma', we begin to open to receiving guidance from our inner Divinity and Higher Self. Only then are we ready to embrace a new awareness rising up from the depths of what used to be the unconscious, or 'unseen', or metaphysical.

The unconscious finding its way into our conscious awareness will initially conflict heavily with many of our rational, logical, left brain assumptions, and a plethora of false beliefs, fears and skepticisms about ourselves and our world, which we have diligently cultivated, and with which we have conditioned and programmed our children for centuries.

Transcendence To Homo Superior

The second step in our conscious evolution from Divine Discontent towards Divine Living is the *integration* of the formerly unconscious with the formerly conscious, in order to achieve *transcendence*. Due to our spiritual awakening we have to overcome the increased tension that will arise between our conscious and unconscious, between the spiritual and the material, between the left brain and the right. The process of transcendence is therefore the foundation of our *Soul Purpose* in this lifetime.

Transcendence is a state of being or existence above and beyond the limits of material experience. When we transcend we excel, surpass or go beyond the limits of the material world, and beyond our Ego perception of reality. To transcend is to escape the confines of the conceptual, rational human world, which only exists in our own minds, in order to become reconnected with the Infinite Conscious Universe.

To evolve our Universal Consciousness and ensure continued spiritual growth and expansion, we must continuously adjust and expand our Consciousness (thinking, sensing) and increasingly access and bring into awareness the Unconscious (emotions, intuition), with the aim of returning ourselves to a state of balance between our spiritual nature and our human condition, and then we must strive to maintain this newfound equilibrium.

Due to the dominant influence of a current worldview based on Rationalism and Newtonian Physicalism, we have no choice but to focus on adjusting and expanding our customary way of *thinking*, as well as how we choose to perceive our world via our five *senses*. The way we currently perceive and think about our world is simply not in line with our inner Divinity; it does not reflect and honor our original spiritual nature.

Concurrently our original Life Plan requires that we become more intimately attuned to the inner guidance and metaphysical attunement function of our *emotions* and *intuition*, because without spiritual awareness and inner guidance from the Higher Self we cannot achieve our Soul Purpose and Life Calling in this lifetime.

The Buddha taught that the establishing of *mindfulness* is the 'direct path' to the realization of Nirvana. In the Buddhist tradition the Sutra on the Four Establishments of Mindfulness offers four layers of mindfulness practice: mindfulness of the *body* (senses), of the *emotions*, of the *mind* (thoughts), and of 'phenomena' (intuition). These four foundations of mindfulness are regarded as the bases for maintaining moment-to-moment mindfulness.

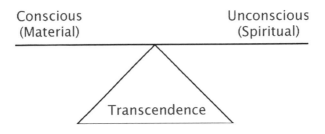

As we become more *mindful* and achieve an increased emergence of the unconscious and the metaphysical, with an accompanying adjustment of the conscious and the physical, we will increasingly transcend the old Material Self, or Ego, and consciously create and evolve a spiritually aligned and metaphysically transformed new version of ourselves, a new and improved species I call *Homo Superior*, the 'Superhuman'.

Individuation To Integration

Thirdly, in conjunction with the process of transcendence and achieving our Soul Purpose, we can create a truly Divine Life by pursuing our original goal of achieving *individuation* in this life-time. Individuation (or self-actualization) enables us to adapt and function more effectively as spiritually co-conscious, co-creating beings in our secular society. It also empowers us to offer increased selfless service to each other, and thus live a fulfilling, purposeful life. Individuation is therefore the foundation of our Life Purpose or *Life Calling*.

Individuation is the process of finding the answer to the age old questions, "Who am I?" and "Why am I here?" Individuation is about becoming aware of your true self, discovering your own original design, and expressing yourself in service to others. To accomplish this we need to integrate and liberate the whole, unique spiritual being that we already are within, before we can make a truly meaningful contribution to the rest of society and the environment.

Jung believed that the process of individuation or development of individuality is simultaneously a development of society when he said, "Suppression of individuality through the predominance of collective ideals and organizations is a moral defeat for society."

Now, at this point you may ask: would it not make more sense to come together as a group in an ideal future world, to work as a collective, or as a 'tribe', towards a shared global ideal, instead of increasingly becoming individualized, specialized, distinctive and fully self-actualized, each marching to our own drum?

The answer is no, for there is a distinct difference between *individuation* and *individualism*. Sol Luckman explains it well when he writes that "acknowledging our inner divinity as a step on the path to embodying it is not to be confused with narcissism or individualism, since we must further admit that everyone's divine birthright is the same limitless creational potential of uncon-ditional love".

Individuation is the process of becoming a fully integrated, balanced and contributing member of society. There is nothing selfish or self-absorbed about embracing your own inner Divinity and your unique identity as a spiritual being in human form, for in this awakened and aware state you have no choice but to automatically acknowledge and value the Divinity within your fellow man, regardless of them being conscious or uncon-scious of its existence.

Being aligned with your Divine Self finds expression in unconditional love, joy, compassion, selflessness and a year-ning for peace. You are individuated when you are able to live in complete wholeness and harmony with yourself, the com-munity, all living creatures, nature and the world. Individuating is therefore a spiritual necessity, not to be confused with the materialistic individualism.

Note that individuation cannot occur in isolation, because our relationships and interaction with others and our environ-ment is obviously a vital part of the process. In fact, Jung is quoted to have said that you cannot individuate far away and alone on Mount Everest!

Individualism, on the other hand, refers to a self-centered and ego-centric state of being that places your own beliefs, needs, desires and preferences above that of everybody and everything else in the world. That kind of thinking and being in the world is the outdated, destructive way of the Material Ego. It is the stale worldview that has created the reality we share today, and it is the foundation of the obsolete structures of the previous millennium. Individualism was the way of Feudalism, Colonialism, Communism, Socialism and Capitalism. In truth it is nothing more than an obsessive state of 'survival of the fittest'. It is what brought us to where we are now, and it was clearly not the answer or solution to the human condition.

The Safe Side Of The Road

In her book *The Way of Individuation*, Jungian psychologist Jolande Jacobi provides a brilliantly simple and spiritually profound description of the process of individuation.

> *Like a seed growing into a tree, life unfolds stage by stage. Triumphant ascent, collapse, crises, failures, and new beginnings strew the way. It is the path trodden by the great majority of mankind, as a rule unreflectingly, unconsciously, unsuspectingly, following its labyrinthine windings from birth to death in hope and longing. It is hedged about with struggle and suffering, joy and sorrow, guilt and error, and nowhere is there security from catastrophe. For as soon as a man tries to escape every risk and prefers to experience life only in his head, in the form of ideas and fantasies, as soon as he surrenders to opinions of 'how it ought to be' and, in order not to make a false step, imitates others whenever possible, he forfeits the chance of his own independent development. Only if he treads the path bravely and flings himself into life, fearing no struggle and no exertion and fighting shy of no experience, will he mature his personality more fully than the man who is ever trying to keep to the safe side of the road.*

Our future survival and evolution will not be found in sameness, alikeness, similarity or coercion. Instead, we must build a new global civilization based on increasing diversity, variety, assortment and multiplicity. But there is one fundamental condition - for it to be successful it must be achieved in harmony with others and our planet.

From the perspective of the old mainstream view of our world, such a future world of diversity appears quite impossible and nonsensical, because that would mean that everybody 'does their own thing in their own way". History has taught us that everyone doing things their own way eventually manifests itself as selfishness, greed, creed, personal preference, chauvinism, dogma and ego-centered beliefs, which has caused our wars, the establishment of our borders, the separation between the rulers and subjects, and the division between rich and poor. It is also the root of the 'haves' and the 'have nots', of crime and corruption, and all manner of misery in the world. We have always had one person, or group, or nation forcing their views, beliefs, desires or ambitions upon another. It is what caused the mess we are in to begin with.

But from a new paradigm and a radically different worldview, which has been gradually surfacing all over the globe, we will discover that through *individuation* we can accomplish a new *integration*. We will find that we can achieve a collective, harmonious existence as Individuated Superhumans in a newly, co-created reality. The only missing link is our current lack of spiritual awareness.

In 1897 Ralph Waldo Trine wrote in *In Tune With The Infinite*, "If you preserve your individuality then you become a master, and if wise and discreet, your influence and power will be an aid in bringing about a higher, a better, and a more healthy set of conditions in the world". There is no need for us all to be alike and think the same way, neither do we need a common enemy to force us come together and reach out to each other.

If we allow ourselves and everyone else the freedom to fully individuate as *spiritual beings in human form*, there will be no need for us to be forced by worldly circumstances to take hands and stand together. Our souls will automatically want to flock together, like moths to the flame of our shared Divinity, yet each with wings covered in the glimmering colors and unique patterns of our individual human expression.

This co-conscious, co-creative approach is now entirely attainable for the first time in human history, because we now have the necessary science and technology to make it perfectly possible and within our reach to 'each do our own thing' - without harming, limiting, bothering or judging each other.

Many clues that the world is ready for this long-overdue, new worldview and scientific paradigm is to be found in recent advances in science and philosophy, including Quantum Physics and New Thought concepts like the Holographic Universe, Reality Tunnels, Quantum Healing, Deliberate Creation and Conscious Evolution. Further evidence is also emerging from our fast evolving technology, which has brought us new levels of connectivity and increased *personalization* and *customization* of many aspects of our daily life, including global social networking with whomever we choose, and instant information distribution geared to our personal preferences and fields of interest. In an extreme example we witnessed in 2011 the vital role these emerging communication technologies played in political protests in Egypt and Libya, the riots in the United Kingdom, and the *Occupy Wall Street* campaign in the United States of America.

Our physical world seems ready and able to accommodate the needs of the spiritually awakened new Superhuman. The constraints or demands of our material world are not the real problem; it is our own spiritual awareness and philosophical wisdom that is lagging behind.

Descending Into The Underworld

There is an additional layer of meaning to the dream I had about Inanna, which further served as a thematic structure for this book. In my research I discovered that this Sumerian goddess is most known for her 'descent myth' - the intriguing story of her journey into the underworld. Inanna's tale is considered to be a primal archetype for *spiritual initiation* or *awakening*, which is the foundation and focus point of Divine Living.

There are four myths involving Inanna, which are interpreted to represent the four stages of human development. The first three are archetypal representations of developing one's own individuality or inner sense of self, then establishing relationships with others, and lastly becoming involved in the external world.

The descent myth represents the fourth and final stage, which is the metaphysical, mystical aspect of our earthly existence. The descent myth is therefore symbolic of our ultimate *spiritual enlightenment*, which is the transcendence of our earthly Ego in order to realign with our universal Higher Identity, or the Divine

Self. It represents our awakening from the Divine Disconnect to Divine Living.

John C. Robinson writes in his paper, *Living the Myth of Inanna*, that the descent myth of Inanna "is most certainly a story of initiation into the mysteries of death and rebirth, for the heroine must die to her identity, authority, and life in order to awaken renewed, perhaps even transformed."

Inanna decided to go to the underworld voluntarily to seek wisdom, understanding and enlightenment. But in order to enter the underworld she had to give up who she was and all that she owned. Inanna had to leave behind Heaven and Earth and abandon her position as holy priestess, as well as her seven temples, and give up all her heavenly powers and earthly possessions. These brave actions represent the spiritual seeker's initial period of Divine Disconnection, followed by the shedding of the former Ego-driven life by letting go of old patterns, false beliefs, and material pursuits, and instead embracing a new, transformed life of greater spiritual understanding, insight, gratitude and wisdom. It also represents the descent into the collective unconscious, to reconnect with the universal code of all creation.

There are several 'descent myths' in various cultures and religions of the world, and they are all archetypes of leaving the old behind and transcending to the new. This archetype is also the foundation of Divine Living. To live a Divine Life is to awaken and reconnect with the Divine Self and to leave behind the old Ego life of Divine Discontent for a brand new Divine Life of purpose, joy and spiritual bliss.

In the Kabbalistic text *Zohar: Bereshith to Lekh Lekha*, Nurho de Manhar writes, "This union with the Divine is the mystery of all mysteries; but ere Abraham could attain unto this high degree of spiritual life and knowledge, it was necessary to subject him to trial and probation."

For some people spiritual awakening comes unexpectedly, like a thief in the night. There is usually no real reason why they should not be prepared for its approach, because there are typically many signs and warnings beforehand.

This dramatic form of awakening is often preceded by all manner of trial and tribulation, even profound suffering, hardship and tragedy. But you do not need to endure trauma, serious illness, a near-death experience or a 'dark night of the soul' to awaken spiritually. You are a spiritual being by nature and your inner Divinity is always ready to reconnect with you, whenever you feel ready. It is your birthright and your true destiny.

In his 1992 article *Initiation - The Descent into Hades,* Dan Sewell Ward writes that the myths of Inanna and her descent into the underworld reveals a series of profound messages relating to, among other, "the concept of a higher self, the abandoning of old values and artifacts, and the ultimate empowerment of voluntarily making the descent, as well as the implications of modern day individuals making their own descent into Hades as a form of spiritual initiation: a seeking of wisdom and growth and the shedding of illusions".

Interestingly, Ward also presents the idea that our world and society may be in the process of making its own descent, by releasing traditional, outdated paradigms in preparation for a new era of accelerated growth. It is another underlying theme to this book, namely achieving and maintaining a Divine Lifestyle in these uncertain times of increasing instability and cynicism.

By creating a Divine Life we personally overcome the challenges of society's persistent clinging to an outdated scientific paradigm, as well as a worldview that disregards our true spiritual nature, and refutes the infinite well-being and abundance that flows through the entire Universe. Divine Living empowers us to navigate through the inevitable collapse of old structures, institutions and traditions as we venture into the 21st Century, and enables us to become pioneers in a global shift towards spiritual awareness that must inevitably reach the point of critical mass.

The Dark Night Of The Soul

Inanna's journey is similar to the myth of the *Dark Night of the Soul,* which originated from the poem with the same name written by the 16th-century Spanish mystic, Saint John of the Cross. It tells the story of the journey of the soul returning from its temporary home in the physical body to reunite with God in Heaven. The concept of the Dark Night of the Soul has come to represent a period of intense loneliness, suffering, darkness and spiritual emptiness, which is the prelude to an ultimate transformation or rebirth into Higher Consciousness and Spiritual Enlightenment.

The Dark Night is a deep metaphysical depression that may affect spiritually awakened individuals who have already progressed far on their spiritual journey, but then suddenly and unexpectedly experience an interlude of profound spiritual disconnection. The sufferer feels overwhelmed by doubt, despair, hopelessness and anguish and the process can last anything from a few days to several years.

The Life Plan of some spiritual seekers may require that they go through such a Dark Night at some point in their life. In many cases this proves to be what ultimately informs and shapes their unique Life Calling later in life. Surviving the Dark Night is closely associated with the archetype of the *Wounded Healer*, namely that one can only become a true healer of others if you have personally suffered and found healing for yourself. Without going through the Dark Night, it is believed that the healer can never truly understand or empathize with his patients.

The Dark Night of the Soul is a concept I strongly identify with, since I have gone through this experience in more than one way, and as I explained in the Preface, it partly inspired this book. If you are currently going through such a profoundly challenging time in your life, know that this too shall pass. Personal suffering inspired me towards much wisdom and compassion, and it can do the same in your life. I now live in constant gratitude and appreciation for all that I have experienced, because it enables me every day to help and support others; to heal broken hearts, transform lives and guide people on their path towards personal fulfillment.

Instead of choosing the role of martyr or victim, know that once you liberate yourself from your Ego-based suffering, you will become a source of great comfort for others. Once your Dark Night has passed, nobody else will be better suited to teach the valuable life lessons that you had to learn yourself through misery and hardship. During trying times do not settle for bitterness, self-pity or resentment. Embrace instead the Divine miracle of your path to greater awareness and understanding. Acknowledge your growing empathy for others and validate and cherish those people who stand by you, for better or worse. There is always much light at the end of every life tunnel, and someday soon you shall find that silver lining. Without the contrasts created by loss, disappointment or suffering, it is unlikely that we will ever truly treasure the real blessings in life, like our health, our talents and our family and friends. If we never experience the chill of a dark winter, it is very unlikely that we will ever cherish the warmth of a bright summer's day. Nothing stimulates our appetite for the simple joys of life more than the starvation caused by sadness or desperation.

In order to complete our amazing life journey successfully, it is vital that we turn each and every dark tear into a pearl of wisdom, and find the blessing in every curse.

The Evil Ego

As beings created in the image of Infinite Intelligence, Divinity, God or the Supreme Source, we have been endowed with a capacity for *divine reasoning*, also known as our *free will*. A focus on the unconscious is therefore only one half of the awareness-transcendence equation, because true spiritual awakening and transformation must involve the *conscious* or *rational mind* and the Ego. This is something that is all too often disregarded, or even disapproved of in the New Age or New Thought movement.

An increasing number of spiritual authors and metaphysical teachers have in recent years been turning the human Ego into some kind of one-dimensional 'New Age villain'. In order to encourage spiritual seekers to embrace their own Divinity and open the doors and windows to the innate wisdom of their unconscious mind and Divine Self, some modern gurus have been over-emphasizing the Ego-aspect of our two-fold beingness.

Of course, one cannot really blame the average spiritual seeker for having this kind of 'knee jerk' reaction, as it is merely a natural response to centuries of Ego domination. A valid attempt is simply now being made at restoring the balance between the Ego Self and the Higher Self, and the conscious and unconscious mind. But in the process it has, like so many other things in life, turned into a pendulum swing from one extreme to the other. A misleading perception or false belief is increasingly being perpetuated that the unconscious or the intuitive is all that really matters in any spiritual endeavor, and that the conscious, rational, logical, analytical mind is the mortal enemy of spiritual awareness and soul growth.

This unbalanced, one-sided approach to spiritual development and personal transformation may get us out of the starting gates, but it will not lead to our ultimate transcendence and individuation. This extreme anti-Ego stance is in fact not so much different from the cynical skeptics who deny the existence of anything mystical or spiritual - it is merely at the opposite end of the spectrum. There is no real evolutionary leap or spiritual transcendence to be found in such a lopsided, fundamentalist approach to the role of the human Ego.

The modern obsession with the 'Evil Ego' has been the source of confusion and frustration for many spiritual seekers. I personally see this problem daily in my practice. Many of my clients struggle to find a balance between their spiritual, intuitive self-expression and the harsh realities of their material, physical reality, as well as their hectic lives, and everything rational and logic they have been taught since their childhood. Then they read books and attend seminars where they are further encouraged to discount or exorcise their 'demonic Ego' for the sake of a more spiritually connected, intuitive lifestyle.

This growing myth of the 'Evil Ego' or 'False Self' is not in accordance with the Laws of the Universe. For there must be duality and balance in everything. Just like we must have night and day, summer and winter, life and death, we must also have the conscious and unconscious, the rational and the intuitive, the spiritual and the physical, the right brain and the left. Think of the Taoist symbol of *Yin* and *Yang,* bound together as parts of a mutual whole. This is what Jung really meant when he referred to transcendental function.

> *Once the unconscious content has been given form and the meaning of the formulation is understood, the question arises as to how the ego will relate to this position, and how the ego and the unconscious are to come to terms. This is the second and more important stage of the procedure, the bringing together of opposites for the production of a third: the transcendent function.*

We have to merge Yin and Yang the way it was always intended to be in this time-space reality. The key to spiritual enlightenment is not to be found in shutting down the Ego, but in transcending the domination of the Ego by reconnecting and realigning with the Divine Self.

Spiritual Fool's Paradise

To truly transcend we cannot just retreat into a spiritual 'fool's paradise' and live in esoteric seclusion from all things secular. Neither does it make sense to spend days in constant meditation or devotion, in an attempt to suppress the ever-present Ego, or to throw out all our current scientific knowledge and technological progress to create some kind of esoteric existence. Saint Irenaeus said, "For the glory of God is the *human person fully alive*; and life consists in beholding God; A *life-affirming*, universal vision of God's cosmic love where everything is sacred."

We dare not exclusively revere the intuitive, symbolic, artistic, spiritual, right brain aspect of human consciousness, like some believers aim to do, while disregard the *balancing, dualistic role* of the rational, logical left brain. It would defy the reason we came here in the first place, for we did not come into this physical time-space reality to have a solely spiritual experience. If that was the case, we would have remained in our original spiritual form. No, we incarnated from a perfect spiritual state to come here and have a physical and profoundly *human experience*.

Yet, at the same time we also cannot continue with the insanity of the greedy, post-modern 'rat race' and remain slaves to our masculine, analytical, rational, practical, egotistical left brain. In this sense the 'Evil Ego gurus' do have a valid point, because it would defeat the spiritual purpose of our human existence. We came here to have a thrilling physical experience for the sake of *spiritual soul growth* and *creative expansion*. But for that to be possible we must have access to our divine reason or free will.

We basically need our Ego to be 'earthly gods'. We need our Ego to be able to *evolve consciously.* We need both the Material Self and the Divine Self to achieve our Soul Purpose and accomplish our Life Calling. The way Inanna was one united goddess with twin, opposing powers, we too must become *individuated* earth-bound deities who have *transcended* the tension between our conscious and unconscious mind, the chasm between our physical and spiritual awareness.

Dr Bernard Butler writes that "Inanna, as goddess of the morning and evening star, represents a form of *consciousness* in which we can join solar with lunar thinking, thus allowing both attention to detail and seeing the big picture."

There are some people attempting to live impractical, purely spiritual or esoteric lives, by trying every day to remain in a state of constant metaphysical attunement with the intuitive mind or the Universe, while there are even more souls all over the world stumbling along aimlessly in a discontented, restless existence that emphasizes 'old thought', false beliefs and all things cynical and skeptical, while ignoring, or even mocking the intuitive, unseen realm they all carry within. Is it any wonder that so many people suffer stress, anxiety, feelings of failure, and a lingering discontent in their own lives?

Somewhere in-between, and beyond these two extremes there lies the truly awakened life of both spiritual bliss and material abundance for all. A life of love, peace, joy, happiness and, most of all, contentment. This is the Divine Life, in harmony with ourselves, each other and our planet.

Your Divine Birthright

When we restore integration and balance of the conscious and unconscious, and develop ever-increasing harmony between the spiritual and the physical, then we achieve transcendence, which is our *Soul Purpose*. At the same time we accomplish individuation, which is our life purpose, or *Life Calling*. Only then do we become truly empowered as the human deities we were always meant to be and we then live in the unified dualism and balanced power of Inanna.

This way of life, that is perfectly aligned with your Soul Purpose and Life Calling is what I call Divine Living. A Divine Life is about making the most of your time here on Earth to achieve the soul growth you crave as a metaphysical being, while ensuring at the same time that you have an exhilarating, abundant and fulfilling physical life experience. None of your personal achievements, enjoyments or satisfaction need ever clash with society and the environment. The Divine Life not only serves the individual, but it also serves the greater good. It calls for a life of service to humanity and contribution to the positive, creative expansion of the Universe. In this book I aim to show you how to achieve this way of life. It is your Divine birthright and the time has come for you to reclaim it.

PART I

AWAKENING
YOUR DIVINE BEING

1

YOUR DIVINE ORIGINS

You are not who you think you are. You are not that face you see in the mirror every morning. You are not someone's child, or someone's parent, or partner or friend. You are not the physical body you admire or criticize when you take a shower, or when you get dressed. Neither are you the profile description on your social networking page, or your impressive title at work, or the name on your high school diploma or your driver's license. You are not defined by your career, or the things you own, or the family and friends you love. You are not a name or an address, or a six-figure salary.

You are one thing and one thing only. You are a Divine Being. An all-powerful creator. You are a deity in jeans and a t-shirt, and within you dwells the infinite wisdom of the ages and the sacred creative force of All that is, will be and ever was.

Do you remember how spiritually aligned, connected and aware you were as a young child? Remember how it felt to be so wonderfully conscious, wide-eyed and receptive? The world was a magical place of adventure, discovery and exhilaration. You then still had a vague memory of being created in the image of the Divine. As a recent arrival on the planet, you still had some recollection of that 'other place' you had come from – that state of Pure Consciousness, of Celestial Power, infinite Creative Intelligence and everlasting Unconditional Love. In that pure, original state you were eternal peace and perfection personified. You were a crystal clear, meta-dimensional snapshot of God's image in high-definition Technicolor.

You still are that original cosmic entity, but you chose to be incarnated as a human being to have a physical life experience. You decided to come to planet Earth for an alternative adventure.

You volunteered for the ride, and your original aim was to experience, learn, evolve, expand and most of all, to have fun!

So, come on, go take another look in that mirror and say 'hello' to the physical incarnation of your Divine Self. There you are - the pure expression of Divinity! Now, take a deep look into your own eyes, for they are the windows of the soul. There you will recognize the 'real you', an incarnation of Infinite Goodness and Joyous Life. Meet your ever-present Higher Self, your True Self, the Soul Essence of where you come from and the reason why you came here. This 'essential you' has been around all this time, since before your birth, and for millennia before that. All you needed was someone to remind you of that fact; to awaken you from the unconscious, habituated fog that was your conditioned earthly life until now.

You are not a human being having a spiritual experience. You are a spiritual being having a thrilling human experience. So, now you know who you really are. No more daily drudgery. No more 'merely surviving'. No more reality coma. No more feeling sorry for yourself. No more excuses. Consider yourself awakened.

The Divine Disconnect

At some juncture in our childhood most of us reach the point where we forget our true metaphysical origins and our Divine legacy. We become increasingly alienated from our Divine Self, and sometimes even completely disconnected from the all-pervading Supreme Source of well-being. We forget about the access and connection we have to this creative metaphysical force of Divine Consciousness that flows throughout the Universe.

Our separation from Spirit, God or Source sometimes becomes so acute that those who find themselves in this state respond with horror, contempt and even aggression towards the messenger who dared remind them of who they really are as spiritual beings. Some who remain under the spell of the 'reality coma' are so determined to disprove the possibility that they might have some kind of spiritual essence, that they devote a whole lifetime of study, research, public protest or professional skepticism to refute these claims. Such fear have they been taught in good faith by their parents and custodians, to ensure their physical survival and acceptance in society, that they become incapable of entertaining any idea that potentially may contradict or question their worldview.

Deepak Chopra writes in *War of the Worldviews* that "skeptics squat by the road like guardians of truth, letting no one pass who doesn't come up to scratch. They never realize that they can see only what their paradigm tells them to look for. If you judge a person only by how well he plays pool, Mozart won't pass scrutiny, but the fault is in your lens."

The separation between man and his Divine origins is the genesis of all religions, cults and belief systems in our world, and it is also the primary driving force behind all science, art and philosophy. Searching for metaphysical meaning and life purpose is a natural attribute of the human condition. Exploring the existence of God or Divine Consciousness beyond our current reality is an innate yearning we all have. No amount of scientific or technological advancement will ever extinguish this urge from human awareness. Whether we admit it to ourselves, or not, we all feel the need within to bridge our disconnection from the Divine.

We begin to separate from the Divine Self the moment we are born. At birth we have no sense of 'self', and we have no awareness of being separate from Spirit or Source, but in time we quickly begin to identify with our new physical environment and with the human Ego or Material Self that we choose to adopt, based on the feedback we receive from others. We gradually also adopt the social role assigned to us by our family, our peers and our community.

In time we completely lose touch with our Divine Self, because as we grow up we are increasingly exposed to the man-made concepts, theories, paradigms, belief systems, cultures, traditions and history underlying our current time-space reality. We become attached to the Material Self or Ego, and we learn to cling to whatever we are taught to perceive as the parameters or limits of our shared reality. Eventually we end up fully conditioned and firmly 'plugged into' the co-created, human 'reality matrix' that forms the foundation for life here on Earth. In the process the memories of our original Divinity often fade completely. This state of separation and 'spiritual amnesia' is the *Divine Disconnect*.

The Data Gathering

Why is our human incarnation cut off from its spiritual origins for a large portion of our life? If we really are such Divine Beings, and powerful creators of our own reality, how is it possible that we lose most of our connection with the Divine after we arrive on the planet? If we really do design our own Life Plan before we come, why do we allow this disconnect to happen?

The Divine Disconnect in the early years of a person's life is in fact a classic concept found in many ancient wisdom teachings, mytholo-gies and religious traditions. One only needs to consider the bio-graphical information of some of the more well-known prophets, ascended masters and spiritual teachers throughout history to find evidence of the proliferation of this phenomenon.

Abraham. The founding father of the three largest mono-theistic religions of the world, namely Judaism, Christianity, and Islam, had an unremarkable life as a semi-nomadic shep-herd and trader, until very late in his life. Somewhere in his 70's God revealed to him his true destiny as the father of a nation and entered into a sacred covenant with him. Today Abraham is honored as the Father of Faith, yet his connection with the Divine happened very late in life.

Confucious. His reforms and teaching is reported to have only begun when he resigned from his position as Justice Minister in the Chinese state of Lu after the age of 53.

Jesus Christ. He lived an ordinary life and worked as a carpen-ter, until his baptism at the age of 30, when John the Baptist recognized him as the long-awaited Messiah. Shortly after, Jesus went into the desert for 40 days to fast and pray, and at this time he was unsuccessfully tempted by Satan. His return marks the beginning of his ministry and teachings.

Moses. The receiver of the Ten Commandments also had his spiritual awakening very late in life. After 40 years of being a humble shepherd, God appeared to him in a burning bush and instructed him to return to Egypt and free the Hebrews from slavery.

Lao Tzu. It is unclear exactly when he had his spiritual awakening, but there is more than one legend about his life that seems to reflect the concept of an initial Divine Disconnect. According to one popular myth he was conceived when his mother gazed upon a falling star, after which he stayed in the womb for 62 years and was born a grown man with a full grey beard and long earlobes, which are symbols of wisdom and a long life. Another legend has it that he grew weary of urban life and became a hermit at the age of 160. It was at this time that the classic Chinese text known as the Tao Te Ching is said to have come into being, when a guard at the city gate asked him to produce proof of his wisdom. The Tao Te Ching founded Taoism and strongly influenced Confucianism and Chinese Buddhism.

Mahavira. He renounced his kingdom, his family and worldly possessions at the age of 30 and subsequently spent twelve years as an ascetic who practiced constant meditation until he achieved *arihant* status, which means that he conquered anger, ego, deception, and greed, and attained perfect knowledge and perfect perception, while becoming passionless and gaining infinite power. Mahavira is known as the sage Vardhamāna who established the Jainism faith.

Prophet Muhammad. The Founder of Islam was orphaned as a child and brought up by his uncle. As adult he worked as an ordinary merchant and shepherd, until he became discontentted with his life in Mecca. He retreated to a cave in the surrounding mountains to meditate and during this time he received his first revelation from God at the age of 40. Three years later he started preaching these revelations publicly.

Siddhārtha Gautama Buddha. He was born into the life of a wealthy prince, set to become king. It is said that he was shielded by his father from all religious education and knowledge of human suffering. Although his father ensured that he was provided with everything he could ever want or need, Siddhartha felt that material wealth was not life's ultimate goal. His spiritual life began around the age of 29, when he left his father's palace and became profoundly aware of ageing, sickness, suffering and death among his subjects. This depresssed him so much that he gave up his life as a prince and initially strove unsuccessfully to overcome human suffering, by living the life of an ascetic. He later changed the direction of his quest and subsequently attained true enlightenment and thus founded Buddhism.

Zoroaster. According to legend he was the son of a mediocre nobleman and he lived a conventional life as a priest, until he had a heavenly vision at the age of 30. In his vision an angel brought him to the god Ahura Mazda, who instructed him to found a new religion known today as Zoroastrianism.

From these examples there emerges a clear pattern of metaphysical awakening and spiritual transcendence, namely that it typically occurs towards the *second half of a human life*, after an initial period of Divine Disconnection.

This initial period of Divine Disconnection is intentional, not coincidental. The preliminary stage of spiritual 'unconsciousness' or disconnection is a period of *physical orientation* and *data collection* in every young human's life. It is the preparatory time in our lives where we learn to adapt, function and survive in the Earth environment.

During this time we also develop our Ego identity and learn to establish and manage relationships with others. Through trial and error we figure out how to use our intuitive and emotional inner guidance system to ensure our survival and we begin to master the knowledge and skills we will need to accomplish our Life Calling later in life. We seem to need this period of Divine Disconnect to truly focus our attention of the demands of the material world, in order to become fully contributing members of society. Only once we have established a firm footing and a solid understanding of our physical reality are we ready to reconnect with our original spiritual mission and realign with the Divine Self.

But life was simpler in the past, when the pace of life was slower and more predictable, and religion provided a firmer spiritual structure to our physical existence. In our post-modern day and age it is increasingly difficult to spontaneously return to our spiritual roots when the time comes and we are ready.

Awakening is easier said than done for many people these days. The Material Ego has mutated over the past millennium into an exceptionally dominant and all-pervasive force that somehow paralyzes modern man's spiritual inclination for much longer periods of time, even whole lifetimes, while enslaving him with fear, superficial materialism and hedonistic pursuits.

The spontaneous spiritual awakening we are supposed to have no longer occurs as it should for everyone. Some of us become deeply stuck in the reality maze of the modern world and find it difficult to 'wake up'. Some of us miss our target date, because of life's distractions and our capacity for free will.

We all *will awaken* spiritually at some point in this lifetime. As spiritual beings in human form it is inevitable. Unfortunately, this day only arrives for some people at the end of their journey, often when they are already on their death bed, because they chose to go through life ignoring the signs and refusing to hear the call. Such a late reconnection means they never have the opportunity to fully self-actualize, individuate and transcend in this lifetime. Therefore they never fully achieve their Soul Purpose, or wholly accomplish their Life Calling. Their Life Plan remains unfulfilled when they depart from this time-space reality.

Not accomplishing your Life Plan is a tragic act of free will. It is akin to charting an elaborate vacation itinerary before arriving at your holiday destination, with all kinds of plans for outdoor adventures and intentions to go sightseeing and shopping, but then ending up spending the whole trip in your hotel room ordering from room service and watching television. In a similar fashion the unconscious soul spends a lifetime in the semi-conscious state of Divine Disconnection and then returns home 'empty-handed'.

Fortunately, all is not lost, because the Divine Self has many innovative ways to remind us who we really are, when the time draws near for us to awaken. At the end of our lives none of us can claim to never have received any signs, messages or warnings to emerge from our disconnected slumber. We are always invited in some way to reconnect. All we need to do is hear the Inner Calling. Yet, despite all the early warnings and signs, many of us choose to remain spiritually deaf and blind and are eventually forced to awaken through trauma or tragedy in our lives.

The Existential Crisis

People awaken to their personal spiritual truth and inner Divinity in diverse and interesting ways. For some it is a gradual process over months or years, while others have sudden or profound metaphysical experiences. For some the Divine reconnection is triggered by a traumatic event, or an internal or external crisis causing them to go through a Dark Night of the Soul, or a 'descent to the underworld'.

Inanna's descent, when she gave up her status as priestess, and St John's Dark Night, in which the soul had to journey through a long, dark night to ultimately reach God, are the primal archetypes for these experiences. But these are just two examples of the essential 'descent to the underworld' theme found in many religions all over the world.

The archetype of the hero, deity or holy person who journeys to the underworld or the afterlife, and then returns with a higher knowledge, increased consciousness or heightened spiritual status, appears to be ingrained in the collective unconscious of all humanity, no matter what religion or spiritual path we may choose to follow. There are a plethora of classic mythological characters who made visits to the underworld. These are merely a select few from a long list.

Hermóðr - Norse paganism

Hunahpu and **Xbalanque** - Mayan mythology

Inanna - Sumerian mythology

Indra - Vedic religion

Izanami - Japanese mythology

Jesus – Christianity

Joseph – Judaism

Kaknu - Native American mythology

Osiris - Egyptian mythology

Psyche - Greek and Roman mythology

Pwyll - Welsh mythology

A well-known modern version of this myth is *The Divine Comedy* by Dante Alighieri. This epic poem is considered to be one of the greatest works in the history of world literature and tells the story of Dante's own journey through the three 'realms of the dead', namely Hell, Purgatory and Heaven.

The phenomenon of an awakening due to traumatic events, a personal dilemma or a Dark Night of the Soul is known in Psychology as the *existential crisis*. It is considered it to be the stage in human development when many of us question the value, purpose and meaning of our lives.

According to Wikipedia.org an existential crisis may result from "the sense of being alone and isolated in the world; a new-found grasp or appreciation of one's mortality; believing that one's life has no purpose or external meaning; awareness of one's freedom and the consequences of accepting or rejecting that freedom; or an extremely pleasurable or hurtful experience that leaves one seeking meaning."

Modern versions of spiritual awakening due to an existential crisis include near-death experiences, being 'born again', having a 'first vision' or the visitation of a divine being, or suffering an 'ego death'. An example in current popular culture is the well-known author Eckhart Tolle, who reported a profound spiritual awakening after he had suffered long periods of intense suicidal depression.

Magical Thinking

The time of the Divine Disconnect appears to be directly linked to the childhood phenomenon Swiss developmental psychologist Jean Piaget calls *magical thinking*. Magical thinking is a common trait found in all children all over the world, between the ages of approximately 2 until 7. This timeframe is also known as the 'pre-operational stage' of child development and it is the period in our early life when we increasingly explore our environment and gradually learn to distinguish between 'fantasy' and 'reality'.

Children at this age initially have all kinds of imaginative ideas and magical interpretations of the world in order to make sense of their external and internal reality. At this age we still believe that we can grow wings and learn to fly; or that animals can talk and sing; or that our shadow is a magical person following us around; or that the Sun goes to sleep in the ocean; that there is a man living in the Moon; or that the wind, the clouds and the trees notice us and obey our instructions. We often also have 'imaginary friends' at this age.

The process of exploring the actual limitations of our time-space reality lasts several years. Most 'magical thinking' typically disappears around the time when a child finally accepts that there is no such thing as the Tooth Fairy, or Santa Clause. As our understanding and knowledge of earthly reality increases we lose our imaginative sense of the magical and metaphysical.

It appears that the only reason magical thinking must fade into the background of our consciousness as we grow up is because it can become inappropriate or dangerous from a *survival perspective*. To live safely in our physical body on this planet in primitive times we had to recognize certain patterns in our environment, for example we had to know that certain berries or plants are poisonous when we eat them, or that we may die should we fall off a cliff, or that wild animals can cause us physical harm. Confronted with the independent forces of nature it is obviously not a good idea for frail young humans to believe that they can fly or give instructions to wild animals.

However, we never fully lose the tendency to see the magical or mysterious in the ordinary. Findings in cognitive science suggest that magical thinking is an *inherent, human trait* that persists into adulthood. For example, humans display *confirmation bias,* meaning we tend to seek confirmation for our beliefs, rather than trying to disprove our beliefs (which is ironically the exact opposite of what we do when we do scientific research).

We also experience what is known as *cognitive dissonance*, which can lead to psychological discomfort. What this means is that we are generally reluctant to change our existing beliefs, even when we are presented with clear evidence contradicting our existing beliefs, because it creates an uncomfortable sense of dissonance. We instead prefer to continue believing what we always believed, rather than change our convictions, because changing it is too unpleasant or traumatic.

Magical thinking remains a part of our adult life and this appears to be prevalent in all societies and cultures. It is also a phenomenon that is found in all civilizations. Throughout recorded human history we find clear evidence that mankind has always believed that some things are *sacred*; that things can be *cursed*; that the human *mind* can *control matter*; that *rituals* bring prosperity or good fortune; that there is power in *words* and the *names* assigned to things; that there is *justice* and *moral order* in the Universe (such as karma or God's judgment); and finally that the Universe is 'alive' or has a *conscious awareness* of its own existence.

The fact that these fundamental beliefs are widespread and common in all cultures is no coincidence or accident. If we accept that we are spiritual beings having a physical, human experience, our tendency towards 'magical thinking' and metaphysical belief makes all the sense in the world.

However, many scientists attach absolutely no metaphysical or spiritual significance to these phenomena. For example, researcher Dr Eugene Subbotsky refers to it as 'magical ideation' and suggests that we retain our preference for magical thinking because "it's much more comfortable to think that your fate is written down in a constellation of stars than that you're one of a certain group of intelligent animals who are lost in frozen space forever". Neuropsychologist Peter Brugger, takes a more positive approach, which goes beyond the mere 'survival' theory. He states that it is not healthy for us humans to be entirely stripped of all our magical thinking. His data seems to show that a lack of magical thinking leads to 'anhedonia', which is the *inability to experience pleasure*.

We were never really meant to feel like 'animals' lost in space. It is clear that we have an innate urge or intuitive desire to find meaning and purpose in our lives, and that we derive a lot of pleasure and joy from the so-called 'magical ideations' we attach to random patterns and coincidences. I propose that although it is necessary for us to initially put our 'magical thinking' into its proper earthly perspective, while we grow up, we should not be encouraged or pressured to relinquish it entirely, for it is an expression of our original spiritual nature. It is also my experience that a true spiritual awakening is always accompanied by the return of so-called 'magical thinking' to our consciousness in some way, shape or form. Without 'magical ideation' true spiritual awareness seems impossible.

Yes, we did come here for a physical human experience and therefore we have to make do with little or no awareness of our 'superpowers' for a large portion of our life. It is part of the deal. One cannot expect to have a truly physical life experience bound by time and space, while retaining your full spiritual capacity. The two states of being are mutually exclusive.

In this lifetime we are like Superman who must remain disguised as the nerdy newspaper journalist Clark Kent, or Harry Potter and his friends who are not allowed to do magic while they are on holiday, away from Hogwarts School of Witchcraft and Wizardry.

We don't mind this compulsory precondition for our current physical incarnation, because being more physical than spiritual is essential to the authentic human experience. It is after all what we originally signed up for! However, we were not meant to completely abandon our metaphysical nature and enter this time-space reality entirely 'unarmed' and powerless. Even Harry Potter and Clark Kent get to tap into their 'special powers' once in a while, especially when the going gets tough.

Impotent Superheroes

Psychologists view the magical thinking period in child development as just another step in our growth, from being a childish, irrational and illogical baby into a mature, rational and logical adult. This assumption is based on the scientific paradigm of Physicalism or mechanistic Newtonian thinking that still dominates conventional science.

Professor Francis Heylighen defines the current dominant worldview as being "based in reductionism, determinism, materialism, and a reflection-correspondence view of knowledge. Although it is simple, coherent and intuitive, it ignores or denies human agency, values, creativity and evolution".

This concrete, inflexible view of reality has become the main reason why we are conditioned to forget our true spiritual nature and relinquish our innate metaphysical abilities. It is the leading cause for many people to remain in the 'reality coma' of Divine Disconnection for much longer than they need to.

Without so-called magical thinking many among us are like superheroes, abandoned in the middle of nowhere, without access to any of our superpowers. In this state we have only the Material Self or Ego and the preconceived notions of the Newtonian worldview serving us as guides. In this unconscious state of being we are ultimately unable to fully serve ourselves, each other or this planet; neither can we truly honor the Laws of The Universe.

The Silly Habits Of Ape Brains

Researchers also maintain that our magical thinking, in both our childhood and adult life, is merely a result of our brains being designed to *recognize patterns*, because making such cause-and-effect connections enabled our ancestors to survive in the natural world. They disregard any metaphysical explanation for this phenomenon and instead describe it merely as "seeing causality in coincidence".

Modern day skeptics thus regard magical thinking as a natural human trait that, since it is no longer really required for our survival, has become nothing more than a *biological weakness* in the way our primitive 'ape brains' are wired. They see our penchant for attaching all kinds of interpretations and deeper meanings to coincidences and accidents as *silly habits* that lead to all kinds of superstitions and false beliefs about the spiritual, the supernatural and the paranormal.

But the metaphysical truth is that we do not begin our lives as mindless clumps of 'irrational animal flesh' with a silly tendency to see patterns in everything. Instead we start out as experienced spiritual beings in a young physical incarnation. We know upon arrival that we are able to influence and shape our reality; that we can control our environment with the power of our consciousness; and that there are many unseen things beyond this limited time-space reality. At the time of our birth we had just arrived here from an alternate dimension or a higher state of consciousness, where all these 'magical powers' or possibilities are indeed very real and perfectly ordinary.

The process of child development is much more than merely developing or becoming a more a rational, logical human being. Instead it is a process of *adjusting* our Higher Consciousness to be able to process an unknown, new reality platform. It is the process of *adapting* to an unfamiliar, foreign environment here on planet Earth.

Children are therefore not merely irrational, illogical young mammals or 'little apes'. Instead, they are wise spiritual sages who have come here by choice on a very specific, goal-oriented life mission. Unfortunately, in the human form they are also very vulnerable as new arrivals in this foreign environment, and we must consider this upon welcoming them into our world.

Have you ever noticed the deep wisdom in a baby's eyes? In the state of Divine Disconnection we call it 'innocence' or 'naivety', as if these babies know absolutely nothing, while we know it all. Imagine how different our society would be if we should adopt a very different worldview which honors children as newly arrived spiritual 'elders' or cosmic explorers. Imagine how differently our psychologists would study the childhood years as being a period of *adjustment* and *adaptation* to a new environment, and a new physical body.

Maybe we should treat the newborn infants of our species with the sophistication that the National Aeronautics and Space Administration (NASA) in America devote to rehabilitating their astronauts after a long period in outer space. During extensive space flights, astronauts develop various neuro-motor impairments that require therapy and special care upon their return to Earth. The effects of not being exposed to gravity for a few months can be so debilitating that some astronauts have to relearn how to walk or to hold up their neck, similar to the way newborn babies learn to sit up and walk.

Keeping It Real

Research based on Jean Piaget's theory of child development has shown that children believe they can *dynamically participate* in the workings of the Universe, for example making the clouds move with their mind. Children also accept without question that all things are *conscious* and alive, which is known as 'animism'. Rocks, trees and lightning bolts therefore all have a life and an innate *awareness* of their own.

Children also accept that all inanimate things have an *internal energy* that enables them to do all kinds of things, similar to the child's ability to use his or her muscles to jump and run around. In the child's eyes a big rock could therefore 'refuse' to be moved by 'pushing back' just as hard when the child pushes to shift it.

Children also take it for granted that everything in the world around them were made especially for the sake of humans and that everything is organized for the good of mankind, known as 'artificialism'. If a child were to be asked how the world came into being, the child would state that it was somehow created by man, or created for man.

Children do not view their world with this kind of magical thinking because they are still learning how to be conscious in the 'real world'. Instead they display this way of thinking because they still need to adjust their former state of Higher Consciousness to a new, limiting environment of physicality that demands a certain level of *realism*. Children arrive on this planet as innovative and curious little 'scientists' who explore and find ways to acclimatize to the new reality in which they now find ourselves.

As a species we remain in the care of our parents for much longer than any other primate species. From an evolutionary, animalistic perspective this makes no sense, because to grow up as fast as possible would ensure greater survival and enable us to procreate and have more offspring much sooner. Experts believe the reason we spend such a long time in a nurtured childhood environment may be due to our very large brains, which presumably requires a much longer time to grow, develop and learn.

From a metaphysical perspective this makes sense, because extensive data collection is required for the purpose of our Life Calling. The period for data collection has also become more lengthy over the centuries as the human species evolved and became more sophisticated. A few centuries ago most children did not receive any formal schooling and were considered to be adults at a much younger age.

Removing The Training Wheels

In time, as we mature from our childhood, we learn as spiritual beings in human form to let go of our 'human training wheels', until we fully adopt adult rational thinking and logic appropriate to this time-space reality. We do this for the purpose of surviving and ultimately to fulfill our Soul Purpose and Life Calling. We understand that in order to complete our earthly mission successfully, and get the most out of this physical experience, we must adapt functionally to the shared reality of our human parents, peers and ancestors.

It is interesting to note that Jean Paiget's theory of magical thinking proposes that the child can initially not distinguish between his internal being and the external world. It is only through *progressive differentiation* that the child's internal identity comes into being and is then contrasted with the external reality.

Piaget states that this is not due simply to children being ignorant of their internal world, but due to the confusion caused by the child's lack of *objectivity*. In the early stages of development the 'self' and the 'world' are perceived or experienced by the child as *one*, and not as separate entities. To become objective, children then have to develop an *Ego identity* from which they can perceive and interpret their external world. By the time the Ego of a child has finally found its identity within this physical reality, the process of establishing the state of Divine Disconnect is also complete.

Unless we grow up in a truly eccentric environment or highly spiritual household, there is a lot of pressure on us from a young age to relinquish all manner of 'magical thinking', because we soon discover that the metaphysical instincts and inner spiritual wisdom with which we arrived in this time-space reality are not entirely welcome in a world driven by realism and the rational Ego.

We are taught from early on that our Higher Consciousness way of thinking is considered irrational or impractical in this new environment. Those of us who secretly hold on to some level of inner spiritual awareness eventually often find ourselves criticized and ostracized for being superstitious, immature or simply weird.

Only once we adopt a more metaphysical approach to how we view human nature and child development will modern science begin to truly grasp the meaning of the infinite Cycle of Life, from birth to death to rebirth. Only then will we truly understand why the physical appearance of elderly people seem to be more and more like that of newborn babies, as they near the final stage of their life. The elderly are not 'deteriorating' or 'decaying' into a physical death; they are merely reverting to their original state of Divine Beingness.

It is interesting to note that the process of becoming aware of this time-space reality after our birth clearly seems to be reversed upon the moment of our death. Shortly before death many people appear to detach themselves from the limitations of this reality and prepare for a journey back to their spiritual home. Medical personnel working in emergency units and hospices often report patients "hallucinating" or "losing their grasp of reality" shortly before their death. This is known as deathbed phenomena or 'death-bed visions'. People who have witnessed these deathbed visions tend to report similar phenomena across different cultures.

According to the Horizon Research Foundation the most commonly reported deathbed phenomenon is the so-called 'take-away' vision in which the dying person sees dead relatives, religious figures, angels or other ethereal beings who come to collect them or accompany them through the process of dying. The dying are often seen reaching out their arms to someone invisible in the room or having conversations with deceased loved ones. These experiences also result in a marked change in the dying person's emotional state and they tend to express a sense of peace, calm, joy and excitement.

Additionally, the dying person also seems to experience extra sensory perceptions in the form of 'heavenly music' or a 'radiant white light' which envelops the room. Some people report the sensation of travelling back and forth between this present existence and another dimension or a new reality. Many dying hospital patients also regain their physical strength and a youthful appearance shortly before they die, despite having been very weak for a long time.

These are but a few examples of widely reported and researched deathbed phenomena that all indicate that we do proceed or return to an unseen metaphysical or spiritual state at the time of our departure from this world.

The Golden Age Of Man

Humanity has been losing its connection with the Divine, God or the Supreme Source throughout the millennia. In the initial 'Golden Age of Man' the disconnect was not nearly as dire for our ancestors, who were basically 'gentle savages'. In those early days we were spiritual beings having a thrilling, yet *primitive* physical experience in this wild, untouched playground that was ancient planet Earth.

Most cultures and religions have in common the myths, legends and traditions describing this original Golden Age of Man. It is remembered as the time when the Gods walked among men, when the people lived organically and in sync with the natural ebb and flow of nature, and the entire world was a wild paradise. There was no need for 'magical thinking' then, only genuine everyday magic and mysticism. Children were not mocked or scolded for singing to the rain or talking to the wind.

Of course, in our vulnerable human form we also faced many practical challenges during that golden age to ensure our physical survival, but that was how it was intended to be. After all, we came for the challenge, thrill and adventure of it all, did we not? It is no wonder that as a species we still love epic, adventure films and fantasy novels. We also love the expression of beauty in the arts and the drama, and the rush and excitement of sports.

In the golden age we found innovative ways to survive the elements and protect ourselves from dangerous animals and plants. We had the ability to do this, because we came into this world equipped with our metaphysical capacity for Divine reasoning, innate intelligence, creative ability, extra sensory perception, intuition and a capacity for communication. We needed these 'godlike' talents or abilities to ensure our free will while we were here. Without free will the whole journey would have been pointless to begin with. For if we were not equipped with free will we would not be able to make decisions and choices that would foster our soul growth and spiritual expansion. Neither would we have much fun in the process.

At first we took from nature, and later from each other, only that which we required for our basic survival. But in time we began to disturb this balance due to our tendency towards greedy pleasure-seeking, our need to learn, understand and know and our desire to increase and expand. Our species evolved as a consequence, constantly growing in secular knowledge, insight and understanding.

We became increasingly skilled and sophisticated, and our worldly needs and desires expanded as a consequence. We wished to experience, learn and know more, but in the process we increasingly lost touch with our origins in Spirit and we gradually drifted further and further away from our Divine essence.

The human Ego evolved as we became more and more aware of our individual consciousness and free will, and it eventually took over. We began to worship the 'false idols' of property ownership, war and material riches. Through these pursuits we increasingly converted our co-conscious Ego into the False Self that is modern man. This False Self reigns supreme in the Newtonian society it has created for itself and is just as synthetic and toxic as its man-made environment. The evidence for this current state of Divine Disconnection is especially compelling when one considers how post-modern pop culture admires, adulates and encourages the traits of narcissism, conceit and greed.

According to recent research at the University of Michigan the empathy levels of American college students have dropped significantly since the 1980's, with an especially dramatic decline over the past decade. To make matters worse, during this same period levels of narcissism among college students has reached new heights, according to research done at San Diego State University. One possible reason for this decline may be our increased social isolation, and the growing dehumanization of people due to technology. You only have to read some of the really cruel and callous comments some young people post on social networks and video sharing sites to find the necessary evidence.

Narcissism is becoming the cult of our current generation. Our society worships those who succeed at the expense of their fellow man. We adore those who are obsessed with their own self-importance; we follow their lead and indulge their whims and vanities. We call them Star, Socialite, Celebrity, Fashionista, Trendsetter, Entrepreneur, Mogul, Guru, Diva, Icon, Genius. And the more selfish, greedy and unkind they act towards others, the more thrilling they are to their Groupies, Hipsters, Followers and Fans. They are the post-modern gods of the False Self.

The Laws Of The Universe

Our *free will* and capacity for *reasoning* are a large part of what truly defines our inner Divinity. The rational mind was originally intended to be our platform for learning, creativity and expansion. We were created in the 'image of God' so that we could literally live like 'human gods'. But using our free will we developed a False Self. The human Ego was intended as a platform of objectivity from which we could successfully navigate our earthly reality, but has instead become the mastermind behind all that is wrong with our post-modern society. It is the reason why we remain in the state of Divine Disconnect, well beyond the intended expiry date, and it is also the cause of our growing sense of dissatisfaction as a species trapped in 21st Century reality.

The human Ego developed out of our wanting to take advantage of our free will in this lifetime. As spiritual beings in physical form we enjoy our creative freedom, our ability to reason and our capacity for free decision-making and choice. That is after all why we came here as spiritual beings - to enjoy this independent, earthly experience.

In human form we enjoy expressing our individual and unique ideas, and doing things our own way. We enjoy seeing ourselves as separate from everything and everyone else. We do it because we can, and because it's fun, but in the process we have also drifted away from our Divine origins and we increasingly forgot our inherent spiritual nature.

The more the Ego began to dictate and drive our life choices, as well as our individual and collective perceptions of reality, the more we began to disregard the Laws of the Universe. These Universal Laws, also known as the Divine Laws or the Spiritual Laws of Nature, are the unchanging principles that govern the entire Universe. It is what keeps everything in metaphysical balance.

These laws are the pillars of our existence in all dimensions, the very fabric of every realm of man and spirit. Without these universal forces there will be no continued creation. Nothing will expand or prosper. The Universal Laws makes everything 'tick' and keeps everything together. They ensure that balance is somehow always restored and that we live in harmony with ourselves, each other and the world around us.

The Ego has increasingly resisted the Universal Laws over countless centuries, since the time of the Golden Age of Man came to an end. Our scientists have uncovered many of the mysteries of nature's physical laws, such as gravity, electricity, chemistry and magnetism, but we have forgotten in the process the need for metaphysical integration, balance and harmony.

Our Ego-driven modern society has now reached a point in its evolution where we seem to think we are above the order and laws of the Universe. We have come to believe that we can continue to violate these laws and do whatever we please, without ultimately doing harm to our species and our planet.

At the same time, many of us increasingly feel overwhelmed by our sense of Divine Discontent, because we have grown weary of this battle of wills our Ego has been waging against our inner Divinity over so many lifetimes. We are exhausted from our constant Ego-driven struggle with ourselves, each other, our natural environment, and the Laws of the Universe. We are yearning for reconnection with the Divine Self and long to once again be in harmony with all.

After many centuries of slavishly following the Ego, we wish to find some way to awaken and realign with our Divine nature here on Earth. We long to reinvent the 'golden age lifestyle' of our ancient ancestors, repackaged for a future Earth and a new golden age of man. This revamped way of life is the art of *Divine Living*.

The World Is Our Playground

In our original Infinite Oneness of Spirit we together invented or co-created the reality of this planet and all its marvels, to serve as some kind of shared 'soul school' or 'cosmic playground' for our own creative, spiritual expansion. Our world was designed to be a magnificent 'adventure resort' intended solely for our existential enlightenment. We created this as a time-space reality outside the other metaphysical dimensions, where we could come and 'rough it in the wild', so to speak, on the ultimate 'educational camping trip'. We each own time-share in this amazing place, it is not reserved just for the privileged few.

Sadly, the more sophisticated we became in our enjoyment of this co-created world, the more detached and confused we became about our spiritual origins. In essence we have never been able to fully answer the mystery of our existence while we are in the flesh, and maybe it is best that we don't. It is not in our best interest to know absolutely everything while we are here. That is not why we came here.

Someday, at the end of this lifetime, when we return to our original Divine state, we will remember everything in full and we will truly understand. We will then hopefully look back with delight at the contribution our physical life has made to the continued expansion of our magnificent Conscious Universe and we will hopefully sign proudly at the bottom of another completed chapter in the Book of Life.

In the meantime it is in our best interest to shield ourselves from full awareness of our Divinity. There is a place and a time for everything. Why spoil the ride?

There is a classic Talmudic myth of the four rabbis, Azzai, Ben Zoma, Elisha ben Abuyah, and Akiva, who met as a group in paradise for the purpose of studying Kabbalah. But they delved so deep into the mysteries of the Universe and God that Azzai went insane, Ben Zoma died and Elisha ben Abuyah destroyed all the plants and left the faith of Judaism to become a heretic. Rabbi Akiva was the only one who "entered in peace and left in peace." It was this legend that led medieval rabbis to place a ban on the study of Kabbalah, by limiting it to people of character who were mature and of a certain age.

In our human form it is intended for us to remain incapable of fully grasping the Divine mysteries of the Universe. This current time-space reality was created as a lucid foundation, a familiar platform, a time-honored podium from which we can act out the physical experience we intended to have before we came. Reality is our stage and we are the actors. It is a familiar playground for the human DNA. It is a matching habitat or matrix that resonates with all the ancient experiences of our species and all the deep-seated memories of our ancestors. It is engraved in our genes and cellular structure in the form of a *collective unconscious*. Our earthly reality is a like a traditional family holiday destination to which we return with every new generation.

To entirely remove the primary structure or scaffolding of this physical, shared reality, by delving too deeply into the mysteries of our spiritual origins, would be to destroy the essence of the human experience. It would be like burning down a cosmic school, or exposing all the secrets of the conjurer during a magic show. We would simply 'spoil' the fun for ourselves and for all future generations. Why organize a treasure hunt for children, and then point out all the places where you have hidden the prizes, gifts and sweets?

If we were to rip open the veil that separates us from the Other Side and suddenly have total recall and full understanding of the nature of our Divine being and metaphysical origins, we would no longer be able to function effectively within this time-space reality. We would become fish out of water, unable to breathe. We would be aliens on a translucent planet. The earthly environment would disappear or disintegrate into a faint cloud of surreal smoke.

If we were to give up our human 'innocence' and lose our trust in the firmness of this earthly platform, we would simply defeat the purpose of this wonderful illusion we call 'reality'. Our collective awareness of, and participation in this shared platform and operating system is what keeps the world turning on its axis. If it were to be fully exposed to the Divine origins of humanity, while we are still here in physical form, there will no longer be much point for us to come into this dimension, nor for it to continue to exist. The spell would be broken.

We did not come here to have a complete and perfect metaphysical or spiritual existence, because we already have that 'back home'. The French author Jules Renard wrote: "We are ignorant of the Beyond because this ignorance is the condition of our own life. Just as ice cannot know fire except by melting and vanishing."

But, if we did not come here to experience a full-blown metaphysical reality, why this book? Why this quest to reconnect with our Divine Self? Would it not then defeat or tarnish the purpose of our current life journey?

The answer is no. Yes, we did come for an imperfect, secular experience, but not to suffer in utter neglect and misery. We were never supposed to destroy, pillage and violate our planet and each other. We do need to be human and vulnerable, but not deficient, self-destructive and powerless. We are children of the Divine. We are all-powerful creators, the owners and heirs to a glorious metaphysical empire, the designers of an extraordinary and constantly evolving species. We came here to discover, explore, experience, learn, grow and have fun. We came here to create and expand as 'gods' in physical form. We came here to experience a Divine Life of balance, harmony, joy, abundance and unconditional love, much like our ancient ancestors did during the Golden Age of Man, but this time with much greater wisdom, insight and sophistication

You and I chose to be here at this time in human history. We came here to experience all of the happiness, joy, purpose and fulfillment a Divine Life can yield. We also came with a specific Life Plan and mission to fulfill our Soul Purpose and Life Calling, and to honor our sacred duty to ourselves. And in order to accomplish that, we need to reclaim that part of our Divinity with which we have lost contact. To achieve these things we have to reconnect with, and embrace the Divine Self.

2

THE DIVINE SELF

Your Divine Self, or Higher Self, is not a remote aspect of you that exists elsewhere, in some distant, transcendental place. Your Divine Self is your true, original state of *consciousness* or being-ness, and it is here inside, and out there and everywhere and beyond everything.

Access to the Divine Self is not limited only to those of us who have achieved certain virtues, or have met certain standards of goodness, faith or holiness. Kathleen Besly writes in *The Divine Art of Living*, "If God is omnipresent there can be no separation between the material and spiritual. With this as an accepted view, we cannot think one thing more wonderful than another because God, the Infinite Perfection, is in and of everything."

The Divine Self is therefore not some kind of special status or process of salvation, or a superior level of spiritual development. It is not something that you can only strive to attain through dogmatic religion, or earn through regimented spiritual practice.

The 'place' we come from, whether you choose to call it Heaven, Nirvana, Zion, Hashamayim, Avalon, Moksha, the Other Side, the Hereafter, Dreamtime, the Spirit Realm, the Ether, or Paradise, is not a far-away geographical location or a physical destination. It is instead the omnipresent, infinite state of *consciousness* we all originate from. It is a separate dimension, an alternate reality, a different plane of being, which exists inside and outside and all around us, and beyond everything. The Divine Self is your doorway or direct 'inner link' to this Original Consciousness. The Divine Self is the true, original you that is within; it is the 'metaphysical you' who always has been and always will be. Your human body and Ego identity is merely a temporary expression of your inner Divinity. You have been created in the 'image of God', or in the essence of the Divine Source, and that is the immaculate core with which you arrived on planet Earth at the time of your birth.

In *Spiritual Growth, Being Your Higher Self*, Sanaya-Orin Roman describes the Divine Self as "eternal, infinite consciousness, free from all attachments and beyond all action; it is constant and unchanging, birthless and deathless." She further describes it as "the Oneness from which all life comes, and to which all life returns."

The Divine Self is known by a plethora of names: the Higher Self, Soul, Light Body, Cosmic Consciousness, Christ Consciousness, I Am, Holy Spirit, Essence of Life, Universal Mind, The Tao, the Inner God.

It is not important which name you choose to use. What is ultimately important is that you consciously *reconnect* and *realign* with your Divine Self, so that you will have a direct experience and greater awareness of your inner Divinity and be more mindful of the daily guidance and comfort you receive from your Higher Being. The Divine Self is your guide, your muse, your teacher, your comforter and your protector. Recognizing and honoring the role of the Divine Self in your life is essential to creating a Divine Life.

The Splitting Image of God

Ralph Waldo Trine writes in *In Tune With The Infinite* that the life of God and the life of man are in essence identical and therefore as One. He further explains that the lives of God and of man differ not in essence or quality; they differ in degree.

> *If God is the Infinite Spirit of Life back of all, whence all comes, then clearly our life as individualized spirits is continually coming from this Infinite Source by means of this divine inflow. In the second place, if our lives as individualized spirits are directly from, are parts of this Infinite Spirit of Life, then the degree of the Infinite Spirit that is manifested in the life of each must be identical in quality with that Source, the same as a drop of water taken from the ocean is, in nature, in characteristics, identical with that ocean, its source.*

If you come from a Christian, Islamic or Jewish background you will be familiar with the concept that man was created in the 'image of God'. And since we were created in God's image we must mirror Divine Nature with our ability to actualize unique, godlike qualities on our own accord. These sacred *qualities* or *abilities* confirm our inherent Divine nature and are the essential components of our Divine or Higher Self.

You Have Divine Reason. You are a rational being with a capacity for *deliberation* and *free decision making*. You also have an inquisitive mind which seeks to attain universal understanding and harmony with yourself, others and your environment. The 17th century French philosopher, René Descartes, expressed this very well when he exclaimed: "I think, therefore I am!" This ability to think, imagine, reflect, reason, consider, learn, judge, contemplate, ponder, deliberate, choose, decide and believe are all expressions of a rational, infinite, eternal Divine Intelligence or Creator God that has existed since the dawn of creation, and this rational ability is more commonly known as your *free will*.

Your free will gives you the unique capacity for moral and spiritual reflection and growth. And since you can think of yourself as a being created in the image of God or the Divine Source, it becomes clear that we are in fact co-creators with the Divine. God or the Divine Source does not reflect on our behalf, or decide or choose or deliberate for us in all things. We are able to attain self-actualization and we are able to participate in the sacred reality of Divinity.

You Have Complete Centeredness. Your consciousness or 'beingness' is experienced from the perspective of a distinct 'I, Me and Myself'. You are aware of your own consciousness in this time-space reality and there is a sense of individuality or separateness from everything around you. Your state of *consciousness* refers to your *individual awareness* of your unique thoughts, memories, feelings, sensations and environment. You possess a certain *self-consciousness* as a separate, living entity. This is also known as the Ego. If you were merely an unconscious component of God's creation, or an oblivious, humble fiber woven into the magnificent tapestry of the Universe, then you would not have had such a clear sense of your own, individual beingness.

However, it is this very awareness of being a separate 'identity' from the rest of all creation that gave rise to the regime of the False Ego, or the Narcissistic Self, which is the underlying cause for more and more souls remaining trapped in a state of Divine Disconnect for most, if not all of their lives. Spiritual awakening and reconnection with the Divine Self happens when we realize that although we have our own complete centeredness we are also holographic, miniature fragments of God and the Conscious Universe. We are more than just ourselves. We are expressions of the Divine Source, reflections of the Omnipresent Oneness of Being.

You Have Creative Freedom And Metaphysical Power. As an expression of Divinity you have been blessed with a creative imagination and you are free to explore all of its limitless possibilities within a Conscious Universe of pure potential and constant expansion. Once you have selected the possibilities you desire, you are able to create, attract and *manifest* those desired possibilities. Your imagined possibilities can be manifested metaphysically in many different ways, which we will explore later in this book. You have the *creative freedom* to be a conscious creator of your life experiences and your physical reality.

To live a truly awakened and abundant Divine Life you must recognize that your external reality shapes and moulds itself around everything you think, say, expect and believe. The 19th-century German composer Richard Wagner once remarked that he was convinced that there are "universal currents of Divine Thought vibrating the ether everywhere and that any who can feel these vibrations is inspired." Your innate creative, metaphysical capacity empowers you to be a conscious co-creator of our reality. Whatever is possible in your mind, whatever can be reasoned, or imagined, or dreamt of, ultimately become reality.

You Have The Capacity For Self-Actualization. The American psychologist Abraham Maslow defined self-actualization as "the impulse to convert oneself into what one is capable of being." As a human being created in the image of the Divine, you are able to realize all of your innate potentialities in this lifetime. Self-actualization is the sacred potential you have as a being of Divine origins to manifest all your latent potentialities and to contribute to society. You are meant to make a real difference in the world and ensure the continued expansion of the Universe. This is more commonly known as your Life Purpose or your *Life Calling*.

You Have The Capacity For Self-Transcendence. As spiritual beings who came forth from a Divine Source we have the inherent desire and ability to improve and better ourselves spiritually. This is our *Soul Purpose*. When you come into this lifetime you are not only seeking the thrill of experiencing and experimenting with your reason and free will, as well as your complete centeredness, your ability to manifest and the challenge of self-actualization. In addition you arrive in this time-space reality with the intention of going beyond the limited state of human Ego, in order to expand your *Divine consciousness, insight* and *wisdom*.

You are a Divine being who arrived here with a 'soul mission', consisting of a list of experiences you intend to have and lessons you hope to learn during this lifetime. The goal is to achieve soul growth and an expansion of wisdom, insight, and consciousness. In certain religions this is known as 'salvation', while others describe it as 'transcendence' or the attainment of 'enlightenment'.

Self-realization in Hindu religion refers to a profound spiritual awakening, where you wake up from an illusory self or Ego to embrace your true Divine Self. The Hindu and Buddhist concept of karma is closely associated with the quest for self-transcendence.

Ego Is An Illusion

But, if the Divine Self is the 'real, true you' created in the image of God or Divine Source, then who is that confused face you sometimes see in your bathroom mirror? That person with the sometimes arrogant attitude and the all-too-often self-absorbed outlook on life?

Well, that individual is your Ego, and the Ego is a figment of your imagination, an illusion, a False Self, and invented Material Self. You are a spiritual being having a physical experience, not the other way around. That face and body you see in the looking-glass is merely a 'fancy-dress costume' that you rented for the occasion.

Ironically, the Ego is a manifestation of our capacity for Divine reasoning, free will, complete centeredness, creative thought and self-actualization – all the inherent qualities that make us Divine beings. The purpose of the Ego is to be a survival mechanism and our 'reality platform'. As non-physical beings in human form we need the self-awareness of being a material entity with its own earthly identity in order for us to makes sense of our physical environment and function 'normally' within this time-space dimension. Without the human Ego we would be like 'ghostly aliens' trapped in a reality we do not comprehend.

Furthermore, to survive in the wild as primitive man the human species had to develop a sense of self to meet its basic needs. This development of the Ego was the driving force behind human evolution, from ancient Co-Conscious Man up to today's Humanic Man. But in time the urge to look out for 'me, myself and I' took on a life of its own, until we have created such a false, illusionary sense of self and separateness from both the natural world and our Divine origins, that we lost all connection with the Oneness of Being that is the very fabric of the Conscious Universe.

We have reached a stage in our evolution as a species where we no longer have the need for primitive survival-based thinking, but we are still dominated in our thoughts, feelings and actions by the temporal illusion of the human Ego. We have created a post-modern world of physical comfort and our primitive survival instinct is no longer a priority.

But because our world has changed, our needs have also changed and many of us desire a 'new way' to be in the world. This is where most people's current sense of Divine Discontent originates. We are no longer finding satisfactory answers in science, religion, materialism or mere hedonism. Although the current mainstream worldview, as expressed in the mass media and popular culture, keeps feeding the selfish False Ego or Material Self, our inner Divinity constantly reminds us that there is more to our life here than mere physical survival, rational knowledge, sensual pleasure and the gathering of material possessions and comforts.

The only way to transcend this tension between the conscious Ego and the unconscious Divine Self is to awaken to our true spiritual nature and expand our current consciousness to incorporate more of that which was previously unconscious. In other words, humanity is ready to shift to a higher and deeper level of consciousness. If we wish to personally thrive in the modern world we have created, and also collectively ensure our survival and evolution as a species, we will simply have to accept that we each need to take personal responsibility for the way we perceive and interpret our world, and for how we express the Ego and its often self-obsessed needs.

In the *Dhammapada*, one of the primary collections of teachings in Buddhism, the Buddha says, "Earnest among the thoughtless, awake among the sleepers, the wise man advances like a racer, leaving behind the hack."

We cannot afford to wait for corporate science and popular culture to catch up with the current global spiritual awakening and dawning new age of conscious evolution. The English evolutionary biologist Julian Huxley said, "Whether he likes it or not, [man] is responsible for the whole further evolution of our planet...man is nothing but evolution become conscious of itself."

Until you accept the fundamental truth that you are a Divine spiritual being, instead of an earth-bound Ego, you will never recognize your Soul Purpose and Life Calling, even if it hunted you down to tap you on the shoulder. Ralph Waldo Emerson wrote, "Every man is a divinity in disguise, a god playing the fool."

All the physical and material things that you may think are you, or belong to you, or define you, are all just a daydream, an outdated survival fantasy. You are a spiritual being on a mission, not a human animal whose only concern is physical survival.

The Triangle of Divine Living

Spiritual awakening and awareness of the *Divine Self* is the first foundational component, or pillar, for creating a Divine Life. Once you embrace your true spiritual nature and Divine origins you will increasingly come back into alignment with your innate Divine potential and receive daily inner guidance from your Divine Self. This will empower you to consciously and more effectively pursue the second and third pillars of Divine Living, namely achieving your *Soul Purpose* and accomplishing your *Life Calling.*

Without the continuous daily guidance and comfort provided by your Divine Self, it would be impossible to fulfill your spiritual mission in this lifetime. Your Divine Self is who you really are in

Spirit; it is your true metaphysical identity and is therefore the mastermind behind your Life Plan.

Before you became the human incarnation you are now, your Divine Self was responsible for choosing when and where you would be born; who your parents and family would be; what life experiences you intended to have; which life events would be pre-destined for you, which soul lessons you aimed to learn; what your human passions, talents and ideals would be; and how you intended to contribute to the evolution of humanity and the continued expansion of the Universe.

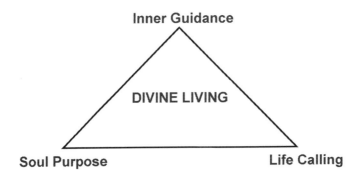

The Divine Self is the original architect of your Soul Purpose and Life Calling. Would it not make sense to follow the direction and advice of your inner 'Life Designer' in achieving your earthly mission? Reconnecting with your Divine Self is like tuning into a television channel or radio station. When you are not properly aligned with the frequency of the signal, the quality of the broadcast will be disturbed, blurred, noisy, and inferior. But when you are sharply tuned-in and aligned, you will experience crystal clear, high-definition insight into your original life design and true purpose. When you are spiritually aware and metaphysically attuned the Divine Self becomes a lucid, unambiguous guiding light towards your true destiny.

Soul Purpose vs. Life Purpose

To create a Divine Life it is important to differentiate between your Soul Purpose and Life Calling (also known as your Life Purpose). I prefer to use the term Life Calling, because 'Life Purpose' is often confused with the concept of 'Soul Purpose'. The most prevalent misconception is that Soul Purpose and Life Purpose describe the same thing and therefore the two terms are often interchanged. There is however a very clear difference between the two concepts.

Soul Purpose is your 'inner' metaphysical purpose. It refers to the *soul growth* and spiritual expansion you hope to achieve in this lifetime. Simply put, it refers to the knowledge, insight and wisdom *you aim to take away with you* when you depart from this reality one day, in order to return to where we came from.

Life Calling, or Life Purpose on the other hand refers to your 'external', secular purpose in this lifetime; it refers to *the contribution you hope to make* while you are here in physical form. In other words, it refers to whatever legacy it is *you hope to leave behind* in this world when you return to the spiritual realm.

Inner Guidance

In *The Hidden Power*, Thomas Troward expressed the belief that if we had to choose from all the spiritual principles the one that is most important, the need for *inner guidance* must rank as our first and highest priority.

> *Looking to this Infinite Mind as a Superior Intelligence from which we may receive guidance does not therefore imply looking to an external source. On the contrary, it is looking to the innermost spring of our own being, with a confidence in its action which enables us to proceed to the execution of our plans with a firmness and assurance that are in themselves the very guarantee of our success.*

Wayne Dyer writes, "If prayer is you talking to God, then intuition is God talking to you." You have been equipped with an unfailing inner guidance system to steer you towards fulfilling your Life Plan. When you reconnect with your Higher Consciousness and realign with the Divine Self you gain access to an inner awareness that will empower you to deliberately tap into your original Life

Plan and manifest a truly exhilarating, meaningful and abundant Divine Life.

Your inner guidance system is the 'voice' of your Divine Self and it consists of two components, namely your *intuition* and your *emotion*. On your journey through life, intuition walks ahead to give you directions and show you the way; your emotions follow behind to track your progress and let you know if you are still on target and moving in the right direction. All you need to do is tap into your intuition to guide you in making decisions and choices, and then to monitor your feelings for feedback on how well you are doing. Simply heed the call and follow your inner voice home. That's all there is to it.

Inner Guidance = Intuition + Emotion

In the next chapters of this book you will discover many powerful tools and strategies you can use to tap into the infinite resources of your intuition and emotions. Reconnecting with the Divine Self is however the key to getting back on track with your Life Plan. Once this is achieved the real work will start when you begin to follow the intuitive guidance and emotional instruction you receive.

When you follow your inner guidance you will gradually become more mindful of your Soul Purpose and Life Calling. Your priorities in life will shift and you will begin to master the power of conscious creation and attracting abundance into your life. The Universe will conspire to pave the way for you through synchronicities and you will begin to 'hit the ground running'. Step-by-step your new Divine Life will unfold by itself in ways you could never before have imagined.

Chasing Rainbows

The state of Divine Disconnect, when you are feeling out of touch, imperfect, inadequate or wanting in your life, it is not a reflection of who you really are, neither is it some shameful personal defect that requires salvation. It is in fact a reflection of who you are *not*, because you have become what you are *not*.

This sense of being disconnected or separated from your Divine Self is not real, it is a distorted phantasm. It is your physical form trying to make sense of the distorted, grotesque image you have of your own Divinity. You are seeing yourself reflected in a house of mirrors lined with rows and rows of limiting fears, self-destructive beliefs and false idols.

In this state you become cut off from your true Soul Purpose and Life Calling. You are no longer aligned with your Divine Self and you lose your direction and purpose. The anxiety, fear and pain that you then feel is your inner guidance system attempting to nudge you back into the right direction.

Trying to access your inner Divine Being from such a limiting, ill-defined state of mind amounts to the impossible task of chasing rainbows. A mission impossible. A road to nowhere.

Instead of chasing an imaginary pot of gold at the end of some rainbow, you have the power to reawaken the flawless Higher Being that you truly are. You can be like a transparent, multi-faceted prism that bends, shapes, reflects and transforms the light of Divinity into the spectral colors of a truly blessed reality, filled with wonder, joy and purpose.

Once you return to this natural state of being, you will no longer feel the need to go chasing after elusive, earthly rainbows, for you would have unleashed the true, multi-hued rainbow of your intended Divine being. You will then *be* the rainbow, the true reflection of your Divine origin.

Thomas Troward explains that our spiritual reawakening from the Divine Disconnect is inevitable and will happen as a matter of course at some point in our earthly existence as it was originally intended, whether we are ready or not.

> *The awakening to consciousness of our mysterious interior powers will sooner or later take place, and will result in our using them whether we understand the law of their development or not, just as we already use our physical faculties whether we understand their laws or not. The interior powers are natural powers as much as the exterior ones. We can direct their use by a knowledge of their laws; and it is therefore of the highest importance to have some sound principle of guidance in the use of these higher faculties as they begin to manifest themselves.*

While you remain spiritually asleep, or out of alignment with your original Life Plan, your Divine Self will constantly try to reconnect with you and guide you towards your intended Soul Purpose and

Life Calling. You will experience this as an inner sense of longing, sadness or nostalgia. It will feel like missing a loved one you do not know or being 'home sick' for a place you have never been.

Once you become aware of your true spiritual nature and recognize the presence of your inner Divine Being, you will automatically begin to receive the comfort, guidance and assistance to transform your life.

Turning On The Light

How do you feel about life right now? What effect, for example, does reading the words in this book have on you? Is it a negative or a positive emotion? Does it make you feel good, or not?

Your unfailing inner tracking system informs you from moment to moment whether you are still on target, or not. And when you feel good you know you are heading in the right direction. Thus, if reading this book is making you feel 'good', or at least just a little curious or intrigued, then you know that you were meant to read these words. You know for sure that this book is somehow serving your Life Plan.

There is no way you can misinterpret what you are feeling at such incredible moments when you feel tuned in and on track. When you feel intensely alive, inspired, interested, excited, optimistic, hopeful, confident, centered, joyful, happy, fulfilled, or calm, then you are in perfect alignment with your Divine Self. You are locked into your Higher Consciousness. You know for sure that you are honoring your Soul Purpose and you are firmly on your way towards fulfilling your Life Calling. You are aware and on track, 'tapped in' and 'locked-on' like a heat-seeking missile.

But when you feel stressed, lifeless, bored, disinterest, indifferent, cynical, desperate, insecure, sad, depressed, disgruntled, stressed, or anxious, it is usually an undeniable sign that you are going off-course and heading in the wrong direction, or that you are simply resisting your true destiny and calling.

Sometimes the Divine Disconnect becomes so intense that you feel like a lost soul trapped in a 'dark, sinister cell', or in a 'deep pit'. The darkness is so all-encompassing that you cannot see anything in front of you; neither can you find the way out. You know intuitively that there must be a door or some opening somewhere. Who knows, there might even be a light you could at least switch on? So you desperately feel your way around, trying to find a way to escape. But the more you search, the darker it becomes. Every time you find something that seems to offer some hope, like a door knob or a light switch, you soon discover that it is not, and you feel even more hopeless.

And so you go round and around, like a dog chasing its own tail. You focus only on what is there right *now*: the darkness, and your frenzied search for a way out. You see only the shadows of the negative reality that seems to be your life at this *present moment,* and that is what you focus on with all your might. In the process you only end up inviting more and more gloom and despair into your life, and each day you recreate that same reality, over and over again. You never break the pattern and you create or attract no new possibilities for the future.

If any situation, plan or project in your life brings with it a lot of darkness, drama or constant uphill struggle, then it is clearly not in alignment with your Divine Self. When you are truly aligned everything in your life becomes more effortless, seamless and synchronistic. In these circumstances your life just seems to *flow* and all the pieces of the puzzle simply fall in place of its own accord. And the more you focus on all the goodness in your life, the more you attract blessings and well-being into your conscious reality. Your life just gets better and better as the days go by. It really is all that simple. If you feel trapped in a dark place or stuck in your current reality, just turn on the light. It is a simple choice, a basic decision. And you can make that decision right now.

Like those clap-on-lights that some people install in their homes, your dark pit also has a 'magical light' light installed. It is there, right above you, in the center of the room. That 'light' is your Divine Self, your source of inner peace, well-being and inner guidance. It is your connection to the Source of All that is, was and ever will be. It will show you where the doors are; it will fling open all the windows and set your spirit free. All you need to do is turn it on. Just one mental 'clap' – the simple flip of a 'mind switch'!

Grounding, Centering And Shielding

Before you attempt any exercises for awakening and realigning with the Divine Self it is recommended that you establish a meditative foundation. It is best to begin all spiritual growth exercises, intuitive development and energy work sessions with a *grounding* and *centering* meditation or visualization to create an *energy foundation* for your practice session. Additionally, you may prefer to incorporate a spiritual protection shield or prayer blessing, depending on your personal belief system.

Centering aims to center your inner, non-physical beingness within your physical body, while grounding refers to strengthening or reaffirming your connection with the physical reality and the secular world. Centering and grounding is therefore aimed at *stabilizing yourself energetically* by firmly setting a mindful, perfect balance between your body and soul, between the spiritual and the secular, between the physical and the metaphysical. Being grounded and centered is to feel safe and securely anchored in the physical world, while opening up to increased energy flow and metaphysical or spiritual input.

You may ask why we would attempt to increase our awareness of our physical bodies and earthly reality when we are going to be engaging in spiritual or metaphysical activity. Why would we want ourselves and the ground beneath us to feel 'more real' and tangible, when we are going to venture into the deepest recesses of our subconscious unconsciousness?

I always liken it to the exploration of a deep, mysterious cave. The best way not to get lost while you are venturing deeper and deeper into that unfamiliar grotto is to tie a long roll of string to the entrance of the cave, so that you can follow it back on your way out. Grounding and centering is like having your sailboat firmly anchored on the open sea, while you are scuba diving nearby to explore the unknown depths of the ocean.

There are many creative ways you can achieve a deeply grounded and centered state of being at the beginning of your spiritual development sessions. I believe it is best to intuitively find what works best for you as a unique individual. In my work with students and clients I have found that no two people are intuitively and spiritually 'wired' the same way. You can use the following guidelines to design your own grounding and centering process.

1) **Find a quiet place** free from distractions to do your spiritual exercises. The best place for this would be the 'sacred space' you created for your daily spiritual practice. More information about this is available in the next chapter of this book.

2) **Sit or lie in a position that is comfortable** and which allows you to fully relax. If you experience any discomfort, adjust your position until your find something that works.

3) **Use music if it aids you.** I like to use instrumental music when doing spiritual or energy work, as I find it helps me to focus. However, it is vital to choose appropriate music that will not be distracting or dominating. You do not want the music to stimulate your imagination and begin to color your intuitive impressions, so that it loses validity or accuracy. If music distracts you, don't use it at all. Also, using music during exercises for clairaudience, for example, makes no sense as it will most likely drown out any auditory impressions you may perceive.

4) **Create a closed energy circuit** by crossing your legs at the ankles and interlocking your hands or finger. This will greatly enhance your grounding and provide a stable basis for energy flow.

5) **Erect a protective psychic shield around you**. Find an image or concept that works for you, anything that you can relate with and will provide you with a sense of safety and security. There are many ways to do this, for example surrounding yourself with a golden 'wall of energy', or creating a 'glass sphere' around you, or seeing yourself in a 'circle of white light', or placing a series of 'mirrors' facing outwards to form a protective ring around you. Whatever 'shield' you choose to use, ensure that you visualize it having two distinct qualities: your mind must perceive it as *impenetrable* and *unbreakable* so that it is strong, safe and secure enough to keep all unwanted influences or negative energy out, while still being *permeable* or *porous* enough to allow all wanted input and positive energy in. For example, instead of putting up an iron 'wall', visualize a steel 'cage' or a metal 'sieve'. It does not have to be realistic or practical. Use your imagination to create what-ever works for you intuitively. The most important thing is that whatever shield you create must be believable to you and must make you feel secure. If it is

not making you feel safe, it will only serve to distract you, which will cause your protective energy to waiver. The aim of these kinds of visualizations is to direct and maneuver energy.

6) **State a suitable affirmation or intention** which you chose beforehand. What is your goal or intention for this particular session or exercise? In this instance your intention would be to reconnect with the Divine Self. State your affirmation in your mind or speak it out loud. If you prefer, you could say a suitable prayer or perform a ritual chant or incantation, whatever you prefer. The following is an example of such an affirmation or statement of intent.

> *I am a spiritual being in a healthy physical body. I am establishing a direct connection to my Divine Self within and realigning my inner awareness with the entire Conscious Universe. I am awakening and reconnecting with my inner Divinity to fulfill my destiny, I am strengthening my bond with my Higher Being to manifest the life I came to live and to ultimately be of greater service to my fellow man.*

7) **Close your eyes and focus on mindful breathing** by diverting your attention to the natural flow of your breath. Become more conscious of your breath. If you find it helpful you can do a specific meditation or yoga breathing exercise to establish a base, before going into natural, mindful breathing. Do not put any further effort into your breathing. Simply allow your breathing to flow easily and spontaneously, while you merely observe it happening.

8) **Progressively relax the different sections of your body**, focusing on one area at a time. Start from your feet and work all the way up to the top of your head. Notice any physical sensations you are having that may be distracting or that may be in your awareness. Focus on your body becoming perfectly calm, relaxed and still.

9) **Solidify your center.** Centering is about finding the quiet, inner core of your being. Simply go within and sense where your center is. I find for most people this is usually in the area of the solar plexus, although I have worked with people who felt it in the root or sacral chakras, or in the heart chakra. Sometimes it is useful to use a visualization if you find it challenging to locate your center, for example, visualizing that you are the core of a lotus flower. Once you have found your center or core, feel it stabilize and becoming *solid* and *fixed*, then attach it to your grounding cord (see next step) and proceed to ground your energy to the earth.

10) **Earth yourself with a grounding cord.** Once again this is up to your creative imagination. The idea is to direct your energy in such a way that you become firmly grounded to the earth below. This can be achieved by simply visualizing a strong cord or 'steel chain' that anchors you to the center of the earth, or imagine yourself as an 'old oak tree' with thick, sturdy roots growing deeper and deeper into the ground. This creates a loop or circuit for energy flow. A misconception about grounding is that it keeps you from somehow being 'airy fairy' or 'ditsy', as if you might levitate and float away giggling into a twilight world of rainbows and unicorns. The real purpose is not to 'tie you down'. Instead it is similar to the earthing or grounding of electricity in your home. Similar to your home's earth leakage all unwanted energy is redirected through your 'grounding cord' and discharged into the earth, which serves to protect you.

11) **Quiet your emotions.** Focus on your emotions and notice any feelings you may be experiencing. How are you feeling, what are you feeling: Anger, Fear, Sadness, Surprise, Joy, Love? Focus especially in the heart or solar plexus areas. Ask your emotions to become calm. Evoke from within a sense of neutral serenity, of inner peace. Become emotionless.

12) **Clear your mind.** Focus on your mind and become aware of any thoughts you may be having. Discontinue all thinking and shut down any 'self-talk' that may be going on in your head. Let your active mind become quiet. Clear your mind of all conscious thought. Use visualization if you find it helpful. For example, imagine your mind being the tranquil, reflective surface of a lake without any ripples, or imagine your mind to be like an empty, white screen. Do not allow your mind to wander. Simply relax and try to think of absolutely nothing.

13) **Disengage your senses.** Stop paying attention to your sight, hearing, smell, taste and touch sensations. Focus on experiencing the stillness. Embrace the silence within.

14) **Proceed with your exercise or activity**. You should now be centered, grounded and shielded and your rational mind disengaged enough for you to be ready to begin your spiritual growth exercise, intuitive development activity or energy work.

Divine Meeting

There is no correct or recommended way to reconnect with your Divine Self. I believe it is best to find your own, unique way of initiating this contact. Let your intuition be your guide. The following exercises therefore only serve as examples or guide-lines.

Please note that for some people the process of reconnecting and realigning with the Divine Self can be physically discomforting and psychologically disorienting in the beginning, until you become more accustomed and acclimatized to the powerful new flow of energy through your body and mind.

However, to acknowledge and open up to the Divine Self does not require any major effort, concentration, willpower or struggle on your part. The Higher Self is who you already are 'within', so you will simply be opening up to that greater part of yourself that is already there. All you need do is have the desire to make the connection. Set your intention and open to all the blessings that Higher Consciousness will bring you when you reconnect with your inner Divinity.

1) **Begin with a grounding, centering and shielding** routine as described above.

2) **Request to be reconnected with your Divine Self.** Throughout your time of Divine Disconnection the Divine Self continued to work behind the scenes to keep you safe and support you in the period of data gathering and human development. However, our free will is a powerful universal law that governs our choices and decisions in life, and therefore we need to request increased awareness and inner guidance when we are ready, for it will not happen without us making the free will choice or decision to allow it. The Divine Self is continually reaching out to us for reconnection, but first the request or intention must be initiated by us.

3) **Focus your thoughts on the intention of making contact** with your Divine Self. If you wish you could visualize your Divine Self as an Angel, or a Spirit Guide, or a religious figure of your choice, or an Ascended Master, or simply a light, or a luminous mirror reflection of yourself. Clearly see your Divine Self at a distance. See how you wave to this Light Being as you are approaching each other from far away, and then how you embrace each other as you eventually come together.

4) **Feel how you open to receiving** the comfort, unconditional love, inspiration and healing energy from your Divine Self. Feel the boost in spiritual consciousness rushing through your physical being.

5) **Become aware of the presence of infinite wisdom and intelligence** you are receiving mentally from your Higher Self, without the need for words, like a telepathic transmission of knowledge and insight. Feel how your awareness is increasing.

6) **Express your needs or questions**. Feel free to ask your Divine Self if there is something specific you need to know or wish to request. You may ask in your mind, or say your

questions out loud if you wish. You may receive an inner message of an external sign or confirmation afterwards.

The time you devote to this exercise can be as short or as long as you prefer. It can even be done within a minute or two. You can also repeat it as often as you like.

Divine Merge

Remember that the Divine Self is the 'authentic you', who you truly are within. The following exercise is another example of how you can open up and establish conscious contact with this greater part of your own being that has always been there, before you became aware of its existence in this lifetime.

1) **Begin with a grounding, centering and shielding** routine.

2) **Request to be reconnected with your Divine Self.** Clearly state your intention in your mind or out loud. You may also do this with a prayer, chant or incantation.

3) **Envision your Divine Self floating far above you** or standing far away from you in the distance. You may imagine your Divine Self in any shape or form you feel comfortable with, for example as a Deity, Spirit Guide, Angel, Star, Glowing Light, Eternal Flame, Energy Orb, etc.

4) **Visualize your Divine Self gradually beginning to move toward you,** until it is right above your head or right in front of you. Greet and welcome your Divine Self and invite your Higher Being to come closer. Ask for your connection with each other to become stronger and more secure.

5) **Merge with your Divine Self.** See your Divine Self embracing you and becoming one with you. Feel how each and every one of your cells, molecules, atoms is united with the radiating, powerful spiritual energy of the Higher Self.

6) **Absorb the unconditional love, peace and serenity emanating from the Divine self**; feel how it surrounds your whole being and how it raises your vibrational frequency higher and higher, as it merges with you. Feel how your energy patterns adopt the superior power and radiance of your Divine Self.

7) **Become one with your Divine Self.** Visualize how you have now become *one* with your inner Divinity. Remain in this state of consciousness and oneness with the Universe for as long as you wish to. In this state of pure beingness you can ask for guidance, receive intuitive impressions, send loving energy to friends and family, do healing meditations for your body, or transform your thoughts and emotions.

8) **Come slowly out of the state of higher consciousness**. Become gradually aware of your body and environment and refocus on your breathing until you are ready to return to normal functioning.

The Chakra System

The chakras are the energy centers, or conduits through which the life energy of the Conscious Universe flows into and out of our aura or etheric body. The same universal Life Force that flows through all the plant and animal kingdom also flows through you via the chakra system.

The chakras have three functions, namely being *receptors*, *storage points* and *transmitters* of energy. Becoming familiar with your chakras is one of the most powerful ways in which you can raise your spiritual awareness and access different levels of *consciousness*. The chakras system may seem simplistic on a rational level, but when one begins to experience it fully in its deeper, intuitive dimension you discover an amazing map to your inner world.

The word chakra means 'wheel' or 'disk', because these energy centers are rotating *vortexes* or spinning *spheres* located along our spinal column at major branching points of the human nervous system, known as the *ganglia*. The seven primary chakras are essentially 'stacked' like a tower to form a column or pathway of energy beginning at the base of the spinal column and moving up to the crown of your head. Through these invisible spinning funnels Universal Energy is received, assimilated and expressed as the Life Force. Each chakra is believed to correlate with a fundamental state of consciousness and spiritual awareness.

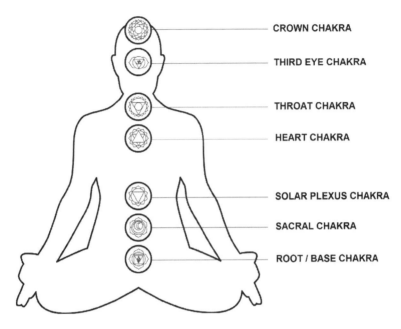

CROWN CHAKRA

THIRD EYE CHAKRA

THROAT CHAKRA

HEART CHAKRA

SOLAR PLEXUS CHAKRA

SACRAL CHAKRA

ROOT / BASE CHAKRA

The Seven Primary Chakras

It is interesting to note that apart from its apparent organization in accordance with the human nervous system, the different chakra points also appear to correlate with the location of the major glands in the human endocrine system.

Each of the seven major chakras further appears to *resonate* with its own *vibrational frequency* for which there are tonal sound correlates. Interestingly, all music in the physical world at its most fundamental level consists of only seven notes.

Chakra Connection

One of the best ways to realign yourself energetically with the Divine Self is to do a *chakra clearing* and *energy reconnection* exercise. This creates a firm foundation for all your other daily spiritual practices and intuitive development activities.

By realigning the chakra system with your Higher Self, and opening the flow of energy, you will be much more empowered to receive inner guidance from within. The goal of this exercise is to reconnect your energy centers with your inner Divinity by extending energy cords from each of the chakras through the center of your body, out through the crown of your head and upward to the Divine Self.

1) **Review the chakra system.** If you are not yet familiar with the chakra system and the location of the different centers in your body, take some time to study the chart above and memorize each location. I find a fast and effective way to remember this is to place your hands onto each section of your body as you work through the chart.

2) **Begin with a grounding, centering and shielding** routine as described earlier in this chapter.

3) **Visualize a bright, powerful source of white light** above your head. This light source is your Divine Self. See the Divine Self radiate and glow, bathing your whole body in a healing white light. Feel your body absorbing this healing light energy until it begins to radiate and glow from within to emanate the same white light.

4) **Clear the chakras.** Visualize each of the chakras starting at the base chakra and working your way up to the crown chakra. First visualize the chakra as a stagnant vortex or disc (windmill, fan, mini tornado) and then consciously 'spin' each chakra in an *anti-clockwise* direction for a few seconds. See how all energy blockages are cleared by this anti-clockwise rotation and how all negative or 'stale' energy is released from the chakra (see the negative energy 'running out' similar to when you unplug your bathtub, or see it blow away like dust or ashes). Once the chakra is cleared, return it to its natural state by spinning it in a *clockwise* direction; see it speeding up until its rotation becomes invisible. Repeat this clearing rotation

with each of the chakras until you reach the crown chakra.

5) **Connect the crown chakra.** Imagine a bright cord of healing *violet* light gradually extending from your crown chakra up into the light of the Divine Self above you and feel it reconnecting and locking into place.

6) **Connect the third eye chakra.** Imagine a bright cord of healing *indigo* light (indigo is the deep spectral color between blue and violet) gradually extending from your third eye chakra and connecting with the Divine Self.

7) **Connect the throat chakra.** Imagine a bright cord of healing *blue* light gradually extending from your throat chakra and connecting with the Divine Self.

8) **Connect the heart chakra.** Imagine a bright cord of healing *green* light gradually extending from your heart chakra and connecting with the Divine Self.

9) **Connect the solar plexus chakra.** Imagine a bright cord of healing *yellow* light gradually extending from your solar plexus chakra and connecting with the Divine Self.

10) **Connect the sacral chakra.** Imagine a bright cord of healing *orange* light gradually extending from your sacral chakra and connecting with the Divine Self.

11) **Connect the root chakra.** Imagine a bright cord of healing *red* light gradually extending from your base chakra and connecting with the Divine Self.

12) **Merge the seven cords.** Visualize how all seven of these connected chakra cords merge or blend into one large, thick cord of *white light* that streams down from the Divine Self into and through your body. Feel how this 'line' or 'port' of connection is now fully opened and ready to receive guidance from the Divine.

13) **Ask your Divine Self for insight, wisdom and guidance.** Due to your capacity for free will, requesting guidance is an important aspect of reconnecting with you Higher Self. You can state this request in the form that you feel most comfortable with, such as an affirmation or intention, or as a prayer, chant or incantation.

14) **Express gratitude and appreciation** for the continued guidance you will receive.

Journey To The Center of The Universe

The following is my adaptation of a fun exercise I discovered many years ago in the brilliant book *Mind To Mind* by the well-known British psychic medium and energy healer Betty Shine. It is one of the very first spiritual development exercises I ever did and to this day it remains one of my firm favorites. The aim of this exercise is to receive instruction, guidance and intuitive input from the Divine Self. This exercise is also ideal for dreamwork and can be done just before you fall sleep. I have had many profound pre-cognitive dreams and insights come to me in this way.

1) **Visualize a small spacecraft for one person.** This craft can be any shape and color you prefer, as long as it is solid. It has a door which magically seals at the seams once you are inside. Inside the craft the environment is very comfortable and fully air-conditioned. Sit or lie down inside your space pod. Relax, feel safe and secure. If you wish you could even start with this visualization and then proceed to do your grounding, centering and shielding routine from inside this imaginary space. Your spacecraft could in this instance become your psychic shield and the craft's seatbelt could become your grounding cord.

2) **Travel to the 'Universal Institute of Divine Living'** located in the far reaches of space, in the center of the Universe. Feel how your spacecraft lifts off the ground and gradually increases speed until you are travelling to your destination through the Universe at the speed of light. Stay relaxed and calm, centered and grounded. Enjoy the ride as you pass many stars and galaxies. In the

distance you begin to see a light which grows and grows in size until you are close enough to see that it is a tunnel. See how your craft flies into this tunnel and travels for a while until the tunnel opens up into large hangar or hall.

3) **Meet your Teacher Guide.** Once you have landed, the door of your craft opens and outside is your friendly Teacher Guide waiting to welcome you at the Institute. Let your imagination decide the appearance of this wise being. Over the years I have had clients and students who based the appearance of their teacher on a sketch made for them by a psychic artist, which they found very useful. See how your Teacher leads you through an impressive hall into a special classroom, where you are then seated opposite your Teacher Guide to receive instruction and guidance. You can stay as long as you feel comfortable. Intuitively I have always preferred to work with a group of teachers and guides, and I therefore visualize accordingly. Instead of placing myself in a classroom with one teacher, I visualize a panel of teachers in a larger room, with me seated in front of them for instruction and guidance. Remain in this state of consciousness as long as you feel comfortable (or until you fall asleep if you are doing dreamwork).

4) **Return home and close the session.** Once the exercise is complete, visualize your Teacher Guide taking you back to your craft. Enter the craft and seal yourself inside like before. Visualize the whole journey in reverse until you are safely back home. Gradually open your eyes and relax.

PART II

ACHIEVING
YOUR SOUL PURPOSE

3

THE ART OF DIVINE LIVING

Creating a Divine Life is not a selfish act. Until we are able to find some degree of personal joy, inner peace and lasting contentment, we are actually of little use to our fellow man. If we are to be effective as our proverbial 'brother's keeper', which is essentially the foundation of our Life Calling, we need to achieve a happier and more meaningful life for ourselves.

We need to be 'tapped in' and 'turned on', both feet firmly on the ground, and our conscious awareness solidly maintained within 'the zone' of Divine Living. We need to lead the Divine Life we were meant to have all along, in order for us to be truly equipped for our transpersonal purpose to serve others and the planet. Only then will we be able to make the many valuable contributions to the world that we are supposed to make in this lifetime.

They say you cannot take anything with you when you die, but this is not entirely true! We do take with us the 'spiritual data' we have gathered through the various life lessons we encounter in this lifetime, as well as the extent of transcendence we were able to achieve. Like eager 'tourists' we will return home one day with all the metaphysical pictures, postcards and souvenirs we collected here on the Earth plane, and we will forever cherish the many wonderful, and sometimes challenging experiences we had on this amazing journey. And if we choose to return for another lifetime or two, we will apply all we have learned in the design and completion of our next 'trip'.

You have a unique metaphysical purpose in this lifetime; you are here on a personal spiritual mission. Your *Soul Purpose* is an extension and continuation of your consciousness throughout various lifetimes and other dimensions of existence. Your Soul Purpose is part of your overall Life Plan, and it was designed to expose you to certain circumstances, conditions, experiences and life challenges, in order to create the necessary opportunities for conscious expansion, soul growth and spiritual evolution.

Before you were born into this lifetime, the planning of your Soul Purpose involved, among other things, the choosing of your parents and family; the establishment of soul agreements or contracts with other fellow travelers; the pre-determination of certain life events and milestones for various reasons; and finally also how you chose to depart one day.

Note, however, that your current life is not entirely pre-destined or laid out in advance. The way your life is to play itself out is not cast in stone. Instead it will be determined by your *free will* choices and decisions from day to day. Your Life Plan is more like an itinerary or a list of highlights, instead of a detailed, pre-written script for a stage play or movie.

Your Life Plan only maps out the highlights or route markers for your journey. These are the pre-destined events and circumstances that will arise throughout your lifetime. It is what some refer to as 'destiny', 'fate' or 'luck'. It is the events and experiences in our lives we cannot control or prevent. We don't arrive here with a step-by-step 'drill' of what must happen every day. Instead we enter physical life with a basic to-do list of events and experiences we will encounter along the way. What happens the rest of the time is entirely up to us as we go about our daily business.

Finding Your Soul Purpose

You cannot 'find' your Soul Purpose. You already know what your Soul Purpose is; it is inscribed in your very being. Your Divine Self is fully aware and informed of your reasons for being here. Your Higher Self is after all the architect and designer of your current life journey.

The details of our Soul Purpose are mostly unconscious for most of us, yet it informs and determines our daily choices, decisions and actions. The Divine Self always steers and guides us towards fulfilling our spiritual mission, with or without our cooperation or conscious participation. However, participating actively is much more fulfilling and yields more profound results.

The only difference between those of us who are completing our mission unconsciously and those of us who are spiritually awakened and keenly aware of our reasons for being here, is that the conscious spiritual seeker will ultimately be more successful and satisfied in their quest. Tragically, too many souls reach the end of their human lives only to discover too late that they have not achieved much in the 'spiritual growth department', nor have they contributed much to the expansion of the Conscious Universe.

The spiritually awakened person is naturally not content with neglecting their Soul Purpose, because they know that we are spiritual beings having a physical life experience and they wish to make the most of their Earth journey. The spiritually aware soul does not wish to return home 'empty-handed' one day. This possibility seems even more unattractive if one considers the notion that you might have to come back and do it all over again! Back to square one. The awakened soul would much rather move on to 'bigger, brighter and better' things, by taking on new journeys into other dimensions, alternate planes of existence, deeper realms of consciousness, or parallel universes.

So, how do you ensure that you stay on track with your Life Plan and ultimately achieve your Soul Purpose in this lifetime? Easy, you simply realign with your Divine Self and follow the instructions of your inner guidance system. There is no pressing need for you to know the exact details of your Soul Purpose. All you need to do is consistently maintain communication and connection with your Divine Self and follow the inner guidance you receive.

To realign and maintain your connection to your inner Divinity you need to establish some form of daily spiritual practice and begin to live a more mindful existence. Mindful living is a raised state of consciousness and awareness that is achieved by engaging in spiritual practices and activities that transform your thoughts, evolve your emotions, sharpen your senses and increase your intuition.

Transcending Dualism

To achieve our Soul Purpose we have to live a spiritually aware and mindful life, making the most of the obstacles, setbacks, problems and challenges we may encounter along the way. The only way we can do this is through transcendence, i.e. by continually striving towards integration of the conscious and unconscious, the left and right brain, the body and the mind, and the physical and spiritual. To truly fulfill our Soul Purpose we need to create a 'best of both worlds' existence, by establishing a *dynamic balance* between our limited physical being and our infinite spiritual beingness. This balanced, integrated existence creates a Divine Life.

We are spiritual beings having a physical adventure. Our aim in human form is therefore not to have a profound spiritual experience, or to be entirely dedicated to our metaphysical development. Quite the contrary, we are also here for more mundane reasons, apart from our soul growth and the expansion of the Conscious Universe. We also came into this world to accomplish a Life Calling, whilst *enjoying* the adventure of being in physical form.

We are therefore perfectly able to achieve our Soul Purpose in this lifetime without consciously knowing the exact, intricate details of our personal soul mission. In fact, in our limited human form we will not be able to comprehend much of the blueprint for our Soul Purpose anyway. We were designed as human beings to be able to achieve our spiritual life goals without having to 'reinvent the wheel'.

For this reason it makes no sense for all of us to spend days fasting and in deep meditation, or live limited lives that revolves entirely around spiritual practice or religious devotion. Neither are we required to adopt an ascetic lifestyle that aims to isolate us from the 'real world'. The real world experience is what we came for in the first place. We did not come here to be exclusively spiritual, we came here to be human and experience physical life.

I am not suggesting that devoted Buddhist monks, for example, are leading pointless or unnecessary lives. In fact, I believe people who lead such dedicated lives of devotion and exclusive religious pursuit serve an important Life Calling in our world. It is my conviction that their daily meditations, prayers and chants are what help to neutralize and balance a lot of the destruction and negative forces unleashed in ignorance or unconsciousness by the rest of mankind. However, this way of life is not destined for all of us. Should this kind of life be a part of *your* Life Plan you will in time be guided towards it.

Achieving our Soul Purpose is therefore about transcending the *dualism* in our earthly existence. We cannot achieve our Soul Purpose by allowing either the rational left brain or the intuitive right brain to dominate. We also cannot achieve our Soul Purpose by separating our spiritual pursuits from our physical lifestyle.

Our spiritual goals cannot come to full fruition if not accompanied by a minimum level of material comfort, mental and sensory stimulation, physical pleasure and an underlying respect for and adherence to the Laws of the Universe. In other words, true soul growth and spiritual expansion cannot be accomplished without a *practical, abundant lifestyle* that is conducive to achieving our Soul Purpose.

We did not come into this life to be exposed to constant lack, extreme suffering or unbearable misery. The lack, suffering and misery we witness on our planet is entirely man-made and self-inflicted. It is the unfortunate byproduct of our Divine Disconnection and the dominance of the Ego. It is manifested by *lack consciousness* and pervasive *false beliefs* about the need for primitive human survival. Many of us prefer to believe that we are meant to struggle and suffer, and that life is nothing more than a cruel, desperate race to ensure the 'survival of the fittest'.

This is where some religious traditions and teachings have failed us, because they prescribe certain taboos, or demand strict adherence to various forms of self-denial and self-inflicted discomfort, in order to achieve spiritual enlightenment, or salvation. This penchant for suffering is known as *asceticism*, which is a lifestyle that abstains from the normal pleasures of life, or rejects personal material satisfaction in order to achieve certain spiritual outcomes.

It is not true that we can only achieve our Soul Purpose by living the life of a hermit or by abstaining from sensual pleasure. Such extremely contrasting experiences can in some instances add value to our soul growth and sometimes they may even be required by our Life Calling, but it makes no sense to make it a lifelong pursuit when it is not needed. We have enough contrasting experiences already built-in into our Life Plan - in the form of pre-destined circumstances and events. There is no need to inflict unnecessary misery upon ourselves in our challenging human condition. A purposeful life is therefore not about depriving ourselves (or others) from the joys of life, neither is it achieved by adhering to a strict list of prescribed, man-made rules. Divine Living is about achieving balance, integration and congruity in our thoughts, emotions, senses, words and deeds.

When we are in this balanced state of being we are aware, peaceful, content, focused, joyful and truly alive.

Divine Living is therefore a practical lifestyle. It is not a deeply philosophical, esoteric quest for salvation or enlightenment. Neither is it supposed to be a struggle. It is actually a way of life that can be achieved by anyone, anytime, anywhere in the world with very little effort. No major sacrifices or financial investments are required.

Does this sound too easy? Well, Divine Living really is as simple or as complex as your choose to make it. Your current lifestyle will most likely experience some automatic or organic changes from the 'inside out', once you begin to embrace the habits and maxims of a Divine Life. As you realign with your Divine Self, shed some of your false beliefs and get back on track with your Life Plan, you will feel the spontaneous need to make some practical adjustments to your lifestyle and daily routine.

No More Excuses

Adjustment and personal transformation is inevitable once you wake up from the Divine Disconnect and begin to realign with the Divine Self. An inner shift will automatically begin to manifest in how you choose to live your life externally. For some the changes in their daily lifestyle are subtle, while others need a complete 'overhaul' of their daily routine. If you are reading this book you are probably more than ready to make some changes, whatever they may turn out to be. Do whatever you feel comfortable doing and make gradual (or radical) changes to your lifestyle when you feel ready to proceed.

If you believe that a more spiritual, mindful way of life may be difficult, or even impossible to achieve within your current environment, think again. No Ego excuses will silence the inner calling of your Divine Self once you have unleashed its powerful energy. You will have no choice but to eventually yield and comply. There is no reason why anyone should be unable to achieve and maintain a Divine Life within their current life circumstances, whatever those circumstances may be.

Viktor Frankl, the renowned psychologist who survived the Holocaust, writes in *Man's Search for Meaning* that "in spite of all the enforced physical and mental primitiveness of the life in a concentration camp, it was possible for spiritual life to deepen".

He continues to share that some of the inmates in his camp, who chose a more hopeful or positive attitude, "were able to retreat from their terrible surroundings to a life of inner riches and spiritual freedom".

Well, if Frankl could do it, and even live to tell the tale, then so can you – no matter what you may be dealing with in life! Blaming our circumstances, or our environment, or our past for our failure to fully embrace a spiritually awakened and abundant lifestyle is nothing more than a feeble excuse, or the fear of failure. Whatever the nature of your physical surroundings or current lifestyle, you can reconnect and realign with your Divine Self amidst absolutely any circumstance. Sure, some conditions may prove more favorable than others depending on where you work and live, and who you work and live with, but no matter how challenging your circumstances may seem, once you begin to follow the inner guidance of your Divine Self, you will find the most miraculous solutions to the most difficult problems.

No matter how disadvantaged, stressed, depressed, diseased, disabled, anxious, lonely, desperate, lost, hopeless, unattractive, fearful, suicidal, abused, unloved, talentless, rejected, or ostracized you may feel at this point in your life, there is no reason why you cannot begin right now to *transform your life* into the marvelous, joyous experience you originally intended it to be. Start small and don't be impatient with yourself when you get it wrong. It took almost a lifetime to condition you to be the person you are now. It will take some more time to get the accustomed to your new, awakened way of life.

Spiritual Development

One of the most profound misconceptions and false beliefs about spirituality and spiritual practice is that we are somehow flawed human 'animals' in need of spiritual salvation or 'deliverance'. Many spiritual seekers believe they must somehow atone for their human imperfection, or they must work hard towards becoming "more spiritual". This is not the truth for those who are spiritually aware.

When we experience true spiritual awakening the realization soon comes, courtesy of our Higher Self, that we are already spirit incarnate; we are of Divine origins. We are not flawed or lacking in our original form. We cannot 'become more spiritual', for we already are spiritual by nature and we were all made in the image of the Divine. We do not come from a state of imperfection or 'lack'. Spiritual development and soul growth is therefore not a process of becoming 'more spiritual'. It is instead a process of becoming *less caught up in the material*, less Ego-bound.

Spiritual development is the process of increasing awareness and consistently realigning with the Divine Self. It is the process of attaining greater levels of sacred awareness; it is the quest for a higher level of consciousness. The more conscious we become, the more illuminated the truth about our reality and the meaning of our existence becomes. Higher Consciousness and alignment with the Divine Self raises our awareness of our role here in on Earth, and empowers us to achieve our Soul Purpose and accomplish our Life Calling. Without spiritual development we are like travelers on a dark country road, with only a candle to light our way. But when we grow spiritually to greater awareness and higher levels of consciousness, our path becomes enlightened by a powerful spotlight.

Working towards spiritual growth is therefore not about transforming yourself into a more 'spiritual person'. You already are that spiritual being by nature. Efforts to develop spiritually is merely a process of *setting your inner spiritual being free*, by shedding the misconceptions, negative thoughts, and limiting false beliefs brought on by your former state of Divine Disconnection. It is a process of liberating your inner Divinity from the rule of the Ego or Material Self.

Spiritual Practice

Awakening, reconnecting and realigning with the Divine Self is no doubt the most important first step in personal spiritual growth, individuation and ultimate transcendence. To rediscover your Higher Self and tap into your Higher Consciousness is usually a very awe-inspiring and life-changing experience. But your new-found spiritual awareness and rediscovered Divine origins may soon lose its power to transform your life if you do not adopt a new lifestyle that includes some kind of *consistent spiritual practice*.

Divine Living and spiritual practice goes hand in hand. A Divine Life is impossible to achieve without some form of regular spiritual practice, in order to increase and maintain your connection and alignment with the Divine Self. What you come to know and believe about your own spiritual origins is meaningless, unless you have a direct and personal daily experience of receiving guidance from your inner Divinity. The only way to achieve this is to practice your new awareness and beliefs on a daily basis.

In our human state we sometimes too easily slide back into old habits, and with the constant onslaught of materialism, misinformation, fear conditioning, scientific skepticism and the distraction of mass entertainment and popular culture, you have a very limited probability of expanding your newfound spiritual awareness, unless you engage yourself consciously in some form of habitual and frequent spiritual practice.

Spiritual practices are actions and activities we undertake on a regular basis for the purpose of cultivating spiritual development. There are a plethora of spiritual practices available, both ancient and modern, that you can apply in your own life to sustain your spiritual awareness and Divine connection. Regular spiritual activity will fine-tune your alignment with the Divine Self, improve the clarity of your inner guidance, and consistently nurture and develop your ability to manifest abundance.

Your spiritual practice of choice may include any of the following:

- Astral Travel & Projection
- Breathing Exercises
- Ceremonies, Rites & Rituals
- Channeling
- Charity & Acts of Kindness
- Cleansing (Fasting, Energy Clearing, Sage burning, Baptism)
- Creating Sacred Space
- Dancing
- Divination (Tarot, Astrology, I Ching, Numerology, Runes)
- Dreamwork
- Energy Work
- Expressing Gratitude
- Healing Practices (Acupuncture, Reiki, Shiatsu)
- Past Life Regression
- Inducing Trance / Altered States of Consciousness
- Mandala
- Meditation
- Music (playing, listening to)

· Physical Activity (Yoga, T'ai chi ch'uan, Aikido)
· Pilgrimage
· Prayer
· Readings (Empathic, Psychic, Mediumship, Akasha, Aura)
· Shamanic Practice
· Singing & Chanting
· Study & Contemplation
· Religious Worship

When undertaking any spiritual practice it is important to bear in mind that we are all different. We all have our own beliefs, temperaments, personalities, interests and personal preferences. Your beliefs and spiritual practices will depend a lot on your personal spiritual journey, your past life experiences, and your karmic quest. Each of us has a unique Life Plan, Soul Purpose and Life Calling to achieve in this lifetime.

A spiritual practice that is ideal for one person's soul growth may simply not work at all for another. Therefore it is recommended that you seek intuitive guidance from your Divine Self on which practices will best suit your unique needs in this lifetime. Ultimately, it does not matter which practice or discipline you choose, as long as you incorporate it into your daily living and apply it consistently.

The Akashic Records

Spiritual activities and consistent mindfulness enables us to consciously explore our Soul Purpose on a deeper level. It enables us to gather knowledge, insight and information about our unique metaphysical blueprint and our soul mission. The source of all this information is the Akashic Records. The Akashic Records offers the seeker a glimpse into their Soul's path and purpose for this lifetime.

The Akashic Records is the metaphysical 'library' or 'archive' of the Conscious Universe; it is a vibrational record of every soul and its journey, containing all the energetic data of each and every human experience, as well as the complete history of the Cosmos. Edgar Cayce described it as the "record that the individual entity itself writes upon the skein of time and space, through patience - and is opened when self has attuned to the infinite, and may be read by those attuning to that consciousness."

The Akasha is like an immense, universal 'supercomputer' or 'cosmic internet' registering the experiences of every living being since time began, including all our thoughts, emotions, and beliefs. It is also a recording of all the choices, decisions and actions of a karmic nature that has ever been made by every human being throughhout time. As a species we have been interacting consciously and unconsciously, deliberately and accidentally, with this cosmic database throughout the history of mankind. We use this database to create our Life Plan before we come into this lifetime and we consistently tap into it, via the Divine Self, to achieve our Soul Purpose and Life Calling while we are here.

The Akashic Record is also known as the Book of God's Remembrance, Hall of Records, Mind of God, Book of Life, Collective Unconscious, Aether, Fifth Dimension and even as the Divine Matrix. Well-known Wiccan author Scott Cunningham describes the Akasha as the spiritual force from which the four elements of Earth, Air, Fire, and Water descend.

Several mentions made of the "Book of Life" in the Bible are believed to be in reference to the Akashic Records. One of the often cited quotes is found in Revelation 20:12, "And I saw the dead, great and small, standing before the throne, and books were opened. Another book was opened, which is the book of life. The dead were judged according to what they had done as recorded in the books. "

A potential scientific basis for the existence of the Akasha is found in Quantum String Theory, which predicts the possibility of the existence of as many as eleven other dimensions, instead of the known three spatial dimensions and the fourth dimension of time we are conscious of here on the Earth plane. Some experts propose that the Akasha embodies the fifth dimension, or that it is an energy field of quantum particles or 'subatomic waves of information' recorded within everything and everyone in our Holographic Universe.

This energetic 'substance' or fifth dimension is beyond the parameters of our current time-space reality and human comprehension and it can only be partially accessed by us through the Divine Self. The Higher Self therefore holds the key to Higher Consciousness. Access to Akashic information can thus be achieved through all manner of spiritual practice or the inducement of altered states of consciousness, which includes prayer, meditation, intuitive development, astral projection, past life regression, energy healing, psychic and mediumship readings, shamanic ritual, divination, channeling, deep hypnosis and dream-work. By accessing the Akashic Records we discover more information about the nature of our Soul and our Soul Purpose. We can also better understand how we created our current life circumstances based on our past choices and previous lives.

However, it is essential to always bear in mind that access to the Akashic records is limited. For example, the memory of our previous lives is restricted the moment we enter into this lifetime. Our Divine Self has full knowledge of our past lives and our current spiritual mission, but our rational, conscious human mind has limited access. We are able to consciously explore our previous lives and discover a few clues to guide us in this current lifetime, but we will not gain complete access, because that will defeat the Soul Purpose of our current life. We will not evolve or grow much spiritually if we had full disclosure of the contents of our Akashic Record.

The Daily Habits of Divine Living

A truly fulfilling and long-lasting Divine Life requires at the very least some minor changes in our daily habits and way of life. There are no real short-cuts around this - to change your life for the better on a permanent basis you need to change your lifestyle. Joseph Campbell said, "We must be willing to get rid of the life we've planned, so as to have the life that is waiting for us. The old skin has to be shed before the new one can come."

However, do not attempt to completely alter your current way of life overnight; it will take time to gradually adopt a new way of being in the world. It does not matter how long it takes you to make these adjustments, as long as you consistently make gradual changes and adopt new habits that are conducive to achieving your Soul Purpose and Life Purpose. Divine Living is in essence a *process* or a journey, not a destination.

The following daily habits of Divine Living have been applied with great success in my own life, as well as in the lives of many of my clients and students. They are also common practice among most spiritually aware people all over the world.

Habit # 1: Seek Solitude

Quiet moments of silence and private reflection is a practice and a recommendation you will find in most, if not all religious teachings. This is no accident. If there is one thing most of us lack in our modern lives it is these small, quiet moments of true inner peace, serenity and silence.

Our daily environment is riddled with a constant flow of news, information, public opinions, marketing messages and entertainment noise that drowns out our inner voice. For spiritual awareness and intuitive guidance to flourish and bloom we simply must spend some time alone in the company of the Divine Self. Paramahansa Yogananda said, "Come into the silence of solitude, and the vibration there will talk to you through the voice of God".

Although our Higher Self is always with us, every second of our life, the best way to truly exercise our spiritual muscles, and cultivate a strong, clear connection with our inner Divinity, is to frequently have times of solitude and contemplation. It is no coincidence that many of the ascended masters and spiritual teachers throughout history often chose to retreat from society for a period of time, to go into the desert or up into the mountains, in order to find enlightenment.

Spiritual seekers need some quality time alone, when they can momentarily disconnect from the demands of the material world and shutdown some of the 'noise' bombarding the physical senses, in order to journey within and enjoy fellowship with the Divine.

Make it a habit to practice solitude for at least 15 to 30 minutes a day, and use this precious time alone to engage in the spiritual practice of your choice, such as meditation, prayer, contemplation, creative visualization, psychic development, journaling, affirmations, ritual dance, dreamwork or simply walking on the beach. It does not matter which spiritual practice you choose, as long as it enables you to shut out the noise of the world and make a direct and powerful connection with the Divine Self.

Personally, I recommend that you spend at least 10 to 15 minutes of this time in *daily meditation*. Meditation has remained popular for millennia because it is so effective and therefore the ideal spiritual activity to engage in during your time of solitude.

By the way, I find that some of my students initially find it very challenging to be alone. Some have grown so accustomed over the years to always having people around that they find it intimidating to be alone, especially without a blaring television set or loud music to fill the void. If you are unaccustomed to silent solitude, then it will likely also be difficult for you at first. However, if you persevere these quiet moments will most likely become your favorite part of the day!

Habit # 2: Create Sacred Space

Set aside a dedicated area or a special room in your home for your moments of solitude, and for your daily spiritual practice. This is known as creating a 'sacred space'. Not only will your new sacred space externalize your spiritual awareness in a tangible form, but it will inspire you to engage in your daily spiritual practice. It is less likely that you will avoid or ignore the spiritual routine you have planned for yourself if you have a set area in your living space that constantly reminds you of what you are supposed to be doing. A designated sacred space will make your spiritual practice an integral part of your daily lifestyle.

Creating a sacred space is a highly personal process and it is unique for every person, so trust your inner guidance and follow your own creative instincts. The following suggestions and guidelines will help you get started.

1. **Find whatever space you may have available.** You can convert a whole room in your house, if you can spare it, or simply create a small, special corner in some quiet part of your home. If you really have no space you could even consider some space outside under a tree, or even clear out a closet and convert that into your sacred nook.

2. **Create a perimeter or gateway.** Some of my clients find it very useful to create a special barrier or *boundary* between the ordinary world and their sacred space. It makes one more aware of leaving behind everyday reality and shifting into the spiritual, intuitive domain of Higher Consciousness. It helps to set the tone and atmosphere, and to focus the mind as you leave the secular to enter into the metaphysical. To create such a 'doorway' or 'veil' to symbolically pass through, you could hang a bead curtain over the doorway, or place a decorative Chinese screen or room divider in front of your scared corner.

3. **Install comfortable seating.** You will need something to sit on in your sacred space for the purpose of meditation, contemplation, or prayer. Seating could range from a few loose pillows or a bean bag to a comfortable chair or couch. The kind of seating is not important, what matters is that it is comfortable and conducive to your practice. If you are going to use your space for small group activities or fellowship with friends you should consider having additional seating available.

4. **Set up an altar.** Please note that an 'altar' in this sense does *not* refer to the traditional or religious concept, namely an elevated structure, mound or platform upon which religious ceremonies are enacted, or on which sacrifices or gifts are offered to the relevant god or deity. Instead the altar in your sacred space is merely a platform or area that will serve as your *central focus point* and display area for your daily spiritual practice. A coffee table, or even a small box draped with a table cloth or an attractive piece of fabric, will do the trick. You can use this platform to display all your favorite spiritual objects, ornaments, charms and souvenirs. Your collection could include candles, crystals, stones, beads, shells, twigs, branches, leaves, flowers, plants, herbs, statues, relics, talismans, incense, essential oils, framed pictures, oracle cards, prayer wheels, beads, sticks, flags, mandalas, religious books, mementos and gifts from loved ones, as well as bells, cymbals and other musical instruments.

5. **Decorate the rest of the space**. Paint the walls in appropriate colors, or drape it with your favorite fabrics. Hang some paintings or pictures of nature scenes, animals, holy places, religious symbols, angels, or geometric shapes. Consider including a water fountain, and some plants, mirrors, drums, sculptures or wind chimes. Install a sound system for playing music and guided meditation recordings. Appropriate lighting is also essential for creating the perfect atmosphere, and you may need a special lamp if you will be reading in your scared space. Decorate your sacred space to your personal taste and be

guided by your preferred belief system. If you have some knowledge of *feng shui,* or know a friend who is an expert, you could also apply the principles of this ancient Chinese art of placement to arrange and decorate your sacred space. The essence of feng shui is the creation of a harmony and a dynamic balance between your 'inner space' and your exterior space, which is ideal for creating the perfect sacred space at home. If you do decide to ask a friend or a professional to assist you with the decorating, ensure that you are hands-on and directly involved every step of the way. It will serve as your sacred space, so it requires your personal energy input.

6. **Honor or bless your sacred space before you begin to use it.** You can do any initiation ritual you choose based on your personal preferences and your belief system. It could range from a simple set of affirmations or a religious prayer to a Native American cleansing ritual using burning sage.

7. **Set up some household rules.** If you have a family or roommates, ensure that you set some rules regarding your scared space and be sure that everyone understands that this area is private, or even off-limits. If you will be sharing the space with friends or members of the family, then arrange the necessary schedule or code of conduct. This will help to prevent unnecessary interruptions or distraction during your times of solitude and contemplation.

Habit # 3: Schedule Your Time

You may feel that setting a schedule or following a routine is not really a very spiritual or esoteric way to live, but unfortunately it is often the only effective strategy to maintain any form of spiritual practice in our hectic modern lives – especially if you are new to a spiritual lifestyle.

The demands of the material world are such that we have no choice but to put at least some planning and discipline into our daily spiritual practice. In my work as coach I have witnessed time and time again that the only people who really make significant progress in their spiritual development are the ones who stick to some kind of *routine*. Of course, if you are not new to spiritually mindfulness and you are already adept at incorporating some form of spiritual practice into your daily lifestyle, then you would have less need for this kind of scheduling.

Some of my clients create elaborate daily schedules which they record on wall charts, while others simply make a few mental notes each morning to orientate themselves with regards when, where and how they will fit their spiritual activity into their day. It does not really matter how you decide to approach your time scheduling, as long as your planning ensures that you *consistently* and *frequently* engage in your spiritual activities.

The following is an example of how a working mom might structure her daily routine of spiritual practice.

5:30 Meditation & affirmations
6:00 Do laundry
6:30 Shower, dress
7:15 Make breakfast & lunches
7:45 Get kids ready for school
8:30 Drive kids to school, drive to work
9:00 Work
12:00 Eat lunch
12:30 Work
5:00 Pick up kids
5:30 Homework,
6:00 Clean house, monitor chores
6:30 Dinner, dishes
7:30 Kids' bath time
8:00 Bedtime stories
8:30 Creative visualization
9:00 Gratitude Journal
9:30 Watch TV, Read

When planning the allocation of your time, bear in mind that apart from your traditional spiritual practice you will also need to incorporate some of the other techniques and exercises for personal transformation included in this book. You should aim to include in your daily routine some work to transform your thoughts, shift your emotions, sharpen your senses, develop your intuition and manifest abundance. How much you include and which components you favor will all depend on your unique needs and where you currently are in your own development.

As you begin to adapt your life to achieve your Soul Purpose and Life Calling, you will find that some aspects that are important to you now will be replaced later by others that may not seem so urgent at the moment. Be prepared to remain flexible in your approach and be sure to consistently consult with your Divine Self through meditation, prayer and intuitive guidance. Remember that Divine Living is a journey, not a destination.

Habit # 4: Meditate Daily

Daily meditation is essential for spiritual development and increased alignment with your Divine Self. Meditation enables us to improve our spiritual equilibrium, clear negative energy attachments, access our intuition, find answers to personal issues, resolve spiritual questions, manifest our desires and enhance our cosmic connection with the Universe and the Divine.

Meditation is defined in many different ways, and there are many diverse styles, methods and approaches. My favorite definition comes from the Trappist monk, Fr. Thomas Keating, who described meditation as 'sitting down in God's lap and being with the Divine'. This statement captures the true essence of meditative practice - it is sheer communion with the Divine Self and the Conscious Universe, Source Energy, or God. Meditation is about disengaging from the Ego or Material Self and being mindful of your Oneness with all that is, was and ever will be. Meditating is like 'phoning home' when you are far away from your loved ones and feeling a little homesick.

Because meditation serves to silence the Ego, so that you can hear the voice of the Divine, it does not involve any form of rational thinking, logical analysis or critical judgment. Those are the activities of the Ego mind. Meditating is the process of entering into an *altered state of consciousness* where you become a witness, observer and receiver. There are three fundamental approaches to meditation.

I.   **Concentrative meditation** is to completely focus your conscious awareness and mental attention on a specific object or focus point for a certain period of time. Concentrative meditation is therefore the *active directing of your attention* towards only the *focal point* of your choosing and not onto anything else. This object of your attention might be a single word, or a mantra, image, concept, question, idea, symbol, feeling, sensation, belief, or a religious figure. This form of meditation can be focused upon simple things, like your breathing, or complex concepts, like 'the sound of one hand clapping'.

II.   **Mindful meditation** is the art of being mindful and receptively conscious of your field of awareness. In this form of meditation you are *not actively directing your attention* or focus. Instead you are merely a witness, or a non-reactive *observer* monitoring the content of your inner experience from moment to moment. It is an acute open *awareness* of the flow of the present moment. Wandering thoughts or distracting feelings are simply noticed, without resisting or reacting to them in any way. Mindfulness meditation is therefore not so much about *what* one focuses on, but rather the *quality of your focus or awareness* in each moment.

III. **Guided meditation** is not meditation in the traditional religious sense. It is akin to the process of creative visualization, the main difference being that it is 'guided' and you therefore need someone else, in the form of a meditation instructor or a voice recording, to guide you through your meditative journey. When you are not being guided but instead 'guiding' yourself, then you are engaging in *creative visualization*. Guided meditation usually 'tells a story' and has a beginning, middle and an end. It basically serves the same purposes as a creative visualization session, such as connecting with the Divine Self, intuitive development, manifesting your desires, transforming your thoughts and emotions, sharpening your senses or improving your health and reducing stress. The possibilities are truly endless. Guided meditation is a great way to start if you are unaccustomed to meditation. There are many excellent guided meditation recordings available on the market today.

Meditation will not only enhance your spiritual development, but it will also offer you many physical health benefits and improve your quality of life. For example, a 1995 report to the National Institutes of Health on alternative medicine concluded that, "more than 30 years of research, as well as the experience of a large and growing number of individuals and health care providers, suggests that meditation and similar forms of relaxation can lead to better health, higher quality of life, and lowered health care costs."

Unfortunately, research has also shown that many people experiment with meditation at some point in their life, but few turn it into a lasting habit. For this reason it is best to have a plan or strategy when you embark on a meditation program, as well as the right mindset. It is necessary to dedicate specific time in your daily schedule to meditation; it must be one of the things on your daily to-do-list, to ensure that it becomes a regular habit.

There are many ways to meditate and I believe it is best to follow your intuition in finding the ideal method or approach for yourself. Trust your Divine Self to show you the way to go. To get the best results from your meditations, it is however important to start from a solid foundation of basic principles recommended for any form of meditation. I recommend the following strategies and building blocks for your meditation practice.

1) **Choose the appropriate time and place.** Ensure that you do your meditation in a quiet, peaceful place where you will not be disturbed. Decide on a set time for meditation in your daily schedule. Most people find that meditating in the morning, before they start the day, is the best time, because your mind has not yet been cluttered by all the hustle and bustle of daily life. You do not need more than 15 minutes per day to begin with; you can always increase the time later if you wish. If you are a complete novice it may be best to start with a shorter time of just five minutes and gradually work your way up to longer periods.

2) **Find a comfortable body position.** It does not matter too much in what position or posture you place yourself to meditate. The most common method is seated on the floor with the legs crossed. It is, however, perfectly

acceptable to meditate while sitting in a chair, lying down on your back or even standing up. The truly important aspect is to ensure that you are perfectly comfortable and relaxed in whatever position you choose. If you experience any discomfort, adjust your position or change to something more comfortable.

3) **Create a closed circuit.** Meditation is greatly enhanced by crossing the legs at the ankles and gently clasping the hands or intertwining the fingers. This creates a 'closed circuit', providing a more stable basis for the flow of energy.

4) **Begin with grounding, centering and shielding.** Always ground and center within your material body and shield yourself energetically, before you enter into an altered state of consciousness (see previous chapter).

5) **Start with relaxation.** Always begin your meditation session with some form of physical relaxation technique or exercise. I recommend progressive relaxation, which is a systematic approach to relaxing different parts of your body, one at a time, simply by focusing on that area and imagining the tension 'flowing out' or 'melting away'. A good way for beginners to learn this process of complete relaxation is to tighten or contract the muscles in each area, holding it for a few seconds, and then letting it go and feeling the area relax. Start with your feet and work your way up, focusing on each body part or area for a while, before you progress to the next area.

6) **Quiet your mind.** Once your body is completely relaxed, the next step is to shut down all your thoughts and let your mental state become quiet, calm and relaxed. Avoid any inner 'chatter' or self-talk. Forget all your responsibilities, worries, concerns and anxieties. The aim is to 'clear' the mind completely. Do not allow your mind to wander. Simply relax and try to think of absolutely nothing. It is also important to reduce the effect of external stimulation of the mind via the five senses. Therefore

it is best to meditate with your eyes gently closed in a quiet, warm and comfortable environment.

7) **Focused breathing is essential.** The main focus of any meditation session should always be your breathing. By diverting our attention to the natural flow of our breath, we are more easily able to transcend the mind and calm our thoughts. Your breathing should not be done consciously; don't focus or put any effort into inhaling or exhaling. Simply allow breathing to occur spontaneously, while you merely observe it happening. Each time you find yourself being distracted, or your mind following a thought process, return to observation of your breathing. You are ready to begin your meditation once you have reached a state of complete relaxation, when the mind is 'thoughtless' and you no longer need to be aware of your breathing.

Habit # 5: Turn It Off

One of the simplest and most profound changes I made to my life-style a few years ago was to become more mindful of what information and sensory input I expose myself to.

As an empath I have always been adversely affected by disturbing news and shocking images on television and the radio. I am also easily distressed by negative people and emotionally toxic environments.

It has always been a challenge to balance my psychic sensitivity with my penchant for altruism and social consciousness. I care about what goes on in the world, and I have this built-in tendency to always look out for the 'underdog' in any situation. I therefore used to make a concerted effort to follow the news and stay abreast of global political and socio-economic developments. I constantly had to pay the price for it, having my spiritual equilibrium disrupted and my emotional and psychological energy disturbed.

In recent years it became especially challenging to watch the news or read the newspapers, especially here in my country. I could no longer stomach all the incessant reports about rising crime, violence, socio-economic decay, environmental destruction and the corruption of politicians and government officials. Something had to give.

The final straw was the global economic recession a few years ago, which broke the spirit of millions of people all over the world. I simply could not endure the international hysteria, cynicism, negativity and fear-mongering that ensued. I had had enough.

One day I simply made a deliberate decision to no longer expose myself to any of it. I turned it off. I no longer read newspapers, I do not follow the mainstream news and in my home the television set is never tuned in for news broadcasts when I am around. I simply no longer expose myself to things that negatively impact my emotional well-being, my spiritual balance and psychic equilibrium.

They say, "You are what you eat". Well, I say, "you are what you read". What you put into your conscious awareness is what you will manifest in your life. Other people's negative views, false beliefs and destructive manifestations will dominate your reality.

It is not my intention to prescribe to you what you should watch, read or listen to, or who you should associate with. However, no matter what you choose to fill your mind and awareness with, always be mindful of how it is affecting your vibrational frequency and your thought patterns. What we think, and what we feel, is what we become. We create our own reality.

Constantly exposing yourself to popular culture and the mass media will ultimately shape your reality tunnel in ways that are not necessarily conducive to achieving your Soul Purpose and Life Calling. Modern society has generally 'lost the plot'. Slavishly following its false gods and idols makes no sense in a spiritually aware life.

The same holds true for toxic relationships and people in your life who consistently indulge in negativity, cynicism, prejudice, fear-mongering, pessimism, and hatred. It may seem very "unspiritual" of me to advise you to avoid such people, and completely eliminate all the 'trolls' from your life if you can, but truth be told, you can be of no real service to them if you allow them to impede and obstruct your well-being and spiritual growth. Sure, as your fellow seekers these people do need your assistance and support, but you can only provide them with the help they need by staying in alignment with your own Soul Purpose and Life Calling. Only by striving towards the accomplishment of your own mission in this lifetime do you become truly empowered to be of service to others.

If you really want to help all the lost souls who have been poisoning your mind with their skepticism, negative attitudes and false beliefs, then get away from them as soon as possible, and first seek your own truth and personal bliss. The people who truly need your help will gravitate to you in time. Don't try to heal the whole world all at once.

Personally, I had to cut loose several acquaintances, colleagues, friends and family members in order to fully come into my own spiritually, and as a consequence I have been a source of guidance and support to hundreds of clients all over the world. I used to be a lost soul myself and therefore I did not always keep the most positive or uplifting company. Had I continued to indulge and tolerate some of those toxic people in my aura on a daily basis, I would have been of little or no use to the many amazing clients and students who I now assist in transforming their lives. I would certainly not have managed to write this book had I allowed all the 'nay sayers' and 'doom prophets' to stick around.

Practicing social censorship in your daily life presents a real dilemma for some people. We have been so conditioned to believe that we must pretend 'to be nice' to get ahead in life, and that we need to stay abreast of the news at all cost, just like we have come to believe that we must be on top of the latest fashions, technologies and lifestyle trends.

I am often asked how I manage to stay informed about what goes on in the world, since I no longer watch, read or listen to the news. My answer often surprises people. I typically have no idea or any real interest what the global media is reporting from day to day. Most of it is drivel, hype, lies and disinformation anyway. Yet, despite the fact that I do not follow the news, I always know just enough of the really important events happening in the world. I remain reasonably well-informed of the most vital international and local developments. This does not happen by accident or coincidence. It is my firm belief that if there is something in the news that I need to know, the most essential information will find me. It is further my conscious intention that the news I need to hear will reach me in a form that will not disturb or upset me. And this is exactly how it manifests in my life. Whatever I need to now, I attract into my conscious awareness. I trust in the wisdom and guidance I receive from the Divine Self and I trust in the power of my own intention as co-creator to draw to me all that I need to live a happy, safe and fulfil-ling life. The things I need to hear or see always come to me in the right way and at the right time.

Why do we have this obsession with "staying informed" about absolutely everything in the world anyway? How much of what you watch on your television screen, or read in your newspaper, truly affects your daily life *directly*, and how much of it can you *change* without some kind of Divine intervention? In my mind the only reason why any spiritually aware soul would want to follow the mainstream news would be to use the information gained to make the world a better place. To follow the news out of fear and uncertainty only breeds further fear and uncertainty.

It is my belief that the only people who should be following aspects of the news consistently should be people who actually need that relevant information for the fulfillment of their Life Calling. Yet, even in those instances modern technology provides us with so many options these days to filter the information that ultimately reaches us. For example, I have set several Google Alerts on my email account that focus on specific news topics that are of particular importance in my professional work. I find it to be more than sufficient.

We cannot be everything to everyone. I cannot possibly do my life's work, while at the same time attempting to solve local crime, world hunger, social injustice and political corruption. There are others who have a Life Calling to address those matters. To each his own. Take my advice and turn off your television set.

Habit # 6: Be Of Service

Make an effort to be of service to others. Acts of service are an important component in any spiritual way of life, and it is worth your while for it has several benefits.

Firstly, it serves your Soul Purpose. Soul growth and spiritual expansion cannot happen in isolation from the world around us. Do not confuse the need for solitude in your daily spiritual prac-tice with complete isolation from the rest of humanity – it is not the same thing. Service and fellowship are very powerful ways to add value and *fulfillment* to our spiritual life.

The second benefit of service is that it can act as *preparation* for your true Life Calling. You may not be able to immediately start doing the work you were meant to do in this lifetime. Maybe you need to first complete your education, before you launch the career you were called to do, or maybe you must first manifest enough money to start a new business, but that does not prevent you from doing volunteer work in your field of interest, or to offer your services free of charge if you already have some of the necessary knowledge or skills.

For example, if it is your intention to become a veterinary surgeon one of the best things you could do is to volunteer at an animal shelter. If it is your dream to work as a physical therapist, how about doing volunteer work for the physical fitness program for senior citizens at your community center. There are many ways we can be of service and we each need to find the way that works best for us. Sometimes you need nothing more than a computer and an Internet connection to be of service to the world.

Not only will you be 'rehearsing' your future spiritual role in life, but you are also speeding up the process of manifesting your new career or business. If you begin to be actively involved in something you love doing, the joy and fulfillment you derive from it will dramatically raise your vibrational frequency and speed up the process of attracting and manifesting the necessary opportunities and material things you need to accomplish your Life Calling.

A third benefit of being of service to others is that it *distracts* us from our own lives. Being of service to others, who may be less privileged, puts our own problems in a fresh perspective. When we concern ourselves more with others who face worse challenges in their lives, there is less time to be concerned with ourselves and many of our petty worries and fears. The more we serve and inspire others, the more substance we add to our own life experience. No matter how lost you are to yourself, you become more significant to the world when you serve, and because you feel more substantial when you serve it becomes easier for you to find yourself, because there is more of you to find.

Habit # 7: Find Fellowship

Make an effort to get together with other like-minded, spiritually aware souls on a regular basis, preferably to engage in some kind of spiritual practice together. You can spend this time in many amazing and stimulating ways, for example attending a metaphysics course, joining a mediumship development circle, going to

Bible study, participating in a spiritual book club, attending a Law of Attraction seminar, participating in a Yoga class, or doing volunteer work.

Even if you are truly unable to physically go out to spend time with others, there are so many alternative options available these days using modern communications technology, including joining social networking groups and online forums, and participating in online webinars, live podcasts, and video conferencing. It doesn't matter so much what you do when you have fellowship with others, it is the mere act of engaging and sharing that benefits us most, because it serves to raise our vibration and increase our awareness. Spending time with other spiritual seekers serves to align us with our own inner awareness.

4

THE MAXIMS OF DIVINE LIVING

A Divine Life is a life of *harmony.* When we live in harmony with ourselves, with others and our environment, as well as our planet and the Laws of the Universe, we are expressing the truth of our Divine nature. Once you come into this place of harmony, you will begin to see the miracle of your Divine origins manifesting on a daily basis in the form of many blessings. Harmony ensures a truly awakened and abundant life.

To achieve this level of harmony in your daily life it is important to adhere to some personal values or rules to guide you, and help you stay on track towards fulfilling your Life Plan. I call these guidelines *The Maxims of Divine Living.* A 'maxim' is a fundamental truth, a rule of conduct, or a universal wisdom.

By always being mindful of these guidelines for Divine Living you will successfully overcome many challenges that will cross your path, and you will attract many more opportunities for soul growth, in order to achieve your Soul Purpose. The personal values below are also vital in your quest to ultimately accomplish your Life Calling, for it would be impossible to be truly of service to others if you did not have these guidelines as your foundation.

Maxim # 1: Seize The Day

A favorite quote I often share with clients is the timeless statement by Jan Glidewell, "You can clutch the past so tightly to your chest that it leaves your arms too full to embrace the present". If there is one valuable commodity humanity has sacrificed for its Ego-driven modern lifestyle, then it is our ability to truly *live in the now*, to just *be in the present moment.*

How many times in your life have you swallowed a quick meal without really enjoying your food? How many times have you had a conversation with a friend and could not recall much of what she said later? Have you ever been guilty of watching the clock and counting the hours while at work, wishing away another day in your life? How many times over the years have you wished for something to come to an end, or for something to happen sooner? And what is the first thing you notice when you wake up in the morning: the time on your alarm clock or the birds outside your window?

We seem to find it impossible in this day and age to be simply mindful in the present. Even our holidays and weekends are devoted to a mad rush, and lists of things to do. Meanwhile, our true life is what is happening to us while we are busy making other plans.

What used to be the most natural and easily attained state of being for our primitive ancestors, has become seemingly impossible to achieve for modern man. Living in the now is a one of the most basic aspects of a spiritually-centered lifestyle. In fact, it is generally consider to be 'Spirituality 101'. It is the foundation of what a spiritually aware life should be, yet even the most metaphysically advanced and spiritually devoted people struggle to achieve and maintain this simple state of being.

In truth, I do not believe that it is entirely possible or healthy for us to fully live only in the present moment. It would probably not be in our best interest to completely and permanently disconnect from the past and future. We possess this tendency or ability to focus on things that are not happening right now, because it allows us to reflect on the past and the future. In enables us to learn from past experiences and to look forward to the future with expectation, and anticipate and plan for tomorrow.

We need to live with a certain level of daily intent and desire in order to grow, expand and manifest all that we need to fulfill our Soul Purpose and Life Calling. It is good to sometimes fondly remember highlights from the past, or think optimistically of the future. It provides us with a sense of continuity, allows us to judge how much progress we have made, and empowers us with hope and enthusiasm for what is yet to come.

Unfortunately, many of us are unable to do reflect on the past and future in a balanced, healthy way. Instead we tend to cling to the past excessively, and obsess over all that went wrong and could have been different. We wallow in all the mistakes we made. Or we wait around idly for better days to come, wishing our lives away, while we indulge in unrealistic fears about what tomorrow may bring.

Some people even make a conscious effort to avoid dealing with the present moment. They dare not acknowledge the reality of their 'now', as it does not resemble what the False Ego demands it to be. These are the people who would constantly talk about "the good old days", or who would rehash their regrets about all that they could have done differently in their past. "If only," you hear them say, while they dote on their future happiness and success, which might emerge if only their "ship comes in one day".

These people are never content or at peace with where they are at this *present moment*, and they invest all their creative energy in either reliving the past, or dreaming of a distant future. Meanwhile their lives pass them by, day by day, like some kind of temporary rehearsal for what is yet to come. The only effort they usually make to focus on the now, is to point out everything that is currently wrong or missing from their life.

Researchers estimate that we spend nearly half of our day thinking about *other things*, instead of focusing on what we are doing right now in this present moment. Psychologists at Harvard University showed that reminiscing, thinking ahead or day-dreaming tend to make people *more miserable*, even when they are thinking about something pleasant. The researchers concluded that a "human mind is a wandering mind and a wandering mind is an unhappy mind. The ability to think about what is *not happening* is a cognitive achievement that comes at an *emotional cost*."

To live a truly awakened and abundant Divine Life you must make every effort to come into the now and embrace the present moment unconditionally. Increased awareness and appreciation of the present moment is the essential core of your personal spiritual growth and realignment with your Divine Self. To create and truly enjoy a Divine Lifestyle, you must be able to savor the present in all its glory. The joy of this ride absolutely depends on it. Eckhart Tolle writes in *The Power of Now*, "Realize deeply that the present moment is all you have. Make the *now* the primary focus of your life."

This may seem tricky to do at first, but the more you come into alignment with your Divine Self, and the more you begin to raise your awareness of your thoughts, feelings, words and actions, you will become more attentive to your daily experiences and the world around you. Through the exercises later in this book you will also develop your sensory sharpness and intuition and become more conscious of the numerous magical moments in every day. By being fully present and aware you will begin to see the signs and synchronicities that will guide you towards fulfilling your Life Plan.

Divine Living is about being more *mindful*. Make an effort to focus on whatever you are doing at different times in the day. Don't just focus on the actual task, but also become aware of how it looks, sounds, tastes, smells and feels. Notice any 'gut feelings' you may have as a result of where you are and what you are doing at that moment. And notice how are you responding mentally and emotionally, what kind of thoughts and feelings does this activity bring to the surface? If you find your thoughts are drifting off into the past or the future, let those thoughts go and bring your awareness back to the present.

Begin to take more notice of the world around you. No matter what you're doing, always try to find something interesting, beautiful or inspiring in your day, wherever you are. You may also have to make some changes to your general lifestyle, by spending less time doing 'mindless' activities, such as staring at your television set, or replacing your habit to indulge in distracted daydreaming with mindful meditation and creative visualization.

Living fully in the moment is not about being passive or 'mindless', it is about being totally focused and conscious of the many special moments in your day. To be mindful, present and aware is to be truly alive and happy. Find your bliss in the *now*.

Maxim # 2: Do Unto Others

Everything you think, say or do affects everyone and everything else in the Universe. The reason for this is that all things originate from the same Divine Source, God or Universal Oneness. This Source or Oneness from which everything emanates is an eternal and unchanging *unified field of intelligence* that underlies everything in the Universe and is pervasive throughout all of creation. It is also known as the Akasha, Aether, Collective Unconscious, Fifth Element, Superstring Field or the Unified Field of Consciousness.

We are all interconnected, we are One. We are all products of, and co-creators in this Conscious Universe. You are not separate from other people, or the world around you. Neither are you separate from nature, the animals and plants, and all inanimate objects. The Universe does not consist of separate things. We see this clearly demonstrated in the concept of 'non-locality' in Quantum Physics, namely that subatomic particles can become 'entangled' with each other or that they may be able to instantaneously communicate with each other over thousands of miles, regardless of the distance separating them. Each particle always seems to know what the other is doing, whether they are a few feet or millions of miles of apart.

Mind and matter are also not separate entities. Consciousness is not generated by your mind; it is something you are 'plugged into'. Our brain merely enables us to perceive reality by acting as an 'interpreter' or 'translator' of the larger stream of consciousness which we are a part of. Consciousness is something you share with everything and everyone else. When one of us experiences suffering or hardship, it affects all of us. When one of us lives in joy and peace, it affects everyone else. We are all miniature versions of the vast holographic Universe. The Universe is reflected in us and we are reflected in the Universe.

A scientific theory perfectly demonstrating this influence we have on our world is the so-called *butterfly effect* found in Chaos Theory. According to this concept even the smallest changes within a complex system can lead to unexpected, large scale results. For example, meteorologist Edward Lorenz speculated that the flapping of a butterfly's wings could create minuscule changes in the Earth's atmosphere which could ultimately lead to a violent tornado elsewhere on the planet. If you consider how harmless and insignificant a butterfly appears to be, imagine the damage one negative or uncaring human being could do? Know that you 'flap your wings' with every thought, word and deed. Become aware of the effect you may be having on the world around you. Every cause has its effect, and in the end we all reap what we sow.

A Divine Life is a life of *unconditional love* for yourself, for others and for every living being, including Mother Earth. The Divine lifestyle is free from obsessive competition, greed, personality clashes and emotional drama. It is the weak who constantly react in anger or frustration when they come into conflict with others. It is also the weak who constantly seek justice, or revenge for every imagined little offense. It is the weak who feel compelled to be tough and defiant at all cost, regardless whether they are right or wrong. Unless it is a matter of life and death, standing your ground on absolutely everything is mostly trivial and has very little to do with your inner strength.

The truly happy, enlightened and wise find their power in unconditional love. Who is right and who is wrong is *spiritually insignificant*. Truly powerful people seldom have any need for excessive self-defense, or forcing their views upon others. It simply does not matter. Do you want to be right, or do you want to be happy? Do you want to be despised for being defensive and confrontational, or do you want to be loved and respected for bringing a sense of 'increase' to everyone you touch with your presence?

Claiming your 'place in the sun' and staying true to yourself does not have to involve any form of violent conviction, dogged persistence, foolish bravery or brute force. There is nothing that you have to prove to anyone. There is nobody that must be resisted or refuted or convinced by you at all cost. Not everything needs to be changed by you; everyone and everybody does not require your supervision or control. Your opinion is not always required. When you are in alignment with your Divine Self, your Soul Purpose and your Life Calling, it no longer matters all that much what other people think, or say, or believe.

What matters is how you respond to others and how you choose to feel in any given situation. There are never any winners if there also has to be losers, no matter what the circumstance. Jesus referred to it as "turning the other cheek" and "doing unto others"; the Buddha talked of cultivating "a limitless heart" and the Prophet Muhammad encouraged the "conquest of self" and "loving our fellow-beings first".

Instead of always focusing on what others say, or do, or believe, turn your attention to your inner being. Focus on your own vibrational frequency. Work on feeling better about yourself and your life and the world around you. Other people are not responsible for how you feel. If the words and actions of someone else are currently determining your state of mind, or your self-esteem, it means that you have been giving away your power, and it is time for you to take it back.

You were born with the basic spiritual right to 'feel good', and to be happy. In fact, you have inherited a Divine right to feel really great most of the time. It is vital that we feel this way, because it empowers us to love others unconditionally. Once you feel happy and centered in your own being, it is so much easier to be kind and tolerant towards others.

With this approach it becomes so much easier to live a Divine Life. You no longer have to deal with all the stress, drama, negativity and destructive emotions of an Ego-dominated reality, because you now choose a different reality. There is also no longer any desire to be constantly affirmed or acknowledged by others. Gone are the regrets and the grudges. Conflict and arguments all but disappear from your life. It really does take two to tango and nobody enjoys dancing solo, especially if there is no music to dance to.

When you are true to your Divine nature and aligned in harmony with the rest of the Universe, people more often become willing to listen and calmly consider your point of view. Even the really tough and deluded folks become a non-issue, because they will eventually give up and move on.

All of this may seem like a lot of hard work, but it does not have to be. Getting into 'the zone' of 'allowing' is much easier than you may think. Deepak Chopra describes it as following the 'Law of Least Effort'. There are three components to his definition of this law, namely acceptance, responsibility and defenselessness, which he outlines in his book, *The Seven Spiritual Laws of Success*.

Chopra explains that "*acceptance* simply means that you make a commitment: 'Today I will accept people, situations, circumstances and events as they occur.' This means you will know that this moment is as it should be, because the whole Universe is as it should be".

Responsibility means "not blaming anyone or anything for your situation, including yourself. This allows you the ability to have a creative response to the situation as it is now. All problems contain the seeds of opportunity, and this awareness allows you to take the moment and transform it to a better situation or thing."

Finally, he describes the most important component, namely becoming *defenseless*. He defines this as "relinquishing the need to convince or persuade others of your point of view. If you relinquish this need you will in that relinquishment gain access to enormous amounts of energy that have been previously wasted".

I also recommend three additional simple rules of thumb. The first is to always *pick your battles carefully* and to let the Law of Karma take care of the rest. The second is to *never buy into other people's drama*. The third is to recognize that you were never supposed to be anybody's doormat, so don't allow yourself to go down that slippery slope in the first place. *Don't give your personal power away* to anyone for any reason.

Does this mean that we should always remain silent when we are made victims, or look the other way when we see atrocities committed? Not at all. Nelson Mandela did not remain silent. Neither did Mahatma Ghandi. But they also came to the realization during the course of their lives that using force to convince others was not the best way to change the world.

"An eye for an eye makes the whole world blind", said Ghandi. "If you want to make peace with your enemy, you have to work with your enemy. Then he becomes your partner", said Mandela. It is not about remaining silent or avoiding reality. It is about remaining faithful to your beliefs and values, without having to force it upon others. Your life and the rest of the world can be changed without violence, or drama, or force. Mandela and Ghandi are two excellent examples of how to achieve personal peace, spiritual wisdom and harmony with others - and yet, they both managed to change the history of the world.

You won't always get it right in moments of weakness. Some 'bullies' just have the uncanny ability to drag you away from your 'path of least resistance' and, before you know it, you are completely out of alignment and back into the Ego, or the False Self. On those occasions one tends to forget all your best intentions and give in to anger, hurt or frustration. But it gets easier with practice and one does become stronger. You will learn to let go more and more each day. International meditation teacher Jack Kornfield states that "a genuine spiritual path is not to avoid difficulties but to learn the art of making mistakes wakefully, to bring them to the transformative power of our heart".

The truism of 'Do Unto Others' is also known as the *Golden Rule*, namely that we should always treat others as we would like others to treat us. This Golden Rule is an ethical code found in many ancient traditions and world religions. For example, in Christianity there is the well-known quote from Matthew, "So in everything, do to others what you would have them do to you, for this sums up the Law and the Prophets".

In Buddhism the *Dhammapada* states "One who, while himself seeking happiness oppresses with violence other beings who also desire happiness, will not attain happiness hereafter". The

Analects of Confucius says, "Never impose on others what you would not choose for yourself". And in Hinduism the *Mahabharata* declares, "One should never do that to another which one regards as injurious to one's own self. This, in brief, is the rule of dharma. Other behavior is due to selfish desires".

Many versions of the Golden Rule is also found in the texts of ancient Babylon, Egypt and Greece, as well as other major religions, including the Baha'i Faith, Brahmanism, Islam, Jainism, Judaism, Native American religion, Neo-Paganism, Sikhism, Taoism, Theosophy, and Zoroastrianism.

This Golden Rule must therefore be the non-negotiable central pillar of a Divine Life. To be able to live a life of harmony with others and our environment it is critical that we adopt a sense of responsibility for our daily thoughts, words and actions. No man is an island, and although popular culture and consumerism would have us believe that it should be "everyone for themselves" and "may the best man win" and "survival of the fittest", we all know on a deeper spiritual level that this is *not* Universal Truth.

It is no accident or coincidence that the Golden Rule is found in most of the major religious and wisdom traditions throughout human history. Accept that you are indeed your *brother's keeper*, and that you constantly have an impact on our environment and planet, as well as all the living beings you share it with. In the 2011 film *I AM*, Professor of Psychology Dacher Keltner, states it very simply, "It's in our DNA. We are born to be a community. We are born to be our brother's keeper".

This maxim of 'Do Unto Others' can be applied in your daily lifestyle without having to sacrifice yourself entirely in the process. It does not require you to be a victim or a martyr. You also won't need to adopt an orphan, or give away your belongings to the poor. It can be as simple as just changing *one negative thought* per day, or by deciding not to participate in the usual gossip at work. It could be as humble as offering a kind word to a cashier at the supermarket, or a friendly smile at a stranger in the street. The possibilities are truly endless.

Maxim # 3: Like Attracts Like

Einstein taught us that all matter is energy. Everything in the Universe has its own energetic vibration. What we perceive as material things or physical reality is actually energy vibrating at various frequencies.

Did you know that your body consists of approximately 7,000,000,000,000,000,000,000,000,000 atoms vibrating at a certain frequency? Each of these atoms consist of a tiny nucleus surrounded by an electron cloud, which means the atom is essentially about 99.9% space or 'emptiness'.

The electrons in each atom tend to vibrate at a specific natural frequency, which is called its *resonance*. Vibration is basically different types of waves that act upon the atoms in a matter with a similar frequency, causing them to vibrate or resonate. These vibrational waves can be acoustic (sound), electromagnetic, nuclear, mechanical or even quantum waves.

For example, when a light wave with a certain natural frequency strikes a material with electrons that have the same vibrational frequency, then those electrons will absorb the energy of the light wave and transform it into vibrational motion. This vibrational energy is then converted into thermal energy, or 'heat'. This is like holding a magnifying glass over some dry leaves. By moving the glass up and down you adjust the frequency of the light waves to match frequency of the atoms of the leaves. When the waves of sunlight and the electrons in the atoms of the dry leaves begin to *resonate* at a certain vibrational frequency, the atoms of the leaves will begin to absorb the sun's light waves and convert it into a different form of energy (heat).

This selective absorption of a wave by a particular material occurs because the frequency of the wave matches the frequency at which electrons in the atoms of that specific material vibrate. Since different atoms have different natural frequencies of vibration, they will *selectively absorb* different frequencies of vibration.

This 'vibrational matching' is also vital in how we perceive our reality. All five our senses rely on vibrational input that resonates within our limited spectrum of perception. For example, the human eye can only see a small portion of the electromagnetic spectrum, known as 'visible light'. Similarly, we can only hear certain sounds or acoustic frequencies. Our perception of reality is therefore nothing more than a *vibrational interpretation* made by our senses.

From Quantum Physics we also know that everything we perceive around us is actually a series of out-of-focus patterns that shift into focus in a certain way when we *observe* it, or when there is a certain expectation for it to manifest in a certain way. The American poet Ralph Waldo Emerson was therefore quite correct when he wrote "people only see what they are prepared to see."

Vibrational frequency and resonance do not only play a role in how we perceive the world around us, but it also determines who we are on the 'inside' and how the world around us will respond to us, or resonate with us. How you choose to 'vibrate' as an entity will determine your *resonance*, or the kind of energy frequencies you will mostly be compatible with and interact with.

Your thoughts, emotions, beliefs and attitudes are all 'vibrations' that have a certain resonance or vibrational frequency, which will determine what kind of external vibrations it will match, attract and absorb. Positive and uplifting thoughts, emotions, beliefs and attitudes have a higher vibrational frequency, while negative and depressing thoughts, emotions, beliefs and attitudes have a lower vibration. This is quite obvious, for example, when you compare the speech and tone of voice of a happy or excited person with that of a sad or depressed person.

Everything you own, every place you go and every person you spend your time with has their own *vibrational signature.* So does everything you think, feel and believe. Everything in your daily life vibrates at its own unique frequency. But all these things also resonate with the *vibrational signal* you send out. That is what makes all these things a part of your daily reality, namely the fact that you have resonance with everything in your life. You are able to interface vibrationally with all these things. By thinking, feeling, and believing more positively you will have a higher vibrational frequency and you will resonate more easily with positive people and circumstances and attract more positive opportunities and experiences into your life.

If you are uncertain about what kind of 'vibrational signal' you have been sending out, simply have a look at whom and what you currently have in your life. You can see what kind of vibration you are sending out simply by noticing what you have been creating, attracting and manifesting thus far.

The measurement problem in Quantum Physics suggests what we think, feel, and believe is what ultimately our reality becomes. What we focus on and what we desire will ultimately manifest in accordance with our expectation, or how we chose to perceive it, because subatomic particles manifest according to the way it is observed.

We also see in Quantum Theory that the observer cannot observe or think about anything without changing what he sees or observes. Several experiments have demonstrated that when a wave is observed it changes to a new state, and also that the intention of the specific experiment determines whether a wave, or a particle will appear. Researchers have conducted a series of experiments demonstrating that our thinking and our intent can change and influence the outcome of events.

We also know that the elementary particles found in Quantum Field Theory do not really exist at all. Instead they are only relationships or tendencies or correlations that have the potential to somehow manifest into reality. In other words, there may be no objective physical reality at all, only a potential reality within a vast 'empty space' that comes into being when we observe it or focus upon it. These phenomena are discussed in greater detail in the final chapter of this book.

The Universe is therefore like an ocean of virtual particles that 'flicker in and out of existence'. In *The Seven Spiritual Laws of Success* author Deepak Chopra calls it the field of "pure potentiality seeking expression from the unmanifest to the manifest. And when we realize that our true Self is one of pure potentiality, we align with the power that manifests everything in nature". Imagine what effect your thoughts, emotions, words and deeds can have on this vast sea of universal potential.

How you choose to 'vibrate' in this world will determine the quality of your life and the kind of people and circumstances you will attract to you. The people and circumstances you *resonate* with is what will become your daily reality. If you choose mostly negative thoughts and emotions every single day, and surround yourself with negative people, and focus only negative circumstances and events in the world, it is unlikely that your life will be some kind of spiritual 'rose garden'. Under such circumstances the vast potential of the Conscious Universe will mostly be a source of fear, frustration or desperation in your life.

The moment you begin to make a change in your own vibration, you will increasingly make decisions and choices that resonate better with a higher frequency. This is why people often lose some friends and give up some of their hobbies and interests when they awaken spiritually. The things that resonated with their Ego or False Self during the time of the Divine Disconnect no longer seem so relevant or important.

The things of the past tend to lose their charm or superficial veneer when you reconnect and begin to realign with the Divine Self. As you begin to realign with your Divine Self your vibrational frequency will be raised and you will begin to attract and absorb more light, love and joy. Your being will begin to resonate with the lighter and finer vibrations of Higher Consciousness.

This does not imply that you should automatically just give up everything and everyone familiar or dear to you. But you will probably find that your change in vibrational frequency will begin to filter out some of those people and things that no longer resonate with you. Fortunately, there are always many other wonderful people and things to take their place.

However, don't try to make these changes happen consciously. Simply let the changes filter through gradually and organically. The only thing you need to concern yourself with is raising your vibration to a higher, more positive level and maintaining this improved energy field around you as your new vibrational signature. This applies to every aspect of your life.

You can 'raise your vibration' by improving your thoughts, feelings, beliefs and attitudes, while shedding false beliefs, negativity and destructive thought patterns from the past. Additionally, you can adjust your vibration to match the changes you wish to see in your life. If you want a better career or a new relationship you will have to 'meet that imagined person or opportunity half-way' with your vibration. You cannot expect to find that someone special, or get that dream job, if you personally do not resonate with that person or job opportunity.

Think of yourself as a kind of *vibrational magnet* that will only attract that which you automatically send out as a signal. If you settle in your thoughts for second best - maybe because you think you do not deserve it, or because you have this false belief that nothing great ever happens to you - then you are very unlikely to attract that which you truly desire and deserve. Even if it were possible for you to still meet that someone new or get that job, without offering a matching vibration, it would probably not last very long. It would most likely be very difficult for you to get along with your new love interest, or you might find it stressful to cope with the new job. It makes no sense to desire a luxurious new automobile if you don't have a driver's license, and have never learned to drive. You cannot expect to receive that which you are not ready or able to offer in return, or be a vibrational match to.

Instead of concerning yourself too much with what you want in a relationship with a future life partner, for example, it is best to start instead by focusing on *what you can offer* as a partner. The first step to do this is becoming aware of your own vibrational frequency and changing your resonance.

Different geographical locations also have an energetic vibrational signature of their own. This is true for different continents, countries, areas, cities and towns. Where you live holds a certain energy of its own that should ideally support and nurture your own vibration. If you do not resonate well with a place or location you will always be aware of feeling restless, detached, uncomfortable or even unhappy.

Also, bear in mind that your presence changes the environment you are in and has an effect on the places where you go. A person entering a room can immediately bring about a change in the vibrational tone of that space. Over the years I have been witness to many clients, who have had a profound spiritual awakening or a change in vibrational frequency, who eventually developed the overwhelming urge to relocate to a place where they would resonate better with their environment. Be aware that this is something that may also happen in your life.

If you want a better life, if you want to live a Divine Life, then you need to *change your vibration* by changing your thoughts, feelings, beliefs and attitudes. The more positive, enthusiastic and optimistic you become, the higher your vibrational frequency will become and the more you will begin to resonate with all that is positive and uplifting in the world around you. In all forms of vibration like will always attract like.

Maxim # 4: Swing Into Action

To attain a Divine lifestyle and change your reality for the better you need more than just appropriate thoughts, feelings, intentions, beliefs, attitudes and words. You also need to back up these 'new vibrations' in your life with some good, old-fashioned *action*. Divine Living requires a *proactive approach* on your part.

Yes, contrary to all those self-help books and Law of Attraction teachings that encourage people to do as little as possible and sit back and wait for the positive results to come and find them, this book encourages you to put your shoulder to the wheel and your nose to the grindstone.

In the 1910 book *The Science of Getting Rich*, generally considered to be the first modern book on the Law of Attraction and manifesting, Wallace D. Wattles explains that "thought is the creative power, or the impelling force which causes the creative power to act; thinking in a certain way will bring riches to you, but you must not rely upon thought alone, paying no attention to personal action. That is the rock upon which many otherwise scientific metaphysical thinkers meet shipwreck - the failure to connect thought with personal action."

Of course, there is no need to devote hours of self-sacrificing blood, sweat and tears. This is not about doing back-breaking spiritual work to somehow redeem yourself or find salvation through some kind of hard-earned transformation. No, once you begin to realign with your Divine Self and become more aware of your true purpose and calling, you will most likely find that you automatically develop the urge to do some 'new things' in your spare time, such as read, visualize, chat, journal, socialize, observe, study, watch, meditate, pray, share, serve, exercise and rest, to name only a few possibilities. Do whatever spiritual practice works for you, and helps you stay on track with your Life Plan. It is not so important what you or how much you do, but just that you do something, anything.

In spiritual matters there are often too many words and too few deeds, plenty of talk and very little action. Do not become tempted to passively absorb the contents of this book, for example, and not apply at least some of its contents in your life in some way. Knowledge cannot be power if it is not accompanied by some form of *practical action* or *application*.

At first you may feel that you are unsure which actions would be most appropriate, but that is irrelevant and should not be your concern. Start small and simple with what you know and already have at your disposal, and let it evolve organically from there. Trust your inner guidance; the Universe will take care of the rest, with your Divine Self as your guide and mentor. You may even make mistakes and stumble a little from time to time, but that is just a natural part of achieving your Soul Purpose – making mistakes and learning those lessons. This is why action in your life is so vital, because without it you will limit your soul growth and you may never achieve your Soul Purpose. We came here to do things, not sit around and wait for salvation.

You do not have to attain it all in the first attempt. Take it one day at a time. Just do something. Every step you take is one step closer to your dreams, and it is one step further compared to where you were before you took that initial step. Lao Tzu once declared, "A journey of a thousand miles starts with a single step".

You have a Life Calling waiting to be accomplished, at the very least start working towards that goal, even if your personal life remains in limbo for the time being. Don't make the mistake so many people make of waiting for the most ideal circumstances or the best future opportunities to arrive. Make it happen today, right now. We really do need all hands on deck. Begin with a few small steps, as long as you just begin. There is no need to wait until you are old enough, skinny enough, wealthy enough, confident enough, or wise enough. The time will never be more 'right' than *right now*. Actions speak louder than thoughts and words.

This book was inspired by thoughts, visualizations, dreams, discussions, inspirations, ideas, signs, synchronicity, spiritual messages and opportunity, but it was certainly not researched and written by the 'elves and fairies', while I lay sleeping on my sofa. In a sense this book did write itself, but only on a non-physical level, because within this physical reality I had to make this book happen through my own action and several late nights in front of the computer. A few practical things needed to be done to get it to market and into your hands.

The same applies to your Divine Life. Don't wait for the metaphysical to manifest into the physical to ensure changes in your life. As I pointed out before, you did not come into this physical reality to have some kind of fantasy, escapist, esoteric or profound metaphysical experience. You are a spiritual being having a very practical, human experience within a highly physical dimension. And that is wonderful! That is what you came here for in the first place, to play in this crazy sandbox and get your hands really dirty. Make it happen!

Not every change or improvement in your new Divine Life will be attained through only your actions or efforts. Some of it will come about spontaneously and all by itself. The Universe helps those who want to help themselves. Spirit will take care of you and see to your needs along the way. You will be amazed to see how much magical manifestation and synchronicity will begin to surface in your daily life once you begin to take steps in the right direction.

When you have reconnected with your Divine Self and begin to realign with your Divine nature you will find that obstacles begin to disappear and opportunities arise to clear the way towards your goals. Once you are in alignment with your Life Plan all struggle and resistance begins to dissolve and everything around you begins to line-up and conspire to make your ride as smooth as it can possibly be in this physical reality.

Maxim # 5: Get Into The Groove

A Divine Life is about taking responsibility for what you think, feel, say and do, and for manifesting that which you desire, but it is *not about controlling* everything and everyone in your world. When you reconnect with your Divine Self you will soon discover that it is best not to constantly interfere with the natural cycles and rhythms of the Universe. To live a Divine Life of harmony with yourself, others and the world around you, you really do need to 'get into the groove' and 'go with flow'.

In my mother tongue, Afrikaans, we have a saying, "Laat Gods water oor Gods akker loop", which literally translates to "Let God's water flow over God's acre (field)", which means that it is best to go with the flow and trust that God will take care of things in the best way possible. The English equivalent is 'Let Go and let God'.

Divine Living embraces the natural rhythms of life. There are seasons, cycles, patterns and stages of development in everything in the Conscious Universe. It is evident everywhere in nature. Divine Living is about rising calmly and confidently above the negative stages of a cycle and expressing gratitude and appreciation during the positive phases. Never allow negative events or people to contaminate your consciousness; don't seek absolute control; and avoid being impatient. Trust always that *all is as it must be.*

Being obsessive about being in control and feeling impatient about future outcomes are the habits of the Ego, the Material Self. In our post-modern society everything seems to revolve around hedonism, materialism, consumerism, narcissism and intense competition for 'limited' resources. We are conditioned from the moment of our birth to find ways to manipulate and control other people, and exploit our environment. We are taught as children not to trust in the ebb and flow of life, but instead to take matters into our own hands at all times.

As a society we are often too eager to control, manipulate and coerce others into being what we expect them to be, or to behave in ways we expect them to behave. Our efforts to control others are seldom for their benefit - we do it for our own gratification. We trust others will make us feel better if they act a certain way; we expect others to meet our demands and expectations. We try to exert this control so that we can feel satisfied and content with the way things are in our corner of the world. Esther-Abraham Hicks refers to this as "all that cumbersome impossibility", which in my opinion is the perfect way to describe it.

If you knew your potential to feel good, you would ask no one to be different so that you can feel good. You would free yourself of all of that cumbersome impossibility of needing to control the world, or control your mate, or control your child. You are the only one who creates your reality. For no one else can think for you, no one else can do it. It is only you, every bit of it you.

The fact of the matter is that it is simply impossible to control others indefinitely, no matter how much we may persist or insist. And, be honest now, it does become quite a burdensome bother to constantly try and exert control over everyone and everything around you, does it not? It is exhausting just to think about it, and yet so many of us continue to try and hold the reigns, believing we will be able to call all the shots.

As an advisor and coach I interact on a daily basis with clients who have yet to discover the truth about "that cumbersome impossibility". So many people who consult me are either hoping to control someone else, or they wish to escape the hold someone else has over them.

If you are in a relationship or an environment where you feel controlled, pressured or intimidated, you need to take action. Only you can make the necessary changes. Never stop questioning. Never be bullied. Do not let others define you, or decide for you. Even if you are physically imprisoned or financially trapped, you can still set yourself free. Each and every personal freedom or material possession can be taken away from you, but nobody has the power to imprison your mind, dictate your emotions or enslave your soul - unless you allow them to do that. And sometimes, when it is within your power to do so, it is best to turn the other cheek, or to simply let it go. If you can, just walk away.

On the flipside, we too often tend to believe that a partner, a parent, a child, or a friend or co-worker holds the key to how we feel now, or how happy we will be in the future. How we feel today or tomorrow should not be dependent on others. Never. There is only one person who should have the right to determine your joy and happiness, and that is you! Nobody else can provide or withhold your well-being, unless you let them. Until you accept that you really do not control everything, you shall find neither peace, nor harmony in your life.

Next to our obsession with control, *impatience* is the other poisonous byproduct of our Ego-driven society. The Dutch say that 'a handful of patience is worth more than a bushel of brains'. Over the years, I have seen how a lack of patience, uncontrolled emotions and rash actions can crush dreams, destroy lives and wreak havoc in relationships.

It does not come as a surprise that patience features as one of the *most valued virtues* in many religions, including Judaism, Islam and Christianity. Buddhism regards it as one of the perfections that must be achieved on the path to Enlightenment.

I constantly advise clients to remain calm, be patient and allow the future to unfold in its own time. To very little avail. Those who do heed my advice always reap the rewards in the end. But they are few and far between. Many simply cannot conquer the urge to act before the time is right; they find it hard to contain their emotions, be it anger, anxiety, desire or desperation. They do not see that patience can sometimes be the *best form of action*. If only they would accept that the human Ego is fueled by fear and petulant self-interest, and realize that when the Ego takes over in any situation you are bound to get way ahead of yourself, and it will usually lead you to make a royal mess of things.

Patience is the antidote to the restless poison of the Ego. Without it we all become ego-maniacal bulls in china shops, destroying our future happiness, as we blindly rush in where angels fear to tread. In these out-of-control moments, we bulldoze through the best possible outcomes for our lives, within a matter of minutes, only to return to the scene of the crime later to cry over spilt milk. Then the process of picking up the pieces begins, trying in vain to salvage what may be left of the opportunities and future prospects we have now annihilated. More often than not

147

the damage simply cannot be undone. How many times have I heard the sad words: "If only I had listened to your advice, if only I waited a little longer?"

Our lack of patience comes from our fear of the unknown, and our intolerance of uncertainty. We are reluctant to accept that nothing is ever certain or secure in our human experience. The only security we really do have in this lifetime is the knowledge that there is absolutely no certainty. There is no such thing as a 'sure thing' when it comes to the human condition, except for the fact that this lifetime will eventually come to an end for all of us. Sir Francis bacon said that "if we begin with certainties, we shall end in doubts; but if we begin with doubts, and we are patient in them, we shall end in certainties."

Our increasingly fast-paced society and constant technological advancement does not serve us well in the patience department. We like to call it 'efficiency' and 'progress', but how are we supposed to teach our children the virtue of patience when they live in a world where just about everything is easily accessible, and often instantly available? All it takes is one swipe of a credit card, or the click of a mouse button. No wonder we have so little forbearance, and zero perseverance. Immediate gratification is what we have come to expect and demand.

Meanwhile Planet Earth revolves around her axis unperturbed and Mother Nature patiently goes about her daily business, as she always has, doing her utmost to heal the damage and destruction we leave in our wake. She will continue to see us come and go, untroubled by our petty human dramas, whilst the Universe will continue to leisurely work in its many mysterious ways.

I deal with the aftermath of impatience almost every day in the work that I do, and I can assure you that there truly is wisdom in having some *patience* and *fortitude*. There is freedom to be found in letting go of our rigid, premature expectations. Stop jumping up and down; do not try to drive square pegs into round holes. Refrain from peeking at the cards of others, before they lay them out on the table, and quit tampering with the unripe fruit of your destiny. Relinquishing your unyielding ideas of how things must be, and how quickly they must come to pass. Cut loose and surrender to the boundless possibilities that await you. Just kick your heels up and run spontaneously wild with the mysteries of life.

To create a Divine Life you need to peacefully wait your turn and be content to give the cycles of life the benefit of your doubt.

All good things will come to you in time, your Divine Self will see to it. The more you realign with your inner Divinity the less you feel the need to pressure the world around you to immediately comply with all your needs; neither will you have the constant urge to want to control everything. You will have lasting inner peace and you will simply trust in the flow of life.

As your Divine Life unfolds you will no longer have the compulsion to act impulsively, before you consider the future consequences of your words and deeds. You will increasingly have *confidence in the successful outcomes* of your manifested desires, even if it seems to be taking a hundred years to accomplish. You will accept that when you ask it will be given to you, one way or the other, and always when the time is right - as long as it is a benevolent outcome and serves the greater good. You will intuitively know that everything is as it is intended to be, every second of every day. Just get into the groove and go with the flow. Trust that all is well.

Maxim # 6: Bite The Bullet

Have you ever noticed how negative, cynical or bitter people always just seem to attract more and more negative people and unpleasant experiences into their life, to make them even more negative, cynical and bitter? And have you noticed how some people just always seem to be happy, cheerful and optimistic – no matter what their circumstances? It is amazing to see how some people can rise above the most harsh or devastating circumstances to bring joy and hope to the lives of others, while others always have something to grouch about.

In May 2006 Mark Inglis became the first man ever to climb to the top of Mount Everest without both legs. Due to his disability his climb took much longer than the average; he had to spend a grueling 40 days on the mountain. Many people all over the globe have successfully taken on the challenge of climbing to the top of Everest, but it is safe to say that very few of these adventurers ever experience the thrilling sense of achievement that this 47-year-old man from New Zealand felt when he climbed the last few feet to the summit of the tallest mountain in the world.

Inglis lost his legs just below the knees, after he suffered frostbite in a climbing accident in New Zealand. Not only did he not give up his career as a mountain climber, but he also used his

Everest climb as an opportunity to raise funds to provide artificial legs for disabled Tibetans. Inglis himself climbed Everest using carbon fiber artificial legs, especially adapted for such climbing. The New Zealand prime minister, Helen Clark said at the time, "To reach the summit of Everest is a once in a lifetime achievement, but for Mark Inglis it will be even more satisfying. He has said it was a childhood dream to stand on the roof of the world, but he thought he had lost it when he lost his legs."

No matter what happens to us in life, we still get to choose how we will respond to adversity. The person who most personifies this for me is the famous psychologist Viktor Frankl. He published one of the most influential books of all time in 1946, after the Second World War, titled *Man's Search for Meaning*. In it he chronicles his experiences as one of only a handful of Jewish survivors in a Nazi concentration camp, and how people around him perished daily, because they simply gave up hope. He firmly believed that the only reason why he managed to survive his ordeal was because he chose life over death, hope over despair, optimism over negativity.

> *We who lived in the concentration camps can remember the men who walked through the huts comforting others, giving away their last piece of bread. They may have been few in number, but they offer sufficient proof that everything can be taken from a man but one thing: The last of his freedoms – to choose one's attitude in any given set of circumstances, to choose one's own way.*

No matter what your circumstances, no matter how bad things may appear to be, no matter what other people may take from you, there is one freedom that you will always have - the *freedom to choose how you will respond to any given situation.*

There are many more incredible examples of people who have overcame adversity and went on to inspire others against all odds. Stephen Hawking is almost entirely paralyzed, due to a motor neuron disease known as Amyotrophic Lateral Sclerosis (ALS), yet he is the foremost theoretical physicist and cosmologist in the world. Hawking has humbly stated, "It is a waste of time to be angry about my disability. One has to get on with life and I haven't done badly. People won't have time for you if you are always angry or complaining".

Another example is Nick Vujicic who was born without legs and arms, but has achieved much more by the age of 28 than most people will in a lifetime. Since age 19, he has traveled around the world to share his story of hope and faith with millions. Although he has no limbs, Vujicic passionately believes that there is meaning and purpose in any adversity we may encounter in our lives, and that our attitude towards those circumstances is the key to overcoming those challenges.

Hawking and Vujicic are merely two examples from a long list of inspirational role-models all over the world living with serious health conditions, disabilities, amputated limbs, or who have survived severe emotional or psychological trauma, or dire material hardship, but who bring hope, joy and optimism to millions of people all over the world. Although their stories may be diverse and their messages varied, they all seem to have one thing in common: their positive *attitude* to life.

Life in this physical reality is not always easy, or pleasant. In every person's life there will be moments when we will experience trials and tribulations. Yet, despite these pre-destined obstacles we still choose to be born into this physical existence, because the benefits far outweigh any of the associated 'risks'.

Please know that you did not come into this life to be 'punished' or 'tested'. Neither did you come into this lifetime to be subjected to constant hardship or suffering, in order for you to be somehow liberated from the limitations of your worldly or flawed humanity. You are not required to attain some kind of spiritual superiority before you 'kick the bucket' and end up in some 'bad place'. You did not come here to somehow 'graduate', or endure the hell of some kind of 'metaphysical military program' that only a select few ever will complete successfully.

There is no hierarchy, elitism, rank, status or exclusivity in the spiritual realm. We are all One, and none of us purposely came into this lifetime to have a bad experience or become an evil person. Some of us just lose our way after we arrive. Some find their way back soon enough; others get there at the end of their lives when it is too late.

If your current life is a 'living hell', have you ever considered that it may just seem that way because you choose to perceive it that way? For many years, I used to say things like "hell is other people", "my life is one of God's cruel jokes" and "if there is a heaven, I will definitely have a place over there one day, because I am already doing my fair share of hell here on Earth". Sure, there had been many experiences and circumstances in my life that I felt at the time justified my cynical, morbid outlook, but I do not regret going through those periods of intense despair and self-pity.

My 'pity party' served its purpose. It was my Dark Night of the Soul, my 'descent into the underworld'. But since I had emerged from it – somewhat scarred, yet mostly intact and unscathed - I now appreciate the abundant blessings in my life all the more. I also realize how I often I chose to perceive life in a negative way, when I could have chosen a very different perspective.

Instead of choosing the role of martyr or victim, know that once you liberate yourself from your Ego-based suffering, you will become a source of great comfort for others. Once your Dark Night has passed, nobody else will be better suited to teach the valuable life lessons that you had to learn yourself through so much misery and sacrifice. Often the adversities in our lives are a part of our data collection process towards fulfilling our Soul Purpose or Life Calling.

Everything in life happens for a reason. What you need to do is find the meaning hidden in your past, present and future life experiences. Then take the wisdom you collect from it and apply it towards your personal growth, as well as for the greater good.

Personal suffering inspired me towards much wisdom and compassion, and it can do the same in your life. I live in constant gratitude and appreciation for all that I have experienced, because it enables me every day to help and support others; to heal broken hearts, transform lives and guide people on their path towards personal fulfillment.

The only obstacle that could ever stand in your way towards achieving a Divine Life is *you*. It may not be easy to read this truth, especially if you are still stuck in the state of Divine Discontent. From that dark place it is often impossible to recognize the truth of your own responsibility for how you think and feel about your life.

Of course, there are certain pre-destined events and circumstances of contrast that we encounter in life, over which we have absolutely no control. This is how we recognize 'destiny' – when an event or experience is entirely beyond our control we know it was pre-determined. These obstacles and adversities are actually challenges and opportunities. They are not 'sent' upon our life path to somehow test us, or punish us. Neither are they due to 'fate', or 'bad luck' or being 'cursed'. In fact, these obstacles and challenges are a part of the Life Plan we designed for ourselves before we came here.

We planned these events or encounters as milestones or route markers along our life journey, like challenging hurdles and cross-roads on the obstacle course of our intended life path. We came here for the unreserved thrill of this physical life experience, and that is why it sometimes feels like a crazy roller-coaster ride. You did not come here to be a 'timid wallflower', to passively cruise along, or 'make the most of it' without breaking a sweat. How boring and pointless would all of that be?

A workshop attendee once asked author and teacher Esther-Abraham Hicks a question that many spiritual seekers would possibly consider superficial or mundane. He wanted to know "why dogs risk getting bugs in their eyes when they stick their heads out of car windows". Her witty response was very telling and most profound.

> *Because the contrast of the bugs in the eye is a small price to pay for the exhilaration of that ride, and it is exactly the same way you felt when you made the decision to come into this physical existence. It is exactly the way you felt when you knew there would be contrast and you said, 'the ride is going to be worth it!*

Yes, we came for the sheer exhilaration of this physical life experience, knowing that we would have to experience both sides of the coin to ensure that we got the most out of it. We all know deep within that we were meant to have a balanced, overall harmonious physical experience, with sufficient *duality* or *contrast* to motivate us, inspire us and ensure our ultimate appreciation of all that is good. Sri Aurobindo explains in *The Life Divine* that from a spiritual perspective the forces of nature we have to contend with, and the survival challenges we face on this planet, are all necessary means of inspiring further progress and expansion. The problems and difficulties we experience in our lives are merely *balancing forces* to ensure our continued evolution and soul growth.

It is an undeniable fact that in our human form we tend to take things for granted very easily. Due to our free will and our inherently inquisitive and hedonistic nature, we have a constant need for excitement and novelty. We tend to lose interest all too soon in all the great things we have going in our lives. We remind each other to 'count our blessings', but we seldom do.

But if we all came here for an overall positive and inspiring experience, why do some people end up in such bad circumstances or leading such evil lives? Unfortunately, the False Self's severe disconnection from Spirit sometimes leads people to become very self-centered and narcissistic, and the further they drift away, the deeper they sink into the quagmire of disconnection and unbalanced, negative contrast, until all contact disappears and they begin to drown in the dark shadows of a nihilistic existence. This is often when people do evil deeds.

Evil is the opposite of Creation. Evil is vast emptiness, non-entity and anti-matter – the exact opposite of why we come here in the first place. What were meant to be the balanced contrasts in a dualistic life experience become under such desperate circumstances the vast, omnipresent shadows of life that drown out of all the Light of Higher Consciousness. In these circumstances people have lost their personal power and their footing as co-creators. But, it is never too late or impossible to change any circumstance, because the Divine Self will always keep reaching out to them until they embrace their inner Divinity and reconnect with the true Divine power within. Any life can be turned around at any time.

The constant balancing act between good and evil is a fundamental aspect of our human condition and the basis of all Creation. It is expressed in the duality found in every important feature of our current time-space reality: dark versus light, night versus day, summer versus winter, Sun versus Moon. Our earthly world was created to be a place of dualism and our human life a dualistic state of being.

Our diverse positive and negative life experiences are like the binary code used in modern computers and telecommunications technology. The binary encoding system features an infinite number of potential combinations, or strings with various values. For example, when you chat with someone on *Facebook* your whole conversation is merely a translation of an underlying binary code. But although binary code offers endless possibilities it amazingly only consists of two digits namely '0' and '1'. Similarly our life experiences on this planet are all composed of a 'binary code' known as *dualism* or *duality*. Our experiences of birth and death, masculine and feminine, young and old, happy and sad, good and bad were all designed to create a more vibrant journey. Herein lays the true wisdom of the ancient Chinese Yin Yang symbol.

Yin Yang Symbol

The Yin-Yang expresses how the contrasting forces and polar opposites in life are always somehow inter-connected and inter-dependent. In fact, these opposites actually give rise to each other and can only exist in relation to each other. Light cannot exist without darkness, just as day cannot exist without night. The natural dualities or dichotomies in this world are all manifest-tations of Yin and Yang, such as dark and light, female and male, low and high, and cold and hot.

For any painting to be a masterpiece it must contain lots of colorful contrast. If we never experience the chill of a dark, frosty winter, it is very unlikely that we will ever cherish the warmth of a bright summer's day. Nothing stimulates our appetite for the simple joys of life more than the starvation caused by lack, mis-fortune and distress. Without these negative experiences we will never learn, grow or appreciate anything, and we will no longer contribute to the expansion of the Universe. It would defy the original purpose of our species and our world.

In order to complete this amazing life journey successfully, it is vital that we turn each and every dark tear into a pearl of wisdom, and find the blessing in every 'curse'. Whatever it is you are going through right now in your life, or may encounter in future, know that it too shall come to an end.

During trying times do not settle for bitterness, self-pity or resentment. Embrace instead the divine miracle of your path to greater awareness and understanding. Acknowledge your growing empathy for others, and validate and cherish those people who stand by you, for better or worse. Bite the bullet. See the glass as half full. There is much light at the end of absolutely every tunnel in life, and someday soon you shall find that silver lining.

Maxim # 7: Count Your Blessings

One aspect of spiritual living too seldom addressed is our lack of true *appreciation* and *gratitude* for all the blessings in our lives, regardless of our circumstances. Some spiritual seekers tend to be very keen on beating the drum of prosperity and obsess over the Law of Attraction and manifesting abundance, which is too often merely a thinly disguised obsession with material wealth and earthly comforts.

Most of us simply *take too much for granted* every day. We experience so many blessings of joy, beauty, forgiveness, protection and Divine grace we seldom acknowledge in our lives. We always have something to be grateful or thankful for, no matter how difficult times may be. As a species we are very good at complaining about what we don't have, but we seem to find it difficult to give thanks for *what we do have.*

We seldom express our gratitude and appreciation towards those we love and cherish, and we hardly ever remember to share what we have with those who have less – not because we feel obligated, but because we feel so much appreciation that we want to share our abundant blessings with others. Charity is not about lending a helping hand; it is about celebrating all that we have, and to share our joy and appreciation.

Research has demonstrated an indisputable connection between gratitude and spirituality. It is no accident or coincidence that gratitude is regarded as a much cherished and valued quality by most world religions, including the Buddhist, Muslim, Hindu Jewish, and Christian traditions. When reviewing the large body of research work done on the subject, gratitude seems to play a much more noteworthy role in our happiness and well-being than most other emotions and personality traits.

Several research studies in recent years have shown that people who have a tendency towards higher levels of gratitude also tend to report higher levels of psychological, emotional and physical well-being. People who are grateful have been shown to be happier, more optimistic and more content with their lives. They also appear to have lower levels of stress and depression and they are more satisfied with their relationships and social interaction with others.

Studies have also shown that increased gratitude increases a person's tendency towards altruism, empathy, helpfulness, and generosity. Grateful test subjects were, for example, more likely to share their money in a financial game with others. It is therefore no wonder that our modern society, with its noticeable lack of gratitude and appreciation, displays such a disturbing shortage of charity, goodwill and compassion.

Another study has shown that grateful people have a greater sense of control over their environment, life purpose, personal growth and self-acceptance. Grateful people also tend to cope well when facing life challenges; they just seem to deal better with problems in general and are much more successful at navigating life transitions. Grateful people also exercise more frequently, sleep better and are even more resistant to viral infections!

It is interesting to note that one study reported major increases in people's 'happiness scores' after they participated in an exercise of writing down their thoughts and feelings of appreciation in a gratitude journal. In fact, the increases in their happiness were so significant during the short experiment of one week that many of the participants chose to continue keeping a gratitude journal.

If you only had time to adopt from this book one simple life strategy or lifestyle technique to apply in your life, I would recommend making gratitude your first choice and main aim. Even if you had to ignore everything else in this book, do make an effort to be more grateful. It will change your life.

Gratitude is no doubt encouraged as a popular religious or spiritual sentiment because of its precious 'side-effects'. The Prophets, Ascended Masters, Teachers and Founders of the diverse world religions brought us messages of encouragement to live our earthly lives with gratitude and appreciation, because they knew its importance in achieving our true Soul Purpose and Life Calling. Living in a state of true appreciation is the key to the expression and fulfillment of your Life Plan. A Divine Life is a grateful life.

When you go to the seaside to enjoy a day on the beach, you do have a choice about how you will perceive and interpret your experience. You may choose to focus on feeling miserable all day and complain about the sand in your shoes, the noisy seagulls, the irritating wind, the smelly seaweed and the hot sun; or you can choose to appreciate the unusual texture of the sand between your toes, mindful of the fact that it was created through mechanical weathering and erosion of rocks, mollusk shells, and coralline algae over billions of years by way of the cycles of the moon and the tides of the ocean. Our planet is indeed a marvel!

And then you can set out to build an incredible sand castle to the delight of all the children that pass by, or use the 'sands of time' to exfoliate the protective organic miracle that is your skin, while you smile at the comical antics of the seagulls fighting in the distance over a piece of food. Don't forget to bask in the warmth of the sun, which is perfectly balanced by the coolness and fresh smell of an occasional breeze from the magnificent ocean. Then take a deep breath in *deep appreciation* and *sincere gratitude* for this amazing experience that is your Divine Life.

Johannes A. Gaertner said, "To speak gratitude is courteous and pleasant, to enact gratitude is generous and noble, but to live gratitude is to touch Heaven". So much to appreciate, and so little time. No need to say 'thank you'. Just live a thankful, grateful life.

5

TRANSFORMING YOUR THOUGHTS

Quantum Physics has shown us over the past three decades that we can no longer simply view external reality and physical matter in the conventional Newtonian way. Reality and our consciousness of its existence is proving a 'tough nut' for science to crack. Nobody has yet found a conclusive answer to this omnipresent mystery.

There are many modern theories and philosophies aiming to explain what reality truly is, and what it is not. Some propose that reality is an illusion; some suggest it is a shared creation or a mental projection; while others maintain that the only certainty in our world is the existence of an external, physical reality, as traditionally studied by our objective observation of it using the five material senses and rational, logical thinking.

But nobody knows for sure what reality truly is, and neither do we know for sure that it actually does exist in the way we perceive it every day.

We are also uncertain about our own physical existence. Some believe that the human body is just a 'clump of animal flesh' that has evolved its own ability to think, while some believe the human body is merely a figment of our imagination.

Whatever your belief system or views may be on the nature of reality and our existence as a human life form, there is one thing that remains an undeniable fact: we are all *conscious, sentient beings*. We know that we must exist in some way, shape or form because of this fact. *We think, therefore we are.* Actually, for the more skeptical among us, we should expand this idea to state that *we doubt, therefore we think and therefore we exist.* The origin of this concept is widely attributed to the 17th century philosopher

René Descartes, who is today regarded as the father of Modern Philosophy.

But Descartes was certainly not the first to propose the idea, because it is also found in the teachings of ancient Eastern traditions, such as Taoism, Hinduism and Buddhism, as well as the writings of classical Greek philosophers like Plato and Aristotle. In the ten books known as the *Nicomachean Ethics*, Aristotle explains that our consciousness of our own perception, and our ability to think, indicate our existence.

> *If one who sees is conscious that he sees, one who hears that he hears, one who walks that he walks, and similarly for all the other human activities there is a faculty that is conscious of their exercise, so that whenever we perceive, we are conscious that we perceive, and whenever we think, we are conscious that we think, and to be conscious that we are perceiving or thinking is to be conscious that we exist.*

The existence of our own awareness or consciousness therefore seems to be the only thing we cannot doubt in this time-space reality; everything else appears to be suspect. Some modern theorists further propose that consciousness, not physical matter, is what holds all of reality together. This is known as the *Quantum Mind* or *Quantum Consciousness* hypothesis which proposes that quantum mechanical phenomena, such as *quantum entanglement* and the *wave-particle duality*, may play an important role in the brain's functioning, and could possibly offer an explanation for the origins of consciousness. You can read more about these quantum phenomena in the final chapter of this book.

According to the Quantum Mind theory *consciousness* seems to be what shapes and drives our Universe. Some believers call this 'The Matrix' to which we are all connected; others know it as the Ether, the Unified Field, the Collective Consciousness, the Fifth Dimension, Spirit, Source, God.

Within this universal consciousness we each have our unique perception of reality, known as our *reality tunnel*. What we as individuals consider to be external reality is in fact limited to our *interpretation* of our sensory perceptions. Our observations, thoughts and beliefs create a highly personal interpretation of our reality perception. What we choose to *focus on*, and what we choose to *believe* and *think*, is what ultimately defines our *reality*.

In *As a Man Thinketh*, an essay published in 1902, James Allen writes that the human mind is creative, and that all our personal circumstances and experiences in life are the result of our habitual or predominant mental attitude.

> *Good thoughts bear good fruit, bad thoughts bad fruit. The outer world of circumstance shapes itself to the inner world of thought, and both pleasant and unpleasant external conditions are factors, which make for the ultimate good of the individual. As the reaper of his own harvest, man learns both by suffering and bliss.*

Science tells us thoughts are merely electrical impulses and chemical signals. The metaphysical community believes that all thoughts are *energy vibrations*. Thoughts are 'things'. Powerful things. And because we are all inter-connected co-creators of the *Hologram of Consciousness* or the *Omnipresent Field of Consciousness* which we call the Universe, or Source, or God, each and every thought we create in our mind produces a *wave-like effect* throughout the entire Universe, much like the ripples circling outward from a stone tossed into a tranquil lake. Your consciousness contributes to the Universal Consciousness, and therefore your thoughts help to shape, influence and expand the Universe.

Our thoughts are the generators of our reality, and they therefore have the power to be the source of much abundance and well-being in our lives, or the cause of much misery and suffering. It all depends on how we *choose to think* and what we *choose to believe*.

Choosing A New Reality

The concept of the 'reality tunnel' was popularized by Timothy Leary and Robert Anton Wilson and it refers to the idea that each and everyone of us create and perceive objective reality in our own unique and *subjective way*, based on our own belief system, as well as our sensory acuity, social conditioning, cultural background and personal life experiences.

Your reality tunnel is therefore the unique world that you live in, based on your sensory perception and *your personal inter-*

pretation of your perception. It is further shaped by your personal beliefs and experience filters. Wilson said "we believe what we see and then we believe our interpretation of it, we don't even know we are making an interpretation most of the time. We think this is reality."

Knowing that you interpret, shape and influence your own reality gives you a sense of purpose and control over your destiny. However, it also brings with it increased responsibility, because no longer will you be able to blame your past circumstances, your environment, bad luck, other people, or God for everything you feel is wrong in your life. Since you are the only one who perceives your reality, you are also personally and solely responsible for all of your life experiences, and for how you respond to each of life's obstacles and challenges.

Happiness is therefore nothing more than a simple choice or decision. If you want to change your life for the better, you need to make the decision to 'recreate' or 'redecorate' the interior of your reality tunnel. Give it a much needed make-over! Throw out all those old thought patterns, false beliefs, conditioned fears and negative self-talk. Replace it with positive thoughts, optimistic ideas, uplifting mental activities and a renewed zest for life.

Change your reality tunnel from the inside out and it will change your life. There is nothing more to it, and nobody else can do it for you. It is all about you and how you choose to think and what you choose to believe.

Is Your Reality Tunnel Being Hacked?

Have you ever considered that your reality tunnel may be 'hacked'? Think about it. Is your reality tunnel currently a pure version of your strongest spiritual connection, your deepest intuitive insight, your true personal conviction, and your direct experience of that which you accept as fact? Or is your current view of reality being shaped by political agendas, corporate-funded research, religious dogma, the mass media, conspiracy theories, online social networks, popular culture and well-meaning friends and family? How sure are you that your version of reality is pure and that you are immune to 'reality tunnel hacking'?

If you feel that your existing reality tunnel is in perfect health and needs absolutely no adjustment or change, think again.

Consider, for example, how cigarette smoking was not only highly fashionable in the previous century but also considered at one point to be excellent for health and beauty! Did you know that the producers of *Chesterfield* cigarettes used to publish advertisements in the New York State Journal of Medicine claiming that their cigarettes were "as pure as the water you drink"? The American Medical Association (AMA) got in on the action by publishing cigarette advertisements for a period of 20 years, from the 1930's onward, in which it stated that "cigarettes were used by physicians in practice." One of the most well-known advertising slogans in those days belonged to *Camel* cigarettes, claiming that "more doctors smoke *Camels* than any other cigarette." These advertisements were all backed up by scientific research and the campaigns were mostly true, because many doctors did smoke in those days.

Consider therefore, while you may believe that you are creating your own reality, you may actually be creating someone else's version of it. Without realizing it, you may be shaping a reality or worldview planned for you by others. If an increasing number of us globally are daily viewing the same propagandistic television footage, or the same apocalyptic movies, and if we are all reading the same brainwashing newspaper reports, how unique or pure is each of our reality tunnels really?

Are you mindful about what you read, and watch, and listen to? And are you selective about who you have conversations and relationships with? The last thing you want to do is surround yourself with 'negative nellies', doom prophets and fear-mongers. Not only do all these potential sources of negative information and input have a lasting effect on your state of mind and your perception of reality, but you also become *entangled with them energetically*, similar to the subatomic particles in a Quantum Physics experiment. This entanglement has adverse effects on your stress levels, emotional well-being and physical health. If you swim all day long in a reality tunnel flooded with toxic waste, you simply cannot expect to remain happy and healthy for very long.

Next time you stroll out of a cinema, after having watched the latest blockbuster, or next time you switch on your television set to watch the evening news, consider what each member of the audience will be doing with the ideas, images, impressions and suggestions they picked up from watching that screening or broadcast. And then ask yourself if you will be joining your fellow audience members in adding the same grey shades of fear, prejudice, violence, cynicism, skepticism, narcissism, hatred and misguided propaganda to the interior of your reality tunnel?

Thought Transformation

To create a Divine Life the first major shift that must be set in motion is to change your point of view, and transform the way you *think*. Ralph Waldo Emerson said, "Great men are they who see that spiritual is stronger than any material force; that thoughts rule the world." In order to transcend a meaningless, ego-driven material existence, and bring lasting abundance, fulfillment, purpose, peace and joy into your life, as well as the lives of others, you must begin by *transforming your thoughts*. To live in a new way you must learn to think in a new way.

Spiritual awakening to overcome the state of Divine Disconnection is pointless if it is not going to result in a new way of thinking. We do not awaken to our Higher Consciousness to be more spiritual, or holy, or ethereal, or to escape earthly reality. We become spiritually conscious in order to live an *awakened* and *abundant* Divine Life while having our feet planted firmly on Mother Earth. This newfound awareness and way of living is what becomes the essence of our *soul growth* in this lifetime.

The moment we reconnect with the Divine Self and a new awareness emerges from the unconscious, we begin to see the world in a brand new light, and we become increasingly aware of many discrepancies between what we now perceive and what we used to think and believe. To resolve the resulting tension we must *change the way think*. We must integrate the right brain with the left brain, the spirit with the mind, the unseen with seen, the physical with the metaphysical, the secular with the heavenly, and bring them back into balance and harmony. Since the current global worldview generally does not support this process, we have no choice but to do it by ourselves and for ourselves. You and I must become the leading-edge pioneers to resolve the conflict between the conditioned Ego or Material Self and the Divine or Higher Self.

Changed thinking starts by changing the way you think about yourself, then you begin to think differently about others, and finally you change the way you view the world. Sadly, some spiritual seekers aim to change the world and others first, before they get around to working on *themselves*. This is typically the way of the dogmatic and the self-righteous, and does not serve the Divine Self.

By changing our thinking we break the patterns of the Ego's negative self-talk and break the strong hold that *fear* and *false beliefs* have over our daily lives. By dismantling self-limiting thought patterns and mistaken beliefs we change our emotional responses to the world around us, which is the next major step in creating a Divine Life.

Eckhart Tolle writes, "To be conscious of Being, you need to reclaim consciousness from the mind. This is one of the most essential tasks on your spiritual journey". In order to change our thoughts we need to become the *observer* of our own mental processes. We must *become aware* of our own thinking by paying attention to how and what we think, and then we need to take action to change the way we think, as well as the contents of our thoughts. This may seem an almost impossible task, especially if you are a natural 'worrier', or a particularly pessimistic, negative thinker, but it is perfectly achievable. For some it takes longer to truly break the spell of years of conditioning and negative input, but changed thinking and thought transformation can be achieved by anyone at any time. All it takes to set the wheels in motion is to start with just *one thought* at a time.

Choosing New Thoughts

We have one simple choice when it comes to our thinking: either we control our thoughts, or our thoughts control us. Proverbs 4:23 in the Bible states, "Be careful what you think, because your thoughts run your life." What we think is what we *choose to think*. This choice becomes easier as you begin to dismantle your under-lying false beliefs, reconsider your *interpretations* of reality, and master your *habitual thought patterns*. The more you adopt new thinking perspectives the more you will find it increasingly easy to simply *choose new thoughts* on a daily basis.

Kathleen Besly writes in *The Divine Art of Living*, "We make our own lives and create our own atmosphere. The spoken word, which is the thought expressed, is the creative power. If we really desire to live the true life, we must guard our words carefully and send them then, to create right conditions. It is both foolish and harmful to give expression to depressive thoughts, just as it is to refer to disease."

As you become more aware of your thinking habits you will find that other people's opinions and beliefs have less of an effect on your outlook on life; and as you begin to realize how your thoughts affect your mood and emotions, you will become more selective with what you choose to think. You will learn which thoughts serve your well-being and happiness, and which thoughts are a waste of time and energy. You will find that you increasingly choose those thoughts that express compassion, kindness and unconditional love towards yourself, others and your environment. How you view and interpret your world will become a *conscious choice* opting mostly for happiness and joy.

Wallace D. Wattles writes in *The Science of Getting Rich*, "To permit your mind to dwell upon the inferior is to become inferior and to surround yourself with inferior things. On the other hand, to fix your attention on the best is to surround yourself with the best, and to become the best."

Why Positive Thinking Does Not Work

Many seekers complain that they have read and studied numerous self-help books and attended a plethora of workshops, seminars and courses to improve their ability to *think more positively* and be more optimistic, but it does not work for them and it has not made any difference in their lives. Over the years I have seen enough evidence to agree that popular techniques and methods for 'positive thinking' do not always work for everyone. In fact, for some individuals the attempt to force themselves to think more positively can actually make things worse, instead of better.

The reason why positive thinking and related self-help techniques tend to fail is because it is pointless to try and cultivate a new attitude or life perspective that is more hopeful, optimistic and positive, without the support of an underlying *belief system* and a *reconnection* with the Divine Self. Without a true spiritual awakening positive thinking is a tall order for most souls.

In *The Master Key System*, Charles F. Haanel writes, "All thought is a form of energy, a rate of vibration, but a thought of the Truth is the highest rate of vibration known and consequently destroys every form of error in exactly the same way that light destroys darkness; no form of error can exist when the Truth appears, so that your entire mental work consists in coming into an understanding of the Truth. This will enable you to overcome every form of lack, limitation or disease of any kind."

Many self-help strategies and techniques fail to produce results because they have no spiritual backbone. These approaches attempt to reconstruct the individual's worldview and beingness by tinkering and fiddling with the Ego, or False Self. But someone who remains in the 'reality coma' under the Ego's semi-conscious spell of Divine Disconnection, will always tend to regress back to the their conditioned false beliefs and negative thinking habits. They remain slaves and devotees to the negative ideas and pessimistic views they have been taught by their parents, the school, the church, popular culture, public opinion, conspiracy theorists, the mass media and the inevitable bad experiences that sometimes come with modern day living.

To change the way we think about our lives and our world we have to begin with an increased *spiritual awareness* and a *realignment* with the Divine Self. We have to be reminded of our innate Divinity and spiritual origins - who and what we truly are, and why we came here. Without a spiritual or religious belief system we remain trapped in the nihilism of post-modern materialism and Newtonian physicalism, which offers us very little comfort and makes it really difficult to think very positively about life in general.

Conquering the Divine Disconnect, and remembering that we are spiritual beings having a physical experience, brings an overwhelming new awareness of our innate metaphysical abilities and our inner truth. It awakens within us the spiritual power we all possess, and increases our confidence in our ability to shape, influence, direct and control our reality.

There can be no true positive thinking and optimism for the future without a spiritual basis or some form of metaphysical awareness. Without spiritual connectedness any self-help strategy or positive thinking technique is nothing more than a temporary 'band-aid' for a much larger problem. It would therefore be best not to attempt to master any of the following thought transformation techniques unless you feel truly spiritually aware and reconnected with the Divine Self. You must *believe* to *achieve*.

If your spiritual awakening has not happened yet, do not feel discouraged. Continue reading and studying. Sometimes we have been sucked so deeply into the Divine Disconnect that it takes a long time to digest and process all the new 'spiritual information' that comes across our path. Several of my own significant metaphysical experiences and spiritual lessons only fell into place years later, while I was not able to recognize them as such at the time. Keep an open mind, do not lose hope and give yourself time. It will come.

Daily Affirmations

The simplest way to begin your journey towards lasting thought transformation is by incorporating daily affirmations into your spiritual self-care routine. An affirmation is a verbal statement that is deliberately designed to be repeated with *conscious awareness* on a regular basis. Affirmations can relate to any aspect of your life and are typically *simple* and *straightforward*. Some examples of affirmations include:

I am confident
I am at peace
I am worthy of love
I love myself for who I am
I am healthy and happy
I am wealthy and prosperous
I am a money magnet
I am free from debt
Everything I do is successful
I am losing weight each day
I am free from addiction
I am in perfect health
I have faith in today

Daily affirmations can be introduced into your lifestyle anyway you choose. For example, you can incorporate them into your daily *meditation* or *creative visualization* sessions, or you can create a *simple ritual*, such as lighting a candle for each of your affirmations as you say them out loud.

I do my affirmations as a part of my morning routine, after my daily meditation, energy clearing and psychic protection exercises. The latter are necessary due to my highly empathic nature. Personally, I find it best to do my set of daily affirmations all together in one session, before I start my day. However, some of my clients and students report that they prefer to do their affirmations dispersed throughout the day, or to repeat them in the evening at bedtime. Find a method that suits your personality and lifestyle, to ensure that you will make it a lasting part of your daily spiritual self-care routine. Whatever you choose to do, affirmations must be *repeated frequently* and this should ideally be done *daily*.

To secure the best possible results you should involve as many of the *senses* as possible when repeating your affirmations. This may include saying your affirmations out loud to yourself; or recording them and playing them back later; or posting your affirmations on flash cards in visible spots around your home, like your bathroom mirror or the refrigerator; or writing them down several times every day.

So, how does an affirmation work? Well, most of our destructive, negative thinking habits center on criticism of self and others, as well as fear, guilt and pessimism. The key in all this is not the content of those negative thoughts that dominate our daily consciousness, but the fact those *thought patterns are habitual.* This is the logic behind the use of daily affirmations. Affirmations replace our old negative thinking patterns and false beliefs with new thoughts about ourselves and our lives. But for these new thought patterns to become a new habit to replace the old habit it must initially be repeated frequently.

Due to the Divine Disconnect we tend to fall into the habit of recreating the negative aspects of our daily existence over and over, because we keep focusing on how things are today, and not how we envision them to be tomorrow. We obsess all day long about everything that is wrong in our lives and we tend to focus most of our attention on the negative aspects in our day, and then we are very surprised to wake up the next morning and find that everything is still exactly the same! Remember that thoughts are things. Thinking is a creative act. By focusing consistently on the negative things in your life you will get stuck in a vicious circle of recreating the same reality over, and over, and over again.

To add insult to injury some people not only stay stuck in the cycle of their existing life, but they also indulge in additional destructive thinking patterns and false beliefs imposed on them by others, which only serve to create, attract and manifest more hardship, misfortune and suffering into their lives.

The aim of implementing a new daily routine of repeating affirmations is therefore three-fold.

I. **Subconscious Programming.** Affirmations are basically an attempt at 'brainwashing' yourself – both on a subconscious and conscious level. If we perceive something often enough and with sufficient repetition it becomes ingrained in the *subconscious mind* and will eventually transform our daily thinking. Dr Ronald Alexander writes in *The Wise Open Mind* that affirmations work because "it has the ability to program your mind into believing the stated con-cept. This is because the mind doesn't know the difference between what is real or fantasy."

II. **Thought Substitution.** Secondly, the only truly successful way to change any habit is to replace it with a new, better habit. That is what daily affirmations are; they are thought substitutions or replacements that are repeated on a regular basis until they become the basis for new habitual thought patterns that are more uplifting, positive and confident. The idea is therefore that at first we say and think these new ideas consciously and deliberately, until they eventually become habitual and automatic; until we have cultivated a lasting new outlook and attitude towards life and have adopted a new way of *being in the world.*

III. **Manifesting Intentions.** Finally, the aim of daily affirmations is to create, attract and manifest the things we wish for and desire. Yes, your affirmations are powerful *statements of intent*, just like the magical words "alakazam" and "abracadabra" children use when performing magic tricks. Your daily affirmations are your 'magic spells'. By the way, *abracadabra* historically was believed to have healing powers when inscribed on an amulet. The word is said to have its origin in Aramaic, in which *ibra* means "I have created" and *k'dibra* which means "through my speech", which translates to "created as I say".

The process of replacing old, negative thought patterns and self-defeating false beliefs with new thoughts, ideas and beliefs benefits us in two major ways. Not only do we end up *feeling better* about ourselves and more positive and hopeful about the future, but we also develop the habit of clearly and deliberately *expressing our intentions* and desires for greater happiness, joy, wellness, abundance and prosperity in our lives.

What we think about and what we focus on is what creates our reality, and it shapes what ultimately becomes our destiny. The words we speak, the things we believe and the thoughts we choose to think today will manifest as the life we will lead tomorrow. Daily affirmations therefore not only make us feel better in the short-term, but it also re-designs and transforms our long-term future by creating and attracting everything we need to enjoy an abundant and fulfilled Divine Life. Siddhartha Gautama Buddha summed it up perfectly when he said, "All that we are is the result of what we have thought. The mind is everything. What we think we become."

A word to the wise is necessary at this point. In my experience implementing daily affirmations as a temporary measure to change negative thinking habits will not bring you lasting results. There is a prevalent myth in self-help programs and literature that propagates the idea that a habit needs a specific number of days to be changed. The most popular, pseudo-scientific number appears to be 28 days, while some experts suggest 21 days or even 18 days.

Recent research by University College London psychologist Phillippa Lally indicates that it takes on average 66 days to change a habit. Interestingly, it took some of her individual test subjects only 18 days to change certain habits, while others struggled for as long as 245 days!

Daily affirmations are therefore like a physical fitness program; it must become a permanent part of your Divine Living lifestyle. A focused gym workout or specialized exercise routine will produce some significant short-term results within only a few weeks, but in order to enjoy the lasting, long-term health and wellness benefits of physical fitness it has to become a permanent part of your lifestyle. The same principle applies to affirmations. An intense, short-term 'program' of daily affirmations will definitely give you the boost you need, but to lead a truly abundant and lasting Divine Life it will have to become a part of your daily spiritual self-care routine, along with meditation and your other spiritual activities of choice.

Another perspective on habits is worth mentioning. Bear in mind that all our habits, whether good or bad, are merely a response to our needs. If we have developed a habit of destructive self-talk or negative thinking, it is very likely that we cultivated it to *fulfill a specific need*. For example, could it be that your constant self-criticism offers you a sense of security, because it replaces the voice of an overly critical parent or partner who is no longer present? Is it possible that your continuous negative self-talk is merely serving as an excuse for you not to live your life to the fullest, because you fear failure? Have you considered the possibility that your self-defeating, negative thoughts are nothing more than your way of casting yourself into the role of victim or martyr, in the hope of obtain the attention or empathy you never received as a child, or was lacking in your marriage? These are some of the questions we may need to ask ourselves when we embark upon the process of thought transformation. To change our thinking habits we often need to first *address the need that created that pattern* in the first place.

No amount of 'positive thinking' will ever change how you think and feel about yourself and your world, while your outlook on life revolves around a set of false beliefs or a nagging tendency towards 'lack consciousness'. Are you someone who always sees the glass as half empty? Affirmations can be very powerful statements of intent and personal transformation, but if you harbor conflicting *false beliefs* that contradict the contents of your daily affirmations, you will be wasting your time and energy repeating those affirmations , because you will be unable to believe them.

Unlike some self-help books, you will not find a long list of recommended or suggested affirmations here. In my experience working with people I have found that the best results are achieved when you *create your own affirmations* to meet your *unique needs*.

To get you started and for your inspiration I am including some of my personal favorites, and also some of the most powerful affirmations I have used with much success in my own life and career.

All is well!
I trust life
I am truly blessed
I am unconditionally loved

I am pure positive energy
I am free to be me
My life is singular, unique and wonderful
Health and well-being is my divine right
I am blessed with patience and grace
I draw all things positive to myself
My friends are my wings
I attract positive-minded people to me
I embrace abundance
I live in an abundant Universe
I am open to receive all I deserve
The Universe provides for me always
Prosperity surrounds me all day, every day
I am happy and grateful for everything I receive daily
I am grateful for the gifts of intuition and insight
I flow with the miracles of life
I am in tune with the wisdom of the universe

Whatever affirmations you choose to use, always ensure that each and every one of them *resonate with you on an emotional level*. If your affirmations do not inspire you emotionally, or at least stir up some kind of positive feeling from within when you repeat them, they are unlikely to yield the best possible results. Merely uttering or mindlessly reading your affirmations every morning over breakfast is pointless. It is vital that you be *mindful* and *emotionally invested* when you engage in the repetition of your daily affirmations.

Personally, I also find it helpful to 'anchor the affirmation' in your body, as you are repeating it. This is done by placing one or both of your hands on the area that felt uncomfortable when you first identified the need or negative belief you wished to change. It is also good to "breathe into" the affirmation while you are saying or writing it down. These simple techniques ensure greater engagement of your whole being and the ultimate embodiment of your daily affirmations.

Creating Affirmations

The following guidelines are recommended when you create your daily affirmations.

1) **Affirmations must be personal and specific.** The easiest way to get started is to make a short list of those aspects of your life you would like to improve or transform. Keep your list short, to ensure clarity and focus. I recommend no more than three to five focus points for beginners. For example, your list might contain three basic wishes, namely:

   I want to be less stressed
   I have to reduce my financial debt
   I wish I had a boyfriend or partner

2) **Convert each of your needs or desires into simple "I am" statements.** You can also use words like "I have", "I know", "I feel" or "I love". Focus on what you *want*, and not on what you *don't want*. However, do not use terms like "I want" or "I wish" or "I need". These statements only confirm what you do not have; it affirms a lack or need in your life, which obviously defeats the purpose of your affirmation. Always state your affirmation in the presents tense, as if it has already happened and is already manifest in your life. Using the three examples above, you could therefore write your affirmations as follows:

   I am calm and relaxed
   I have enough money
   I am in a loving relationship with the perfect man

3) **Check your affirmations for negativity**. Affirmations are always positive statements and should never contain negative terms like *no, never,* or *not*. Your affirmations should also not contain any words or concepts that may evoke negative associations or unpleasant emotions. For example, instead of stating *I don't have any fear,* it would be more appropriate to say, *I have great courage.* Also, be authentic and stay true to yourself. Don't use fancy or

unusual words that you cannot relate to, or terms you will never use in your daily life. If you feel more comfortable with "hug" instead of "embrace", then use it instead!

4) **Do not limit yourself.** Feel free to create affirmations about absolutely anything that may be of importance to you. You can be, have or do anything you wish - anything you can imagine. Don't get caught up in the practicality of "how" you're going to make it happen, or if it is viable or possible. Do not pose questions you probably won't have answers for, such as "when", "how", "where" or "who". Be specific and clear about what you want, but don't concern yourself with how you will achieve it or how it will manifest. However, it is best to also be somewhat careful what you wish for, because it may come in a way, shape or form that you least expected. Ensure you consider this possibility when you word your affirmations, to avoid nasty surprises!

5) **Include at least one affirmation that expresses** *appreciation* **or** *gratitude*. This is an aspect many people neglect in their lives, yet without it no spiritual practice is complete. It is no accident that gratitude is advocated in most, if not all religious traditions. You can express gratitude in general, or for something specific in your life, for example "I appreciate each and every blessing in my life", or "I am grateful for perfect health". You can also direct your gratitude based on your personal religious beliefs, for example "I thank God for a wonderful life".

Overcoming Self-Limitation

If you are struggling with self-limitation and false beliefs, or if you find it challenging to embrace the truth in any typical affirmation, it may be helpful to rephrase it in a way that is more "acceptable' to your skeptical mind. One way to do this is to make your first affirmations very simple and to take smalls, realistic steps. You do not have to transform yourself overnight from being a pessimistic, somewhat cynical person into a 'belle-of-the-ball Pollyanna' bursting at the seams with happiness, joy and positivity! Instead start with *simple affirmations* that you feel are more achievable and within your reach. In time you can then move yourself gradually up the scale until you reach your ultimate goal. For example, instead of starting off with a sweeping affirmation like, "I radiate infinite peace and happiness", try something simpler like, "I am calm and content".

Another approach that is helpful for people who need a little more convincing or gentle persuasion is to *soften your affirmation* so that it becomes easier to adopt, such as changing, "I am wealthy and prosperous", to something like, "I am open to receiving more".

It is also helpful to use affirmations in the beginning that are *already true* in your life. By repeating these affirmations that are already manifest in your life you may not achieve anything new, but you will grow used to repeating daily affirmations that are in fact true, and very real, and you will thus be training your mind to be more open and accepting of new affirmations you will introduce later, when you feel ready.

The power of affirmations only becomes truly manifest once we have *cleared the subconscious* of its limiting *false beliefs*. The only sure way to do that is to have a profound spiritual awakening, reconnect with the Divine Self and transform the interior of your reality tunnel. To change limiting self-beliefs we need to change what we 'feed our senses' on a daily basis. Vegetating in front of your television set or chasing after the materialistic trappings of the modern rat race will ultimately not serve that goal. When it comes to your thoughts the principle is very simple: garbage in, garbage out. If you constantly feed your mind with the negativity, skepticism and nihilism of modern society you will not manifest a life of abundance and true fulfillment.

Thought Substitution

Certain thoughts and attitudes tend to creep up on us and slip into our conscious mind when they are least wanted. Many people struggle to change a long-held, negative point of view, or stop a habitual thought pattern. The more they try to see something differently, or try to eliminate a specific negative thought, the stronger and more overpowering that thought becomes. It is like having the impulse to laugh while you are in a situation that requires you to be very serious and formal – the harder you try to suppress your laughter, the stronger the urge is to burst out and laugh hysterically.

To stop such a persistent, nagging thought is easier than it may seem. Sometimes it is best not to try too hard, or resist too much. Instead, simply *replace* the negative, unwanted thought with a different, alternative thought. That's it! Simply think of something else that is more positive, or totally unrelated. This technique is based on the premise that two thoughts cannot occupy the mind at the same time.

Substitute the unwanted thought with a better thought and then concentrate on the new thought with a positive attitude, and as much enthusiasm as you can muster. Let your thinking follow this new thought down its natural path, and let the one new thought lead to the next, and the next, and so on.

If you find yourself jumping back to where you started, keep repeating the substitution, until you get into the flow of the substitute thought process. A good way to start with this technique is to either daydream about the future, or to remember a happy, pleasant event from your past.

Note that thought substitution tends to be a temporary solution or strategy during particularly stressful or emotionally difficult times in life. These substitutions are helpful in alleviating anxiety and tension, until our circumstances or state of mind improves.

Can You Remember?

The easiest way to substitute a persistent negative thought is to replace it with a happy, pleasant memory from your past. Try a few of the following ideas to help jog your memory when you need to get your thinking back on track.

Can you remember a time when you:

Enjoyed the company of friends
Felt enthusiastic about a new idea
Felt great about the way you were dressed
Had a lot of fun by yourself
Had a pleasant holiday
Helped someone effectively in a time of need

Laughed out loud after you heard a joke
Received a really special gift
Received praise or recognition for something you did well
Won something nice in a contest
Achieved a significant success
Mastered something you always wanted to do.

Three Positive Images

Another technique to use if you are stuck on a repetitive, negative thought is to think of three positive images you can focus on as substitutes. These positive images can be actual memories or life experiences, or they can be fantasies made up using your wildest imagination.

Image 1: *a moment of confidence, safety, strength or power.*
Image 2: *a moment of happiness, joy or peace.*
Image 3: *a moment of unconditional love and acceptance.*

Visualize each one of these positive images very clearly. Once they are firmly established in your mind's eye, use them to shift from your negative thought to each of the positive images, and then back again to the negative thought.

Repeat the cycle by flipping back and forth between your negative thought and one of the three images until you feel comfortable ending the exercise with your favorite positive image firmly set in your mind.

Getting Active

Another way to replace negative thinking is to distract your mind by engaging in an activity that requires you to *concentrate* or pay *attention*. Make sure the activity is enough to hold your attention for an extended period of time. Mindlessly watching television, for example, will not do the trick. Try different activities, until you find something that truly engages you and makes time fly. Choose something constructive and uplifting. You will soon leave the negative thought pattern behind.

Shifting Perspective

We only perceive that which we choose to perceive, and we only think that which we choose to think. Perception is not an objective process where we passively observe ourselves and the world around us. Everything you see, hear, taste, smell and feel is not perceived in exactly the same way by every person in the world. We each have our own, unique way of looking at the world. Perception is an *active process*, which is based on how we *choose to perceive and think* about our reality. Therefore, when you begin to change the way you perceive the world, the world around you begins to change.

Most of the negative thinking in our lives tends to come from limiting beliefs and judgmental attitudes we hold towards ourselves and others. Many people are either overly critical, cynical, bitter or negative, or they see themselves as victims. These thinking pat-terns are mostly due to fear, poor self-esteem, or a sense of feeling powerless in the world. They are the products of the Ego, or the False Self. The following are some typical faulty Ego perspectives people tend to have of the world and their place in it.

> **False Beliefs**. Erroneous, self-deceptive ideas that act like a *negative mental filter* which blocks out everything else except all the things that support the underlying false belief. For example, you choose to view every little mistake you make in life as proof that you "can never do anything right", but you never take much notice of any of your successes and achieve-ments.

> **All-or-Nothing**. A very one-dimensional view of the world, where there is only wrong or right, true or false, black or white. From this extreme, exclusive perspective there are no grey areas, no room for human error, and no flexibility. From this perspective your thoughts often contain words like *have to, ought to, should,* and *must.* For example, "you are only a winner when you finish first and receive the gold medal"; or "there can only be one winner". Finishing the race in a good time is therefore not considered to be a form of winning with this kind of thinking.

Generalization. This is the perspective where your thoughts revolve around sweeping statements that contain words like *everyone, everywhere, always, never* and *forever*. For example, "you can never trust anyone but yourself".

Prejudice. Pre-judging people, making assumptions and jumping to conclusions about matters you know nothing about. People who are prejudiced in their thinking jump to conclusions and make up their minds without knowing any of the facts regarding the matter at hand. The most extreme form of prejudice is bigotry, which is an obsessive, strong belief or conviction based on a prejudice. For example, "all men are jerks".

Magnification. A thinking perspective where one tends to constantly exaggerate things, or interpret matters unrealistically or out of context, and thus make mountains out of mole hills. The urban slang term for this kind of thinking is known as being "a drama queen". For example, you oversleep, miss the bus and say, "my life is a complete disaster".

These erroneous and exaggerated thought perspectives are a *choice or decision*. That is all they are. A choice. And you can choose to think differently starting right now. By choosing to think differrently you choose to change your reality. What you think is what you get. To change the way you think about yourself and the world, you need to step outside the confines of your limited, *subjective point of view* and see things from a *different perspective*. Sometimes this can be as simple as climbing onto the roof of your house, to see the world from a different vantage point, or lying down on the floor and looking up at the ceiling.

If you are trapped in a 'negative thought binge', like a drug addict, take a break by going to an unfamiliar place where you can experience new people, places and things, or stop talking for one day and make an effort to truly listen to others – no matter how mundane the conversation may be. Read a book about a subject you know absolutely nothing about. Spend an afternoon with people who are different from you, or in a different stage of their life – toddlers, the elderly, homeless people. It helps to see life through the eyes of another.

Another approach is to simply start changing one thought at a time. If you find yourself thinking that you are unattractive, for example, because a co-worker said something about your appearance earlier today, then stop the negative thought process as soon as you become aware of it. Decide to think about it differently. Adopt a different perspective. If this choice or decision does not come easily at first, train yourself to change your perspective by gradually shifting your thinking from the bottom-end of the scale up to a more positive place on the 'thinking barometer'.

I cannot believe Janet made such a nasty comment about me today! I guess you cannot please all the people all the time. I am not going to allow her to upset me this way.

⇩

Actually, now that I think about it, she constantly has some issue with me, and she is not exactly an 'oil painting' herself. Maybe it is jealousy...or fear?

⇩

Maybe she is just scared. Maybe she is worried about that promotion, and that I might be getting more attention at work than she does? I remember how John complimented me on my appearance yesterday morning. Maybe she overheard?

⇩

Coming to think of it, many people have found me attractive over the years. It is silly to base my self-worth on one person's critical and unkind comment.

⇩

You know what...I feel sorry for her; I am going to be more kind and friendly towards her in future. She will feel better about herself, and be less critical of others, if more people are more kind to her.

The perspective shifting approach prevents you from going 'down a rabbit hole' of negative emotion, because once a thought becomes a strong emotion it is much more difficult to turn the tide. It actually creates a *safety buffer* or *time gap*, which forces you to carefully consider what just happened, and prevents you from reacting in ways that will just cause further upset and damage. It is basically a more sophisticated way of 'counting to ten'. By refraining from allowing a thought to become an internal or external 'drama', we conserve a lot of energy that can be put to good use for much more constructive purposes. Changing your perspective increases your *personal power*.

By teaching yourself this process of 'perspective shifting' it will eventually become second nature and ultimately an instant and unconscious process. It will also help you to differentiate more easily between the thoughts and events that deserve your attention, and those that you should disregard.

We truly are our own worst enemies. The way you think about your appearance was not caused by Jane; it was due to what you decided to do with the details of the event and how you chose to think about it. Every thought you entertain is a choice. Don't allow those negative thoughts to take on a life of their own. Prevention is better than cure.

Defensive Pessimism

For one in every three people it is near impossible to shift their perspective through sheer will. Some people find that the more they try to think differently about something the more stressed and anxious they become. These individuals are so affected by their *Ego anxiety* that it would be pointless for them to try and achieve any form of positive thinking or a more optimistic perspective. They worry about everything that could go wrong, expect the worst and simply are not able to find hope or faith in anything.

If this applies to you it is best to start your thought transformation process with a *smaller shift* through the use of *defensive pessimism*. This technique is basically a kind of 'negative thinking' in which you confront your fears, worries and anxieties, instead of trying to ignore them or trying to view them differently.

Defensive pessimism is about *envisioning the absolute worst* case scenario of everything that could go wrong in a given situation and then to come up with a *plan of action* for how you will deal with it should it become necessary. It is therefore a form of perspective shifting where, instead of working on seeing things more objectively, you go the opposite way and indulge in seeing it as *subjectively* as possible, in order to prepare yourself for what may come. This process aids the habitual worrier, or person who struggles with anxiety, to confront their worst nightmares and offers them a sense of confidence and control.

"Trying to adopt a positive outlook when we are anxious - an outlook that discounts our anxiety - can backfire," says Julie K. Norem, author of *The Positive Power of Negative Thinking*. "An anxious business person who denies or ignores her anxiety before a presentation actually increases the likelihood that she'll stutter, fumble, and lose her train of thought before a live audience". Norem explains that defensive pessimism is a strategy that helps us work through our anxious thoughts rather than denying them, so that we may achieve our goals.

Don't Worry, Be Happy

Try the following questionnaire to work through some of your anxious thoughts or habitual worries. Complete the following statement:

I often worry that I ......

Now answer the following questions:

1) If this worry of yours is indeed true, what does it mean to you? Why does it bother you so much? Why is it so important to you?

2) If what you just answered to the above question is indeed true, what does it mean to you? Why does it bother you so much? Why is it so important to you? *(yes, again...)*

3) If what you just answered to the above question is indeed true, what does it mean to you? Why does it bother you so much? Why is it so important to you? *(yes, yes, again, again...)*

4) What's the worst thing that could possibly happen in this context? What do you fear most of all about this worry?

5) When you think of the worst thing that could happen, do you really believe that it is likely to happen?

6) If the worst thing does happen, would you be able to find some way to cope with it?

7) Considering your answers above, what do you think you may be getting out of this worry? How does it work to your advantage, what is the "pay off" for thinking this way?

8) Pretend that your best friend has the same worry or fear that you have and you really want to help him, and make him feel better. What compassionate and rational advice or guidance would you offer him if these were his worries, and not yours?

6

EVOLVING YOUR EMOTIONS

Our emotions are spiritual by nature and they are an important part of our inner guidance system in this physical reality. Our emotions are part and parcel to the 'internal GPS system' we brought with us to serve as a spiritual compass during our brief stay here on Earth.

Our emotions tell us when we are still on track and going in the right direction towards achieving our Soul Purpose and accomplishing our Life Calling. Likewise, when we stray from the Life Plan we designed before we came here, our emotions are there to remind us that we are off course and heading in the wrong direction.

Raising Your Vibration

You will often hear spiritual experts and metaphysical practitioners refer to the concept of "raising your vibration". Raising one's vibration is an important key to all forms of conscious creation and deliberate manifesting. Like attracts like in all things, and therefore we will attract into our lives experiences and outcomes that resonate with our *vibrational frequency,* also known as our *resonant frequency*.

In metaphysical terms negative energy is a *lower vibration,* because it is more dense, murky and heavy. Positive energy on the other hand is much *higher in vibration,* because it is more open, clear and light. Your emotions and feelings are all 'vibrations' that have a certain resonance or vibrational frequency, which will determine what kind of external vibrations it will match, attract and absorb. Positive and uplifting emotions have a higher vibrational frequency, while negative emotions have a lower vibration.

Why is our energy vibration important in the process of manifesting a truly Divine Life? Well, we want to have a vibrational frequency that will create and attract those things we truly desire. We want a level of vibration that will *resonate* with the better things in life. The Laws of Creation and Attraction teaches us that a certain level of energy on the spiritual plane will create and attract corresponding physical manifestations on the earthly plane. The principle is simple: if you are positive in your thoughts and feelings, more good things happen to you, and when you are negative in your thoughts and feelings, more bad or undesirable things tend to come into your life.

For example, you cannot be a miserable, negative person and hope to meet a desirable partner or find that sought-after job opportunity. By their very nature these 'good things' in life will not resonate with your negativity. Even if you manage to somehow attract that partner or job temporarily, it is very unlikely that your negativity will keep them in your life. When you are in a bad place mentally or emotionally, the good things in life are simply out of your league, and therefore out of your reach. And the good things you might manage to grab hold of will soon slip through your fingers.

I see this problem most often in romantic relationships. There is no doubt that we tend to attract partners that match us in thoughts, feelings, perceptions, attitudes and beliefs. Birds of a feather really do flock together. I remember Oprah Winfrey once saying on one of her television shows that we tend to "marry what we know" or something to that effect. I could not agree more. In my practice I have seen how people get into destructive, violent, abusive, co-dependent relationships over and over again. Then they come to me and ask, "Why is it that I always get involved with abusive men"; or "Why do emotionally manipulative women always know where to find me"; or 'Why do all my relationships end in disaster?"

In my work with thousands of people over the years, experience has taught me that successful, lasting and truly happy relationships start with a good, hard look in the mirror. I always say, we must "marry our own soul first, before we can marry our soulmate". You cannot hope to attract someone with a higher vibration if your own vibration leaves much to be desired.

So, how do you raise your vibration to create and attract the better things into your life? The answer is simple. You become spiritually aware by reconnecting and aligning with your inner Divinity, and then you begin to change the way you think, perceive and feel using the emotional and intuitive guidance you receive from your Divine Self. In order to fulfill our Soul Purpose and Life Calling it is vital that we remain connected and in alignment with our inner Divinity. When we are not aligned with the Higher Self we struggle to create, attract and manifest the things we need to fulfill our Life Plan.

Our emotions and intuitions are the result of our conscious connection to our soul, or spirit or the Divine Self, or our lack thereof. When we experience positive emotions it is because our energy vibration is raised to resonate more with our Divine Self, but when we have negative emotions it means our vibration is lowered and we are more disconnected from the Divine Self. No wonder we have the saying in English that someone is "beside themself" with anger or frustration. In those moments of extreme negative emotion we are literally 'outside' our true nature and completely disconnected from our Higher Self.

Raising your vibration does not imply that we should be ignoring negative emotion. Our emotions are our inner guides, our signposts to indicate the direction we should be going. Both positive and negative emotions should be taken note of and acknowledged. Living in a state of disconnection from your own emotions is impossible once you have experienced spiritual awakening. The spiritually aware become increasingly mindful and conscious of their own thoughts, intuitions and emotions. Negative emotions are symptoms and they will not disappear unless they are acknowledged and their root cause is addressed and rectified. Negative emotion is your Divine Self telling you that something is wrong.

In *Molecules of Emotion: The Science Behind Mind-Body Medicine,* Dr Candace Pert explains, "The tendency to ignore our emotions is 'old think', a remnant of the still-reigning paradigm that keeps us focused on the material level of health, the physicality of it. But the emotions are a key element in self-care because they allow us to enter into the body-mind's conversation. By getting in touch with our emotions, both by listening to them and by directing them through the psychosomatic network, we gain access to the healing wisdom that is everyone's natural biological right."

A life dominated by negative, destructive emotion is the by-product of the state of Divine Disconnect coupled with *lack consciousness*, a *scarcity mentality* and pervasive *false beliefs* about ourselves and the need for primitive survival.

Dr Pert further explains that fear, anger and grief are in fact vital for our survival. "We need anger to define boundaries, grief to deal with our losses, and fear to protect ourselves from danger. It's only when these feelings are denied, so that they cannot be easily and rapidly processed through the system and released, that the situation becomes toxic. And the more we deny them, the greater the ultimate toxicity, which often takes the form of an explosive release of pent-up emotion. That's when emotion can be damaging to both oneself and others, because its expression becomes overwhelming, sometimes violent."

To achieve a higher vibrational frequency we must therefore not only focus on consistently *shifting* ourselves into a state of *positive emotion*, but we must also *acknowledge, process* and *express* all our *negative emotions*. However, merely acknowledging and processing our negative emotions, through psychotherapy, for example, is not enough for us to attain a truly awakened and abundant Divine Life. Higher Consciousness and a lasting *evolution of our emotions* are vital to creating a Divine lifestyle. The key to achieving this state of being is spiritual awareness and reconnection with our inner Divinity.

Why is positive emotion so vital to Divine Living? Well, emotional energy attracts more energy of the same kind into our experience. In his 1917 book *The Master Key System*, Charles F. Haanel writes that what we feel on the inside is what we will see on the outside.

> *Harmony in the world within will be reflected in the world without by harmonious conditions, agreeable surround- dings, the best of everything. It is the foundation of health and a necessary essential to all greatness, all power, all attainment, all achievement and all success.*

When we are connected and aligned with the Divine Self, we raise our energy vibration and we feel on top of the world, which then brings forth more positive emotions. Positive emotions ultimately attract more positive people, events and things into our life experience. These positive emotions must however be *authentic* and not merely an attempt to mask or avoid hidden negative feelings we may harbor.

Similarly, 'misery loves company' and when we become out of sync or disconnected from our own Divinity our energy vibration is lowered and we begin to feel all manner of negative emotions, which in turn attract more negative, unpleasant and undesirable people, events and things into our life experience. This key concept is too often neglected by abundance gurus and self-help experts. Some Law of Attraction practitioners tend to place great emphasis on how they create with their thoughts, desires, wishes and intentions whatever they ultimately hope to manifest, while they neglect the role of their emotions and their intuitions to empower them to actually attract those things into their lives.

Tracking Your Emotions

Your emotions are vital to living a truly awakened and abundant life. Our emotions tell us when we are aligned with the Divine Self, and when we are not. Esther-Abraham Hicks states it very simply, "Whatever it is you are feeling is a perfect reflection of what you are in the process of becoming".

When we are aligned with our inner Divinity we are assured that our vibrational frequency will be a match to the things, people, events and experiences we need to manifest in our lives in order to fulfill our Soul Purpose and Life Calling. Think of your emotions as your internal 'homing device' or tracking system. From moment to moment the Divine Self uses your emotions to signal to you whether you are currently synchronized and in harmony with your Life Plan, or not. This may sound complicated, since we have so many complex emotions, but it is actually quite simple to apply.

There are many complex theories of emotion and all manner of scales and graphs that attempt to capture the essence and complexity of human emotion. However, we all know that our emotions essentially boil down to either one of two feelings, namely *positive* or *negative.* One of my favorite teachers and role-models, Esther-Abraham Hicks, agrees that there are only two basic emotions and that they give us a very clear message of how well we are doing, or not.

One feels good and one feels bad. You call them all sorts of different things, but essentially, all of those negative emotions, whether you call it guilt, or anger, or frustration, all feel much the same. They do not feel good. And all of those are guidance saying, "that which you are thinking about right now is not in line with what you are really wanting"... The one that feels good, that feeling of hope, or happiness, or love, that good feeling, that positive emotion, is guidance saying, "that which you are thinking right now, is in alignment with what you are wanting.

W. Gerrod Parrott, Professor of Psychology at Georgetown University proposes a tree-structured list of emotions, which I have found very useful in my practice. Parrot states that we experience six basic or primary emotions, namely the positive emotions of Love, Joy and Surprise, as well as the negative emotions of Anger, Sadness and Fear.

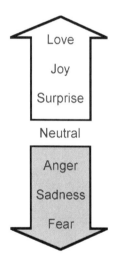

These six primary emotions provide us with ongoing feedback about the state of our vibrational frequency. When you are experiencing Love, Joy or Surprise you have a *higher vibration* and you are in greater alignment with the Divine Self and your Life Plan, but when you are feeling Anger, Sadness or Fear your *vibration is lower* and you are shifting out of alignment with your inner Divinity and you are no longer on course towards fulfilling your Soul Purpose and Life Calling.

Shifting Negative Emotion

In order to maintain our vibrational frequency at a higher, more positive level we need to become more *mindful* of our *emotional state* and our *general mood* on a daily basis. When we experience the beginnings of negative emotion, we must find and resolve the underlying cause, and replace the negative feeling with a more positive emotion as soon as possible.

Replacing negative emotions with better feelings is accomplished by reaching for thoughts, perceptions, beliefs, ideas and attitudes that will bring about a *more positive emotional state.* Your aim should be to work towards a lasting, permanent shift in your emotional awareness and well-being. In order to manifest a truly awakened and abundant Divine Life we need to build and maintain a *higher vibrational frequency* on a permanent basis.

The aim of the following exercise is to shift negative emotion up the emotional scale and achieve a more positive emotional state. Use it whenever you feel that negativity is getting the upper hand in your life.

1) **Identify your current emotional status.** How are you feeling right now? What emotion is dominant? How would you describe your mood in one word? The answer to these questions may be simple or more complex, depending on your level of awareness and the nature of your emotional state. If you are very clear about how you are feeling you will most likely be able to identify whether you are in a state of Fear, Sadness or Anger. If you are not sure in which category to place your current emotion, you need to review the list of emotions in the Tree of Emotions table at the end of this section. Find the *Tertiary* emotion that best describes your current feeling, and then work from the left column to the right to identify your Primary emotion, for example:

   Boredom ⇨ Irritability ⇨ **ANGER**
   Guilt ⇨ Shame ⇨ **SADNESS**
   Uneasiness ⇨ Nervousness ⇨ **FEAR**

2) **Identify your target emotion.** This is done by identifying the opposite emotion to what you are current feeling

using the following table of opposites. For example, if you identified you current emotional state as one of Anger, then you need to focus on shifting it to a feeling of Love.

Negative	Positive
Anger	Love
Sadness	Joy
Fear	Surprise

3) **Find a quiet place, and sit or lie in a comfortable position.** Close your eyes and slow down your breathing.

4) **Breathe deeply in and out.** Focus on becoming centered and relaxed. Shut down any negative self-talk that might intrude.

5) **Think of a person, place, event or past experience that evokes your target emotion.** Who or what do you associate with feeling of Love, or Joy, or Surprise? This could be fond memories of time spent with a loved one or friends, your children, or a favorite pet, or your dream vacation, or an unexpected gift you received. Choose any memory that evokes the *target emotion* you identified in step 2.

6) **Visualize the person, place or event.** See the scene of your positive emotional memory very clearly in your mind's eye. Breathe into the memory, feeling your attention focused in the area of your heart.

7) **Feel how the memory evokes feelings** of Love, Joy or Surprise. How would you describe the feeling you are experiencing in one word? What are your feeling? Caring? Tenderness? Sentimentality? Desire? Passion? Infatuation? Bliss? Jolliness? Enjoyment? Happiness? Satisfaction? Excitement? Triumph? Hope? Relief? Amazement?

8) **Imagine you are breathing in these positive feelings.**
See the positive feelings flow into your heart, and then let
it radiate and spread throughout the rest of your body.

Once you have practiced this technique a few times, you will soon
be able to instantly trigger it within your body whenever you may
need it. Whenever you feel negative emotion creeping into your
consciousness, simply relax, take a few deep, mindful breaths, and
summon your happy feeling back to you. Feel the positive emotion
bubbling back up. This will quickly activate your *positive feeling
state* and *shift you up the emotional scale* into a higher vibrational
frequency.

It is however very important to note that this exercise only
serves as a temporary spiritual 'band-aid'. Our emotions do not
'lead us', they 'follow us'. Temporarily shifting negative emotion in
order to raise your vibration mostly serve to enhance our quality
of life and to speed up the process of manifesting, but it does not
create lasting results to ensure that we fulfill our Life Plan in this
lifetime.

To truly follow our bliss, and find inner peace and abundance,
we must follow the road map provided by our intuition. Our emotions tell us when we are going off course, but they do not show us
which way to go. To meet our true destiny me must follow the
instructions provided by our intuition. Positive emotion will automatically follow.

TREE OF EMOTIONS		
TERTIATY ⇨	**SECONDARY ⇨**	**PRIMARY**
Adoration • Fondness • Liking • Attractiveness • Caring • Tenderness • Compassion • Sentimentality	Affection	**LOVE**
Arousal • Desire • Passion • Infatuation	Lust/Sexual Desire	
Longing	Longing	
Amusement • Bliss • Gaiety • Glee • Jolliness • Joviality • Joy • Delight • Enjoyment • Gladness • Happiness • Jubilation • Elation • Satisfaction • Ecstasy • Euphoria	Cheerfulness	**JOY**
Enthusiasm • Zeal • Excitement • Thrill • Exhilaration	Zest	
Pleasure	Contentment	
Triumph	Pride	
Eagerness • Hope	Optimism	
Enthrallment • Rapture	Enthrallment	
Relief	Relief	
Amazement • Astonishment	Surprise	**SURPRISE**
Aggravation • Agitation • Annoyance • Grouchy • Grumpy • Crosspatch • Boredom	Irritability	**ANGER**
Frustration	Exasperation	
Anger • Outrage • Fury • Wrath • Hostility • Ferocity • Bitter • Hatred • Scorn • Spite • Vengefulness • Dislike • Resentment	Rage	
Revulsion • Contempt • Loathing	Disgust	
Jealousy	Envy	
Torment	Torment	
Agony • Anguish • Hurt	Suffering	**SADNESS**
Depression • Despair • Gloom • Glumness • Unhappy • Grief • Sorrow • Woe • Misery • Melancholy	Sadness	
Dismay • Displeasure	Disappointment	
Guilt • Regret • Remorse	Shame	
Alienation • Defeatism • Dejection • Embarrassment • Homesickness • Humiliation • Insecurity • Insult • Isolation • Loneliness • Rejection	Neglect	
Pity	Sympathy	
Alarm • Shock • Fear • Fright • Horror • Terror • Panic • Hysteria • Mortification	Horror	**FEAR**
Anxiety • Suspense • Uneasiness • Apprehension • Worry • Distress • Dread	Nervousness	

Sensate Focusing

One of the most powerful methods for improving our emotional well-being is to concentrate or focus our attention on our internal feelings and bodily sensations. When we consciously focus on harmful feelings and unpleasant sensations we empower ourselves to conquer the forces of negativity and unhappiness in our life.

Eckhart Tolle says "whatever you fight, you strengthen". This is very true. Whatever we resist tends to persist, but when we become fully aware and conscious of our feelings and inner sensations, we are able to better master our emotions. Sensate focusing enables us to achieve *mind, body* and *spirit integration*, without which true personal transformation is impossible. By focusing on the sensations of the body we release negative energy and we are empowered to reprogram the mind.

It may sound like this is something you already do every day. We are all aware of our negative moods, unpleasant feelings, and unwelcome physical sensations and symptoms in varying degrees. But the truth is that many people are very disconnected, or have very little conscious awareness of what they sense and how they really feel on the inside.

Whenever some people feel bad or experience anything negative they tend to shy away from it, or they try to *repress* it. There is much truth in the popular saying that someone is 'not in touch with their feelings". We often tend to ignore what we feel and hope that it will somehow resolve itself or just go away, but this usually just serves to make things worse.

Sensate Body Scan

1) **Sit or lie in a comfortable position.** Focus on your breathing for a while and relax.

2) **Scan your body for any unpleasant feelings or sensations.** Start at your feet and work your way up to the crown of your head. You may find more than one affected area, for example stiffness in your shoulders, tightness in your chest and a knot of tension at the pit of your stomach.

3) **Spend sufficient time focusing your attention solely on each problem area** as you progress through your scan. Pay careful attention to each region and section of your body, and the various organs involved. What do you feel? Is it pleasant or unpleasant, or neutral? Is the feeling becoming stronger or weaker when you focus on it, or does it stay the same? Is it a physical sensation or an emotion, or both? For example, a sensation of tension in your stomach may be linked to a feeling of anxiety. Don't try to find words to describe what it is you are feeling. Simple feel what your body is telling you *intuitively*. Some people find it helpful to imagine themselves as a caring parent with their inner child telling them from the inside what is wrong. Continue until you have scanned the whole body.

4) **Relax for a few moments** and focus once again on your breathing. Clear your mind and just relax completely.

5) **Gain deeper insight into what you are feeling.** Once you feel refreshed, return your attention to the one area that you felt was most affected, or where you felt the most intense feelings or sensation during the scan. It is usually in the area of the head, neck, chest or abdomen. Focus your attention on this main problem area for a couple of minutes. Imagine that you are touching this area with your index finger or the palm of your hand. What do you feel? Keep monitoring every small change in what you feel or sense in that area.

6) **Immerse yourself into the feeling or sensation.** Go *with* the feeling, not against it! Do not try to resist or suppress what you are feeling. Instead go deeper "into" the feeling. If it intensifies or expands, simply *embrace* it, instead of resisting it. If you find your mind begins to drift off, or tries to avoid the unpleasant sensation, bring yourself back to the affected area of your body and *refocus your attention*. If you find it difficult to concentrate, or you begin to feel very uncomfortable, take a break and try again a little later. Note: if you begin to

feel overwhelmed or extremely anxious at this point it is recommended that you stop the exercise and seek professional assistance.

7) **Concentrate on the main problem area**. What is it trying to tell you? What is the cause of this feeling? What do you see in your mind's eye when you focus on this feeling? Ask your inner child to tell you what is wrong. Keep focusing on this main area until the feeling or sensation begins to dissolve or reduce in intensity, then move on to the next area you picked up during your scan. You may continue until you have touched on every problem area you identified during the scan, or for as long as you feel comfortable. Stop or take a break whenever you feel the need to do so.

8) **Repeat this exercise several times over a period of a few weeks.** Don't worry if the original feeling does not disappear entirely. It often takes time to reprogram the mind-body-spirit connection. Often the more intense feelings or sensations are persistent and may return after a session of sensate focusing. This is perfectly normal. To produce more lasting results you should repeat this exercise. Each time you repeat it, you will feel a marked improvement.

Please note: sensate focusing can cause some people to have very intense physical and emotional responses. High risk individuals, who are repressing a lot of childhood trauma or who have an underlying psychological condition, for example, may find that this technique could temporarily intensely magnify unpleasant feelings or sensations, or even elicit additional, related feelings and sensations you may not have been aware of before. It may even trigger psychiatric emergencies or panic attacks, especially in people who are very susceptible to anxiety. Should you suspect that you fall in this category, you are advised to not attempt this technique on your own. It is best done with the help of qualified therapist or medical professional.

Gratitude & Appreciation

In my work with thousands of seekers and believers all over the world, I have found that gratitude is the one common element missing from most people's lives. Sadly, our lack of gratitude is something none of us can truly afford. You designed this amazing Life Plan of yours with great anticipation of all the wonderful experiences and thrilling sensations you would encounter on this incredible journey. Why on earth would you arrive here at your destination and then proceed to sulk, complain, protest, whine, moan, nitpick and criticize?

We can all do with a little more appreciation and thankfulness for all the wonderful blessings in our lives - from the mundane and humble to the truly miraculous and awe-inspiring. Trust me, if you want to make a radical difference to your general well-being and personal happiness, make a determined effort to include frequent thoughts and feelings of gratitude in your daily routine. It is the one simple lifestyle change and spiritual sentiment that will make the most instant and significant difference in your life.

My all-time favorite personal affirmation that I use almost daily is: "Today I will find something to be grateful for, something to appreciate and someone to thank". Without gratitude a Divine Life is impossible. The Prophet Muhammad said, "Gratitude for the abundance you have received is the best insurance that abundance will continue." Living in the now and inviting abundance and prosperity into your life can only come to complete and full fruition in a state of sincere gratitude and appreciation. The Lebanese-American writer Kahlil Gibran wrote, "You pray in your distress and in your need: would that you might pray also in the fullness of your joy and in your days of abundance."

In 1910 Wallace D. Wattles wrote in *The Science of Getting Rich*, the famous book which is generally considered to be the first modern text on the Law of Attraction, that gratitude is essential to manifesting an abundant and prosperous life.

> *Many people who order their lives rightly in all other ways are kept in poverty by their lack of gratitude. Having received one gift from God, they cut the wires which connect them with Him by failing to make acknowledgment. It is easy to understand that the nearer we live to the source of wealth, the more wealth we shall receive; and it*

is easy also to understand that the soul that is always grateful lives in closer touch with God than the one which never looks to Him in thankful acknowledgment. The more gratefully we fix our minds on the Supreme when good things come to us, the more good things we will receive, and the more rapidly they will come; and the reason simply is that the mental attitude of gratitude draws the mind into closer touch with the Source from which the blessings come.

This is where many so-called "practitioners of the Law of Atttraction" go off the rails. They are so busy with deliberate intentions and mindful creation to manifest their self-centered wishes and desires, usually revolving around material wealth, that they never stop to give thanks for the abundance already present in their lives. If only they would turn their focus and attention to all the wonderful blessings and little miracles around them every day, they would get much better results from their efforts to manifest the things they are so determined to have. For what they do not understand is that the Law of Attraction and the process of manifesting revolves around two key magic ingredients: your *energy vibration* and your *spiritual awareness.*

If you want to create and attract the material manifestations of your wishes and desires, you need to raise your vibration to a level of happiness, joy and excitement that resonates with the object of your intention. And the only truly lasting way to achieve such an elevated frequency of vibration is when you are spiritually aware and aligned with your Higher Consciousness. In this state it is impossible to be anything but grateful for the wonders and miracles of life.

If you intend to manifest the perfect job or the perfect partner, you need to consistently adopt a *vibrational frequency* that matches that desire. Waiting for the perfect job or partner to arrive, before you allow yourself to become truly fulfilled, happy and joyful, is pointless and foolhardy - you are bound to wait a very long time, if not forever. Perfect jobs and perfect partners unfortunately do not go around looking for spoiled, sulky, discontented, ungrateful people as their ideal and preferred company to keep.

So, how do you become more grateful? Well, to live with appreciation is not so much about saying "thank you" all the time, or by expressing how grateful you are to all who care to listen. To truly live in a state of gratitude and appreciation is to replace all your negative thoughts, feelings, words and actions with a more appreciative and mindful outlook on life. When you live in appreciation and gratitude, the urge to complain and criticize subsides, and a yearning to savor and enjoy all the wonderful things in your life and in the world around you emerges.

Gratitude Journaling

Keeping a gratitude journal is one of the simplest and most effective ways to realign with your inner Divinity and increase your levels of appreciation and gratitude in as little as one week. A gratitude journal is basically a diary that you keep of all the positive things in your life that you are thankful for.

1) **Buy a blank notepad or journal.** A spiral-bound book that opens flat is a popular choice, because it is easier to write in. If you wish you can cover and decorate your journal to your liking. It does not matter what your journal looks like, as long as it reminds you of the good things in your life and inspires you to write in it on a regular basis. Instead of using an actual book, you can also post your gratitude entries online on one of several gratitude communities or social networks, or on your Facebook or Twitter page. You can even use something like your iPhone or Amazon Kindle, because there are apps available for this purpose.

2) **Decide how often you will add entries** to your gratitude journal. Will you write every day, once a week or just whenever you feel the need to do so? Personally I recommend two or three times per week. In the beginning it might be a good idea to try and do two or three entries for every day, but don't keep this up for too long, as it will lose its magical effect if you overdo it.

3) **Look out for things to be grateful for throughout the day.** The actual writing down of the entry is not really the most important aspect of gratitude journaling. By shifting your focus and attention during the day towards finding

things that you are thankful for, you automatically begin to adopt a more positive, grateful outlook on life. Begin to find the silver lining around every cloud, see the hidden blessing in every obstacle or challenge. Try and find positive angle in everything that comes your way. Keep mental notes of the things you come across during your day, or save keyword reminders on your smart phone. You will need this information later when you make you next entry in your gratitude journal.

4) **Record your entries in your journal.** Gratitude journal entries are simple, brief and to the point. Typically they are nothing more than a single sentence or phrase about anything you feel grateful for – from the mundane to the really life-changing. If you are religious you can direct your statements of gratitude in the form of single sentence prayers to the deity of your choice. The following are a few examples of what an entry could look like:

The sun is shining so brightly!
I am grateful for all my cool friends
Thank you God for this wonderful day
My boss being so demanding is a blessing in disguise
I love smelling the first roses in the garden...
Just heard one of my favorite songs on the radio

5) **Make use of the following tips** to make your gratitude journal more powerful:

   o **Personalize your journal** using pictures, dried flowers and leaves, magazine clippings, receipts and tickets, quotes, cardboard frames and other decorations, or post online videos made from pictures of the people and things in your life that you are grateful for.

   o **Truly immerse yourself.** Make a conscious decision to become more grateful; don't just go through the motions. When you write your entries light a candle, play your favorite happy music and put a smile on your face. These little rituals all help to make it more real and impactful. Use your senses to visualize the things you are writing about and remember the events of the day. What did you hear, see, smell, taste and feel?

o **Play the 'what if' game.** For every entry that you make, consider for a moment what your life would be like without that thing or person, and then erase those thoughts with a warm wave of inner gratitude that those things are indeed still present in your life. Visualize and consider the difference that person or thing makes in your life, and then thank them for being there.

o **Try to write about people in your life** more often than just about material things. Focus on the way whoever you are writing about makes you feel; close your eyes and journey into your feelings towards that person for a moment. Become aware of the real depth and intensity of your gratitude.

o **Begin to expand your thoughts and write in greater detail** about the things you are grateful for, as you become more experienced in journaling. Instead of trying to write in great depth about various things, focus on one thing or person per day to journal about.

7

SHARPENING YOUR SENSES

Increased sensory awareness is essential to Divine Living. To be spiritually awakened is to be acutely aware of your physical, exterior reality, not only the inner world. Without sensory acuity there can be no soul growth. It is only through acute sensory awareness of the material, secular world that we can truly gain complete insight into the deepest spiritual truths of human existence.

Sensory awareness refers to a sharp, intense perception of everything around us. Our senses are our windows to the world; they are the channels or messengers that bring the external world within. Enjoying our sensory experiences is one of the fundamental reasons why we came here as spiritual beings in the first place; it is central to the exhilarating human adventure we signed up for. We are supposed to use all five of our senses to their full extent – sight, hearing, smell, taste and touch – to truly experience the magical world around us. In every moment of our daily life there is something new or special waiting be noticed and appreciated, if only we were paying more attention.

To be sensory aware is to be *present in the now.* Being present in the now is not about focusing on something or actively thinking about something, or taking some sort of deliberate action. Being in the present is about simply *being there*; to be completely open to what is happening right now. Sensory awareness is therefore about being *mindful in every moment.*

But what does it mean to be 'mindful'? Mindfulness is a state of beingness in which we are deeply aware or conscious of everything that is going on inside of us, as well as around us. Mindfulness is the constant conscious awareness of our thoughts, emotions, sensory perceptions, intuitions, our physical body and everything and everyone we come into contact with in every moment of the day - from moment, to moment, to moment.

You may be thinking, "but I am aware, my senses are pretty sharp, I notice things." The truth is that most of humanity is in a deep trance of Divine Disconnection, the state of awareness I call the 'reality coma'. Post-modern civilization has taken on a reality of its own. It is a strange, technologically driven reality where adults talk into little gadgets stuck to their ears, while their children believe that milk comes from factories. Breathtaking sunrises have been replaced by electronic billboards. Bird song and the howling of the wind have been drowned out by the morning news on the television and rock music on the car stereo. Our taste buds have become slaves to artificial flavorings; with our eyes closed we can no longer recognize the taste of many natural foods the way our ancestors were able to. We pump our atmosphere full of pollutants and lace our homes with synthetic air fresheners. A cool breeze or a hot day leaves many of us unaffected, because our homes are insulated and our air conditioners run day and night.

We have shut ourselves off from the natural world. Our senses have become dull and jaded. Is it any wonder that so many people remain in the state of Divine Disconnection most or all of their lives? They are walking this planet like zombies; they are sleep-walkers, running the rate race with their senses shut down and blacked out.

My students sometimes react with surprise when I point out to them that spiritual awakening is not simply about a reconnection with the spiritual realm and the Higher Self. Awakening to the physical world around us, and coming fully into the present, is an important part of that process. In fact, I believe the one is impossible without the other.

Believers who have had a profound spiritual awakening will often tell you that immediately following their profound experience they immediately began to perceive the world with a much more vivid, intense awareness. It is as if one's senses suddenly become sharp and alive! Spiritual awakening is not just a state of heightened awareness of the unseen or metaphysical, it is also a sharpened, more mindful perceptiveness of the physical, material world. For the natural world around us is an expression of the Divinity that dwells within us all.

We simply take too much for granted every day; blessings of Joy, Beauty and Divine Grace are seldom acknowledged in our lives. How spiritually aware can we truly be if we hardly ever stop to smell the roses? To be spiritually aware is to be sensory acute. These two states of being are mutually inclusive; the one cannot exist without the other. True spirituality is not about being totally ethereal and supernatural; it is also about being in the 'here and now'. Spiritual living is about being fully grounded in the body and the senses.

Pearls Before Breakfast

Have you heard the true story of the internationally acclaimed violinist who disguised himself as a street busker with a baseball cap, and then proceeded to play Bach undercover at a metro subway station? An email outlining this intriguing story has been circulating on the Internet since December 2008. There have been claims that it may be a hoax, or an urban myth, but it is indeed a true story. The event was actually captured on video with a hidden camera.

Washington Post columnist Gene Weingarten created an interesting social experiment, with the assistance of renowned violinist Joshua Bell. He wanted to find out if people would notice music played by a celebrated artist, compared to that of an ordinary street musician. Would they even bother to stop and listen?

Joshua Bell was awarded the Avery Fisher Prize in 2007 and has sold more than 5 million copies of his first recording, which remained at the top of the classical music chart for over 50 weeks. Surely, a classical instrumentalist of his caliber performing in public would instantly be noticed, or even recognized by many people? But sadly that never happened. Weingarten got way less than he originally bargained for.

Bell played for 45 minutes at *L'Enfant Plaza* in Washington, D.C. on January 12, 2007. More than a 1000 people passed by in that short period, and they all basically ignored the virtuoso. Only *seven* people stopped for a moment to listen, and only *one* recognized him at all. Bell collected a whopping $32.17 from 27 charitable passersby. Just three days prior, he played at the Symphony Hall in Boston, to a sold out audience who paid around $100 per ticket for the relatively good seats.

Gene Weingarten later won the Pulitzer Prize for feature writing in 2008 for his article *Pearls Before Breakfast*, which he wrote about this simple, yet profound experiment. Audio and video recordings of the event are available at the Washington Post website. For me the most significant paragraph in the email that has since been circulating reads as follows:

> *The one who paid the most attention was a three year old boy. His mother tagged him along, hurried, but the kid stopped to look at the violinist. Finally the mother pushed hard and the child continued to walk turning his head all the time. This action was repeated by several other children. All the parents, without exception, forced them to move on.*

The question is, if our senses have become so jaded that we are unable to somehow recognize or appreciate one of the best musicians in the world playing the best music ever written, how many other things are we missing?

Playing Fetch

I am reminded on a daily basis of the thrill and magic to be found in being fully conscious and engaged in the present moment. I am reminded of this fact during one of the most mundane activities, namely when I play with my dogs. Have you ever observed dogs playing 'fetch'. Have you noticed how they can just keep running after that stick or that ball - over, and over, and over again, without every growing bored or weary?

Every single time I show my dogs their favorite tennis ball they act as if they have never seen it before. To them that ball is the most magical, spectacular and amazing thing they have ever seen. The alpha dog of the three has a heart defect, but if I would allow him he would literally keep on playing with that ball until his heart stopped. There is simply no end to his enthusiasm for fetching that worn out old thing. No matter how often I throw it, that little dog is always ready and eager to go fetch it!

Well, truth be told, my dogs know an essential life secret that most humans will never discover in their lifetime. Have you guessed what the key is to their inexhaustible, never ending enthusiasm? Well, of course! It is a dog's ability to truly *remain in the present moment*, to live in the *now*. They maintain a wonderful 'freshness of perception' and an acute awareness of every moment while they are playing with that ball.

Animals have this natural ability to be fully present in the moment because, unlike you and me, they have not been *conditioned into constant distraction*. From a young age the human child is encouraged to be always busy, to be always hurried, to be always doing something, to be always preoccupied, instead of simply remaining *open to the present moment*.

These days the ability to 'multi-task' is considered a sign of competence, the trademark of the truly accomplished and successful. From the moment we arrive of this planet we learn to feel we should always be doing something, and the faster the better. We have become accustomed to *doing while perceiving* and we have acquired many modern lifestyle habits that restrict our ability to be truly mindful and open to the present moment.

Teaching Old Dogs New Tricks

So, how does one achieve and maintain a constant state of mindful sensory awareness? Well, this is one of the fundamental mysteries of the human condition that philosophers, yogis and gurus have been attempting to answer for millennia.

The problem with the human condition is that we tend to be extremely habit-bound, and with our modern daily routine set to a clock it is no easy task to make changes to the way we perceive our world. Until we have come together as a species to collectively change the way we live and restructure our economy, our culture, our lifestyle and our society, we have one of two options: we either become one of the pioneers who abandon the rat race in exchange for a simpler, more mindful existence, or we do the best we can within the hectic modern lives we lead to achieve a more mindful existence. Either way will require changing our lifestyle. One cannot expect to keep up your old habitual way of living if you hope to create a new kind of life that is more aware, mindful and fulfilling.

Fortunately, there are ways to start small. The first step towards increased sensory awareness is to change your general outlook on your daily life. Begin to seek that which is 'new' or 'unusual' or 'special' in everyday things that have become stale and habitual to you. Our daily routine offers many unexpected opportunities for rediscovering the world and sharpening our senses.

The principle is simple. Make every moment fresh and new, take a new look at your old, stale habitual way of life. See the world through new eyes, from moment, to moment, to moment. Perceive the small, mundane things in your life with the same level of attention and focus you would invest in the more important things in your life.

For example, brush your hair with the same amount of conscious awareness as you would otherwise give to driving on a wet road in a heavy rain storm. Sit in a quiet corner of your garden and observe the plants and birds with the same amount of absorption you would devote to watching am excellent film in the theater.

Improving Sensory Awareness

The following exercises are simple, easy ways to introduce increased sensory acuity into your daily lifestyle. If you find it difficult to make time for these sensory awareness activities, you can combine some of them with your daily meditation.

Our senses operate on a non-verbal level. The aim of any sensory awareness activity is therefore to experience things directly and intimately, rather than merely thinking about it or using the analytical function of our mind. Sensory acuity is *not* about thinking or analyzing.

Take your time when you are working on your sensory awareness. We are used to being hasty and impatient; everything must be done quickly in our modern lives. This is part of the reason why our senses become so dull; we are rushing around too much. In everyday life we tend to split our attention between the task itself and our sensory experience of it. To sharpen our senses we must *integrate the action* with our *sensory experience* of it.

These exercises should therefore be done at a leisurely pace. Do everything with a sense of wonder. Instead of merely going through the motions, allow your senses to fully explore everything at their own pace. The mere act of picking up a glass or a pencil should be done very slowly, for example, while being completely mindful of each moment of the action.

1) **Object Observation.** Take some time to observe objects in a familiar room in your home. Focus on imprinting the

room and its contents on your mind, but do not memorize anything. This is not a test. Merely observe the room with your full attention, just let it all stream in without thinking about any of the objects that you see. Now leave the room and ask a friend or family member to remove just one object from the room. Do you notice which object is missing? The same exercise can be done with a variety of small objects on a tray. Observe the objects and then let someone remove one of the objects.

2) **Blind objects.** Wear a blindfold and examine the same tray of objects, using all your other senses, except your sight. Tap and shake each object, what sounds to you hear? What does each object feel, smell and taste like?

3) **Blind Path.** Spend some time walking in your garden or down a path somewhere out in nature or in a park. Choose a safe, quiet place. Untamed nature trails are not recommended, instead try a paved path in your local public park. It is also a good idea to take someone with you to keep an eye on you, or at least a cane or walking stick. Walk slowly down the path a few times, while being truly mindful and in the moment. Then walk down the path again, this time closing your eyes at regular inter-vals. Become aware of what other sources of sensory feedback you use to stay on course, when you can no longer use your vision. Practice this until you get good at knowing exactly where you are, then try keeping your eyes closed for longer periods of time.

4) **Feeling Self.** Sit or lie comfortably, with your eyes *open*. Begin to 'feel self with self'. Feel your feet with your feet. Feel your feet in your shoes and your shoes on your feet. Feel your clothing on your legs and your legs inside your clothes. Feel your clothing on your chest and your chest inside your clothes. Feel you finger inside your ring and your ring on your finger. Feel your tongue inside your mouth and your mouth around your tongue. Feel your whole body touching space and feel how space is touching your body, etc.

5) **Sounds of Silence.** Sit or lie comfortably in a quiet place and close your eyes. Become aware of any and all sounds that may be present around you. What do you hear? Do you notice how much sound there is around you, even in a place you thought was quiet. What sounds can you discern? How far away are they? Focus on the sounds close by. What do you hear? Now focus on sounds that are very far away. What do you hear? Now listen to the sound of your own breathing.

6) **Self Report.** Sit or lie comfortably in a quiet place and close your eyes. Become conscious of your breathing. Then begin to 'listen' to your body internally. Now begin to verbalize each and every feeling and sensation you are picking up inside your body. Say what you are feeling and sensing, describe each sensation in words. Try not to stop talking, except to take breaths between sentences. Calmly keep taking, describing every single thing you feel, starting from your feet and working your way up to the top of your head.

7) **Sensory Meditation.** You can devote some of your daily meditation time to concentrate purely on your *senses*. I find the most effective way to do this is to focus on only one sense during a meditation session. My meditations typically last between 15 to 20 minutes. Each meditation can be different; use your imagination and play around with different approaches.

- Collect a selection of fabrics and textures, such as cardboard, paper, tree bark, plastic, metal, nylon, silk, velvet, cotton. Select items with different qualities: smooth, rough, soft, hard. Take your time touching and stroking each one, allowing your mind to explore each texture.

- Listen simply to whatever is happening around you in that moment. Explore the sounds around you without giving thought to them or labeling them.

- Put your fingers or a pair of earplugs in your ears and listen to the sounds inside your body. Apart from your breathing and heartbeat, what else do you hear?

- Meditate on the sound of a bell or small cymbal. Listen repeatedly to the ringing sound when you strike it, and listen to the sound fading, until it is silent.

- Meditate on a fragrant flower, such as a rose, or a whole spice from your kitchen, like vanilla, nutmeg or star anise. Notice in particular if the fragrance is changing your mood or your state of mind.

- Taste different kinds of fruit. Put a piece of each into your mouth, and leave it there for a while. Explore the flavor of it as you move it to various parts of your mouth, before you bite into it. Do you notice any change in its flavor? Do certain fruit flavors affect your mood?

8

INCREASING YOUR INTUITION

You are more than your physical body. You are a non-physical, conscious being in physical form, and because you are this pure expression of Divine consciousness you are directly connected to the Divine Source, or God, or the great I Am, and everything else in the entire Conscious Universe.

Intuition is a key component of the powerful *inner guidance* system with which we arrive on this planet at the time of birth. This connection to Universal Consciousness is however mostly *unconscious* in the human condition and in our daily lives we are generally unaware of our intuitive insights, especially when we are in the state of the Divine Disconnect. But by awakening our innate ability to tap into our *intuition* we can quite easily regain conscious access to Infinite Intelligence, Higher Consciousness, Sacred Knowledge and the Ancient Spiritual Wisdom of the Past, Present and Future.

Lao Tzu, the Chinese philosopher and father of Taoism said, "The power of intuitive understanding will protect you from harm until the end of your days." Your intuitive ability enables your Higher Self or inner Divinity to *communicate* with you, and *guide* you towards achieving your Soul Purpose and accomplishing your Life Calling. Your intuition steers you towards fulfilling your Life Plan. Intuition connects you with the Divine Self, and when you are connected to your inner Divinity you are *aligned* with the Conscious Universe, God, Spirit, Source Energy, Infinite Intelligence, the All Knowing, the Omnipotent, the origins of All that is, was and ever will be.

The famous American psychic medium, Edgar Cayce was once asked during a reading how a person could stay in touch with the "highest psychic forces" to aid them in fulfilling their purpose in life. Cayce replied that the best starting point would be to establish what your ideal is, and next to know and accept that the kingdom of God was *within*. Cayce further stated that the "highest possible psychic realization" is that "God, the Father, speaks *directly* to the sons of men – even as He has promised."

What Is Intuition?

Intuition is simply defined as having *instant perceptive insight* without any rational analysis or logical reasoning. It has also been described as a capacity for *vibrational cognizance*. The word intuition comes from the Latin word *intueri*, which means to 'to look inside" or 'to contemplate'.

Intuition is an effortless, immediate *knowing* or *sensing* of the 'unseen' or the 'unknowable'. It is an awareness that comes from within; an inner knowledge and wisdom that comes to us in the form of intuitive impressions, hunches and insights. It is also known as the 'sixth sense', 'inner voice' or having a 'gut feeling'.

We do not gain access to intuitive information by applying cognitive reasoning, emotional judgment or physical perception using the normal five senses. The things we know and sense intuitively are *not evident* in our environment, and these impressions are typically *not very logical*. Carl Jung described it as "perception via the unconscious". Instead of using our normal senses of sight, hearing, smell, taste and touch to perceive, intuition relies upon extra sensory perception (ESP), or what is also known as the 'psychic senses' or 'clair senses'. Intuition is very similar to using your normal senses to observe or perceive incoming information. With the five normal senses we are able to see, hear, smell, touch and feel without having any knowledge or rational understanding of how our senses work.

Research psychology prefers to view intuition as an evolved form of natural survival instinct, similar to that of animals. However, the spiritually awakened soul knows from direct, personal experience that intuition is much more than a mere survival mechanism. Intuition is an invaluable and absolutely *essential resource* for living an awakened and abundant Divine Life. It is our direct 'phone line' to God; it is an inner 'satellite dish' that connects us with the Divine Source and the Universal Consciousness.

We cannot achieve much here on Earth as spiritual beings in human form without this *built-in guidance system*. Edgar Cayce said, "for through self man will understand its Maker when it understands its relation to its Maker, and it will only understand that through itself, and that understanding is the knowledge as is given here in this state". The 'state' Cayce was referring to is the altered state of consciousness or meditative trance state that he would enter when he did readings, in order to tap into his intuition and the collective unconscious. For this reason he was nicknamed 'The Sleeping Prophet'.

Developing your intuition is to learn to honor your Higher Self. Intuitive guidance and insight from the Divine Self is the fundamental expression of our own Divine consciousness. You radiate with this ancient inner wisdom; you carry within you a doorway to all the answers to the mysteries of the Universe.

To create an awakened and abundant Divine Life you must learn to *trust* this inherited spiritual wisdom and tap into your own intuitive insight on a daily basis. Neale Donald Walsch writes, "Built into you is an internal guidance system that shows you the way home. All you need to do is heed the voice." Divine Living is very much about finding the courage to follow these intuitive insights. It is after all your Divine Right.

Language Of The Soul

Intuitive perception is not something that was hidden or disconnected from human consciousness until now. In fact, primitive man greatly relied on his intuition, because he thought in images and symbols, and listened to his 'inner voice' and trusted his 'gut'. Early man fluently spoke the language of the intuitive mind, the language of his spiritual origins. Man was born intuitive, because man is of *spiritual origin*. Intuition is the earthly *language of Spirit*; it transcends the limitations of this time-space dimension.

Ralph Waldo Emerson, the American transcendental philosopher, noted in his 1824 essay *Self-Reliance*, that our intuition is the source of genius and virtue, and the essence of life.

We denote this primary wisdom as Intuition, whilst all later teachings are tuitions. In that deep force, the last fact behind which analysis cannot go, all things find their common origin. For, the sense of being which in calm hours rises, we know not how, in the soul, is not diverse from things, from space, from light, from time, from man, but one with them, and proceeds obviously from the same source whence their life and being also proceed. We first share the life by which things exist, and afterwards see them as appearances in nature, and forget that we have shared their cause. Here is the fountain of action and of thought. Here are the lungs of that inspiration which giveth man wisdom, and which cannot be denied without impiety and atheism. We lie in the lap of immense intelligence, which makes us receivers of its truth and organs of its activity.

Some scientists argue that intuition is merely an aspect of our normal human intelligence that developed out of primitive man's animalistic survival instincts. The concept of "relying on your instincts" and "following your intuition" is often used interchangeably in the same context, because many people assume that *instinct* and *intuition* is the same thing. This is however an incorrect assumption.

As spiritual beings in human form we do have physical bodies with certain natural instincts, such as the 'fight or flight response' when we sense danger, or the urges to seek pleasure and avoid pain. These instincts have not evolved or changed much since prehistoric times. As technologically advanced and intellectually sophisticated as we have become, we remain subject to our primitive instincts to this day. It therefore makes no sense to propose that our intuition is an evolution of our instinct. There is more to our innermost being than mere physical survival.

Instinct is the *unconscious language of the body*; intuition is the *unconscious language of the soul*. The body speaks the dialect of 'urges' and physical needs, the soul speaks the dialect of symbols and imagery and archetypal wisdom. Intuition is what gives us access to our inner Divinity and creative spiritual origins. Ralph Waldo Emerson said, "Belief consists in accepting the affirmations of the soul; unbelief, in denying them." We cannot access the Soul or the Divine Self through intellect, reason or analytical thought.

Through consistent evolution of our species we increasingly experienced Divine Disconnection as we began to focus on cultivating the intellectual, rational mind at the expense of the intuitive, symbolic mind. We replaced symbols and images with words and concepts. We increasingly banished the innate intuitive capacity of our ancestors to the realms of our *dreams* and the *subconscious mind*.

In *Metaphoric Mind: A Celebration of Creative Consciousness*, Bob Samples says," Albert Einstein called the intuitive or metaphoric mind a sacred gift. He added that the rational mind was a faithful servant. It is paradoxical that in the context of modern life we have begun to worship the servant and defile the divine."

In the 1980's the Harvard Business Review conducted a survey of the top 100 CEOs in the USA. Each participant was asked to name the *one major factor* they feel had contributed most to their business success. Amazingly, all 100 subjects reported that it was their reliance on their *intuition* that brought them all the way to the top of the corporate ladder. More interesting is the fact that many of them confessed to keeping this fact secret, because they feared disapproval or ridicule from their shareholders, colleagues and staff.

Modern man often chooses to ignore or deny his intuitions, referring to it as "just my imagination" or "new age woo-woo". But whether we choose to accept it, or not, we are constantly receiving non-physical information and spiritual guidance via the intuitive mind. To create a truly Divine Life we need to relearn the finer nuances of this subtle and symbolic inner language of the Soul.

Intuitive Development

Intuitive development simply means to develop your ability to make the unconscious more conscious. The aim of intuitive development is therefore to enhance and strengthen your *unconscious connection* with Infinite Intelligence, or the Divine Source, or God, and to bring this connection into your consciousness through *extra sensory perception*. Note that in the literal sense intuition cannot actually be 'developed'. The truth is that we can only learn to *reconnect* with our intuition and then practice ways to consciously be *in command* of our intuitive experiences.

Edgar Cayce once explained when someone asked him how intuition can be developed, "Train intuition? Then, how would you train electricity - save as how it may be governed! By keeping in self those thoughts, those activities of the mental mind, those activities of the body that allow spiritual truths to emanate through. To train such! Not train, but *govern!*"

Intuitive development is therefore not so much about 'learning' as it is about 'unlearning' the internal doubts and blocks we have created to stifle or suppress the flow of our natural intuitive awareness. Carl Jung explained, "The Western mind tends to shut out intuitive prompts because it falls under the domination of that tyrant, the *intellect*: it becomes *stagnant* and inwardly *insensitive*."

To become more intuitive we must relearn how to once again be a receiver of spontaneous and natural inner guidance in the way our ancient ancestors used to receive Divine direction. Intuition is always with us and it remains unlocked and continues to flow to us while we are in the state of Divine Disconnect, but in this state we are like a radio that is not fully tuned into the radio signal. In some instances we may be fully tuned in, but the volume is turned down or on 'mute'. Some people's station may just be poorly tuned in causing them to get vague or scrambled messages, while others are simply not tuned in at all and they hear nothing more than 'white noise' or even complete silence.

The key to tuning or tapping into your intuition is to quiet both your 'head' and your 'heart'. The intellectual mind and emotions must become silent *observers* of your intuitive percep-tion. The most effective approach to speed up development and get faster results is therefore to enter an *altered state of consciousness*, because this lowers the barrier or filter between the conscious and unconscious.

The most common altered state of consciousness approach is of course *meditation*, because it is especially helpful for quieting the mind and emotions, so that we are more open to freely and easily access intuitive information. In a sense one could describe meditation as a form of *self-hypnosis* to unlock the intuitive mind. For this reason meditation is recommended as a spiritual practice and daily habit you should aim to establish permanently in your newly awakened lifestyle.

To increase your levels of intuition significantly you need to get to know yourself very well. Intuition is all about *self-awareness*. You must get to know your Divine Self intimately, in the same way that you would spend time getting to know a wonderful new friend. Embrace your 'inner voice' and explore the unique intuitive language and communication style of your Higher Consciousness.

Note that intuitive development is a highly personal process, because no two people speak the same intuitive language. In our physical incarnation none of us are identical (except for identical twins). It therefore makes no sense to expect that our souls or spiritual blueprint would be similar, or identical. We are each perfectly unique expressions of Divinity and therefore we each speak an 'intuitive dialect' that is one of its kind. This is partly the reason why dream dictionaries and books citing psychic symbols and their intuitive meanings are usually not very effective in interpreting our intuitive impressions and dreams. The meaning I intuitively attach to a particular symbol would most likely be entirely different to your unique interpretation.

The Rational Mind Is Not The Enemy

Intuition is most powerful and unrestrained when we are in an altered state of consciousness, because it allows the subconscious mind and infinite pool of wisdom of the collective unconscious to 'rise to the surface' and express itself more fully, *without being filtered* or *inhibited* by the conscious, rational mind. Many famous prophets, spiritual teachers, healers, gurus, channelers, psychics and mediums throughout history are all known to have entered into some form of trance or altered state of consciousness as part of their metaphysical practice.

There is of course a reason why the subconscious and unconscious is monitored and *kept in check* by the rational mind. It is in fact a prerequisite for human survival in this physical time-space reality. If the subconscious and unconscious aspects were allowed to express itself freely, or even reign supreme and dominate our everyday consciousness, all humans would technically become 'unstable', 'illogical' or even 'insane' in terms of the current time-space reality, and therefore we will be unable to function effectively in the 'real world'.

Our earthly reality was cleverly created to serve as a reality platform for the physical, human life experience; it was designed to be a natural habitat for the rational mind and Ego identity. The subconscious and unconscious are however not restricted by the rational human concepts of 'time' and 'space' and 'reality'. The barrier between the conscious, rational mind and the subconscious, intuitive mind therefore serves as a *protective mechanism*. Psychiatrist and intuition researcher Daniel Cappon proposes that this barrier or censor between the conscious and unconscious was designed to protect and ensure concentrated attention of *clear, alert reasoning*, which we need to function normally in our daily reality. Cappon explains that "we now know that these barriers become *porous* during dreaming, defective in psychopathology, and collapse altogether in senility".

Unrestricted access to the unconscious would lead humanity to be lost in a 'twilight zone', somewhere between the seen, physical, secular reality and unseen, non-physical, spiritual realm, which would make us unfit for daily human living. Remember therefore that your intuitive perceptions may often not make much sense to your rational thinking, but your rational mind is *not* 'the enemy'.

When you tap into your intuition the tables are turned on the rational left brain, because your conscious intellect must now stand back and learn to trust your intuitive perception. The mind must learn to trust the 'gut'.

Always aim to eliminate critical thinking, analysis and judgment when you go into the 'intuitive state'. Simply allow intuitive impressions to flow into your consciousness without it being filtered by the logical mind. Initially you may find that your intuitive impressions come in infrequent 'flashes' or sudden 'bursts', but in time you will find that the flow becomes more natural and organic. In time and with regular practice, you will find that intuitive perceptions will increasingly come to you spontaneously, while you are in a normal state of consciousness.

Emotion vs. Intuition

Some metaphysics teachers and intuition coaches claim that our emotions and intuitive impressions are the same thing, or that personal emotions are a form intuitive perception. This is not entirely accurate and I have found this prevalent myth to be a source of great confusion among seekers. Intuition is *not* primarily about accessing and interpreting your emotions. Nothing could be further from the truth. Intuition is *not about your emotions* at all. In fact it is essential to be as *neutral* or *unemotional* as possible when working with your intuitive impressions. Many people at my development courses find this surprising, because they tend to associate feelings and emotions with intuition and psychic ability. The fact is that the most accurate intuitive perceptions come when one is most neutral or even emotionless.

Learning to distinguish between your thoughts, emotions and normal sensory perceptions, as opposed to the perceptions you receive intuitively, is an important aspect of developing conscious intuition. Sure, you will use your thoughts later to make rational decisions and choices about what you have perceived, and your emotions will guide you in the process of putting those choices and decisions into action. But before you can begin to think, feel, create, attract and manifest, you first need to tap into the infinite, intuitive wisdom within.

Emotions are therefore *not* intuitive impressions, they are our inner, spiritual *responses* or *reactions* to the thoughts we think and the actions we take. When we experience positive emotion we know we are on track with our Life Plan, when we feel negative emotion we know we have gone off course and we are no longer following Divine guidance. Our emotions tell us if we are still in vibrational alignment with all the life experiences and physical reality we wish to manifest, or not, in order to achieve our Soul Purpose and accomplish our Life Calling. Our emotions however do not tell us what we need to do to get back on track, or how we went off track to begin with. Emotions do not guide us by 'walking ahead' or by 'showing us the road', they merely follow us to 'cheer us on' or 'call us back' when we lose direction.

Three Levels Of Intuition

In recent years there has been growing controversy and debate in metaphysical circles over the difference between intuition versus psychic ability. Some argue that it is one and the same thing and that no distinction should be made, others maintain that using your intuition and being psychic are two totally different processes. Although much of this debate is nothing more than semantics, I have found it helpful when working with students to differentiate the *three levels of intuition.*

Level 1: Instinct. The most basic level of intuition is present and active in all living things on the planet and is better known as survival *instinct*. Our instincts are our internal mechanisms for physical survival that have been perfected and recorded over the ages in our cellular DNA. Our instincts are the result of an unconscious, animalistic urge for self-preservation innate to the human form. The physiological 'fight or flight' response is a perfect example of instinct. Another example is the fact that we are programmed to pay attention to other people and animals more than to non-living things, even if inanimate objects are the primary hazards in our environment. Experts do not agree on a set list of human instincts, since they do not agree on what should be considered an instinct, as opposed to merely being a biological or physiological impulse, or a learned or conditioned behavior. Instinctual behavior is however generally considered to be *automatic* and it *cannot be modified*. Try as you might, you may be able to suppress the urge you feel to act in a fight or flight situation, for example by pretending to stay calm, but *your body will respond* physiologically and it is very likely that you will ultimately lose control over the urge to either run away or take aggressive action to neutralize the threat you are perceiving. Instinctive actions are beyond our control and they are triggered by some event in the environment. Instinct is present in every human being.

Level 2: Intuition. Intuition is the *inner sensing* or *spontaneous knowing* that often remains unconscious or subconscious in many people, but is experienced by everyone on a conscious level from time to time. We all experience moments in life when we know the phone is going to ring; or that someone we love is in danger; or we hear an inner voice whisper our name; or we suddenly know where a hidden object is; or we are able to perfectly time boiling eggs without watching the clock; or we accurately anticipate what happens next; or we meet someone and immediately know we will marry that person; or we correctly sense we are doing the right or the wrong thing; or we have a hunch or 'gut' feeling that turns out to be right, or we know what caused something without being told, or we know where to find someone without knowing where they went. In whatever form our daily intuitive perceptions come, they are always timely and useful, and they are also essential in manifesting and maintaining an awakened and abundant Divine Life. Intuition is our spiritual *inner guidance system*. It is not an automatic survival impulse, nor is it a learned or conditioned behavior. It is instead the bridge between our physical survival and our spiritual mission. Some of us receive our inner guidance by seeing images, symbols or visions, or by listening to our inner voice, while others perceive by sensing it in our bodies, or simply through sudden flashes of knowledge, insight and inspiration. Interesting intuitive phenomena that many aware people experience at some point in their life may include:

- **Anomalous cognition**. Having knowledge without any logical explanation of where the knowledge came from; knowing answers to questions and solutions to problems without any rational explanation of how you could have known this information (also known as *claircognizance*).

- **Déjà vu**. Being in an unfamiliar place or situation, or meeting someone for the first time, and then having an overwhelming sense that the place, person or situation feels very familiar, or that it has happened to you before.

- **Precognition**. Perceiving information about future events before they occur; knowing what a future outcome will be.

- **Premonition.** Having a foreboding or forewarning of an impending future event (also known as a 'hunch' or a 'gut feeling').

- **Prophetic dreams** . Perceiving future events in dreams.

- **Retrocognition**. Inexplicable knowledge of past events; the opposite of precognition.

- **Telepathy**. Inexplicable transference of information from one person to another; 'mind to mind' communication; knowing what someone else is thinking or feeling without being in their presence or communicating with them.

We all experience intuition, because we are all spiritual beings in a human body. Most people, however, are in the state of Divine Disconnect and therefore they tend to remain mostly *unconscious* of their intuitive perceptions.

Research has shown that psychic phenomena are most often experienced in an altered state of consciousness, such as when we are sleeping or dreaming, under hypnosis, in a trance or under the influence of mind-altering substances like LSD. This indicates that each of us must have some level of natural or built-in capacity for extra sensory perception.

According to researcher and author Dr Diane Hennacy Powell surveys across several nations suggest that around one fifth of the general population report having clairvoyant experiences. Many of us also have spontaneous intuitive experiences in our childhood, but we are often conditioned not to pay attention. Sometimes children are even punished or reprimanded for allowing their "imagination to run wild".

Level 3: Psychic Ability. The third level of intuition is what is known as *psychic ability*. This form of intuition extends beyond the range of mere personal guidance to also encompass spiritual or metaphysical guidance *for the sake of others*. Natural intuition as described earlier is highly personal and mostly about taking care of our own *personal needs*. Psychic ability on the other hand shifts extra sensory perception from the personal sphere into the realm of the *impersonal*. Intuition is our direct inner guidance from our Divine Self towards achieving our unique Soul Purpose and Life Calling. Psychic ability on the other hand dwells in the realm of the *selfless, prophetic* and *archetypal*. Psychics, mediums and healers are *channels, messengers, conduits* or *surrogates*, which means that they do not only receive personal inner guidance from their own Divine Self, but they also have access to receiving guidance on behalf of their fellow man. These perceptions or messages may come from the other person's Higher Self, or from non-physical entities, or from the Divine Source, God, or Collective Unconscious. Psychics, mediums and healers have the natural ability to allow energy to flow through them to others, and on behalf of others.

Intuitive vs. Psychic

It is my belief that psychic ability is an innate talent or gift aimed at a specific Life Calling, while intuition is a highly personal aspect of our inner spiritual guidance system. We all possess our own, natural intuition, whether we are conscious or unconscious of it, but not everyone is psychic.

In my experience psychic ability is *hereditary*. There is however much disagreement on this subject. Some feel there is an undeniable *genetic link*; others feel that psychic ability is merely developed intuition and that anyone can achieve this level of perception, while others are of the opinion that a combination of *nature* and *nurture* is required to produce a talented psychic.

My conviction that there is a genetic connection is based on the fact that I am a hereditary psychic myself. I inherited this ability from my paternal grandmother. Many fellow psychics also report knowing of psychic family members, especially grandparents. For some reason the ability often skips one generation in some families. Many colleagues I have spoken to all report that they had exceptional extra sensory experiences in their childhood, or that they knew from a very young age that they were different from other children. You often also find a strong extra sensory bond between twins and siblings, and in some cases an incredible psychic connection is shared by identical twins, such as the USA's Terry and Linda Jamison and Chinhee and Sunhee Park. This psychic connection often found with twins suggests that there must be an underlying *genetic component* to psychic ability.

I am often asked why some psychics only discover or develop their ability much later in life, if they were born that way. In my experience from psychic development courses I have conducted over the years, some people are born exceptionally gifted and simply don't know it, or they suppress it initially, when they first discover it. For this reason some people only develop their psychic ability much later in life, often due to significant life events. In many cases it even seems that these life events may in fact happen to force them to become aware, or to accept their calling. For example, people who have had a near-death-experi-ence (NDE) sometimes report an increase in their psychic ability after the event. For others their psychic abilities surface during or after times of severe physical or emotional trauma, such as intense stress, serious illness, major accidents, or exposure to extreme physical danger. There are also known cases of psychics whose paranormal abilities surfaced or intensified due to brain injury. For example, the famous psychic medium Edgar Cayce fell off a fence post on his parents farm around age three and reportedly hit his head on a piece of wood with a nail protruding from it. The nail punctured his skull and caused injury to his brain, but there were no serious consequences, except that he became the most documented psychic in human history.

I do agree that psychic ability is a combination of both *nature* and *nurture,* as is the case with any other talents or genetic predis-positions we may be born with. What this means is that psychics are born with a *latent hereditary* or *genetic capacity*, but their ability is further developed by their upbringing, their childhood environment, education and life experiences.

In my case, however there was very little 'nurture', because I grew up in a society and home environment where my psychic abilities were not encouraged. In fact, I got into serious trouble for it in school, during my early teens. Adults were often shocked or annoyed when I blurted out their deepest secrets in front of strangers, and children were fearful because I sometimes pointed out the presence of entities or things they did not see. I eventually believed that my psychic ability was something to be ashamed of and I suppressed it for many years. I did have a near-death experience in my late 20's. I also experienced several other major life events that have contributed to the sharpening of my psychic abilities. But none of these experiences were the original source or cause of my extra sensory ability, because I was aware of having paranormal perceptions from a very young age. I have never attended any psychic development courses or mediumship circles.

Psychic DNA

It is my view we are all born with varying degrees of intuitive or metaphysical ability, the same way we are all born with an aptitude for playing music, creating art, doing math or participating in sports. We can all learn to develop our innate abilities; it does not necessarily mean we will all excel at it. Most of us can learn to play the piano, or draw pictures or play basketball and soccer. Some of us will even learn to do these things extremely well, but not all of us have the kind of talent that can be nurtured for us to become the next Ludwig van Beethoven, Pablo Picasso, Luciano Pavarotti, Barbra Streisand, Meryl Streep or Michael Jordan.

I do not, however, support the idea that hereditary psychics, mediums and healers are somehow spiritually superior or highly developed. I do not believe in hierarchy or a chain of command in the spiritual sense. There is no pecking order on 'the other side', because that would imply that in our original spiritual state some of us were 'imperfect' or more 'flawed' than others, before we came into this lifetime. It is my conviction that in our original spiritual state we are breathtakingly perfect, completely harmonious and utterly flawless. Some of us are not 'better' spiritual beings than others. That kind of thinking smacks of the values of the 'old think' Ego or False Self. Rank, status, levels and hierarchy are all man-made concepts often used to oppress, suppress, control and exclude others. In my mind these things are not of Spirit.

So, if psychics are not spiritually more evolved, why are they born with 'psychic genes' or into 'psychic families'? And what does genetics or hereditary have to do with spirituality anyway?

Well, it is quite simple really. To have exceptional psychic ability is a Life Calling and therefore a purpose or mission that the psychic, medium, channeler or healer chose as part of their Life Plan, before they came into this lifetime. A soul on a mission to act as an *energetic conduit* or *surrogate* on behalf of others will need the right kind of *physical instrument* or *material form* for the job, as well as the ideal *nurturing environment*. They will need a human body that is genetically equipped with the necessary capacity for receiving, processing and transferring significant amounts of metaphysical energy at high frequencies and intensities.

In other words, the soul who plans to enter into the Life Calling of a psychic, medium, channeler or healer chooses before birth a set of parents from certain families with a history of psychic talent, who will provide the ideal genetic and environmental influences needed to ultimately fulfill their Soul Purpose and Life Calling. Similarly, Beethoven, Picasso, Pavarotti, Streisand, Streep and Jordan also chose their parents and genetic heritage, which ultimately enabled them to do what they did best.

Intuitive development is therefore not about becoming a psychic reader, prophet or stage medium. It is instead a personal journey towards Higher Consciousness and a better quality of life.

Extra Sensory Perception

There are forms of perception that go beyond the five classic senses, which enable us to 'see' the previously 'unseen'. These intuitive or psychic pathways are known in parapsychology circles as extra sensory perception (ESP), or more commonly as the 'psychic senses', or 'clair senses', or 'astral senses' or simply as the 'sixth sense'. One could think of the sixth sense as an extension of our normal five senses of sight, hearing, smell, taste and touch.

ESP is much more common than most people realize and it impacts our lives on a daily basis. It is interesting to note how our extra sensory perceptions have found their way into our everyday language. How often do you hear people say the following words when they are trying to communicate a gut feeling or share a deeper, intuitive insight?

I smell a trouble

It was a bitter-sweet moment

Do you see what I mean?

It just feels right

Then suddenly, out of the blue...

It does not ring a bell

Do you also smell a rat?

I get the picture!

I can taste the success

We just clicked

I don't feel good about this

I knew that was going to happen!

Things are looking up

The pathways of ESP enable us to perceive that which is *beyond the normal range of perception.* Everything in the Universe consists of energy vibrating at different frequencies. Some energy vibrations, however, are at frequencies that are above or below our *normal spectrum* or range of perception. In other words, there are vibrations that we generally cannot see, hear, smell, taste, sense or feel. A simple example of this would be a dog whistle which cannot be heard by the naked human ear. In fact, our normal human perception is very limited, because we know that animals can often smell or hear things we humans cannot. The pathways for intuitive and psychic perception include:

- **Clairvoyance** *(clear seeing).* Seeing what is hidden from ordinary sight, or to see things the naked eye cannot see. It includes a variety of mental imagery, symbols and inner visions. Some people use this term to mean the same thing as 'being psychic', but it really describes only a specific type of extra sensory experience. A person who is clairvoyant receives inner guidance in the form of visual images or through 'inner vision'. It involves *mental imagery* perceived in the mind's eye. Some people report seeing brief visual 'flashes', while others experience animated visions that can be described as a 'mental movie'. Clairvoyant visions can include diverse imagery that varies from person to person and is more often than not symbolic and unique to that person. On an intuitive level these impression are mostly vague and fleeting and they may include among other things archetypal symbols, colors, numbers, letters, geometric shapes, people's faces, or actual scenes or events. The images may come suddenly in a flash, or develop over time as you focus on retrieving it.

- **Clairaudience** *(clear hearing).* Clairaudient impressions come to us as a clear message or sound in our mind in the form of an 'inner voice'. These mental sounds, or inner voices, can best be described as *audible thinking.* So it is kind of like of thinking aloud in your 'mind's ear', but note that it does not involve rational, logical thinking. Clairaudient impressions may also come as humming, whistling, vibrations, musical tones (bells ringing, flute sounds), buzzing, singing, ringing in the ears, or clear and distinct words. Intuitive clairaudience is most commonly experienced in dreams, or in altered states of consciousness, for example, just before going to sleep or waking up.

- **Clairsentience** *(clear sensing).* Energy perception experienced as a tactile or physical sensation. It is the ability to receive information or spiritual messages through intuitive 'sensing' or 'feeling', either by feeling the energy with your hands, or by sensing it emotionally or energetically in your body. Clairsentience is often the first psychic ability to surface in gifted children and normally it is the first experiences adults have who develop psychic ability later in life. It forms the *basis* or *foundation* of all intuition and it is the most prevalent psychic ability among professional psychics and mediums. Typical clairsentient experiences include 'hunches', 'gut feelings' and other physical sensations, such as itching, chills, goose bumps, temperature changes, hair standing on end, and pressure on the crown of the head.

- **Clairtangency** *(clear touching)*. A distinct form of clairsentience, which is the ability to touch an object and 'read' its energy imprints, or to know information about the person who owns the object. Clairtangency is used to practice *psychometry* and is often used in crime scene investigations. Healers and medical intuitives can often also scan a patient's body with their hands to read the energy of their patients.

- **Clairempathy** *(clear feeling)*. Another distinct form of clairsentience which refers to the extra sensory perception of *emotions* and *physical symptoms* in others. The empathic person or 'empath' is an *energetic surrogate* or *conduit* for the feelings of people, animals and plants around them, directly experiencing their emotions, and in some cases also feeling somatic symptoms including pain, nausea, vertigo, fever and congestion. Unconscious empaths, who are unaware of their clairempathic ability, typically absorb all kinds of unwanted emotional and somatic energy wherever they go without understanding, for example, why they suddenly feel nausea or vertigo; or why they are suddenly overwhelmed with extreme sadness and anxiety, when there is nothing in their environment for them to be sad or anxious about. However, do not confuse clairempathy with normal human empathy. Normal empathy is an affective (emotion) and cognitive (thought) process based on observation, logical thinking, perspective-taking, reasoning and an appropriate emotional response. Normal empathy therefore is the ability to 'place yourself in another person's shoes' or the knack to truly understand where others are coming from; to see things from their perspective and relate to how it is making them feel. Clairempathy however is an energy perception or a claisentient response that typically has no rational, logical or sensory origin.

- **Clairalience** *(clear smelling)*. Also known as Clairolfaction or Clairessence, it is the extra sensory perception of smells or odors with no explicable origin. According to a recent survey among more than 2000 mediums worldwide, it is estimated that approximately 90% of all mediums experience psychic smelling from time to time. The most commonly reported smells are tobacco smoke and the smell of roses or perfume.

- **Clairgustance** *(clear tasting).* This sense typically accompanies clairalience and it refer to the extra sensory perception of tastes or flavors. Clairalients often experience associated tastes, along with the particular smells. It makes sense that this partnership exists, since our normal physical sense of taste and smell also go hand-in-hand.

- **Claircognizance** *(clear knowing).* Spontaneous 'knowing' or insight. This pathway enables us to intuitively access or receive *intrinsic knowledge* in the form of ideas, concepts, or answers, as well as knowledge of things from the past, present, or future, without having received the information in any normal manner of transfer. You simply just "know" the answer to something, but you can't back up your statement with any proof or facts, or you cannot explain how this information came to you. The knowing is just there. Claircognizance often comes in the form of sudden insights and or a clear understanding regarding a question or situation in life, with a clear certainty of the correctness of the information. The claircognizant also has inexplicable knowledge of certain places, events, or people. Author and angel intuitive Doreen Virtue describes claircognizants as those people who are often known as "know-it-alls". As children, they seem to know too much and always have an answer for everything. Claircognizants tend to finish other people's sentences or change the subject, because they often already know what you are going to say.

Identifying Your Dominant Clairs

How we receive intuitive guidance is a highly personal matter that differs from person to person. No two people perceive intuitive impressions in exactly the same way and therefore a 'one-size-fits-all' approach is impossible when it comes to intuitive development.

Most people typically have one or two dominant or preferred intuitive 'channels' through which they perceive beyond the physical senses. In my experience, our preferred or dominant pathways depend on both our *genetic predisposition* and our Life Calling. For example, if your Life Calling is to be a composer of music, it would make most sense for your preferred pathway to be clairaudience, as you would need to develop a capacity for extra sensory auditory input when you receive *intuitive inspiration* or channeled compositions from a Higher Source.

An excellent example of how we differ from each other in our perceptions is a well-known prism experiment where they cast light through a prism to project the full spectrum of rainbow colors onto a blank sheet of paper. Test subjects were then asked to mark the borders of each color on the sheet as it appeared to them. Amazingly, some people saw more red, while others saw a larger violet section, and so forth. We are all unique and we all perceive differently, even within the normal range of perception.

Our pathway for intuitive perception is also connected to our preferred learning style. Teachers will tell you that around 40% of students prefer to learn visually, while 20 to 30% prefer auditory information or listening, while the remaining 30 to 40% are more drawn to kinesthetic or tactile input. We don't all perceive the world in the same way. We all have a preferred way to access information. To help you identify your dominant intuitive sense try the following questionnaire.

Imagine each of the following real-life scenes and note your first and most spontaneous impression for each. You will need a notepad and pen for this. I find it helps with some of my students to first read the brief description for each scene and then to close your eyes to create an imaginary version of that scene in your mind. What is the first impression or perception that you become aware of?

For example, if the description is, "you are walking on a beautiful beach at sunset", what is the first thing that comes to mind: do you see the waves crashing, or do you hear the roaring of the ocean, or do you feel the sand between your toes, or do you smell the fresh sea breeze or do you taste the salt in the air? If your first impression was that you "heard the roaring of the ocean", then you make note of it.

1) *Walking on the beach*

    See ☒ Hear ☐ Feel ☐ Smell ☐ See

2) Sitting near a waterfall

    See ☐ Hear ☐ Feel ☐ Smell ☐ See

3) At a friend's birthday party

    See ☐ Hear ☐ Feel ☐ Smell ☐ See

4) Taking a bubble bath

    See ☐ Hear ☐ Feel ☐ Smell ☐ See

5) Finding a parking space at the supermarket

    See ☐ Hear ☐ Feel ☐ Smell ☐ See

6) Making coffee

    See ☐ Hear ☐ Feel ☐ Smell ☐ See

7) Driving to work in peak traffic

    See ☐ Hear ☐ Feel ☐ Smell ☐ See

8) Buying fast food at a drive thru

    See ☐ Hear ☐ Feel ☐ Smell ☐ See

9) Eating out in a restaurant

    See ☐ Hear ☐ Feel ☐ Smell ☐ See

10) The last time you went on a holiday

    See ☐ Hear ☐ Feel ☐ Smell ☐ See

11) Your first childhood memory

    See ☐ Hear ☐ Feel ☐ Smell ☐ See

Add up the number of 'checks' you have for each kind of sensory impression. It is very likely that you will have a variety of senses checked depending on the nature of the particular scene, but you will find that one or two of your senses will have received the most the checks, indicating that this is probably your dominant mode of receiving intuitive information.

Requesting A Symbol

The following exercise is a fun way to explore your unique intuitive language. The aim is to ask your Divine Self a direct question and then receive an intuitive answer in the form of a sign or a symbol. Note that intuitive symbols are not necessarily images or shapes. It could be a sound, a smell, a feeling or even a taste. The kind of inner symbols or signs you receive will depend a lot on which of your intuitive senses are most dominant.

1) **Ground, center and shield yourself.** Start with your usual grounding and centering routine. Remember to include a psychic protection exercise and an appropriate affirmation or intention, for example:

   I am connected to the Divine Self. My inner vision is free from the restraints of time and space. I am intuitively connected to the past, present and future. I see all that I need to guide me toward my highest good.

2) **Clear your mind of all thoughts and distractions.** Imagine your mind to be a tranquil lake. See it as a peaceful, silent sheet of water that extends to all sides around you and off into the horizon.

3) **Visualize above your head a bright guiding star or spotlight**. This star or light is your Divine Self. Ask your Divine Self to communicate with you and feel it shining its gentle, warm and reassuring light on you. Feel yourself opening to receive inner guidance.

4) **Ask your Divine Self whatever question you wish to ask.** Phrase it carefully so that you can understand the symbolic answer when it comes. Remember the soul

speaks in symbols, so don't expect a simple rational or logical answer. It might be a good idea to spend some time beforehand to formulate your question appropriately. Avoid "yes or no" questions, because the answer will probably disappoint or confuse you. Instead of asking, "Will I find a better job soon?" it will be more effective to ask, "What can I do to find a better job soon?" or "How will I find a better job soon?"

5) **Become quiet inside and wait for the answer.** When a symbol or sign appears, accept it as your message. If you do not receive any sign or symbol, it may be that you are blocking the process with your rational mind and it may help to create a 'catalyst'. Simply tell yourself that when you hear a loud tone the symbol will appear, or when you clap your hands a sign will surface. Then imagine the sound of the tone in your mind, or clap your hands, and perceive what symbol comes to you.

6) **Express gratitude and thank your Divine self** for the meaningful guidance you have received.

Developing The Clairs

The following exercise is designed to develop your intuitive senses. You will find that some parts of the exercise are easier than others, simply because some of your senses are more dominant than others. This exercises aims to involve all of the 'clair senses'. It is a long exercise, and can be broken down into shorter sessions if preferred.

1) **Ground, center and shield yourself.** Start with your usual grounding and centering routine. Remember to include a psychic protection exercise and an appropriate affirmation or intention.

2) **Visualize above your head a bright guiding star or spotlight**. This star or light is your Divine Self. Ask your Divine Self to communicate with you. See how the light above you shines down on you and envelopes your whole

body. You are basking in the bright light of your Higher Being. Feel yourself opening to receive guidance.

3) **Become aware of your physical sensations**. What do you feel? What do you sense? Are there traces of tension or discomfort anywhere in your body? What is it trying to tell you? Do you feel cold or warm? Do you feel light or heavy? What is your gut telling you?

4) **Imagine your mind is a radio.** See how your mind radio is currently silent because it is switched off. Visualize above your head a satellite dish or radio tower that is transmitting a powerful radio signal. This tower or dish is your Divine Self. Ask your Divine Self to communicate with you. Switch on and tune into the radio station. See the signal transmission from your Divine Self intensify as it reaches the antenna of your mental radio. Feel the gentle warm and reassuring buzzing vibration of the 'radio transmission' as it travels through your whole body. Feel yourself opening to receive inner guidance. Keep turning the radio dial searching for the perfect wavelength or bandwidth to clearly pick up the broadcast from your Higher Self. Listen for any inner sounds, voices, whispers, or tonal impressions you perceive.

5) **Imagine your mind as a blank screen.** You are in a movie theatre or an art gallery, and in front of you is a white screen or blank canvas. Visualize your Divine Self as a bright light above your head coming from a projector. See how each of the colors of the chakras is being projected onto the empty screen in front of you in the form of a sharp laser light. Starting at the top with the crown chakra, spend a minute or two on each color: violet, indigo, blue, green, yellow, orange, red. See how each color is projected onto the blank screen in front of you and how it begins to form a basic shape. What do you see? Is it a triangle, a square, a circle, a rectangle, a spiral? Then see how the basic shape begins to 'shape shift' into a symbol or an image. What does it become? What do you see projected on the screen? Imagine each of the final images or symbols materializing into tangible matter on

the screen and reach out to take the object that it has become. See yourself picking up and placing each object on the floor in front of you. Return to the blank screen and repeat the process with the next color.

6) **Explore the manifested objects on the floor in front of you**. Pick each object up and bring it closer to your face. Study it carefully in its finest detail. Is it dull or bright? What color is it? Is the texture complex or simple? Now smell the object. Does it have a distinct smell? What does it smell like? Touch it with your tongue. Does it have a taste? What does it taste like? Press it against your neck or your cheek. What does it feel like? Is it cold or warm? Hard or soft? Rough or smooth?

7) **Imagine gathering all the objects together and then pressing them together in a ball.** Keep working on crunching it all together into a ball. Gradually see how the ball becomes smaller and smaller. Finally roll the little ball between the palms of your hands and feel how it becomes even smaller. When the ball reaches the size of a pea, imagine placing it in the middle of your forehead and how it becomes your 'third eye'.

8) **Express gratitude** and thank your Divine self for the meaningful guidance you have received. Slowly return your attention to the world around you and gradually open your eyes.

Dreamwork

One of the best ways to develop your intuitive ability and receive profound inner guidance is to explore your dreams. Dreaming is 'Intuition 101'. Dreams are probably the most important way in which the Divine Self guides us *unconsciously,* while we are still in the state of Divine Disconnect.

Dreams serve *three essential purposes* in our life experience. They serve the *past* by helping us to process events of the day, come to terms with outstanding issues from the past and rehearse and store new skills we have recently learned. Dreams serve the *present* by attempting to resolve issues or concerns we currently face in our lives, as well as reviewing our daily progress report on our path towards fulfilling our Life Plan. Dreams further serve the *future* by acting as a 'virtual reality workshop' in which we can explore future possibilities and create our destiny.

I know personally from numerous direct experiences that we definitely do dream the future. In fact, I use dreams in my work almost every day. I believe we either create our own future in our dreams or the Divine Self reveals future events to us in our dreams. Either way, I believe this is the reason why we sometimes experience moments of *déjà vu*. When we are experiencing déjà vu during the day it is merely dream recall, often years after we envisioned or foresaw today's event in our dreams.

There are many examples of famous precognitive dreams in history. In 1865, two weeks before he was assassinated, Abraham Lincoln had a precognitive dream about his own funeral, and when the Titanic sank in 1912 several people came forward reporting they had prophetic dreams about the event before it happened. Napoleon's defeat at Waterloo was foreseen in a dream. There also many accounts of prophetic dreams in the Bible and Joan of Arc also predicted her own death in a dream.

Many people believe they seldom or never dream, but research has shown that *everybody dreams.* In fact, we enter the dream state every 90 minutes throughout the night. On average we dream about five times per night and our dream time ranges from three minutes to as much as 45 minutes. Scientists have also found that dreaming definitely serves a vital role in our health and normal functioning. For example, in a recent study subjects were not allowed to dream all night long. They were allowed to get their normal eight hours of sleep, but they were awakened at the beginning of each dream cycle. After only three days of this 'dream deprivation' they showed symptoms irritability, hallucinations, lack of concentration and even signs of psychosis. When they were finally allowed to dream again, they all spend longer periods of time in the REM dream state to make up for lost time, and their functioning returned to normal.

Dream Journaling

The best way to explore your dreams, and gain greater access to its intuitive and prophetic content, is to start keeping a dream journal or diary. A good way to start is to recall the last thing you saw or felt, just before you woke up. Review your notes from time to time. You will be surprised at how much of what you dream actually does come true later. You will also find that many solutions to life problems come up in your dreams and you will be amazed at the inspirational ideas you will gather from your dreams.

If you do not have enough time in your day to spend on intuitive development, at least make an effort to include dream-work in your daily spiritual practice. Becoming more aware and conscious of the contents of your dreams is essential to a more intuitive way of life.

Dream Recall

To effectively keep a dream journal, and to also do deliberate dreamwork, such as 'dream incubation', we must first improve our *dream recall.* Dream recall is initially often a problem for many people, but it can be easily improved with just a little bit of patience and effort.

To improve your dream recall you must be motivated and deter-mined to improve your recall ability. It is a known fact that after we wake up we forget approximately half of our most recent dream *within five minutes.* After only ten minutes we forget as much as 90% of what we had dreamt. Be patient, it won't come without some work at first, but over time, and with frequent practice, it will become much easier.

Dream recall is a natural ability we all have. If you think back you will remember that as a child you used to remember your dreams quite vividly and in much greater detail. You still have that ability; you just lost touch with it during the time of the Divine Disconnect. Now the time has come for you to reawaken your dream consciousness.

1) **Set your intention to improve your dream recall.**
   During your daily meditations or other spiritual practices, make some time for manifesting a higher level of dream

recall. Set your intention to increase your recall by adding a dream recall affirmation to your daily set, or do a daily prayer to ask for assistance in your dream recall efforts, or visualize your dream journal filled with pages and pages of detailed dream notes. Imagine clearly in your mind's eye how well you will remember your dreams every morning and experience the intense sense of satisfaction you will feel when you successfully recall all of your dreams.

2) **At bedtime review your dreams from the past few nights.** I usually do this in cycles of one week's worth of dreams. This quality time with your dream notes stimulates your dream memory and allows time for you to interpret your dreams based on the events of the day. Try to identify patterns and synchronicities.

3) **Do your usual grounding, centering and shielding routine** when you are getting ready to go to sleep.

4) **Ask your Divine Self to help you remember your dreams more clearly and accurately.** Visualize how you will wake up and remember everything you dreamed. See yourself writing everything down in great detail in your dream journal. It is recommended that you wake up without an alarm clock, as this tends to negatively affect recall. Set your alarm clock for 15 minutes later than your usual time and visualize how you will wake up at the normal time *without* the alarm.

5) **The moment you wake up, keep your eyes closed and stay in the same body position.** Immediately shut your eyes if they are already open. If you already moved or shifted your body, return to the position you were in when you woke up and then relax and remain motionless.

6) **Recall as many details of your dream as you can remember.** Make a mental list of as many images, feelings and sensory impressions as you can recall. Immediately record everything in your journal. Include everything, no matter how vague or insignificant it may

seem. As you write your notes down you will find that you will remember even more details. Remember to add any symbols, images and drawings you may recall or may help you remember or interpret the dream better.

7) **Express gratitude and thank your Divine self** for the meaningful guidance you have received.

Dream Incubation

Dream incubation is a *deliberate dreamwork* technique in which we 'set the stage' or theme for a specific dream to occur. The aim is to make intentional use of the intuitive potential of your dreams to create a more awakened and abundant Divine Life. You can use dream incubation simply to improve your intuitive awareness or you can apply it to receive guidance, answers or solutions to current life challenges or spiritual questions you may be facing.

Dream incubation enables you to more consciously direct the inner guidance you receive, instead of being merely a passive receiver of intuitive information from the Divine Self. You may be interested to know that a significant portion of the contents of this book is based on guidance I received through dreams, both spontaneous and deliberate.

1) **Focus on improving your dream recall ability first**, before attempting any kind of deliberate dreamwork. It is pointless to set up intentional dreams and then being unable to recall those dreams the next day. Practice your *dream recall* for a few days, or even weeks if necessary. Be patient with yourself and take your time.

2) **Set your intention for your dream incubation.** Decide what it is you hope to achieve or receive in your incubated dream. What is your goal? Perhaps you are seeking the answer to a spiritual question, or the solution to a problem at work or in your relationship. Maybe you need guidance on a particular health issue, or assistance in making a decision about a major financial investment. Or maybe you need an inspirational idea or creative concept for your next artistic project. Try to find some-

thing significant that applies directly to your life at this present time.

3) **Do your usual grounding, centering and shielding routine** when you are getting ready to go to sleep.

4) **Conceptualize your incubation question or problem clearly.** Ask your Divine Self to provide you with clear guidance and request that you will be able to remember everything in your dream in detail.

5) **Focus on your incubation until you fall asleep.** As you drift off to sleep, keep your question firmly focused in your mind. If you find that you are having other distracting thoughts, simply witness them without paying attention and return to your incubation focus point.

6) **Record as much as you can remember the moment you wake up.** Follow the same guidelines for waking up and for initial recall as described earlier in the dream recall exercise. Do not try to analyze or interpret any of the dream content at this point. Suspend all logic and reason and do not judge what you write down. Merely record everything you can recall, whether it makes sense or not. Once you have finished recording your dream put your journal away for a while. Go about your normal daily routine. Revisit your journal later when you have time and read through your notes.

7) **Reflect on the content of your dream and identify any associations and interpretations that may arise.** The answer is often very clear and obvious, especially the more experienced you become at dream interpretation. If it still makes no sense, leave it for another day or two. Repeat your incubation if necessary, sometimes there is a simple missing link that you did not recall the first morning. Even if you don't remember your dream or you were unable to interpret it, know that your efforts are never in vain when it comes to intuitive work. Your deliberate dreamwork always has an effect on your life. Often the answer is merely being processed on a subcon-

scious level and it may come to you as an unexpected insight or sudden revelation later on.

8) **Express gratitude and thank your Divine self** for the meaningful guidance you have received.

Everyday Intuition

Intuitive development should not be restricted to a small portion of your day, or only as a part of your regular spiritual practice. Intuitive awareness is not an exercise or visualization, it is a *lifestyle*. In fact, inner guidance from the Divine Self is one of the three *foundational pillars* for creating a truly awakened and abundant Divine Life. Inner guidance is key to accomplishing the other two pillars, namely achieving your Soul Purpose and Life Calling.

To live a fulfilling and purposeful life we first need to learn to trust and follow our intuitive 'vibes' in everything we do and everywhere we go. Being intuitively aware is our *natural state* of being in the world. When we engage in intuitive development, we are not learning a new skill; we are merely awakening an ability that has always been within us. We are simply returning to our former way of being, when we were children and before we entered into the state of Divine Disconnect. Becoming increasingly in tune with your intuitive awareness should therefore become a *new way of life*.

Practicing your intuitive awareness is something you can do all day and every day. You are constantly receiving a *stream of inner guidance* from the Divine Self. All you need to do is become more attuned to that inner stream of consciousness. Become more *mindful* of your inner perceptions during your normal daily activities. When you 'feel something' like a hunch or a gut feeling, or you hear an 'inner voice' or you see a visual impression flash through your mind, or you pick up an unexpected smell or a very unusual taste in your mouth, do not disregard or ignore it. Instead, *focus* on the perception, *zoom in* on that impression. Don't over-analyze or rationalize your impressions, merely observe them with deliberate attention. Take your perceptions seriously, even if you have no idea what they mean. In time you will begin to notice patterns and unique symbolic meanings to the impressions you get. You will begin to understand the language of your soul and the meanings of what you perceive will become clearer.

Your intuitive perceptions might urge you to take some kind of action or inform you of things that may be coming up in the future. You might know what to expect before you enter into certain situations, or you might have a distinct 'gut reaction' to people you meet or places you go to. The more you become aware of your intuitive impressions, and the more you acknowledge them and experiment, the more you will increase your intuition, until it becomes an automatic and organic part of your life.

A great way to introduce intuition into your every day routine is to play the "I wonder game". I was introduced to this game through the work of Sonia Choquette, one of the world's leading experts on intuitive development. It is also a wonderful game to play with your children, to teach them intuitive awareness at a very young age. The game is very simple. Basically it is a game of conjecture in which you ask yourself questions beginning with the words "I wonder...." The aim is to become more mindful of the world around you and to just let your mind wander. Try to look at the world through 'new eyes'. Ask questions like the following.

I wonder who is calling me on the phone?

I wonder who will greet me first when I arrive at work?

I wonder what color car will drive by next?

I wonder what will be on special at the store today?

I wonder what the first song will be that I hear on the radio?

Another version of this game I find very effective is what I call "I wonder what's on TV?" The best way to do it is seated with your back to your television set, or you could blindfold yourself, or simply close your eyes while facing your television set. Without being able to see the screen, begin to flick through the channels one at a time using the remote control. Pause on each channel and spend a few seconds listening to the sounds and voices coming from the television speakers. Then focus for a moment on any intuitive impressions that you may perceive. What do you see, hear, feel, smell, taste or sense? What do you perceive in your mind's eye? Be careful to not rationalize or over analyze, merely witness your impressions. When you are ready, guess who or what is on the television screen.

What do the people or places look like?
What is their hair color?
What is their skin tone and their appearance?
What clothes are they wearing?
What scenery or buildings are in the background?

Once you are ready, open your eyes and see how accurate you were. Keep playing this game, even if you are not very successful at first. You will be amazed how much your success rate will improve over time.

Synchronistic Signs

We do not only receive intuitive guidance on the inside, we also receive it from the outside world. The Divine, God or Source will provide you with guidance and confirmations through external signs and synchronicities, and will teach you many profound and valuable spiritual lessons in the process. Once you become spiritually awakened it becomes essential to raise your awareness in everyday life. Each and every person, event or experience is a synchronicity. There are no 'accidents' or coincidences. Every-thing happens for a reason.

For example, one of my clients received very compelling confirmation of the signs she had been questioning for years. She was in the midst of a major life transition and a personal trans-formation. For quite some time we had been discussing the signs she was receiving in the form of popular songs. She kept hearing them: over the radio, in the gym and the shopping mall. Once she even heard it on the phone, after she was placed on hold by a call centre. The signs kept coming consistently; every time she asked for them, she received them in the form of a song. But the doubt secretly crept back into her mind soon after. What if it was just her imagination?

There was a specific song she has always associated with a certain special person in her life, for a very particular reason. She had now heard this song on three separate occasions at very sig-nificant moments. Each time it happened, she was either with this person, or she was specifically thinking of him, or she was asking for a sign about him. I explained to her that we sometimes receive the same signs more than once, in order to overcome our doubt or fear. In her case she was getting her signs in three's. But I also knew that she had to see proof of this for herself, before she would feel truly content. I therefore suggested she ask for a confirmation of the fact that important signs come to her in three's.

The answer came sooner than anticipated. She was in a public place when she received my response via text message. She did not even have to ask for confirmation. The minute she opened my message on her cell phone, even before she had finished reading all of it, she discovered three pennies on a seat she was about to sit down on. She immediately sent me the news and I then assured her that pennies are a well-known sign for many people all over the world. I also urged her to keep the pennies in a safe place and have another look at them later, because sometimes the dates or other engravings on them also have special meanings.

The next day I received a follow-up: "Thanks Anthon! You wouldn't believe this, but later yesterday I saw three feathers. Well, actually four, I saw one at first and did a double take – but dismissed it, then an hour or so later saw a cluster of three feathers together on the floor."

An interesting example I read about very recently is of a 13 year old boy, Addison Logan who lives in Wichita, USA. He bought an old Polaroid camera at a garage sale on Thursday, May 24, 2012 and when he got home he opened it and discovered an old photograph still stuck inside. He showed the picture to his grandmother, Lois Logan, who asked where he had found the picture, because she did not recognize it. Addison said, "In that old camera." Lois at first did not believe him, she was too shocked and surprised, because the picture was in fact of her son and Addison's deceased uncle, Scott Logan, and a girl he dated when he was about 17 years old. Scott died in a tragic car accident in 1989, years before Addison's birth. Scott's older brother Jeff later told *The Wichita Eagle* newspaper, "When you get something like that, that's almost like a sign telling us, 'Hey, everything's all right, I'm still here."

Messages from the spiritual realm are potentially life-changing, but they so often pass us by, unnoticed, mostly because of our lack of awareness. In fact, some of us are so stubborn or oblivious to our metaphysical reality that we first have to receive a pebble, then a rock and finally a 'ton of bricks', before we eventually sit up and pay attention! First there is a message, then a lesson and finally comes the crisis. To experience the wonder of witnessing the effect of such miraculous signs and intuitive symbols in your life, all you need to do is be more mindful and increase your awareness. Don't allow yourself to let your mystical reminders and spiritual signposts pass you by forever.

Signs and signals from the Divine Self always have a purpose. Most often they are important guideposts or 'traffic signs' along our life path, confirming our choices, decisions and actions. Sometimes we receive these messages from the spiritual realm to console us in times of distress or sadness, while at other times they come as warnings, urging us to proceed with caution. Receiving your special signs and reading your special symbols is your Divine right, and a basic awareness that anyone can develop. Some gurus would have you believe that this is a complex art or science, or that it requires special psychic abilities or years of study and practice. The truth is that this is a blessing freely available to all of us, regardless of whom we are or what we believe in. All you need to do is ask, and you will receive.

The best way to start reading signs is by simply becoming more aware. Take more notice of the small wonders that happen in the world around you every day. Look out for patterns and synchronicities, because there are no 'coincidences' in life. Everything happens for a reason; there are no windfalls, only godsends. Soon you will begin to discover your unique set of personal symbols and patterns. Your special signs could come in the form of dreams, colors, words, numbers, sounds, songs, computer messages, clouds, images, animals, people, places or specific objects, like coins and feathers. They could also come in a certain order or they may be repeated a certain number of times. The list of possibilities and combinations is truly endless. It is also very different for each individual, depending on your belief system, as well as your cultural background and your unique personality and interests.

Always keep your expectations simple and don't expect weird riddles or complex messages. The message is always very clear and direct. The intention of the Divine is after all to communicate with you and guide you, not to confuse, frighten or mislead you. Also, use some common sense. If you never listen to the radio, you certainly cannot expect it to become a conduit for spiritual communication. Your signs will show up in accessible ways that complement your lifestyle, or match your personal outlook. All you need to do is become more aware and be open to the process.

The Universe is an abundant and interactive place of wonder and magic; it is ready and waiting to respond to your needs. You can heal your life and make all your wishes come true. Your inner Divinity wants the opportunity to guide you and protect you on your journey through life.

Acknowledge your Higher Being and learn to trust your intuition. You have inside of you a deep well of wisdom and you are connected to everything in the Universe. You are part of an infinite and ever-expanding grid of spiritual consciousness. Use your signs and godsends to redesign your life and create the destiny you truly want. Learn to apply your Divine 'early warning system' to avoid unnecessary obstacles and setbacks along the way. All you need to do is ask. Reclaim what is rightfully yours.

PART III

ACCOMPLISHING
YOUR LIFE CALLING

9

MANIFESTING YOUR DESIRES

Deliberately creating, attracting and manifesting the abundance and prosperity you need to lead a joyous and fulfilling life is essential to Divine Living. You are a powerful creator of your own reality and the master of your own destiny. You can be, do or have anything your Soul Purpose or Life Calling requires in this lifetime.

Now that you are well on your way to realigning with your inner Divinity, through daily spiritual practice and shifting your thoughts, emotions, senses and intuition to a higher level of consciousness, you are better equipped and ready to apply the art of manifesting in your daily life. Your thoughts, emotions, senses and intuition will be your 'power tools' for creating and attracting all that you wish for and desire.

The ability to create, attract and manifest all manner of life experiences and material things is one of the 'superhero powers' you brought with you as a spiritual being when you incarnated into this lifetime. But you have lost touch with the ability to consciously create and attract that which you desire when you gave up 'magical thinking' in your childhood and instead embraced the rational 'reality coma' of the Divine Disconnect. But now that most of your data gathering is complete and you have awakened spiritually, you are ready to embark on the next stage in your physical life experience. It is time for you to reclaim your sacred birthright and begin to lead a truly charmed and prosperous life as it was always intended.

The Truth About Manifesting

The Law of Attraction must be the Universal Law that is currently most misquoted, misrepresented and misunderstood in the self-help industry. The Universal Law of Attraction has become highly fashionable in recent years, since its rise to stardom in 2006 with the release of the inspirational film, *The Secret,* and the subsequent publication of the book by the same name a year later. Life coaches, motivational speakers, get-rich-quick gurus, psychic readers and even practitioners of ritual magick have all taken to tossing the term about - too often without a clear understanding of the true nature and meaning of this profound Universal Law.

The most important distinction that many people fail to make when applying the Law of Attraction in their lives is that the act of manifesting is in fact *dual in nature*, like all things in the Universe. Few of the modern proponents of the Law of Attraction - especially those who are merely out to attract wealth, success or romantic love - seem to know that there are in fact two universal laws that govern the process of manifesting, namely the *Law of Attraction* and the *Law of Creation.*

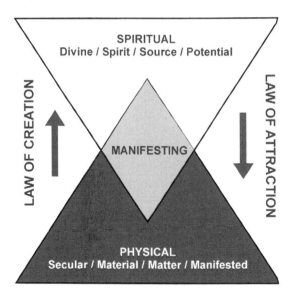

Manifesting is actually a *two-way process* of sending and receiving. Ernest Shurtleff Holmes wrote that "creation is first spiritual, through mental law, and then physical in its manifestation." To manifest something in this physical time-space reality two things need to happen. Firstly, we must create whatever it is we desire on a spiritual level, and then we must attract it into our physical life experience. The Law of Creation governs the *process of creating*, while the Law of Attraction governs the *process of attraction*. The end result of these two processes is *manifestation*.

By the way, I prefer to distinguish between the terms *manifestting* and *manifestation*. I often hear people speak of "the art of manifestation" or how to "master manifestation". The correct term should be "manifesting", because it is a verb referring to an action, namely the *process* of creating and attracting, while the term "manifestation" is a noun referring the ultimate *end result* or *outcome* of the process. Manifesting is something you do, while a manifestation is something physical or material you can see, hear, smell, taste, touch or feel.

The Law Of Creation

The Law of Creation is also known as the Law of Manifestation. I have also seen it referred to as the Law of 'Beamed Energy' and the Law of 'Action'. Esther-Abraham Hicks calls it the Law of Deliberate Creation. The Law of Creation states that *Consciousness is the Source of all Creation*. In other words, everything that exists in both the material and spiritual world, or the seen and unseen realms, is created through Universal Consciousness or Infinite Intelligence.

What this further implies is that we as co-conscious, sentient beings of Divine origins are also co-creators in this shared reality. Because we are all connected and created 'in the image of the Divine', or because we are holographic subcomponents of the Web of Consciousness, we all carry within us the same Divine creative power or ability to manifest. We create with our thoughts, words and beliefs, both consciously and subconsciously, intentionally and unintentionally.

The concept of the Law of Creation is found in many religions and spiritual traditions. One of the most often quoted examples is the Bible verse from John 1:1, "In the beginning was the Word, and the Word was with God, and the Word was God." A powerful, yet simple description of the Law of Creation in action can also be found in the first paragraphs of the Bible, in the book of Genesis, "The earth was without form and void, and darkness was upon the face of the deep; and the Spirit of God was moving over the face of the waters. And God said, "Let there be light"; and there was light."

Jesus Christ is an excellent example of someone who achieved his Soul Purpose and Life Calling during his lifetime. He lived in perfect harmony with the Laws of the Universe and continuously taught his followers how to practically apply the Laws of Creation and Attraction in their daily lives. Some examples of what he said about the Law of Creation include quotes from Matthew 9:29, "According to your faith will it be done to you"; Matthew 7:7, "Ask and it will be given to you; seek and you will find; knock and the door will be opened to you"; and also Mark 11:24, "Therefore I tell you, whatever you ask for in prayer, believe that you have received it, and it will be yours."

Another major advocate of the Laws of Creation and Attraction was Siddhartha Gautama, the founder of Buddhism. The Buddha said, "We are what we think. All that we are arises with our thoughts. With our thoughts we make the world." The Law of Creation is also found in Hinduism and the Vedic tradition of Karma. According to Karmic Law we shall reap what we sow, and what we send out into the world in the form of thoughts, words, and deeds - both the good and bad – will return to us in equal measure. Teachings involving the Laws of Creation and Attraction are also present in varying forms in Taoism, Shintoism, Judaism, Kabbalah, Neo-Paganism, Wicca and Shamanism.

New evolving theories and recent discoveries in science, particularly Quantum Mechanics, increasingly offer potential explanations for how the Laws of Creation and Attraction might work.

- Energy can be converted to matter

- Matter can become energy

- Matter consists of subatomic patterns of energy vibration

- Matter also exist as waves of probability

- The behavior of both matter and energy is influenced by our conscious observation of it

- Time and space may be an illusion

- Matter can exist in several places or dimensions at once

- There is an inter-connected, co-conscious oneness that underlies all matter

- The Universe is a web of consciousness

- The Universe is a hologram in which every subcomponent contains the encoding of the larger whole

All these theories in the 'new science' seem to support the ancient spiritual knowledge that *when we think, we create*. Thinking and believing is creating. Everything that exists in the material world originated as an intelligent thought and was *willed* into existence. New thought teacher Nona L. Brooks said, "Every created thing is Idea in Divine Mind before it is expressed."

This process of creation through ideas or thoughts takes place in all dimensions, planes and realms in the Universe. Intelligent creation through willful thought occurs on both the spiritual and material level. All matter that we physically perceive in the 'seen' world originates from a thought in the 'unseen' realm. Before a concrete, material object can be created or shaped through sheer will into material form, it must first exist as an abstract, intangible thought form.

Unfortunately, in the state of Divine Disconnection, while we are mostly focused upon basic physical survival, we confine ourselves to unconsciously creating only that which we need to stay alive from day to day and therefore we remain disempowered to fulfill our true Life Calling. We are spiritual beings experiencing a material existence, and we were not meant to fully relinquish our metaphysical capabilities when we arrive on this planet. We are meant to fully express our inner Divinity and our Higher Self in this lifetime, and we are destined to creatively expand the Universe through our thoughts, inspiration, imagination and desires.

In the early 1900's the New Thought author Thomas Troward explains the basis of Divine, or Cosmic Co-creation in the book *The Creative Process in the Individual.*

One of the earliest discoveries we all make is the existence of Matter. The bruised shins of our childhood convince us of its solidity, so now comes the question, Why does Matter exist? The answer is that if the form were not expressed in solid substance, things would be perpetually flowing into each other so that no identity could be maintained for a single moment. To this it might be replied that a condition of matter is conceivable in which, though in itself a plastic substance, in a fluent state, it might yet by the operation of will be held in any particular forms desired. The idea of such a condition of matter is no doubt conceivable, and when the fluent matter was thus held in particular forms you would have concrete matter just as we know it now, only with this difference, that it would return to its fluent state as soon as the supporting will was withdrawn. Now, this is precisely what matter really is, only the will which holds it together in concrete form is not individual but cosmic.

Troward refers to the "will which holds all matter together" as being *cosmic* and *not individual*. This is where many commercial proponents of deliberate creation go off track. They confuse the process of *individuation* with selfish *individualism.*

The Laws of Creation and Attraction are first and foremost *spiritual laws* reflecting the inherent selfless nature of the Divine. Our ability to create only extends as far as we are able to be truly reflective of the unconditional love, compassion and harmony that define our inner Divine origins. In other words, without a solid spiritual foundation and true alignment with the Divine Self our metaphysical creative power will remain limited and mostly unconscious; and the results of our manifesting efforts will leave much to be desired, or bring us very little happiness, or lasting contentment.

Unfortunately, true spiritual awareness and Higher Consciousness cannot be taught in weekend workshops and seminars. There are no "10 easy steps" to becoming a truly awakened spiritual being. Spiritual awareness cannot be bought, neither can it be faked or forced. It can only come spontaneously, sincerely and truthfully from within.

Thomas Troward states that the only effective way we can unleash the creative process is to have reverence for the Universal Law of Harmony and to be truly mindful of our Divine origins, which would prevent us from playing irresponsible "psychic pranks" with the godlike creative force we carry within, and instead we would use it only to meet our actual requirements or real needs.

When our eyes begin to open to the truth that we do possess this [creative] power the temptation is to ignore the fact that our power of initiative is itself a product of the similar power subsisting in the All-originating Spirit. If this origin of our own creative faculty is left out of sight we shall fail to recognize the Livingness of the Greater Life within which we live. We shall never get nearer to it than what we may call its generic level, the stage at which the Creative Power is careful of the type or race, but is careless of the individual; and so at this level we shall never pass into the Fifth Kingdom which is the Kingdom of Individuality.

Please note that the "Kingdom of Individuality" he refers to is not self-serving individualism, but instead it refers to "passing into" a Divine Life on Earth through the process of *individuation*. Troward thus makes it clear that true *individuation* can only be found in *spiritual awareness*.

In similar vein Robert Collier wrote in *The Secret of the Ages* that the Universal Mind expresses itself largely through the *individual*, but adds that true creative power can only become manifest when it is applied *in service* to others.

[The Universal Mind] is continually seeking an outlet. It is like a vast reservoir of water, constantly replenished by mountain springs. Cut a channel to it and the water will flow in ever-increasing volume. In the same way, if you once open up a channel of service by which the Universal Mind can express itself through you, its gifts will flow in ever-increasing volume and you will be enriched in the process.

The mistake many practitioners of deliberate creation and attraction make is that they attempt to create and attract the manifestation of all kinds of desires that are *outside the context of their Life Plan*. Yes, we can all do, have, or be anything we wish, as long as it serves our Soul Purpose and Life Calling. There must be balance, harmony and order in all things. It is Universal Law. Collier further explains that we often struggle to harness our inherent creative power because we have never focused all our diverse desires into "one great dominating desire".

You have a host of mild desires. You mildly wish you were rich, you wish you had a position of responsibility and influence, you wish you could travel at will. The wishes are so many and varied that they conflict with each other and you get nowhere in particular. You lack one intense desire, to the accomplishment of which you are willing to subordinate everything else.

This is why it is so vital to make an effort to identify your Soul Purpose and Life Calling, for until you have *clarity* on your *life mission* it will remain difficult to raise your vibrational frequency to a matching level where you will begin to create and attract the experiences and things you truly need to serve your own soul growth, as well as be of service to the rest of the world. Creating and attracting only becomes manifest to its full extent when it is applied *in line with our original Life Plan.*

At this point you may feel the need to ask, "But what about me, what about my personal needs, and wishes, and desires? How can I be, do, or have anything I desire, and then you tell me that it will not manifest if it does not serve the greater good?"

The answer is simple. The answer is in fact what this whole book is about. When you are truly awakened as a spiritual being in human form you will consistently and intuitively strive to align with the Divine Self and you will automatically desire only that which is in harmony with your Soul Purpose and Life Calling. Divine Living is a life of harmony with the self, others and the Universe. Remember the seven maxims of Divine Living?

Confucius said, "The more man meditates upon good thoughts, the better will be his world and the world at large." When you are living a truly Divine Life you simply will not have any overriding selfish needs and desires that are not in service of the greater good. That which you desire on the outside will reflect your connection and alignment with the Divine on the inside.

The Law of Attraction

The Law of Attraction in its most basic definition states that "like attracts like" and what this means is that "birds of a feather flock together". This Universal Law represents the magnificent magnetic power of the Conscious Universe to draw together similar energies for the purpose of creating, expanding and becoming. And because we are spiritual beings of Divine origins we also have this magnetic, creative force within us, which draws into our reality those things, people, events and circumstances that match our inner state of being. In other words, we attract life experiences that are consistent with our beliefs, thoughts, feelings and perceptions.

Deepak Chopra writes in *The Seven Spiritual laws of Success*,"Inherent in every intention and desire is the mechanics for its fulfillment. And when we introduce an intention in our pure potentiality, we put this infinite organizing power to work for us."

Everything you experience in your daily life comes to you because of the workings of the Law of Attraction. It is essential to gain a clear understanding of how the Law of Attraction works, because without this insight it is not possible to enjoy a purposeful, abundant Divine Life. Evidence of the effects of the Law of Attraction can be found everywhere in your immediate surroundings. Consider for a moment some of the people in your life, your friends, family, colleagues. Can you see how their personal outlook, attitudes, beliefs and typical state of being in the world reflect the reality of their life?

For example, those who always seem to be confident and assertive about their right to have money and to gather wealth, and who are truly generous in sharing their subsequent blessings, are the people who are usually the most prosperous and fulfilled. Meanwhile the ones who are constantly complaining about their lack of money, or are penny-pinching and always fearful of being cheated out of their money by others, or who persistently warn others of the 'evils of money', are also the people who never have enough money and are often over their ears in debt.

Many of us are also familiar with the stereotypical elderly aunt or uncle in the family who is always complaining of illness and therefore is constantly suffering poor health. And what about your widowed mother, divorced sister or single girlfriend who whines about all men being "abusive idiots or chauvinistic fools", and how she hates them, and then she simply cannot understand why she always meets the worst kind of men.

Arielle Ford writes in *The Soulmate Secret*, "If we believe that there is plenty of love in the world and we are worthy of giving and receiving that love, we will attract a different quality of relationships than someone who believes in scarcity or feels unworthy of happiness. If we believe the world is a loving and friendly place, then most of the time that will be our experience. If we believe the world is a chaotic, stressful, and fearful place, then eventually that will become our reality. So, believing and knowing that your soulmate is out there is a critical first step in the formula for manifesting him or her into your life."

What we think, believe and perceive is what we become, for if we think, believe and perceive in a certain way we generate emotions that match those thoughts, beliefs and perceptions, and how we feel emotionally lowers or raises our vibrational frequency, and how we vibrate will determine which life experiences we will attract, and which we will repel. We attract those things, people, events and circumstances that *resonate* with our *vibrational frequency*. Like attracts like.

In Matthew 7:16 - 18 Jesus says, "By their fruit you will recognize them. Do people pick grapes from thornbushes, or figs from thistles? Likewise every good tree bears good fruit, but a bad tree bears bad fruit. A good tree cannot bear bad fruit, and a bad tree cannot bear good fruit."

In *As a Man Thinketh* James Allen writes, "Good thoughts and actions can never produce bad results; bad thoughts and actions can never produce good results. This is but saying that nothing can come from corn but corn, nothing from nettles but nettles. Men understand this law in the natural world, and work with it; but few understand it in the mental and moral world (though its operation there is just as simple and undeviating), and they, therefore, do not co-operate with it."

Resonant Frequency

Resonance is an *increase in energy* which we attract and absorb into our life experience and our reality, when the frequency of the energy we attract matches our own internal frequency of vibration. This is known as your *resonant frequency* or your 'level of vibration'. Resonance occurs at a particular energetic frequency, when our level of vibration and the energy of the things we want (or do not want) are of *equal magnitude*. Like attracts like.

Intuition and emotion are key elements in establishing the appropriate resonant frequency for successful attraction and manifesting. It is not enough to simply wish for something, you must first desire that which you intuitively know is in accordance with your true purpose and calling, and then you also need to match it with a truly strong desire and faith that will manifest what you want. Attempting to manifest things outside the scope of your original Life Plan is pointless and will bring you little contentment. And filling your mind with worry, fear and anxiety will only bring more stress and unhappiness into your life experience. Filling your mind with happy, joyful thoughts will attract happiness and joy into your life. It will bring you the good things in life you truly need and desire.

There is no distinction between the way we attract positive or negative experiences. Our mental and emotional state defines our particular energetic frequency. If we think about negative things we do not want; or we believe that bad things always happen to us; or if we believe that we are victims of lack and scarcity and that we have to compete with others for limited resources; or if we go through life focusing most of our attention on all that is unpleasant and undesirable in this world, we will automatically generate matching emotions and feelings of fear, deprivation, anxiety, depression, anger, skepticism and despair. These negative feelings and beliefs change our resonant frequency, which in turn attracts negative or undesirable energy of equal magnitude into our lives and ultimately manifests as negative, unpleasant, or undesirable things, people, events and circumstances.

Similarly, if we think positive thoughts about the things we desire and wish for; or we believe that only good things always happen to us; or we have an abundance consciousness believing there is more than enough resources and well-being in this world for everyone to share equally; or if we go through life focusing most of our attention on all that is pleasing and desirable in this world, we automatically generate matching emotions and feelings of enthusiasm, gratitude, joy, serenity, inner peace, faith, hope and happiness. These positive thoughts, beliefs and feelings raise our resonant frequency, which in turn attracts more and more positive energy of equal magnitude into your reality, which then manifests in your life as positive, pleasant, and desirable things, people, events and circumstances. Like attracts like.

In *The Law of Attraction: The Basics of the Teachings of Abraham* Esther and Jerry Hicks explains this principle of 'non-exclusion' in the Law of Attraction.

Without exception, that which you give thought to is that which you begin to invite into your experience. When you see something you would like to experience and you say, "Yes, I would like to have that," through your attention to it you invite it into your experience. However, when you see something that you do not want to experience and you shout, "No, no, I do not want that!" through your attention to it you invite it into your experience. In this attraction-based Universe, there is no such thing as exclusion.

Unconscious Attraction

The universal Law of Attraction is not something we must learn to use. In fact, most people are unconscious of its existence. But that does not mean it does not affect their lives. The law of Attraction affects all of us. It is a natural part of how our Universe operates.

In our infancy we do not have to "learn" about the Law of Gravity, for example, to learn how to walk, run or jump. The Law of Gravity is simply a natural phenomenon we gradually discover and adapt to as we grow up. However, as we mature, those of us who are not content to spend our lives doing nothing more than walking or running, go on to develop and master more and more ways to apply or defy the effects of gravity on our body. Those of us who desire more than the obvious become highly skilled athletes, dancers, aerospace engineers and astronauts. We are not content going through life remaining unconscious of the role of the Law of Gravity in our lives. For when we remain unconscious of the effects of gravity, there are limitations to what we can do and what we can experience and achieve. The same holds true for the Law of Attraction.

Hale Dwoskin writes in *The Sedona Method*, "The secret that everyone already knows intuitively within themselves is that we are all whole, complete and perfect as we are, in that we can manifest whatever we choose by simply focusing on what we would like and letting go of everything else."

But we do not have to be consciously aware of the Law of Attraction in order for us to attract and manifest any of our life experiences. Most people attract their life experiences while being completely oblivious to their ability to attract and create their own reality. They are *unconscious creators*.

Some unconscious creators are in fact very successful at attracting amazing life experiences and prosperity, because they learned from their parents and ancestors "how to be in the world". It is no accident or coincidence that wealth or fame often runs in families. If you trace back the origins of the money in most wealthy families you will most likely find a great grandparent in the family tree who was a *conscious creator.*

While many souls remain in the state of Divine Disconnect and therefore never become conscious of the effects of the Law of Attraction in their lives, some of us do discover its existence and choose to master this innate creative power we all possess to manifest a truly purposeful, abundant, fulfilling Divine Life.

Unfortunately, not everyone who discovers the Law of Attraction is equally successful in harnessing its power for a better life. Some get caught up in selfish greed and an obsession with material wealth and status, which they erroneously believe will bring them happiness and contentment, while others constantly slide back into false beliefs, lack consciousness, a scarcity mentality or a negative outlook on life. The missing key in these cases is a *lack of spiritual awareness* and the *absence of true purpose* that serves the greater good.

Conscious creators who do not live in alignment with the Higher Self and who are not synchronized with their Soul Purpose and Life Calling will never be able to fully harness the metaphysical power of the Law of Attraction. Some may be able to generate great wealth or fame, despite their lack of spiritual awareness, but it is unlikely that their life will offer them much joy, fulfillment and lasting contentment. They will restlessly chase after another pot of gold under the next rainbow, never stopping to appreciate the real splendor of the magical spectrum of light waves and colorful display above them.

Destiny vs. Free Will

Do you believe that your life path is entirely pre-destined? Some people do. They prefer to see themselves as helpless puppets on a string, hanging around, while fate takes its course. For them the future is firmly cast in stone. Their destiny is pre-determined and their life path non-negotiable. The writing is on the wall. Period. They show little or no interest in the possibility that they may have much more control over their destiny, and that they can make great things happen for themselves and by themselves. Neither do they realize that they can get what they want from life so much sooner, and enjoy those outcomes for so much longer.

Your future is not entirely pre-determined. There is also no such thing as 'fate' or 'bad luck'. There is only destiny and free will. Destiny is the cards we are dealt in this lifetime. Free will is how we play them. Any successful card player will tell you that the secret to success lies in a combination of *opportunity* and *strategy.* They will also tell you that it is possible to win the jackpot with a weak hand, or lose millions with a royal flush. It is all about the attitude, the faith, the patience, the confidence, the self-control, the focus and, most of all, the timing.

Yes, the major events in our lives are often pre-destined. You can identify them easily, because they are the events and circumstances that are usually beyond your control. These are the signposts and pit stops we had planned for ourselves like an elaborate obstacle course, before we came into this lifetime. These pre-determined events and outcomes serve as the *life lessons, challenges* and *opportunities* for soul growth and are an integral part of our thrilling roller-coaster ride through life.

The remainder of our life experiences, both the opportunities and the challenges, are what we create, attract and *manifest* in this lifetime. We are the masters of our own true destiny and the creators of our own reality. We choose how we wish to live our lives. We create most of our life experiences with our thoughts, words, beliefs and actions (Law of Creation), and we attract these creations into our life experiences by virtue of our intuitions, emotions and our vibrational frequency (Law of Attraction). We become what we think, feel and believe. We have free will, and therefore we are able to decide what our *strategy* or approach to life will be.

Remember that you are a spiritual being having a human experience. You are of Divine origin, which means that you are an extension of Higher Consciousness or the Divine Self in this physical time-space reality. Therefore you have several inherent Divine qualities, namely the *ability to reason*, and the capacity for *deliberation* and *free decision-making*. You are also *aware* of your own consciousness and you have *creative freedom* and metaphysical power to *manifest.* Finally, and most importantly, you have the capacity for *individuation* (self-actualization) and *transcendence* (enlightenment, salvation).

Why Bad Things Happen To Good People

I am often asked why bad things sometimes happen in our lives. Did we cause or create these events ourselves, or are they merely a part of our original Life Plan? Well, most of the negative things that happen to us in our lifetime are our own Ego creations; they are not pre-destined in our Life Plan. They are not the work of the Divine Self, they are in Troward's words the "psychic pranks" of the Ego Self. In *As a Man Thinketh* James Allen writes that every man is where he is in his life by the "law of his being".

> *The thoughts which he has built into his character have brought him there, and in the arrangement of his life there is no element of chance, but all is the result of a law which cannot err. This is just as true of those who feel 'out of harmony' with their surroundings as of those who are contented with them.*

We did not come into this lifetime to suffer and endure all manner of hardship, pain and deprivation. In fact, if you look very carefully you will notice that the majority of misfortune, scarcity and calamity that people endure is mostly *man-made*. They are our own creations. They are very seldom so-called "acts of God" or natural disasters. Even the natural disasters we sometimes face are due to our own choices and decisions, because we interrupt the natural flow of rivers by constructing dams, we build our homes below water-lines, we suppress natural fires, we contaminate our groundwater with deadly chemicals while fracking for shale gas, and we inject greenhouse gasses and aerosol particles into the atmosphere. Some experts even speculate that human activity may be the cause of some earthquakes.

Very few of the bad things that happen to good people are a result of their pre-destined Life Plan. It is perfectly within your power to prevent many negative events and experiences in your life. All you need to do is accept responsibility for your own negative acts of creation and set out instead to consciously manifest a Divine Life.

Your Life Plan is a list of experiences and lessons you hope to encounter during this lifetime. The goal is to achieve an expansion of your wisdom, insight, growth, and consciousness. Your Divine Self was the mastermind behind many of these life events. They are destined to happen to you, one way or the other. But how good or bad the actual experiences are, how much time they require and what route you take to get to each of them, all depend on what you choose to think, feel, decide, and ultimately do. It will be determined by your thoughts, emotions, sensory acuity, intuitions and your conscious manifestation of solutions to these life challenges.

If you are aligned with the Divine Self you will stay true to your original Life Plan and the Divine Self will guide you through each of these life challenges and opportunities. The pre-destined life events that make up your Life Plan are meant to challenge you towards achieving your Soul Purpose and accomplishing your Life Calling. In order to complete this amazing journey successfully, it is vital that you turn each and every dark tear into a pearl of wisdom, find the *blessing* in every curse.

Do You Feel Lucky?

Does luck exist and is it something we cause or create, or is it merely something we attract or earn? Is it true that some people are just more lucky than others? Do we sometimes just have bad luck?

These questions always reminds me of my dad. It was the inside joke at family dinners that he would always get the fillet of fish with the most bones in it. It was always the first thing he said, after he ordered fish in a restaurant, "Wait and see, mine will be the one with the most bones". Of course, as expected, he always did get the most bones! He tried many strategies to avoid getting all those bones. Sometimes he would switch plates with one of us, before we started eating, in hopes of exchanging his 'bony fish' for one of our 'bone-free' delights. Or he would deliberately order a type of fish that is supposed to have fewer bones. Yet, no matter what he tried, my dad *always* got the fillet of fish with the most bones. It was sometimes so bad that we would turn the 'counting of the bones' into a game. But the truth is that my dad did not have 'bad luck. His belief was simply so strong that he actually manifested his fear time and time again.

There are four pathways by which we can attract positive or negative life events and experiences into our lives. The sketch below illustrates these four pathways of manifesting.

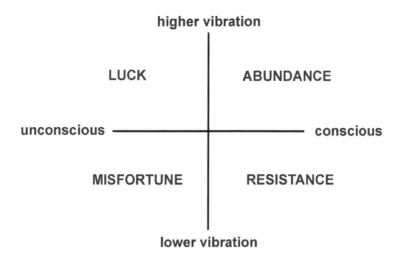

The Path of Luck

When we experience moments of "good fortune" or something happens to us that make people say, "You are so lucky" it is likely that we invited this unexpected providence into our experience through the pathway of Luck. Luck happens when we *unconsciously create* something and then attract it into our life through a positive *higher vibration* or *resonant frequency*. I find the most interesting aspect of Luck is that it most often comes to people who expect or need it the least. How many times have you heard someone say, "Why did he have to win, he does not even need it!" Once again proof that like attracts like.

The Path of Misfortune

Misfortune or 'bad luck' happens when we are *unconscious creators* who attract unpleasant or undesirable experiences into our life through a negative, *lower vibration* or *resonant frequency*. Once again the most compelling aspect of Misfortune is that it so often tends to happen to people who can afford it the least! With some people it seems that the more 'bad luck' they have, the more they attract even worse calamity into their lives. Hence the popular saying "it never rains but it pours".

A Bible quote from Mark 4:24 also comes to mind, "Whoever has will be given more; whoever does not have, even what he has will be taken from him." The only way to reduce the amount of misfortune in your life is simple solution: *become a conscious co-creator.* You may at first not be able to avoid absolutely all misfortune, but you will certainly have less of it! Carl Jung said, "Until you make the unconscious conscious, it will direct your life and you will call it fate."

The Path Of Resistance

Resistance to manifesting is one of the major challenges that many practitioners of the Law of Attraction seek to address and overcome. It is often the central discussion point at manifesting seminars and workshops, and it can be a great source of frustration for those who consistently struggle to create and attract the things they truly want, which ironically only *adds to their resistance* and further impedes their ability to manifest.

The effect of resistance on manifesting is two-fold. In the first scenario we *consciously* create something good or positive and then fail to attract it into our lives because of *negative, lower vibration* emotions. Although we created that which we desire, we are not offering a vibration that matches that creation; therefore we are unable to act as a magnet to draw it towards us, or unable to keep it.

For example, you cannot expect to attract the life partner of your dreams if you are offering very little to that wonderful person in return. We are often so busy manifesting the perfect mate that we seldom stop to think what we will be bringing to that relationship. To find the perfect partner, you have to become the perfect partner. No 'perfect mate' is going to be out there looking for a partner who is sad, pessimistic, unenthusiastic, skeptical, angry, frustrated, discontent, unhappy, distrustful and cynical. Victims and martyrs simply do not make the best marriage material. The only potential partners you will attract with negative emotion are people who resonate with your low vibration, which is clearly not the beginnings of a very happy and fulfilling long-term relationship.

The second form of *resistance manifesting* is when we *consciously* create something negative or bad, and then proceed to attract it into our lives by offering a matching vibration of *negative emotions.* This often happens when we are constantly focusing on all the negative things in our life. When we think negative thoughts and we indulge in the negative emotions that accompany them, we are literally inviting more and more misery and disappointment into our lives.

The Laws of Creation and Attraction is a double edged sword. Not only do we create and attract the things we do want, but we also tend to create and attract the things we *don't want*, by focusing our attention on those things. Esther-Abraham Hicks describes the problem perfectly, "The thoughts that you think, regarding those things that you want, set into motion the creation, and eventual fulfillment, of that which you want. And likewise, the thoughts that you think, regarding those things that you do not want, set into motion the creation, and eventual fulfillment, of that which you *do not want*."

Wallace D. Wattles writes in *The Science of Getting Rich,* "The moment you permit your mind to dwell with dissatisfaction upon things as they are, you begin to lose ground. You fix attention upon the common, the ordinary, the poor, and the squalid and mean; and your mind takes the form of these things. Then you will transmit these forms or mental images to the Formless, and the common, the poor, the squalid, and mean will come to you.

Resistance is often also caused by our lack of faith and our constant attempts at controlling the outcome. Esther-Abraham Hicks explains, "When you talk about what you want and why you want it, there's usually less resistance within you, than when you talk about what you want and how you're going to get it. When you pose questions you don't have answers for, like how, where, when, who, it sets up a contradictory vibration that slows everything down."

The Path Of Abundance

This is the path of manifesting for the spiritually awakened. It is the path of deliberate creation and intentional attraction. We manifest abundance when we are *consciously* creating and attracting everything we need, want and desire into our lives through maintaining a consistent positive, *higher vibration* emotional state.

Charles F. Haanel writes, "If you see only the incomplete, the imperfect, the relative, the limited, these conditions will manifest in your life; but if you train your mind to see and realize the spiritual ego, the "I" which is forever perfect and complete, harmonious; wholesome, and healthful conditions only will be manifested."

The Origins Of The Secret

Deliberate manifesting is nothing new. It is not a modern concept that only recently became available to the 'spiritually privileged' because of a plethora of Law of Attraction books and films like *The Secret* (2006). In fact, in popular culture books about conscious creation and deliberate manifesting go back over a more than a century, including *As a Man Thinketh* (1902); *The Science of Getting Rich* (1910); *The Master Key System* (1917) and *This Mystical Life of Ours* (1919). These are but a few of the many books that came forth from the New Thought movement at the turn of the previous century.

But these were not truly the original texts on the Laws of Creation and Attraction. To find the real original 'teachings' on this subject all you need to do is have a look at the scriptures and texts of most of the major world religions. In all of them you will find evidence for our ability to consciously manifest. Manifesting is an underlying principle in many traditional reli-gious practices, including meditation, prayer, ceremony, rite and ritual. The art of manifesting is truly as old as time. We are powerful spiritual beings having a human experience and we have been *enforcing our free will* using the purposeful path of abundance manifesting for millennia.

Being A Co-Creator

To create, attract and manifest is an innate metaphysical function we all have access to as Divine beings. Jane Roberts writes in *The Nature of Personal Reality*, "You are given the gifts of the gods; you create your reality according to your beliefs. Yours is the creative energy that makes your world. There are no limitations to the self except those you believe in."

To be a creator is a function of our *free will*. The truth is that we are co-creators of our shared reality throughout our entire lives, even during the time of our Divine Disconnect. We all create our own reality and shape our own destiny in every single moment of our lives. What you think, feel, believe, wish for and desire in this very moment, is what you will become tomorrow, and the day after, and the day after that.

As entities of Divine origins we are inter-connected mirror reflections of a holographic Universe; we have no choice but to act as co-creators of our shared reality. However, most of our co-creating takes place on the *unconscious level*, without us being aware of it. Ernest Shurtleff Holmes explains this very well in his book *Creative Mind and Success* published in 1919:

> *Man does not really create. He uses creative power that already is. Relatively speaking, he is the creative power in his own life; and so far as his thought goes, there is something that goes with it that has the power to bring forth into manifestation the thing thought of. Hitherto men have used this creative power in ignorance and so have brought upon themselves all kinds of conditions... today hundreds of thousands are beginning to use these great laws of their being in a conscious, constructive way. Herein lays the great secret of the New Thought movements under their various names and cults and orders. All are using the same law even though some deny to others the real revelation. We should get into an attitude of mind wherein we should recognize the truth wherever we may find it. The trouble with most of us is that unless we see sugar in a sugar bowl we think it must be something else, and so we stick to our petty prejudices instead of looking after principles.*

In ancient times our ancestors used their metaphysical powers to shape, transform and control their physical life experience throughout their lifetime. The demands of their shared reality in those days did not require such a severe and complete disconnection from their inner Divinity. The ancients lived in much greater harmony with their Higher Self. They understood the innate cycles of life and they trusted in the flow of Spirit. They lived and breathed in synchronicity with the heartbeat of their planet and the pulse of their spiritual heritage and Divine origins. Sure, they knew hardship and the challenges of earthly survival, but they also knew the joy of love, laughter and connection to the

Divine Source. As spiritual beings having a physical life experience, they recognized their innate metaphysical power and they put it to good use.

Survivors And Sinners

Unlike our ancestors, most of us have lost our inner awareness of our spiritual gifts and metaphysical potential. In the post-modern era most people create, attract and manifest the basic things they need in their lives without ever becoming aware that they are in fact the *architects of their own reality* in this lifetime.

Being an unconscious creator is usually not a problem if all goes well, but when matters get out of hand and we end up being not as happy, prosperous or content as we somehow know deep down we deserve to be, it becomes a real dilemma. Often the unconscious creator would then turn to self-pity, blame or rage, believing that their partner, family, friends, teachers, peers, co-workers, society, the environment, nature or God is somehow responsible and accountable for their personal misfortune and misery. Unconscious creators are often slaves to their own *lack consciousness* and they tend to make sweeping statements based on false beliefs they cling to regarding their own worth or the lack of justice in the world.

It must accept my fate.
I have such bad luck.
Things never go my way.
I must be cursed.
God is punishing me.
I am such a loser.
It is what it is.
My life just sucks!

Unconscious creators often go through a lot of unnecessary pain, suffering and misfortune in their lifetime. Much of it can be prevented, or at least be alleviated. Sometimes in my coaching practice I feel like a helpless bystander, having to witness some of my more stubborn, cynical clients turn themselves into powerless victims of their own circumstances. They either choose to become martyrs to their own fear, laziness or indecision or they are in such denial that they are unwilling to change their self-destructive ways. They come to me for help, because they are not content to let Fate, Chance, Luck or Destiny drag them by the hair along their pre-written life path, but yet they also make very little effort to accept responsibility for the catastrophe they have thus far chosen to manifest.

The most troublesome problem with unconscious creators is that they are unaware of how their creative actions impact their own lives, as well as that of others. Apart from the damage these unconscious creators cause in their own lives, they are also of very little use to the welfare of their community, or the well-being of our planet. They often do more harm than good, because all their unconscious acts of creation serve mostly only their own selfish needs and are not in harmony with the rest of the world.

There are two kinds of unconscious creators, namely the *Survivors* and the *Sinners*. For the survivors unconscious manifest-ting is mostly geared towards their own *survival as human beings*. These people usually only manifest enough on an unconscious level to get by for yet another day. They are so entirely caught up in 'scraping through' and 'keeping head above water' that they are blind to any other possibilities in their lives. Nothing else matters much to them. Ironically, the more aware they become of their own lack and hardship, the less and less they seem to have. We truly do become what we think of and focus on, and when our attention is centered on what we *don't have* and how bad things are in our lives, we automatically create, attract and manifest even *more of the same*. We simply become what we think, say and believe. If your daily focus in life is on being sick, poor or lonely, you will be diseased, deprived and desperate. You are merely creating more and more of the same.

The main risk that the typical Survivor creator runs is not that they are missing out on some of the best things life has to offer, but that they are most probably not achieving their Soul Purpose or Life Calling. In the survival mode we are unable to accomplish our true destiny.

This principle is perfectly demonstrated by Maslow's Hierarchy of Needs. Abraham Maslow introduced the world to his hierarchy in 1943 with an essay titled, *A Theory of Human Motivation*. Maslow used his proposed 'hierarchy of needs' to describe the typical pattern of human motivation. His theory suggests that as humans our most basic, lower level needs must first be met, before we will have a real desire or motivation to fulfill any of the higher level needs. Maslow also wondered why some people seem to go the extra mile to achieve something in their life, while others lack the drive or motivation to pursue anything beyond daily survival. For this purpose he coined the term *metamotivation* to describe the motivation of people who go beyond the scope of their basic needs and strive for constant personal growth and self-actualization.

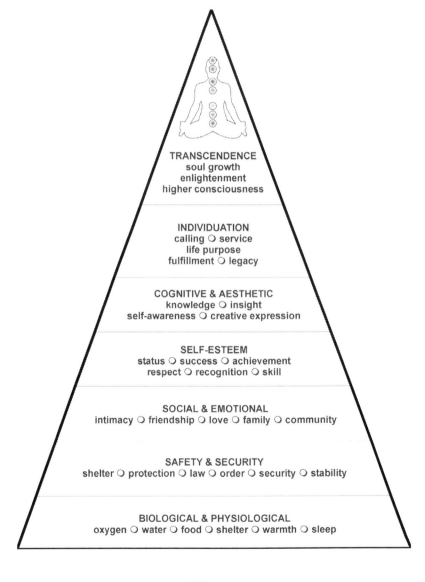

TRANSCENDENCE
soul growth
enlightenment
higher consciousness

INDIVIDUATION
calling ○ service
life purpose
fulfillment ○ legacy

COGNITIVE & AESTHETIC
knowledge ○ insight
self-awareness ○ creative expression

SELF-ESTEEM
status ○ success ○ achievement
respect ○ recognition ○ skill

SOCIAL & EMOTIONAL
intimacy ○ friendship ○ love ○ family ○ community

SAFETY & SECURITY
shelter ○ protection ○ law ○ order ○ security ○ stability

BIOLOGICAL & PHYSIOLOGICAL
oxygen ○ water ○ food ○ shelter ○ warmth ○ sleep

Survivor creators lack Maslow's metamotivation. They focus on their most basic needs and typically do not create or attract much beyond the three lower levels of Maslow's hierarchy, namely their physical needs, safety and security, and love and relationships. It is therefore unlikely that they will achieve their Soul Purpose or accomplish their Life Calling in this lifetime, for basic human survival is not the fundamental reason we incarnated as human beings.

For the *Sinners* manifesting tends to revolve mostly around the lower energy frequencies on the scale of human emotion: pride, vanity, narcissism, selfishness, anger, envy, jealousy, hatred, gluttony, sloth, discontent, despair, egotism, conceit, self-importance, arrogance, snobbery, greed and the lust for power and control.

I call them the "sinners" because many of the motivations that drive their unconscious manifestations remind me of the Seven Deadly Sins found in the Catholic faith, also known as the Cardinal Sins or the Capital Vices. Now, this may seem like an unfair generalization at first glance; it may even appear to be somewhat judgmental! Of course, I admit that not all unconscious creators are purely self-serving, egotistical 'evil-doers'! Some of their unconscious acts of creation do sometimes bring positive, useful manifestations into our shared reality, despite their lack of spiritual awareness. Furthermore, many of their self-centered and malevolent creations are fortunately prevented or limited from manifesting due to the overriding effect of Universal Law, which ensures continued order, harmony and balance throughout the Universe.

But think about it for a moment But think about it for a moment. If you observe the typical desires and manifestations of spiritually unconscious people, how much of what they bring into our shared reality serves their fellow man or the planet they share with us? Would their typical manifestations, for example, reflect the Seven Virtues of the Catholic faith? How many people do you know who consistently lead a life of true charity temperance, diligence, chastity, patience, kindness and humility? Most likely you do not know many, if any at all. And I am sure the few you might know all have one thing in common: they are either devoutly religious or they are spiritually highly aware.

I have never been able to comprehend why anyone would be judgmental or disapproving of the religious beliefs and spiritual practices of others. Thank God for all the Christians, Muslims,

Hindus, Buddhists, Sikhs, Judaists, Spiritualists, Neo-Pagans and millions of dedicated followers of all the other world religions who profess the values of unconditional love, peace and harmony. Their beliefs and practices contribute much to our continued expansion and evolution as a species. They make our world a safer and more pleasant place than it would otherwise be.

Every religious prayer, meditation, trance, initiation, song and dance that sends positive, higher vibration energy into the Conscious Universe every day bring balance to all the negative, immoral and destructive acts of creation that we sometimes commit as fallible human beings, whether conscious or unconscious. For those among us who are unconsciously creating that which may be negative and destructive in the world, often because of fear, resistance, lack consciousness or spiritual disconnection, there are many other spiritually aware souls who create all that may be positive and constructive in our world, because of their belief in kindness, compassion, selflessness, harmony, peace and unconditional love.

In everything in the Universe there is always *perfect balance*. It is Universal Law. I am therefore thankful for every religion and act of worship in the world that serves the continued expansion of our Universe and invites joy, peace, goodwill, charity, compassion and unconditional love into our shared human experience. These religious acts of creation serve to maintain, support and improve our physical life experience for ourselves and the generations to come.

Why Play God?

The Universe will continue to expand and we will continue to evolve, mostly without our own conscious awareness of how we contribute and participate in this magnificent process. Yet, if this is the case, why would we want to consciously create and manifest? Would it not be better for us to remain on 'auto-pilot' and let the Divine Source take care of everything?

The reality is that we were never meant to be unconscious creators. As born co-creators we have always had a duty to our fellow man and to all of Divine Creation to contribute to the formation of an increasingly better world and a brighter future. We were given *free will* to choose how we wish to live and how we prefer to evolve. To enable us to exert our free will and make it manifest, we were given a profoundly Divine Gift, namely the ability to create, shape, mould, direct, attract and manifest our needs and desires. We are expected to apply this Gift in service to the greater good. Our earthly life is not a free ride. We must 'earn our keep'. In fact, we have reached the stage in our development as a species where it is has become our Divine duty to consciously participate in our own evolution.

Thomas Troward writes in *The Creative Process in the Individual* that because we are created in the image of the Divine it logically follows that when we have become truly aware and appreciative of our Divine origins we would automatically reflect in turn the innate qualities and objectives of the Divine, which obviously includes our capacity for creative freedom and the ability to manifest.

> *We have seen that the Spirit's Enjoyment of Life is neces-*
> *sarily a reciprocal - it must have a corresponding fact in*
> *manifestation to answer to it; otherwise by the inherent*
> *law of mind no consciousness, and consequently no enjoy-*
> *ment, could accrue; and therefore by the law of continu-*
> *ous progression the required Reciprocal should manifest*
> *as a [human] being awakening to the consciousness of the*
> *Principle by which he himself comes into existence... A*
> *being thus awakened would be the proper correspondence*
> *of the Spirit's Enjoyment of Life at a stage not only above*
> *mechanical motion or physical vitality, but even above*
> *intellectual perception of existing phenomena, that is to*
> *say at the stage where the Spirit's Enjoyment consists in*
> *recognizing itself as the Source of all things. The position*
> *in the Absolute would be, so to speak, the awakening of*
> *Spirit to the recognition of its own Artistic Ability.*

We have matured as an evolving species and have put a lot of our creative potential to good use thus far. We have, for example, expanded our science and technology beyond anything we could have possibly imagined a hundred years ago. This achievement is a noteworthy expression and celebration of our Divine origins. God, or the Divine Source revels in this material expression of expanding Infinite Intelligence and celebrates our secular achievements as a species. However, as our scientific and technological expansion continues, and increasingly speed up, many of us are also becoming less and less fulfilled and content as inherent spiritual beings, and our planet and the environment is in serious jeopardy. In this sense we did not regard the "grand harmony of the Originating Spirit" which Troward describes.

> *[The] All-Originating Mind we may picture as the Great Artist giving visible expression to His feeling... If the grand harmony of the Originating Spirit within itself is duly regarded, then the individual mind affords a fresh center from which the Spirit contemplates itself in what I have ventured to call its Artistic Originality - a boundless potential of Creativeness.*

As co-creators we have fulfilled most of Maslow's lower level needs of our species. All our science and technology has brought us great comfort and ease of survival, yet it has offered us very little happiness, purpose or lasting joy. Our modern comforts have also come at a high price in the form of an ongoing and gradual destruction of our natural resources. We have become a threat to ourselves and the planet. We are even making use of our Divine-inspired technology to our own detriment.

Clearly, we are doing something wrong. The world today is not the pleasant, safe or healthy place that it should be. A lot of what we have created is not a worthy reflection of our Divine origins. We have somehow lost our way and it is now our duty as an evolved species to turn the tide by beginning to more fully express and honor our Divine origins and innate metaphysical capacity.

Robert Collier writes in *The Secret of the Ages,* "But to every man of vision the clear voice speaks. Nothing splendid has ever been achieved except by those who dared believe that something inside them was superior to circumstance." The time has come for us to reclaim our sacred birthright and to walk once again in the power of who we are and where we come from. If we become empowered as the human 'deities' we were always meant to be, we can make the most of our time here on Earth, in order to achieve the soul growth and life calling we always intended. And we can do all of that whilst ensuring an exhilarating, thrilling and abundant physical life experience for ourselves. The Divine Source offers us complete and endless abundance. All we need to do to tap into this infinite stream of well-being is to consciously and deliberately create, attract and manifest that which we require to serve our Soul Purpose and Life Calling for the greater good.

The Metamotivation Of A Species

As a species the time has come for us as a collective to take on our higher level needs on Maslow's pyramid. More and more people around the world are becoming aware of the fact that as a species we are now developing a strong metamotivation to expand and thrive beyond the scope of our basic human needs. Our science and technology has addressed most of our lower level needs. The time has come for us to strive towards not only our own individuation and transcendence, but also the spiritual evolution and ascension of our whole species to *homo superior,* the Divine Superhuman.

If we are to continue to evolve and prosper as a species, we need critical mass to tip the scales. We need a greater number of spiritually awakened souls who can act as constructive, conscious co-creators. We need souls who can actively and deliberately shift the tide and save mankind from what seems to be its current path of self-destruction. The world needs us now to become spiritually awakened. Manifesting is not merely about attracting a romantic partner, finding a glamorous job or lining our own pockets with more money. Sure, such things do empower and enable us to serve others better, but they should not be our main concern. Ultimately we must create, attract and manifest *in service* to others and our planet. A partner, job or lots of money cannot bring you lasting happiness and contentment. The path to true fulfillment lies in achieving your Soul Purpose and accomplishing your Life Calling.

The real purpose of our ability to manifest is spiritual in nature, not material or secular. The Bible expresses it very aptly in 2 Corinthians 9:8, "And God is able to bestow every blessing on you in abundance, so that richly enjoying all sufficiency at all times, you may have ample means for all good works." The Hindu spiritual teacher Swami Sivananda said, "Giving is the secret of abundance." So does the Qur'an, "God will reward those who have faith and do good; he will enrich them from his own abundance."

This is the essential aspect of co-creation that many proponents of the Law of Attraction tend to forget. Manifesting is not a purely self-serving act and should never be governed by greed and selfish gain. We are all inter-connected and inter-dependent incarnations of one original Divine Source. We are co-creators of the Holographic Conscious Universe. Every single thought, emotion, wish and desire we manifest as individuals impacts the rest of the Universe.

Becoming a deliberate, conscious co-creator therefore brings with it the spiritual responsibility towards our species, all living creatures and the whole planet. None of our personal achievements, enjoyments or satisfaction need to ever clash with society or the environment. But we must ensure that our acts of creation are in harmony with the Laws of the Universe and that it is serving the greater good. In his famous book, *The Science of Getting Rich* published in 1910, Wallace D. Wattles describes the true purpose of material manifesting and prosperity.

> *That which makes you want more money is the same as that which makes the plant grow; it is Life, seeking fuller expression. It is essential, however that your purpose should harmonize with the purpose that is in All. You must want real life, not mere pleasure of sensual gratification. Life is the performance of function; and the individual really lives only when he performs every function, physical, mental, and spiritual, of which he is capable, without excess in any. You do not want to get rich in order to live swinishly, for the gratification of animal desires; that is not life. But the performance of every physical function is a part of life, and no one lives completely who denies the impulses of the body a normal and healthful expression. You do not want to get rich solely to enjoy mental pleasures, to get knowledge, to gratify ambition, to outshine others, to be famous. All these are a legitimate part of life, but the man who lives for the pleasures of the intellect alone will only have a partial life, and he will never be satisfied with his lot. You do not want to get rich solely for the good of others, to lose yourself for the salvation of mankind, to experience the joys of philanthropy and sacrifice. The joys of the soul are only a part of life; and they are no better or nobler than any other part. You want to get rich in order that you may eat, drink, and be merry when it is time to do these things; in order that you may surround yourself with beautiful things, see distant lands, feed your mind, and develop your intellect;*

in order that you may love men and do kind things, and be
able to play a good part in helping the world to find truth.

The Divine Life not only serves the individual, but it also serves the greater good. It ensures a life of service to humanity, as well as the creative expansion of the Universe. A Divine Life is a life of *harmony.* When we live in harmony with ourselves, with others and our environment, as well as our planet and the Laws of the Universe, then we are expressing the Truth and the Essence of our Divine nature.

Once you come into a place of harmony in your daily life, you will begin to see the miracle of your Divine origins manifest on a daily basis in the form of many Divine blessings, and a truly awakened and abundant life. To achieve this level of harmony it is important to adopt and implement the *Maxims of Divine Living.* By always being mindful of these Divine truths you will become a creator of many miracles in your own life and the lives of others.

The Scarcity Mentality

It is the natural and inherent impulse of all Life to strive towards growth and expansion. Our Conscious Universe is constantly in the process of becoming, increasing, and extending. All Life is an act of Creation, a product of Infinite Intelligence. It is the innate nature of all consciousness and intelligence to constantly seek greater extension and expansive expression. Without this natural urge to live more, express more, become more, and expand more, stagnation and destruction eventually sets in, and ultimately barrenness, non-being, anti-matter and death.

To be a co-creator, whether conscious or unconscious, is there-fore not a choice or an obligation. The ability and inclination to manifest is inherent in our spiritual beingness; it is simply in our Divine nature to create and to want more, do more, have more and become more.

The natural environment here on planet Earth was designed for one purpose only, namely the advancement of Life for the sake of Universal Expansion. The same holds true for all other dimensions, planes, or realms of the Universe. For there are many other realities beyond this material world. Everything that is, was and ever will be is in existence to serve the deliberate, expansive expression of the Infinite Intelligence of the Divine Source.

Because our planet and our natural environment is designed for growth and the promotion of Life, everything we could possibly need to survive, grow, expand and express ourselves is more than *bountifully provided* and made *available to us all.* We do not live in a world of scarcity, lack or deficiency. If you witness signs of shortage in the world around you, you can be sure that it is a man-made illusion. We live in an *abundant place* designed to serve all our human needs, fulfill our wishes, support our desires and bless us with bounty and *infinite well-being.* Remember this the next time you cut into the deep magic of a fully ripened fruit. Our world is meant to be a happy, generous horn of plenty in which we are all meant to share to our hearts content. There truly is *enough to go around* for everyone.

The only true sin of mankind is our global indulgence in an unrelenting *lack consciousness* and a *scarcity mentality.* This is a tragic weakness of the human condition, and it is due to our instinctive urge to survive in a material world. The need to violently compete with each other and plunder the environment is a result of the Divine Disconnect. The more spiritually unconscious and unaware we have become as a species, the more we have developed a *fear of scarcity* and an *obsession with lack.* Mahatma Gandhi said, "There is enough in the world for everyone's need; there is not enough for everyone's greed."

I consider this lack consciousness and scarcity mentality as our only true "sin", because it is the foundation of all manner of evil, immorality and destruction in our world. Without going into an in-depth discussion of the 'nature of sin', let us look at just one example by simply considering once again the Catholic faith's Seven Deadly Sins: Greed, Envy, Lust, Gluttony, Sloth, Wrath, and Pride. Mull over these human weaknesses for a moment and you will notice that they are all merely the expression of man's *fear of lack and scarcity.* When we believe that there is not enough abundance for everyone to share, our human survival instinct urges us to seize more, demand more, compete more, steal more, cheat more, consume more, possess more, and command more. And as if that is not enough, we sometimes do not only want what we can get for ourselves, but we also want what others have.

Some seekers at times wonder why their earnest attempts at creating, attracting and manifesting their desires are not always as successful as they had hoped it would be. The answer is simple. Abundance will only fully become manifest in your life once your vibrational frequency resonates the *opposite of lack consciousness and a scarcity mentality.* To successfully manifest the good things in life we must replace greed, envy, lust, gluttony, sloth, wrath, and pride with Temperance, Charity, Diligence, Chastity, Patience, Kindness and Humility.

Divine Living cannot fully manifest and flourish if you indulge in a scarcity mentality. Having this kind of outlook only serves to disrupt the natural flow of all well-being and abundance in your life. Instead you must indulge in the opposite sentiments; embrace the natural bounty that is automatically your Divine inheritance. Have faith in the bountiful generosity of the Universe. Trust in the flow of well-being that abounds in all that is, was and every will be. Wallace D. Wattles explains in *The Science of Getting Rich* that we must rid ourselves of the concept of competition.

> *You are to create, not to compete for what is already created. You do not have to take anything away from any one. You do not have to drive sharp bargains. You do not have to cheat, or to take advantage. You do not need to let any man work for you for less than he earns. You do not have to covet the property of others, or to look at it with wishful eyes; no man has anything of which you cannot have the like, and that without taking what he has away from him. You are to become a creator, not a competitor; you are going to get what you want, but in such a way that when you get it every other man will have more than he has now.*

Instead of an obsession with lack and scarcity, express your appreciation and gratitude for all that you already have and shall receive, for these sentiments are the true expression of your inner Divinity. There is no real lack or scarcity in this world except that which is created by the greed and ignorance of man. We did not come into this lifetime to suffer deprivation or misery. There is only well-being and bountiful abundance. There is supposed to be more than enough for everyone.

Let us be trusting and thankful that all our needs, wants, and desires will become manifest for the greater good. For when we live a life of gratitude and appreciation and we embrace the abundance that abounds in all that is, we begin to truly thrive and prosper. In order to do more, know more, and be more in this lifetime and beyond, we must also *have more*. Apart from emotional and psychological abundance, we must also have material prosperity. We must have every material thing we need, not only to survive, but for our soul growth and spiritual expansion. For we need material things in order to learn, and do, and become. And when we are blessed with such prosperity and well-being we are empowered to fulfill our Soul Purpose and Life Calling. Lao Tzu said, "When you realize there is nothing lacking, the whole world belongs to you."

The Buffer Of Time

I am often asked by my students why the things we consciously create do not come to us sooner. Why do we so often have to wait for our needs and desires to manifest? The answer is simple. Manifesting is mostly meant to be slow and measured, because of our human condition and the nature of our time-space reality.

Imagine a world where every weird and wonderful thing we desire instantly manifests. Imagine the chaos and confusion that would ensue. I always tell my clients to be careful what they wish for. Even with the built-in protection mechanism of a time and space delay between creation, attraction and actual manifestation, some people still get it wrong. Imagine if they were able to randomly manifest their wishes instantaneously!

Some Law of Attraction authors and teachers would have you believe that the delay in manifesting is due to something you are doing 'wrong', or that you are not correctly applying their recommended techniques. Sure, there are things that we can 'do wrong' when it comes to manifesting, but the act of creation is not some foreign skill we must learn or acquire. We are all natural co-creators by virtue of our Divine origins, but because of the Divine Disconnect and the dominance of the Ego or False Self, many of us lose touch with our metaphysical abilities. Yet, even during that time of disconnection we still remain *unconscious creators*. It is therefore pretty much like riding a bicycle. The moment we re-awaken spiritually and align with the Divine Self, we tend to take to our role as co-creators like 'fish to water'.

All the Law of Attraction books and manifesting seminars available these days are therefore *not teaching us how to create*. We already 'know' how to do that as spiritual beings. Instead they are actually 'unteaching' us in order to 'delearn' all the *false beliefs* and *ego attachments* we assembled during the time of the Divine Disconnect. These false beliefs and ego attachments disturb our resonant frequency and therefore prevent us from attracting the things we hope to resonate with. This is the reason why some books and courses are less successful than others in bringing people lasting fulfillment. They are often too steeped in upholding the false beliefs and material obsessions of the Ego or False Self, namely money, success, fame, sex, and power. These things only serve our worldly, human needs. They do not bring us into closer alignment with our Divine Self, and they do not necessarily serve our Soul Purpose or Life Calling.

It is simply in our best interest not to instantly have everything we think we want; it is not good for us to manifest things too quickly. We do not always create and attract what is good and uplifting. In our human form we sometimes create and attract negative, unpleasant and even destructive things into our reality. Instant manifesting might sound like a good idea when your resonant frequency is high and you are busy creating and attracting positive things, but what happens when the Ego or False Self steps in and takes over the process of manifesting? How many of your most negative, undesirable thoughts and desires would you really want to enter your life experience?

In *The Law of Attraction: The Basics of the Teachings of Abraham* Esther and Jerry Hicks explains that it is fortunate that "here in our physical time-space reality things do not manifest into your experience instantaneously. There is a wonderful buffer of time between when you begin to think about something and the time it manifests. That *buffer of time* gives you the opportunity to redirect your attention more and more in the direction of the things that you actually do want to manifest in your experience."

We also cannot always have exactly what we want, when we want it, because of a potential *conflict of interest*. What you wish for may be to the disadvantage of someone else, or what you desire may be damaging to the environment, or what you create may ultimately disturb the equilibrium that exists in the Universe.

Although there is duality in the Universe, everything is always in perfect balance. The flow of universal energy is much like the swing of a pendulum, constantly swinging to and fro to maintain perfect harmony. Day follows night, Sun follows Moon, Summer follows Winter, peace follows war, health follows illness, happiness follows sadness, and *receiving follows giving*. There is a constant *exchange of energy* and what we receive with one hand we will always give with the other, whether we wish to, or not. It is Universal Law. Your personal or individual human needs will never take priority over Universal Law. There is much truth in the popular sarcasm, "The Universe does not revolve around you".

Without duality, energy exchange and the constant correction of universal balance our Universe cannot function effectively and efficiently, neither can it continue to expand. We are all inter-connected co-creators of this *Hologram of Consciousness*. Our individual consciousness shapes, influences and expands the Universal Consciousness, and vice versa. We are one great collective and together we manifest all that is, was and ever will be.

Your personal acts of creation and attraction are therefore subordinate to the greater good of the 'collective'. To understand this better, it helps to imagine the Conscious Universe as a 'doting Mother Hen' who is always looking out for the best interest of all her little chicks. As a caring and responsible mother it is her duty to ensure that each and every baby chicken gets enough to eat, so that they will all survive and grow up healthy and strong.

When you create and attract, the Conscious Universe jump-starts a process of collective action to begin to shift, and shape, *transform and rearrange energy*, so that the right people, events, experiences and material things will all conspire to enter your life at the *best possible time*, in order to manifest whatever it is that you need to fulfill your Soul Purpose and Life Calling. This process takes time.

The smaller, more mundane things we create and attract usually manifest within days or weeks, sometimes months. However, in my experience the process of manifesting our major desires, such as meeting the perfect life partner, owning a dream home, getting a big promotion at work or making a complete career change typically takes about two to three years to manifest. Consider your own life until now. Think back on some of the important things you dreamed of and wished for that did eventually materialize in your life, and then consider how long before you began thinking about it, wishing for it to come true. It is very likely that many of the blessings in your life only came along a after a couple of years, if not more.

But if the Universe is conscious and omnipotent, why does it take so long for the really good stuff to manifest? Well, it is not really the Universe that is 'slow' to get it all together. No, the sluggish pace of manifestation is due to the limitations of time and space and the restrictions of the human condition. If it were up to the Universe alone, everything would manifest faster than the blink of an eye, but because everything needs to be 'lined up', while at the same time also adhering to and fulfilling all the hopes, dreams, wishes and desires of *everybody else* who may be affected by your single act of creation, things tend to move at the natural pace of time-space reality, which must remain a stable platform. The metaphysical or spiritual act of creation is immediate and instantaneous, but it is the process of attraction that slows the manifesting down to the physical, material pace of human reality.

Ralph Waldo Trine advises in *This Mystical Life of Ours*, "No matter what comes, be glad; and live in the conviction that all things are working together for good to you. As your conviction is so is your faith; and as your faith is so it shall be unto you. When you live in the conviction that all things are working together for good you will cause all things to work together for good, and you will understand the reason why when you begin to apply the real science of ideal living."

Mindful Manifesting

There are many methods and techniques we can apply to harness our innate metaphysical ability in order to deliberately create and manifest our desires. The methods I use most frequently with my clients include daily *meditation*, *affirmations*, *gratitude journals*, *vision boards* and *creative visualization*.

Bear in mind that we cannot be taught how to manifest, as it is an innate, natural aspect of our inner Divinity. The power to manifest is a spiritual talent we all bring with us into this physical reality. Manifesting techniques and methods are therefore mostly man-made techniques to bring our innate ability to create and attract back to the surface. Ability or potential means very little if your do not acquire the necessary skills to make the most of your natural talent.

In order to deliberately and successfully manifest for the greater good we must first of all have a spiritual awakening. Spiritual awareness brings with it an openness to understand and truly embrace the underlying principles of the Laws of Creation and Attraction. Manifesting is a mission impossible without a true reconnection and realignment with the Divine Self. Spiritual awareness and Higher Consciousness brings with it faith, love, hope, trust and the inner knowing that our Universe is conscious, bountiful and abundant. Without *faith* our attempts at manifesting will be erratic and will yield disappointing results.

Also remember that manifesting is not the result of a once off technique or exercise. You cannot expect to do a manifesting exercise once a week, or even once a day, and get the best possible results. Truly powerful manifesting is a *way of life,* it is a lifestyle. To deliberately manifest is to lead a *mindful* life; it is the key to an awakened and abundant Divine Life filled with joy, happiness and prosperity.

Mindfulness means to be truly *present in the moment*, in the now, while being fully aware of our thoughts, emotions, sensory perceptions, intuitions and body. Mindfulness helps us to come back to the here and now, to be aware of what is going on in the *present moment*, to be in touch with the enchanted stream of life mindfulness means to flow with the miracles of Life; it is the *magic key* to manifesting and creating a truly awakened and abundant Divine Life.

The famous monk Thomas Merton provides the most profound description for mindfulness in *The Inner Experience: Notes on Contemplation*. His words reveal the true magical secret behind manifesting a Divine Life.

> *The life of contemplation in action and purity of heart is, then, a life of great simplicity and inner liberty. One is not seeking anything special or demanding any particular satisfaction. One is content with what is. One does what is to be done, and the more concrete it is, the better. One is not worried about the results of what is done. One is content to have good motives and not be too anxious about making mistakes. In this way one can swim with the living stream of life and remain at every moment in contact with God, in the hiddenness and ordinariness of the present moment with its obvious task.*

Before we can truly manifest we must become more mindful. We achieve this by consistently transforming our thoughts, evolving our emotions, sharpening our senses and increasing our intuition. With mindfulness come patience, inner peace, appreciation and gratitude. Mindfulness raises our resonant frequency to soaring new heights, which ensures that we create, attract and manifest the life experiences we most desire.

Creative Visualization

Creative visualization is probably the most popular method for deliberate manifesting. Contrary to what some people believe, visualization practices are traditionally also a common form of *spiritual practice*. In Vajrayana Buddhism, for example, complex visualizations are used to attain Buddhahood.

Visualization is the technique of using our *imagination* and a *mindful state of being* to visualize and conceptualize the material things, people, events, circumstances and experiences we wish to create and attract into our lives. Unconscious creators often engage in creative visualization without even realizing it - we refer to as "daydreaming". The difference between daydreaming and creative visualization is however that the latter is *mindful, aware, conscious* and *deliberate*. The key steps I recommend in the creative visualization process are as follows:

1) **Decide what you want to manifest**. Be very clear about what it is that you want to create or attract into your life. The most important key element to this first step is to be extremely careful what you wish for, because you will often get exactly what you ask for, and what we sometimes ask for is not exactly what we really want! Make sure that you will not have any regrets later. Also, do not even consider manifesting things or experiences that negatively affect the well-being of others, or the environment. Always manifest for the greater good only. I find in my practice that the most effective method to gain clarity and certainty about what you want to manifest is to draw up a "shopping list" or "cosmic order". Stick to one subject or concept. Do not try to manifest a new relationship, a new career, a new house and a new car all in one visualization. Keep it simple and stick to one thing at a time. I sometimes encourage clients to spend a few days or even weeks preparing their list, until they have fine-tuned it to perfection. Try to keep your list short and concise, because it is easier to remember when you begin to visualize. Creating a one column spreadsheet works best for

most people, because you can constantly keep changing and improving it.

2) **Start with breathing or meditation.** Sit or lie comfortably in a quiet, comfortable place. Begin your creative visualization 'playshop' with at least 5 to 10 minutes of breathing and meditation. The aim of this is to shutdown the noise of the material world around you and become truly mindful in the moment. It is acceptable to play soft meditation music, as long as it does not distract you from the meditative process. The correct choice of music is vital. The purpose of your meditation is primarily to raise your resonant frequency.

3) **Connect with your Divine Self** and ask for intuitive guidance in the process of manifesting. Remember to spend a few minutes giving thanks and express gratitude for all the abundant blessings already in your life. Be truly mindful of these blessings, feel how they make you feel. This will help to raise your vibration.

4) **Visualize what you wish to create or attract**. The aim is not to merely see the things you want to manifest, but to actually experience it as a real-life event. The idea is to take the bullet points on your shopping list and combine it into a fantasy or "mind movie". I find that closing your eyes is most effective. Try not to refer to your list all the time, as this breaks the flow of your imagination and reduces your mindfulness during the process.

5) **Include all your senses.** Once you have visualized the basic "mind movie" keep focusing on the whole scene. What do you see? What do you feel? What do you hear? What does it smell like? What can you taste? Fully engage with your mind movie, become absorbed and heighten your awareness. Become increasingly mindful. I find that the visualization stage also greatly benefits from using a "movie soundtrack". Choose uplifting and inspiring music to accompany your mind movie. Music adds a powerful dimension to the visualization process, because the right kind of music raises your vibration. I prefer not to use

music with lyrics. Use the same piece of music every time you repeat this particular visualization. You can also carry this music with you and listen to it at least once or twice a day between visualization sessions; think of your mind movie as you listen to it in the car or while washing the dishes.

6) **Become mindful of your emotions.** How do you feel while you act out your mind movie? What is your emotional response to whatever you see, hear, feel, taste and smell in your created scene? Take note of every emotion. Truly experience the love, joy, happiness, peace, serenity, contentment, gratitude and appreciation of each and every moment of your imagined experience.

7) **Observe your intuitive responses** to your mind movie. While you are absorbed in your fantasy, does the experience "feel right"? Is there an inner knowing that this is truly what you want? Please note that if you experience a 'gut feeling' or ominous foreboding that something is "off" or "not right" with whatever you are visualizing, your Divine Self is telling you that you are not going in the best direction for your greater good. It could be that your desire does not serve your Soul Purpose or your Life Calling; or maybe you are not yet ready to welcome this manifestation into your life, because you feel unworthy or you lack faith, or you lack the confidence; or maybe what you desire is not in the best interest or harmful to others. Whatever the reason may be, it is vital that you discontinue the visualization at this point and instead focus on identifying and resolving the underlying issue first. Do not return to your visualization until the problem is truly resolved or until you have designed a more appropriate shopping list to replace the existing one.

Note that the main aim of your visualization effort is not to simply create things in your mind. Instead it is about *imprinting* how those things *make you feel.* Research has shown that our subconscious mind cannot distinguish between reality and imagination. When we visualize a fantasy our subconscious mind believes it is really happening and it becomes a *memory imprint.*

We need this imprint to repeatedly *raise our vibration* and ultimately *attract* the experiences we visualized. In other words, by imagining the things you desire you create a cognitive, emotional, sensory and intuitive imprint of your desire. This imprint can then be called up into your conscious awareness on a regular basis to repeatedly raise your vibration, in order to *keep you resonating* with that which you desire and will ultimately attract.

Perfect Partner 'Playshop'

The following is an example of how a typical creative visualization may be conceived. The aim of this particular visualization will be to attract your perfect life partner.

1) **Design your shopping list.** What does this person look like: height, eye color, body type, health? What are their demographics: age, intelligence, education, income, interests, hobbies, lifestyle? What do they do for a living? What are their most prominent characteristics: intelligent, educated, wealthy? What is their personality like: quiet, serious, sensitive, kind, conscientious, independent, original, funny, charming, calm, adventurous, analytical, determined, passionate? How do you envision your relationship with this person? Think about your parents' relationship or other role-models and what you witnessed as you grew up. Think about your friends and relatives, and their relationships. What was it about them that impressed you? What did they do and have with each other that you thought was great? However, *do not focus* on what you *do not want*, for you will attract that also!

2) **Create your mind movie**. Visualize yourself walking on a beautiful beach on a lovely summer day. What do you see, feel, hear, taste and smell? Feel the wind in your hair and the warmth of the sun on your skin. Smell the fresh sea breeze and taste the saltiness in the air. In the distance you see your perfect partner walking towards you. At first they are a just a tiny figure in the distance, but as they come closer you begin to see them more clearly, exactly as you had imagined. See their face, their smile, their eyes, their body. See how their way of walking reflects the

qualities of their personality. What clothes are they wearing? Keep walking towards your perfect partner until you are standing face to face. See how you greet each other and then embrace and kiss. What do you see, hear, feel, taste and smell? What emotions are you experiencing? How do you feel intuitively when you are with this person, what does your "gut" tell you, etc.

3) **Repeat this visualization as often as you wish**. Recall your memories of it while you are driving to work, or when you are in the shower. Bring back the way it made you feel. Keep the feeling and the vision alive in your daily vibration as much as you can.

Vision Boards

Vision boards are a fun way to *externalize* the process of creating, attracting and manifesting and make it *more tangible* or real, especially for people who are new to the concept of deliberate creation. Many of my clients and students have made use of vision boards with great success.

Vision boards are basically a *visual representation* of the desires and wishes you are intending to create, attract and manifest in your life. In a sense you could describe a vision board as affirmations or intentions in a *picture format.* All these images and words are combined into one cohesive collection to form a collage or artwork to be used in your manifesting process. It is basically a 'story board' of your dreams and aspirations.

Vision boards are powerful because they speak the language of your intuition and your subconscious mind in the form of images and symbols, and they evoke positive emotions to raise your resonant vibration to a level where it matches your desires.

Traditionally vision boards are made using a simple poster board decorated with some magazine and newspaper clippings, drawings and personal mementos. You will also need some scissors, glue and color pencils, paint or markers. Many people prefer this 'old-fashioned' approach, because it is hands-on and more tangible. However, more and more people these days are opting for the use of computer technology and the Internet to create their vision boards. You can easily put together a vision board on your computer using a wide range of software you will find on most standard systems. Some innovative people even prefer to create 'vision videos' with matching music soundtracks, which they publish on sites like YouTube and Dailymotion.

There are no set rules to making a vision board and the only real limit is your own imagination. If you are not sure what a vision board looks like, simply do an Internet search for images of "vision boards" and have a look at what other people all over the world have been putting into their vision boards.

1) **Decide what you wish to manifest**. Put together your 'shopping list'. Although many people use their vision boards to display all of their intentions for all aspects on their life at once, I recommend focusing on one main concept or aspect of your life. What is your major goal? Choose the main theme for your vision board. Is it a new relationship, a new career, a new lifestyle, a family? Spend a few days or even weeks preparing your list. For example, if you are aiming to attract your dream job, ask yourself questions about how you envision this new job.

   What is the title of your dream job?
   What kind of work will you be doing?
   How good will you be at doing this job?
   How will doing this job make you feel?
   How much will you earn financially?
   What additional benefits will this job offer you?
   What will your lifestyle be?
   Where will you work, what is the work environment?
   What clothes or uniform will you wear to work?

2) **Collect pictures and clippings that express and represent your intention.** Find images, photos, quotes, phrases, power words and small objects that symbolize and embody everything that you have listed in the first step. You can look for pictures and clippings in old magazines, or search the internet and print out what you need. Collect as much as you want to. Another good idea is to add some of your daily affirmations, print them out or make it up out of words clipped from magazines. Some people prefer to take their time and collect their materials

over a long period of time, which can be a very *powerful way to manifest*. Remember that working on your vision board is equally as important as the end product. It is all part of the process of manifesting, because you are constantly busy focusing your attention and thoughts on our desires. While you are collecting pictures, do not filter or edit anything at this stage. Do not analyze, judge or rationalize. Select images based on the strength of your emotional and your intuitive response to them. Just collect and cut out whatever resonates with you in the moment, even if you do not immediately understand why you feel it is appropriate for your project. If you like something just clip it out.

3) **Review your collection and complete your layout.** Be mindful of your intention while you sort through your collection of images and first select the main, larger pictures and clippings you want to use. Arrange everything according to your intuition. Each image on your vision board should evoke a positive emotional response and a strong intuitive reaction from you. The mere sight of your vision board should raise your vibration to match that which you intend to attract and manifest. Once you have put a basic layout together, add other smaller images and clippings that support the main theme and highlight certain aspects of your aspiration. If some components do not feel 'right', simply discard them and find something that does work for you. Keep rearranging until you are happy with your final design. Paste everything neatly onto the poster board and add some finishing touches and decorations with paint or color markers if you wish. Remember to include at least one sincere expression of gratitude and appreciation somewhere on your vision board!

4) **Place your vision board strategically in a prominent spot where you will often see it**. Your vision board must be placed in a location where you will have constant exposure to it. A good place to put up your vision board would be on your refrigerator, on your bathroom mirror, the back of your clothes closet, or in front of your desk at

work. If you created a vision board on your computer, you can use it as your screen's wallpaper, or download it onto your mobile phone.

5) **Keep improving and fine tuning your vision board over time.** Your vision board is never final or complete. Keep adding to or changing your vision board as you discover new images and clippings that you feel are more appropriate. Your vision board is a work in progress. Keep improving your board until your intentions become manifest, at which time you can replace it with a new vision board.

10

YOUR SPECIAL MISSION

Do you know where you are going in your career? Does your work make you happy? Do you know what you really want to achieve in your lifetime? Do you know why you are here? Do you feel fulfilled? Is your life's work meaningful? Do you feel you are meant to have a bigger purpose?

These are questions that many people ask themselves from time to time. We all have this urge to seek true purpose and a deeper meaning in our lives, because we know intuitively that we came here to *fulfill a mission*. Sadly, many people never discover their true Life Calling, and they return to their spiritual home with-out completing the task they originally set out to fulfill.

Oliver Wendell Holmes said, ""Many people die with their music still in them. Too often it is because they are always getting ready to live. Before they know it time runs out." Accomplishing our Life Calling is not so much about the end result as it is about the process of getting to that destination. It is in fact this 'journey' of creativity and physical achievement that we came to experience and enjoy, not the ultimate outcome. Life truly is a journey.

The starting point to truly accomplish your Life Calling is to accept and embrace the inner knowledge that you are indeed different and very special. You are an extraordinary and unique human miracle! There has never before been anyone in the entire Conscious Universe exactly like you, and before you came into this world you equipped yourself with a remarkable toolbox of talents, aptitudes, skills, abilities, ideas, insights and inspiration.

Right here, right now, you have the capacity within you to accomplish anything you can imagine. You can be, do and have anything you can set your mind to. You are designed to be a powerful creator of your own life experience. You are correct; you are indeed meant to do something wonderful with your life. And if you do not yet remember what your special mission is, it is time for you to find out!

Clarity And Focus

I have read numerous biographies and autobiographies over the years. I have always been fascinated with people's destiny, their life choices and how it contributes to their subsequent achievements, success and personal fulfillment. I was intrigued to see just exactly how many highly successful and celebrated people throughout history often *knew from a very young age* what it is they were supposed to accomplish in their life, and they often become completely devoted to this mission very early on. Even those who did not initially know for sure what exactly they were meant to do, tend to report that they always knew they were meant to *do something special with their life* - something significant or memorable.

Most of us know that we came here to do something meaningful with our lives. We all feel an inner 'calling' at some point, but we tend to forget our original mission, or we become so distracted by the demands of modern life that we somehow lose direction and focus. This appears to be a deciding factor in the lives of successful and celebrated people – *clarity* and *focus*. They have a unique focus, ambition or drive from early on, and many also report a vivid clarity about what direction they need to take.

Along with *clarity* and *focus,* the third aspect you tend to find in the life stories of exceptional people is that they report a certain amount of *luck, good fortune* or *opportunity* that came along at just the right time, to catapult them from an average existence to an extraordinary life. But as we have seen there is no such thing as fate, luck or chance. The synchronistic events or opportunities that these people experienced were something they *created for themselves,* by applying their own power of conscious creation.

The lesson to be learned from this is simple. To accomplish your Life Calling you need to first *identify your true calling*, then you must *pursue it with clarity and focus*, and finally you must apply your innate ability to *attract and manifest all that you need* to make your mission possible. When you do this, the Universe shall conspire to bring about the ideal circumstances, opportunities and encounters with key people, places and events to make your mission a reality. What you focus upon and what you think about is what ultimately will become your future.

From The Inside Out

The reason why many people fail to recognize their Life Calling is of course due to the Divine Disconnect. They lose touch with their spiritual origins and eventually get stuck in the data gathering phase of their Life Plan.

I am sure you know of at least one ambitious friend or family member who has been concocting or coming up with all kinds of grandiose schemes and plans for projects, new careers or start-up businesses for years. Yet, they never seem to get anything off the ground. This is often due to the person being stuck in the data gathering mode and taking a purely *materialistic approach* to their life calling. The main problem is however not that they have too many vague plans, or that they are too greedy or power hungry. The foremost concern is that that they set themselves up for failure because they *start at the wrong end* of the process.

Your Life Calling is not really about what kind of work you do or which career you choose, or how much money you will make. It is not about *what* you do for a living, it is about *who you are* on the inside. It is about how you express yourself in the world as a *spiritual being* in human form. Even people who manage to achieve success in a field that is contrary to their true calling, or reach great heights in any career despite their lack of spiritual awareness, often reach the point later in their lives where they wake up to the knowledge that their money, fame and power bring them no lasting contentment, joy or inner peace. Tragically, this realization or awakening sometimes comes in the wake of a traumatic event or crisis in their lives.

Unconscious individuals tend to approach their lives from a purely *secular* or *materialistic perspective*, viewing themselves as highly evolved animals who need to *compete* with their fellow man for a higher-up position in the food chain. The less ambitious focus their attention mostly on *survival* or comfort from day to day. They see their career or business merely as a means to put a roof over their heads and food on the table, whilst inside their soul there remains a void, a yearning for a life of real purpose and meaning. These unconscious souls will however not become aware of their true Life Calling until they shift their focus away from mere physical survival, or from their obsession with material gain, and instead look towards a more *spiritually inspired* career approach.

In truth there is only one true Life Calling. Once you strip away all the trappings of modern materialism and lack consciousness, there remains only one purposeful mission in everything we do, no matter which career or field of work we may choose. In fact, in a sense we are all born to fulfill the same Life Calling. It is called *service*. You and I are *called to serve* each other and our planet. Without being of service in some way, shape or form your life can never be truly purposeful or fulfilling. A Divine Life is a life *dedicated to service.*

The 'Struggle For Life' Myth

It is a myth that we are by nature competitive and selfish in order to survive. Aggressive business tycoons and narcissistic modern day celebrities often uphold the concept of 'survival of the fittest' to justify their competitive drive. Most of us were schooled in the Darwinian paradigm to believe that we are highly evolved 'monkeys' who somehow got to where we are because of natural selection, intense competition and our general superiority as a species. We therefore tell ourselves that it is perfectly acceptable to express our 'naturally animal urges' to callously trample and destroy each other in our stampeding rush to the 'top of the pile'. Yet, nothing could be further from the truth.

Dutch primatologist Frans de Waal believes we instead have an overriding, natural instinct for *compassion*. We are not here to merely serve our own interests. In his book, *The Age of Empathy* he explains how empathy comes naturally to both humans and animals. This view is based on fieldwork and laboratory research on, among other, chimpanzees, elephants and dolphins. According to De Waal many animals are instinctively predisposed to assist and support each other, take care of one another, and even take direct action to save lives. Similarly, De Waal believes that every human is destined to be *humane.*

> *Don't believe anyone who says that since nature is based on a struggle for life, we need to live like this as well. Many animals survive not by eliminating each other or by keeping everything for themselves, but by cooperating and*

sharing…What we need is a complete overhaul of assumptions about human nature. Too many economists and politicians model human society on the perpetual struggle they believe exists in nature, but which is a mere projecttion. Like magicians, they first throw their ideological prejudices into the hat of nature, then pull them out by their very ears to show how much nature agrees with them. It's a trick for which we have fallen for too long. Obviously, competition is part of the picture, but humans can't live by competition alone.

What we focus on and what we think about is what becomes our reality. If you approach your life and your career from a paradigm of 'lack consciousness', and if you subscribe to the belief that work is just something you have to do to pay the bills or 'keep up with the Joneses', then you will never be able to see the real value of what you can contribute and where your true talents lay.

And if you prefer to believe that a fulfilling and successful life is reserved only for a lucky few celebrities or wealthy tycoons, then a humdrum existence and boring routine may be all that your life will ever amount to.

Many successful scientists, inventors, entrepreneurs, artists and other remarkable people will tell you that they never started out with the aim of making lots of money, or to become famous or honored. They will tell you that they merely *followed their true passion*, their heart's desire. They simply started doing what they have always enjoyed doing, and somehow the recognition, success and money just followed.

The 'Fame And Fortune' Myth

There is a major fallacy about life purpose that some inspirational speakers, life coaches and celebrity biographers propagate without even realizing the damage they are doing to the lives of others. It is also a serious misconception that many Law of Attraction gurus preach as the 'gospel truth', and then they have no clear answers when their followers fail to make their first million or are unable to become the next Kim Kardashian. The truth is that the Law of Attraction is not about making more money than you will ever be able to spend in one lifetime, neither is it to be on the cover of every magazine in the world. The myth of celebrity and wealth does not a *true Life Calling* make.

No spiritual being ever put together a Life Plan aimed solely at 'getting rich quick', or making it into the Hollywood gossip columns. If a Life Plan is meant to include fame and fortune, which it sometimes does, it is never for its own sake but always for the purpose of *being of service* to others. There are many celebrities who are sincerely engaged in various causes, charities, community service, or some form of social or spiritual upliftment. Well-known stars like Bono, Bob Geldof, Oprah Winfrey, Madonna, Lady Gaga, Paul Newman, Angelina Jolie, Brad Pitt, Ellen Degeneres and Beyoncé Knowles are but a few of the names that come to mind.

Not only do many of these celebrities sponsor various causes financially, or through generating publicity with their involvement, they often also express their support in their work in order to create awareness and change the way people think about certain issues. These celebrities do not merely entertain the masses; they often also make a real, tangible difference in the world. Their career success is a means to an end that goes beyond mere fame and fortune. The ones who don't serve society usually fade from our memory very quickly.

Fame and fortune is in essence not the meaning or purpose of any life. It never will be. It is nothing more than a *false belief* maintained by the mass media, and sold to 'ordinary' people based on a post-modern culture of consumerism. These myths are the inventions of the Ego and the False Self, the trappings of a secular society devoid of the miraculous and stripped of the truly meaningful. These myths sell more products, by creating a distant ideal few of us are supposed to ever achieve.

Some spiritual gurus will try to convince you that fame and fortune come to those who have a special calling, unusual talent, good karma or a superior mission in life, but this is not true, as there is no superiority, status or hierarchy in the spiritual realm. Those are all *man-made concepts*, and this is becoming increasingly clear in our current culture where we now see highly talented artists and entertainers rub shoulders on the red carpet with reality stars and 'ordinary people' who become famous (or notorious) for no apparent reason except that the media has placed them in the public eye. Never measure your Life Calling based on popular public opinion or the materialistic, hedonistic values of secular society. The myths of fame and fortune are mere illusions and they cannot bring lasting joy and fulfillment.

So, what are the keys to happiness then? Numerous studies have been done in recent years to discover the mechanics of happiness and a list of common characteristics shared by happy people have been identified in various studies.

Happy people....

- consistently express appreciation and gratitude
- are committed to their life goals and ideals
- are altruistic and always willing to help others
- spend a lot of time with family and friends
- express optimism and excitement for the future
- do daily physical activity or exercise
- truly enjoy life's pleasures
- live in the moment

True happiness simply cannot be found in your bank account. If you don't have a lot of money your first instinct may be to disagree, but consider that our standard of living has increased dramatically over the past century, yet our levels of happiness has not increased at all, and in some cases it has even diminished slightly, according to Professor Daniel Kahneman of the University of Princeton, "There is a lot of evidence that being richer isn't making us happier."

The Smart Seeker's Bucket List

It is said that we all have a 'bucket list'. In case you are not familiar with the term, a bucket list is all the things we hope to do or achieve in our lifetime, before our death. The term has its origins in the old idiomatic expression "to kick the bucket", which means "to die". For most of us our bucket list is merely a few random thoughts, ideas or loose mental notes.

If you had to quickly make a bucket list for yourself right now, what would the top five things be that you still want to do? It is very likely that the item "spending more time at work" will *not* appear on your list. Life is essentially not about 'work'. To work is to *survive.* To *serve* is to *live and thrive.* Your Life Calling is not to have a career or a job to 'make ends meet'. We have only one Life Purpose or Calling and that is *to be of service* in whatever we may do. It does not matter who or what we serve, be it our fellow man, animals, nature, or the environment, as long as we are of serving the Greater Good. Being of service is an expression of our inner Divinity. Apart from achieving our Soul Purpose as spiritual beings, being of service is our only other duty that we need to fulfill in this lifetime. None of the other human obsessions, trifles and absurdities we chase every day are of any lasting significance or importance in the greater scheme of things.

The 2006 General Social Survey (GSS) at the National Opinion Research Center at the University of Chicago found that people who were most happy and satisfied with their careers were all in professions that focus primarily on *serving other people.* The study further indicated that the most satisfying jobs were mostly the *professions,* especially those involving care-giving, teaching, protecting others and various creative pursuits. The top three jobs for satisfaction were clergy, firefighters and physical therapists.

Other highly satisfying jobs in this survey included education administrators, artists, teachers, authors, psychologists, special education teachers, operating engineers, office supervisors, security and financial services salespersons, architects, actors and directors, science technicians, mechanics and repairers, industrial engineers, airline pilots and navigators, hardware and building supplies salespersons and personal housekeepers. Interestingly, some jobs that have a high degree of social status and prestige, such as medical doctors and lawyers, did not make the list of the top twelve most satisfied or happy careers. The researchers believed this was due to those jobs involving immense responsibility and very high levels of stress.

So, how important is your career or job truly in the greater scheme of things? Is it really so important *what* we do, or is it more important *how* we do it? Kathleen Besly writes in *The Divine Art of Living*, "A man's daily business at his office can be made a channel of spiritual power if he consecrates each minute of time to the highest expression of spiritual life of which he is capable, always doing his work from the highest and most honorable standpoint. The same method may be applied to every form of occupation."

In 2012 Bronnie Ware, an Australian palliative nurse, published a book, *The Top Five Regrets of the Dying*, after she recorded the dying epiphanies of her patients over several years. 'Palliative care' refers to caring for patients in the final weeks of their lives. Ware's discovery was quite remarkable. People in their final days did not report any regrets about not earning more, not being more successful, not being more attractive or glamorous, not being sexually more active, not gratifying the senses more often, or not collecting more material possessions or social prestige. None of the typical obsessions of humanity one would expect seemed to be of any importance to people on their deathbed.

Instead the dying people Ware spoke to wished they had not always worked so hard and such long hours. They wished they had lived a *more authentic life* by being more *true to themselves* and *expressing their emotions*, instead of living according to the expectations of others. They wished they had *gathered the courage* to stand up to the pressures of their peers and society in order to stay true to themselves. They wished that they had stayed *more in touch with friends* and made more of an effort to *cultivate lasting relationships.* Most of all they wished they had allowed themselves to be happier and truly content. Ware reports that the *wish for greater happiness* was surprisingly common among the people she interviewed, "Many did not realise until the end that *happiness is a choice.* They had stayed stuck in old patterns and habits. The so-called 'comfort' of familiarity overflowed into their emotions, as well as their physical lives. Fear of change had them pretending to others, and to their selves, that they were content, when deep within, they longed to laugh properly and have silliness in their life again."

Your career or your job is not the thing you will miss the most when you come to the end of your life. In fact, you career decisions and job choices may be the very thing that you *regret the most.* Ralph Waldo Emerson said, "The crowning fortune of a man is to be born to some pursuit which finds him employment and happiness, whether it be to make baskets, or broadswords, or canals, or statues, or songs." Find whatever makes your heart sing and then share it with the rest of the world. Time is of the essence.

A Life Of Increase

Am I suggesting that we all stop working and become lazy lay-abouts? No, not in the least. In fact, personally I cannot imagine not having something meaningful and constructive to do with my day. I love my work. I did not enjoy my earlier jobs in life, but I certainly do now. For a long time I felt very unhappy and frustrated; I really had no clue what I really wanted to do with the rest of my life. I was getting ready to give up all hope forever, when the breakthrough finally came in my mid-30's. I knew deep down that there was something else I was supposed to be doing with my life. Had it not been for my own spiritual awakening, I would probably still be doing a job I did not really care for, while denying my true psychic heritage in the process.

If you are still searching for your true calling, know that there is something you will be extremely good at, something you were designed to do before birth, even if you don't know what it is at this point in time. You may have a single calling, or you may have multiple, sequential life purposes to fulfill. And do note that a Life Calling is not necessarily a job or career. It could be something you do in your free time, when you are *not working* or something you do as a part of your work, and not the actual job itself.

Don't define your own success based on the expectations of your friends, family or society. Success and achievement manifests in different ways for different people. Some of us are meant to become the best in *one single pursuit* or skill, while others are meant to be 'jacks-of-all-trades-and-masters-of-none'. Some of us are meant to become rich, or famous, or highly educated, while others are meant to lead frugal, humble and more simple lives. All of it serves a purpose; all happens for a reason, all is as it must be.

We are *supposed to love what we do* for a living and the only way to achieve that is to ensure that whatever you are doing is serving the greater good. Ensure that every time you of service you touch the world around you with the energy of expansion, growth, advancement, improvement and becoming.

That is your true Life Calling in a nutshell: to expand the Conscious Universe by *serving the greater good*. Wallace D Wattles captures this sentiment perfectly in *The Science of Getting Rich*.

> *And in so far as your business consists in dealing with other men, whether personally or by letter, the key*

thought of all your efforts must be to convey to their minds the impression of increase... Doing what you want to do is life; and there is no real satisfaction in living if we are compelled to be forever doing something which we do not like to do, and can never do what we want to do. And it is certain that you can do what you want to do; the desire to do it is proof that you have within you the power which can do it. Desire is a manifestation of power.

To become more, to expand, and to seek more complete expression is inherent in our human condition, because it is an innate quality we possess due to our original *spiritual nature*. 'Increasing' or 'becoming' is what drives the expansion of the entire Conscious Universe. We are each of us a mirror reflection of the Universal Source; we are created in the image of the Divine. We are a perfect imprint of the magnificent Holographic Web of Consciousness. And because we are spiritual beings who reflect the Divine in physical form, we also possess the innate qualities of Divinity. We are *self-aware* and *conscious*; we have the *capacity for reason*, sentience, imagination and creative thought; we command *creative freedom* and the metaphysical *power to manifest*; and we have the capacity for complete self-actualization, *individuation* and *transcendence*. All these qualities are the expression of our inner Divinity, a direct reflection of the Higher Self.

To live a truly awakened and abundant Divine Life that will ultimately culminate in the achievement of your Soul Purpose and your Life Calling, you must honor these Divine qualities within. To achieve your Soul Purpose you must strive to become more conscious, continuously reaching for a higher state of being and higher level of consciousness, and for unconditional love, peace and harmony. This is the *process of transcendence*, the process of achieving a superior state of being, or an enlightened existence above and beyond the limits of our material experience.

To accomplish your Life Calling you must figure out who you really are and begin to differentiate that which makes you truly unique from the rest of the Conscious Universe. For while we are all made in the image of the Divine Source and we are all reflective fragments of the Universal Hologram, we are each of us also unique in our individual make-up and in how we are meant to contribute to the expansion of the Universe.

It is vital that we identify who we are, what our unique talents and interests are and what we can offer in service to the greater good. It is our duty to figure out what makes us special. For without the process of individuation we are of no use to our fellow man and the planet. Without individuation we fail to achieve our mission to planet Earth.

It is our mission and our duty in this lifetime to create more, attract more, manifest more, become more. It is our task to create new things, and to reshape and redesign the world as we know it. It is our assignment to increase, expand and improve what is, was and ever will be. In the words of Wallace D Wattles, "You are a creative center, from which increase is given off to all."

Individuating Your Life Calling

The process of identifying your true Life Calling or changing careers requires that you believe you can mould the work you do around your goals, and not the other way around. Successful people *first set personal goals* and then they set out to find a career or job to match those goals. Creating your ideal vocation requires trusting that you can follow your dreams and passion and that successful will follow, because you are doing what you love to do. Many people who do not follow their passion choose to do so not because they are incapable of being successful, but because they *fear failure*. They will only consider chasing their dream if they are guaranteed to be successful.

How do you find your true passion? How do you remember your Life Calling? By going within, not by searching outside. Look inward and let your intuition and emotions shape your career path. Your Divine Self knows which direction is most fitting for you. Let your inner guidance take the lead and the practical solutions and opportunities will manifest. Most of all do not fear change, because we usually find our true direction in the midst of change and upheaval. Change is what brings new opportunity. Where a door closes a new window always opens.

Before they come to me for assistance, many of my clients have spent many hours of their precious time here on Earth attempting to figure out what their true Life Calling might be. Few are successful in this endeavor. In my experience they usually fail due to the following four reasons.

Unconscious Prematurity

I have discovered that some people attempt to pursue their true Life Calling too soon in their life, before they are truly ready. Our Life Calling can only be identified once we are truly equipped to pursue it. The principle is much the same as the words of the Buddha, who said, "When the student is ready, the teacher will appear."

It is difficult to accurately identify your Life Purpose while you are still in the state of Divine Disconnect. In this state of 'reality coma' it makes no sense to try and delve into spiritual purpose of your life. In the state of Divine Disconnect our being is centered on material survival and Ego fixations. In the state of Divine Disconnect the Ego with all its false beliefs and material obsessions reigns supreme. To try and uncover your spiritual truth from this unconscious condition is futile. A true spiritual awakening and reconnection with the Divine Self is required to tap into one's true mission and destiny.

We also need significant *life experience* or a *relevant education* if we are to take on certain callings. You are setting yourself up for failure and frustration if you proceed with your true calling before you have gathered all the knowledge and experience you will need to get the job done. If you have to 'flip burgers' at a fast-food restaurant in the meantime, make the most of your time there. Everything happens for a reason and there is something you are supposed to learn or achieve in your current job, before you can move on.

Become more *mindful* and *appreciative* of where you are now, in the present moment, and make the most of it for the time being. Meanwhile keep your eye on the target and keep working towards your goal. I hated most of my earlier jobs, but today I am using all the skills I learned in each and every one of those jobs. There was method in all the madness.

Secular Materialism

Many people who are unhappy in their careers tend to approach the search for their true Life Calling from a materialistic or secular perspective. They allow the Ego, or the False Self, as well as the expectations of friends, family and teachers to command the process. Others seek for their personal truth among the many meaningless pursuits and obsessions of modern society. They seek purpose in the opinions of others and the external, material world, instead of going within to find their own intuitive truth.

Ralph Waldo Emerson said, "Be yourself; no base imitator of another, but your best self. There is something which you can do better than another. Listen to the inward voice and bravely obey that. Do the things at which you are great, not what you were never made for."

It is unlikely that you will find your true Life Calling if the main focus of your search is how much money you will earn, how glamorous your work will be, or how much recognition or fame it will bring you. The original Life Plan you designed before you incarnated into this lifetime did not consider such trivial human fixations. If money, fame or power is an actual part of your Life Plan (sometimes it is) it will come to you in its own good time as it was pre-determined. And when these things come to you as pre-destined, it would not be for their own sake or purely for your indulgence, but in service of the greater good.

It is no accident that some of the rich and famous live truly charitable and socially conscious lives once they achieve success, while others suffer the 'misery' of their many blessings. One only has to watch a few talk shows or flip open the latest edition of any lifestyle magazine to find news of yet another celebrity or business tycoon who have fallen from grace, because of drug addiction, alcoholism, sexual misconduct, violence, failed relation-ships or suicide. The stresses and pressures of a life of fame and fortune become unbearable if one has no sense of true direction, purpose and fulfillment.

The spirit within us constantly craves reconnection with the Divine Self, the soul yearns to stand within its Soul Purpose and the mind hungers for a sense of meaning and fulfillment that only our true Life Calling can provide. Therefore one must focus the exploration of your Life Calling on what matters within, not what the external world considers important. Uncovering your Life Calling is a *spiritual quest*, not a material pursuit.

Linear Logic

The third mistake people make in the hunt for their Life Calling is to approach the search from a linear perspective, starting from the beginning of their life up to where they are now. To them it is a matter of their childhood background, their education and their work experience until now making some kind of sense or forming a logical pattern which will show them where to go next. They stick with the familiar and safe, poking around with a stick in the comfort zone of their current life. They believe that somewhere in there they might find what it is they have been missing, the magical key to unlock their true destiny. In my experience this is a fruitless pursuit.

To reveal your true Life Calling I find it is much more productive and effective to consider your life from its ending, instead of its beginning. When you get to the end of your life, what would you have wanted to achieve? This is where your quest should begin.

Permission Denied

You may find this odd, but I have found with many of my clients that the one and only thing that holds them back in life is a 'lack of permission'. It is amazing what happens with some people when you simply give them permission to pursue their dreams. It often changes their lives dramatically within just a few weeks.

Many people are pressured from an early age to fulfill the expectations of their parents and society. Subconsciously they believe they have to do what others expect of them. They often seek approval or recognition from others to affirm that their dreams are not silly or impractical. And because they never get clear confirmation or permission from the key people in their lives, they never get very far with anything. They lack the courage of their own conviction. They talk about it, but they don't do much, always waiting for someone else to give them the 'thumbs up'. These people have never been granted the freedom to truly be themselves and express their heart's desire. Many people have a lost inner child who is merely waiting for permission from an adult to go ahead and fully express themselves. If this sounds like you, know that you are hereby granted unconditional permission to take on that dream you have been waiting to fulfill. I am giving you full permission to make your dream real. Take action right now, you may proceed!

Career Myths

More often than not the problem with accomplishing your true Life Calling is not due to an inability to identify what you want to do, but in what you believe you are *not supposed to do*. In my work with people who wish to change their career paths I have found many of them held back by certain myths, misconceptions and false beliefs.

Myth #1: You must be sure what you want to do. Many of us fear taking the first step towards a new career because we firmly believe that we first have to be 100% sure of what we want to do before we begin to do anything. Many of my clients over the years started out with this *all-or-nothing approach.* People often have this idea that they need to stop one career and then move into the next all in one big leap. They believe they cannot make this leap until they are absolutely sure they want to do it and that they definitely will be successful in their new career. The truth is that many of the most successful people started out by first *experimenting,* or trying out small projects in their spare time, or attending night school, or working part-time or on weekends. You don't have to wait until you have officially resigned from your current job, or until you have enough money to attend a training course, before you can take steps to manifest a shift in your career. You can start today, right now. Simply researching your field of interest on the Internet is already a step in the right direction. Often your original idea transforms over time as you discover new information and ideas. Don't wait for better days. Do something today.

Myth #2: Work is not about passion. Many people believe that to be truly successful in this day and age one must make a career decision based on *social status* or *potential income.* Many of us allow ourselves to be pressured into so-called 'sensible' career decisions believing it is in our best interest, while completely ignoring our true passion. The truth is that the most successful people are usually the ones who follow their true passion. If you are one of those people who at some point buried your passion for the sake of a so-called 'smarter' career choice, it may be time for you to reconsider. If you have been trying to continue building on that false career foundation, you will continue to build on sand and look for needles in haystacks. Instead dig deep below the sand to find that *original passion* you laid to rest so long ago. We all know at a very young age what we want to do with our lives. We arrive with that innate knowledge, but we lose it due to social conditioning and the Divine Disconnect. Go back to your roots. What was it that you loved doing as a child or teenager? What were your original interests and hobbies? What were your childhood passions? I find 90% of the time that this is where people rediscover there true passion and the way forward.

Myth #3: Work now, play later. Many people believe the best approach to their career decision is to choose a career that will pay well, which will enable them to first grow rich and save enough money, which will then allow them to pursue their true passion later in life. Unfortunately, this approach is often disastrous for most, as you eventually become trapped in a life you never really wanted to begin with. Truly successful and fulfilled people do not postpone their dreams. They live in the moment and they often become absorbed and committed to their career very early on, because they love what they do. Working just to make money, and postponing work enjoyment and career satisfaction until later, will not ensure your commitment and ultimate success. 'Follow your passion and the money will follow' is the mantra of many people who are content and fulfilled in their careers. To find your ideal career you have to look at the world through new eyes and from a *fresh perspective.* Explore your childhood passions, experiment with new skills, research ideas you were always too afraid to consider, try out different things. Do not allow false beliefs, other people's ignorance and career myths to block your path to accomplishing your true Life Calling.

Myth #4: The future is a linear upward rise of science and technology. One of the foremost reasons why some people are struggling to find their niche and calling in today's world is because they are trying to apply old-school, traditional approaches and solutions to a fast-changing, modern world. Many of the preconceived ideas we hold about careers paths, economic survival, technology and the future are no longer applicable or relevant. It has not been for years. Too many of us are still trying to be 'square pegs in round holes'. Our world is rapidly changing and herein lays a potential goldmine of future career and business opportunities. Attempting to make your way in the world in the manner of your parents or grand-parents is fast becoming a dead end street.

Ralph Waldo Emerson described the problem very well when he said, "I see young men, my townsmen, whose misfor-tune it is to have inherited farms, houses, barns, cattle, and farming tools; for these are more easily acquired than got rid of. Better if they had been born in the open pasture and suckled by a wolf, that they might have seen with clearer eyes what field they were called to labor in."

Sohail Inayatullah explains in an essay titled, *Eliminating Future Shock*, "The shape of the future is thus not merely a linear upward rise of more science, more technology and more modernity, i.e. the end of history, of religion, of tradition. Indeed, individuals and communities throughout the world have seen the linear future and said, 'No, we don't like it." Inayatullah further explains that "history is not merely linear, it can be cyclical, or move like a pendulum".

The globalized, post-modern world we have collectively created over the past century is increasingly being questioned and challenged by spiritual seekers. There are several shifts in modern society's outlook that will increasingly create new spiritual business opportunities and alternative career paths never dreamed of before. And contrary to the 'information age' myth of future careers all being driven by hi-tech materialism, we may be surprised in years to come when our children will be doing unusual new jobs that do not fundamentally revolve around technology. Will technology become obsolete in this New Age? Absolutely not! Modern technology and communi-cations media will empower us to do these 'New Age' jobs, but they will not be central to our economy. Technology will merely be a means to an end, not an end in itself.

Back To The Future

To uncover your true Life Calling, or at least find some accurate clues of which direction you should be going, try the following exercise. You will need a quiet place to meditate and a notebook or writing pad and pen. I find the most of my clients also benefit from listening to meditation, new age or classical music. Baroque music is ideal, but don't play it during the first step while you are meditating.

1) **Start with your grounding, centering and shielding** routine.

2) **Enter into a state of meditation** and connect with your Divine Self. Guidelines and exercises to achieve this are available in Section II of this book. Withdraw your mind from the 'noise' of your daily life and discontinue any thought process or self-talk that you may become aware of. Focus purely on connecting with your inner Divinity.

3) **Ask your Divine Self to guide you** in indentifying your true Life Calling. Then spend a few minutes giving thanks and expressing gratitude for all the abundant blessings in your life. The purpose of any meditation or prayer is primarily to raise your vibration. If we do not feel good or happy, we cannot truly commune with the Divine; neither can we attract the things we wish to manifest.

4) **You can also perform the first two steps as dream-work** the night before, just before you go to sleep. Ask your Divine Self to reveal your Life Calling to you in your dreams. Make notes of any dream content you can remember the next morning, the very moment you wake up. Then repeat these first two steps when you do the exercise. Once you have completed your preparatory meditation proceed to the next step.

5) **Draw up a 'bucket list'** of all the things you would like to do before you die. Write down at least ten things. At least five of the things you want to do must be purely for *enjoyment and adventure*. They do not have to be serious or solemn, for example "Learn to play the guitar" or "Visit Disney World". The other five things must be your *important life goals*. What are the really important things you would like to achieve? For example, "Complete my college degree" or "Start a non-profit organization". Please

note the emphasis here is on activities or "things to do", not on material things you wish to own or titles you would like to have. Do not limit yourself in any way. Forget about money and material possessions. Also, do not concern yourself with the how, when and where you will be able to do these things. Imagine you have just won the lottery or that you have discovered a magic lamp that is granting you ten wishes. You can do whatever you please, absolutely anything! This is *your* bucket list, so allow your imagination to run wild!

6) **Review your bucket list.** Are you happy and satisfied with the things you chose? Do these things on your list make you feel excited? Do you feel energized and inspired? If not, you may need to make some changes. A bucket list should make you feel enthusiastic and motivated!

7) **Review your list a second time by going 'back to the future'.** This time observe your list from the perspective of the end of your life. Pretend for a moment that you have already done all of the things on your list. You have completed your bucket list exactly as you had planned to. If this was your final hour on the planet and you are about to 'kick the bucket', and you have done all these things on your list, would you feel satisfied and content that you had made the most with your life? Would you feel that you have done all the really fun stuff you always wanted to do, as well as all the truly meaningful things you ever wanted to? Would you feel that you have been really *true to yourself*? Would you also feel on your last day that you have truly *served* humanity or the planet? If your answer is a resounding "yes!", then your list is complete. If it is "no" or "maybe", then you need to go back and make some changes. Refine your bucket list until you feel it is truly meaningful to you.

8) **Write a mission statement for your life.** Take the essential keywords and concepts from your final bucket list and write out a 'mission statement' for your life. Look for a common thread that runs through your list. Look for similarities; try to identify the pattern of your desires. All

the things on your list are basically an expression of your personality. What is it that makes you tick? Once you have identified a common thread or theme convert it into a 'mission statement' by completing the following sentence: "My mission in this lifetime is....." For example, the following bucket list could be translated as follows:

- *Ride an elephant*
- *Feed the sharks*
- *Go on a trip around the world*
- *Be a contestant on 'The Amazing Race'*
- *Work with animals*
- *Make the world a better place*
- *Save an endangered species*
- *Learn to speak another language*
- *Inspire and motivate others*
- *Make peace with my family*
- *Start a non-profit organization*

My mission in this lifetime is... *to travel the world working with people and wild animals in other countries in order to make the world a better place.*

9) **Identify career paths or business opportunities** that would fulfill your mission statement. For example, from the above mission statement the following possibilities and opportunities come to mind:

Animal Behaviorist
Animal photographer
Animal Trainer
Conservation Biologist
Conservation Officer
Ecologist
Environmental Activist
Environmental Risk Assessor
Environmental Travel Operator
Game Farmer
Game Warden

Marine Biologist
Tour Guide
Wildlife Biologist
Wildlife Filmmaker
Wildlife Researcher
Wildlife Veterinarian
Zoo exhibit designer
Zoo Keeper
Zoologist

10) **Begin to make it real.** Once again, do not concern yourself with the how, when or where. You have the rest of your life to manifest all the things you may need to fulfill your Life Calling. Your focus at this point is to first identify your direction or goal. Once you know where you are going, it will be easy to create, attract and manifest all you need to make it real. So, what if the person in our example is currently working as a cashier at the supermarket? Does that prevent her from beginning to manifesting whatever it is she needs to fulfill her calling as an Animal Behaviorist? A great place to start an environmental or wildlife career might be to read about it, do research on the Internet and most of all to *volunteer*. My next suggestion would be for her to get out of the supermarket and start working in place where there are live animals, even if it is initially only part-time or in her free time. Imagine how being near the animals would raise her vibration and how fast she would begin to attract the people and opportunities she may need to progress forward.

PART IV

THE NEW AGE
OF CONSCIOUS EVOLUTION

11

THE PARADIGM SHIFT

We are standing on the threshold of a brave new world, a new era in human history. The Age of Aquarius is upon us and at times our world seems to be in cultural and environmental chaos. Although there has been increasing excitement over a global shift that seems to be taking place, many seekers and believers all over the world are struggling to cope with their fear for the future and the many challenges of these trying times. I personally talk to many discontented and downhearted people every day.

However, I do believe that we are living in a truly great era. Despite the many challenges we face as a species, we are currently living in an age which heralds the advent of the next leap in human evolution. We are witnessing the dawning of a New Earth and the awakening of a New Age of global spiritual consciousness.

The post-modern world is something we have co-created, with each other and our ancestors, but it can hardly be described as the earthly paradise of Shangri-La. Although many of us have woken up to recognize our true spiritual nature and have become aware of our own metaphysical contribution to our external reality, very few among us can claim to be living a life of perfect Nirvana at all times. The reason for this is the glaring incompatibility of our newfound spiritual awareness with the external, daily reality we share as co-creators. We are beginning to see what a mess mankind's Ego or Material Self has made.

Yes, the world does seem to have gone somewhat mad, and Divine Discontent seems to be at an all-time high for many people all over the world. But there is also some method in all this madness. The mess the human Ego has made is merely a part of our evolutionary process. Maybe the frog had to drink up almost half the pond it lives in, before it could manage to leap across it?

The Age of Metaphysical Man

Have you ever wondered how we arrived at this juncture in our evolution as a species? Many years ago the philosopher Gerald Heard offered an interesting explanation. He speculated on the evolutionary growth of our *cultural consciousness* and the psychological make-up of modern man.

In Pre-historic times we were for the most part primitive and content with our day-to-day existence. We were merely *pre-individuals*. It was a time before the Ego ruled the minds of men. It was the time of *Co-conscious Man*. There was little awareness of 'me, myself and I' and everybody managed to find ways to live together in harmony, for the sake of our collective survival. But it also marked a humdrum existence. It must have been remarkably uninspiring, because everyone was thinking along the same lines and no new ideas were really coming to the fore.

Of course, this state of affairs had to become really dreary in time. Due to our growing intelligence and our innate spiritual impulse to expand, the need for adventure, exploration and novelty grew, which made the way clear for the *proto-individual* or *Heroic Man* to emerge. We began to strive for more. We set out to become bigger, better, stronger. It was an era of rebellion, child-like adventure and wild exploration. But once again all the heroic conquest and victory brought us very little contentment. At least our mental capacity increased.

Our consciousness eventually turned away from outward adventure toward inner discovery. Humankind had now reached its 'adolescence'. As expected with any 'teenager' the world had suddenly become a very confusing place for *mid-individual man*. We needed answers, we needed a renewal of our inner guidance, and we had become so caught up in our exploration that we gradually began to lose touch with our true spiritual nature and origins. We needed something to replace what we had lost; we needed belief systems and moral values. Thus, *Ascetic Man* emerged and created the great religions of the world. Sadly, in the process he also destroyed many of his fellow men to promote or protect that which he came to believe. Through this ideological conflict we inherited much guilt, shame and confusion.

Humanic Man came to the rescue with the development of the arts and sciences. As *total-individuals* we now escaped the confines of the collective tribe mentality and claimed greater independence and individuality. We pursued logic, rational analysis, which required a subjugation of the subconscious, and the spiritual. The collective unconscious was increasingly being dismissed, our Divine origins devalued, and the metaphysical essence of mankind began to suffer. The Ego and our out-of-control *free will* now increasingly ruled our newfound, self-obsessed consciousness, which was not its original purpose.

Eventually we began to lose control of our man-made ideologies and technologies, while we increasingly indulged the senses, and succumbed to more greed and Ego corruption. We initiated the systematic destruction of our planet and our environment, in order to feed our narcissistic, superficial needs. Today we face the potential collapse of our global society and many of our natural resources.

Nell Minow recently asked Tom Shadyac, producer of the 2011 documentary film *I AM*, why some indigenous peoples seem very peaceful, while others are very aggressive and violent? Shadyac responded, "That wasn't the overriding indigenous way. They had conflicts and no one would suggest that a new society wouldn't have conflict. But the conflicts were limited. If a person was hurt or a piece of land was taken, payment had to be made for that, a warrior against a warrior. But not genocide. Not what's happening today. There's an ideology underlying that about our disconnection that's run amok and it allows us to do all kinds of insane things".

One of the most prevalent false beliefs today is that we must at all cost control other people, based on our fear of diversity. We feel threatened by everyone that seem different from us, or do not think feel, believe or do as we do. This false belief stems from primitive times when our main priority was *survival*. 'Survival of the fittest' is however a modern myth. Renowned primatologist and animal sociologist, Frans de Waal writes in *The Age of Empathy* that we need a complete overhaul of our assumptions about human nature.

> *Too many economists and politicians model human society on the perpetual struggle they believe exists in nature, but which is a mere projection. Like magicians, they first throw their ideological prejudices into the hat of nature, and then pull them out by their very ears to show how much nature agrees with them. It's a trick for which*

*we have fallen for too long. Obviously, competition is part
of the picture, but humans can't live by competition alone.*

According to Tom Shadyac the solution to our post-modern inclination towards greed, selfishness, conflict and superficial materialism is not in "changing who we are; it's about waking up to who we are. We know external things bring us joy to a certain point, but beyond that it doesn't. How about competition bringing us together instead of separating us. Ignorance comes from the word 'ignore'. We experience heaven when we serve each other... When we feed others, we feed ourselves".

Gerald Heard explains that Humanic Man is characterized by a society "that is completely self-seeking, because it is completely individualized into separate physiques that can have direct knowledge of only their own private pain and pleasure, inferring but faintly the feelings of others. Such a race of ingenious animals, each able to see and to seek his own advantage, must be kept in combination with each other by appealing to their separate interests."

With our modern technology the tolerant and democratic way of life Heard suggests is entirely within our reach as a global community. We have the necessary knowledge, facilities and expertise to embrace a completely diverse and democratic society, where everyone can be truly individual, yet still co-exist in absolute peace and harmony. The only missing ingredient appears to be the *will* to do it, a lack of *global awareness*. The solution begins inside of us, it must come from within. Shadyac adds that it "isn't as much about what you can do, as *who you can be*. And from that transformation of being, action will naturally follow."

Until one nation ceases its attempts to dominate another, there will never be true freedom. Until one religion relinquishes its quest to prove its god superior to that of another, there shall never be world peace. We will never truly prosper or experience lasting harmony, until we refrain from preaching the gospel of our own moral values and our personal preferences by forcing it upon others. We are not supposed to all be the same, feel the same, think the same, and believe the same. The key to continued expansion of our Universe lies in diversity, not in conformity and coercion. Conventionality is the death of creation.

You and I are now living on the cusp of this new age of man. We are transitioning from the Ego-driven era of Humanic Man to what

Heard calls the *post-individual* age of *Leptoid Man*, derived from the Greek word *lepsis*, meaning "to leap". As a species we increasingly face the opportunity to 'take a leap' into a considerably expanded new culture of co-consciousness. I prefer to call this new era the 'The Age of Metaphysical Man', or 'The Age of Indigo Man', because in this new age we will experience a great expansion of our consciousness, and all aspects of our spiritual awareness and psyche will become much more integrated.

In a sense we will be coming full circle, recapturing many of the qualities we had lost since the golden age of the primitive co-conscious man. This time around we will once again be co-conscious, but with an advanced level of *metaphysical insight,* understanding and wisdom. We are set to become a *spiritually evolved*, *highly intuitive* and *co-creative tribe* of beings who will live in *global harmony* and use our science and technology to work for us, and not against us. It is either that, or we may be facing calamity.

The Mass Extinction of Man

There are those who believe we may be facing extinction as a species - if we don't change our ways. This idea is not as far-fetched as it may seem. The mass extinction of entire plant or animal families is something that has happened on several specific occasions in history.

The most well-known of these extinction events is the end of the 'golden age of the reptiles', when most of the dinosaur species disappeared. The small percentage that survived ultimately became the bird species that today still roam our planet. I have often wondered about the fascination children all over the world seem to have with dinosaurs. It is a subject that is a source of great enthusiasm for both boys and girls. Could it be that they intuitively remember the past, that the traumatic events of that time remains ingrained in our DNA to this very day?

It was only 73,000 years ago when humanity also faced the possibility of complete extinction. This happened when the Toba super volcano erupted on the island of Sumatra. It caused such a colossal explosion that entire ecosystems were disrupted and most of humankind perished, leaving only an estimated 10,000 survivors alive on the planet. Although this event is not considered to be one of the 'big five' mass extinctions, it is more than enough to demonstrate the true fragility of mankind, and how vulnerable we really are to the innate power of the natural world.

But what does all of this 'doom and gloom' have to do with our spiritual awakening, and your potential happiness as an individual? Well, because we do have a choice in all of this. When you face the real possibility of your own extinction, it is no longer so important how many cars you drive, whether you are wearing the latest fashion, or whether your jewelry is more expensive than your friend's. Finally meeting that boy-next-door will probably not make it all seem worthwhile either. Neither does it matter much if you get that house, or that promotion, or that award. No longer will it be all that important to acquire more material possessions, or attain greater business success, political achievement or sensual satisfaction.

If most of us could fully embrace our capacity to co-create a new reality from our collective consciousness, and if most of us would choose to pool our efforts, we could ultimately choose to evolve our species and rise above the possibility of our own demise.

False Prophets and False Idols

Too many members of our global community remain stuck in the age of Humanic Man. They continue to search for answers by applying only left brain reason, exerting excessive control, following old regimens and establishing rigid rules and regulations. Many of our artists, philosophers, innovators, scientists and entrepreneurs have been swept away by the tyranny of linear thinking, Newtonian science, the mass media and increased materialistic pursuit. We continue to wage wars, and in spite of everything we have suffered there are yet more rumors of wars – across borders and in our streets. Corporations, traders and media moguls have become our false prophets. Technology and luxury items our false idols. Meanwhile, our imagination-deprived children are increasingly being medicated or emotionally incarcerated to sedate the soul and suppress the spirit.

Fortunately, all is not lost. Over the past few decades some of us have been awakening to a new consciousness and as a collective we have gradually been gaining critical mass towards global change. This universal awakening had a slow start in the

60's and 70's, but has been gaining incredible momentum since the begin-ning of the 21st Century. Over the past decade, especially due to the hype surrounding the date of December 21, 2012 marking the end of the ancient Mayan calendar, there has been much specu-lation about increased spiritual awakening. There has also been talk of a much anticipated paradigm shift finally arriving in full force, and of a new level of human consciousness and the dawning of a new 'golden age' for mankind.

More and more awakened believers and seekers around the world now personally observe profound spiritual occurrences in their daily lives; encounter paranormal phenomena that defy the laws of nature; receive astonishing validations for the existence of unseen dimensions, non-physical beings and the afterlife; enjoy the remarkable results of energy healing and metaphysical thera-pies; experience impressions of extra sensory perception; observe the future in their dreams; witness spectacular miracles; enjoy the fruits of conscious creation; transform their lives through delibe-rate intent; find true fulfillment in service to others; and embrace the bliss of spiritual enlightenment and a purposeful life.

Yet, the jury is still out among the mainstream scientific community, and the general public. Skepticism and cynicism remain widespread. This prevailing doubt regarding all things spiritual and metaphysical is the tragic by-product of a post-modern culture that is entirely devoid of the mysterious, and the miraculous. We live in a society where it has become increasingly shameful to be in any way associated with anything 'other worldly'. In many instances metaphysical beliefs and personal paranormal experiences are kept secret from family, friends and co-workers, while civilized and educated people point scornful fingers at the mystics and sages in their communities. Present day prophets and shamans are ridiculed and disparaged. Professional psychics and mediums feel the need to conceal their true identities behind silly stage names and subtle semantics like 'intuitive' or 'sensitive', for fear of being publicly embarrassed or disgraced. The compelling research findings of parapsychologists, holistic healers, and even some quantum physicists and other scientific pioneers, are disregarded as biased 'fluff', because it does not comply with an outdated scientific paradigm. Yes, there is a new kind of prejudice in town known as the 'spiritual closet'. And if you follow the media reports, skeptics blogs and online social networks, you will find that many members or our society are still hunting witches and stoning people in the streets.

Mad Scientists and Snake Oil Sellers

There have always been two kinds of science in our world. There is the conventional, mainstream science that makes your car run on fuel, allows your computer to process data, enables your cell phone to connect to a signal and keeps the processed food in your fridge fresh for longer. Then there is the so-called 'fringe science' which conjures up visions of mad scientists, green smoke in dungeon-like laboratories, and snake oil sellers at carnival side-shows. Fringe science is however the science of tomorrow.

History has shown repeatedly that what may seem weird or improbable today often become the mainstream conventions of the future. It is important to bear in mind that all scientific facts are little more than temporary truths. Despite the fact that a mainstream scientific community may have reached some kind of consensus, their findings will always be provisional. Scientific knowledge is impermanent by nature and continuously expands and changes as we evolve. This is clearly evident from how science has developed throughout history.

TheFreeDictionary.com defines the term *paradigm* as "a set of assumptions, concepts, values, and practices that constitutes a way of viewing reality for the community that shares them, especially in an intellectual discipline". The dominant paradigm of a certain era will therefore determine or prescribe what will be studied, how scientists will ask questions, how these questions will be structured, how the results of studies should be inter-preted, and how experiments would be conducted.

In *The Structure of Scientific Revolutions* the science historian Thomas Kuhn explains how a scientific paradigm evolves from the 'old science' to the new. Kuhn defines the term paradigm as "universally recognized scientific achievements that, for a time, provide model problems and solutions for a community of researchers". Kuhn further explains that there are three phases to the process of scientific revolution, or the adoption of a new paradigm. The first is the *pre-paradigm phase*, in which there are several incompatible and incomplete theories and no consensus on any of these theories. In time the scientific community begins to adopt one particular set of theories over the others, until they reach a widespread consensus. This is the beginning of the second phase, known as *normal science*. Most scientific studies now become focused within this dominant paradigm, and continue undisturbed for as long as there is consensus among researchers. But in time progress in normal science usually reveals certain *anomalies*. Anomalies are scientific facts and research data that cannot be fully or properly explained within the framework of the current paradigm.

One of the best examples of an anomaly in current science, which directly impacts all of us in our daily lives, is the so-called *placebo effect*. A placebo is basically an inactive or harmless substance, such as salt water or a vitamin tablet, given to a medical patient as a treatment, instead of an actual drug or medication. Countless studies have shown that a placebo can cause clearly measurable improvements in a person's health or well-being. For example, a patient might be told that a simple starch tablet, with no medicinal properties whatsoever, is in fact a very powerful, new painkiller. Amazingly, the subject's headache would disappear soon after they have taken the starch tablet.

Studies have confirmed that the anomaly of the placebo effect is possible in many areas of medicine. Placebos have been shown to alleviate pain, anxiety, depression, Parkinson's disease, inflammatory disorders and even cancer. One of the most famous studies often cited in cancer research is the report by psychologist Bruno Klopfer titled, *Psychological Variables in Human Cancer.* In this 1957 study a patient known only as "Mr. Wright" was told that he would be treated with a new miracle anti-cancer drug called "Krebiozen". Mr. Wright was dying from cancer of the lymph nodes and his doctors had tried all other available treatments without any success. When he received the first injection of "Krebiozen", Mr. Wright's condition was critical and he was completely bedridden, but within only three days he was up and about, cheerfully joking with the nurses on duty. Tests soon revealed that his tumors had shrunk by half and a few days later he was discharged from hospital.

Another fascinating study, which sent some shockwaves through the scientific community, was the work done by Fabrizio Benedetti of the University of Turin in Italy. Benedetti not only showed that he could effectively manage pain in a patient by replacing morphine treatment after a few days with simple saline solution (salt water), but also that he could *neutralize the effect of the placebo*.

After showing that he could effectively treat pain with salt water, Benedetti added Naloxone, a drug that blocks the effects of morphine, to the same saline placebo. Incredibly, the pain-relieving power of the saline solution disappeared! The Naloxone blocked the effects of the salt water in the same way it would block morphine. Benedetti's results therefore show that the placebo effect may somehow be *biochemical,* which implies that our minds can indeed affect our body's biochemistry. Such a finding is contrary to the generally accepted assumptions found in mainstream medi-cal science and is therefore an *anomaly*.

In his analysis of the evolution of scientific paradigms, Kuhn further contends that the existing paradigm in normal science eventually becomes 'stretched to its limits' in its attempts to explain an increasing number of anomalies. Initially anomalies are often dismissed as errors in observation or measurement, and a variety of other factors. According to Kuhn most scientists will continue to hold on to the current paradigm, despite a growing number of anomalies, because no *credible alternative* is available to them to replace it with.

But fortunately, in any community of scientists there are those individuals who are more daring or brave than the rest. These scientists realize that there is a problem with the current paradigm and they then initiate the third phase of Kuhn's model, known as *revolutionary science*, by exploring alternatives to the old, obvious assumptions. For a time, a rival paradigm or parallel science may emerge, and this 'new science' often would have many anomalies of its own, because it is still a novel and incomplete framework. Kuhn states that most scientists will continue to support the old paradigm, and this is a good thing. For science to truly develop and grow there must be the more conservative individuals versus the more progressive, to create the necessary balance and to ensure that the new science will have a firm foundation going forward.

Marja de Vries writes in *The Whole Elephant* that despite history showing repeatedly that new concepts and theories will always replace the old, and although this is generally accepted to be essential to the process of scientific development, "it still happens that independent scientists, who have the courage to 'go public' with such new, deviating perceptions are branded as kinds of modern-day heretics by the representatives of the 'established doctrine."

This sometimes narrow-minded tunnel vision of some members of mainstream society, especially with regards the possible connections between science and spirituality, is reminiscent of the prosecution of Galileo Galilei. He had to stand trial on suspicion of heresy in 1633, because he claimed that the Earth revolved around the Sun. This theory was considered to be contrary to Holy Scripture and Galileo was found "suspect of heresy". He was instructed to denounce his views on the matter and placed under house arrest, where he remained for the rest of his life. Today Galileo is venerated as the father of modern science, physics and observational astronomy.

Galileo's *Heliocentrism* (the Sun is the centre of our galaxy) is not the only fringe theory that eventually became mainstream science. Other controversial ideas that were later proven include *Continental Drift*, which explains the movement of the Earth's continents relative to each other, and the *Big Bang Theory*, which is currently the most prevalent cosmological model for the creation of the Universe.

With the story of Galileo in mind, one cannot help but wonder what our descendants will one day make of controversial contemporary theorists, scientists and philosophers who have been breaking away in ever increasing numbers from the conventional, mainstream worldview over the past century.

Will the people of the future, for example, acknowledge physicist Fritjof Capra's work on the decline of the former mechanistic, reductionist paradigm of Newton and Copernicus and the dawning of a new *Holistic Culture*? Will scientist Robert Lanza be remembered mostly for his work on stem cell technology, or rather for his theory on *Biocentrism* that ultimately became the new paradigm that integrated all of physics?

And what will our children call Nassim Haramein? Will he continue to be mocked as a fraud, or will they hold him in the highest regard as 'The New Einstein', who developed the unified hyperdimensional theory of matter and energy, known as the *Holofractographic Universe*?

And will future generations honor Brian David Josephson, the Welsh physicist and Nobel Prize laureate who has on several occasions in recent years publicly defended *Parapsychology* and paranormal research, claiming that there is conclusive evidence for unseen phenomena that is simply still being ignored. What value will our children attach to the work of American astronomer and astrophysicist Carl Sagan, who wrote about life on other planets and encouraged the search for *Extra-terrestrials*? And what will they make of British biologist Rupert Sheldrake, whose theories about *Telepathy* and the brain's *Morphic Fields*, which can interconnect and trade information, may eventually change our understanding of the human mind. Would future generations even remember the Sheldrake critics who had called for his books to be burned?

Will the people of the future remember Edgar Cayce as a psychic 'quack' or the founder of the *New Age Movement* which ultimately changed the history of man as we know it? How will Dr Helen Schucman, author of *A Course In Miracles* be labeled in the future; will she be known as a spiritual menace who spread a false revelation, or a saint who brought *spiritual transformation* to the world?

What will become of the slogans of courageous, innovative minds like Duane Elgin, the author and activist who has been encouraging us since the 80's to replace our mass consumption lifestyles with *Voluntary Simplicity*, a lifestyle of simple living with balance in order to find a life of greater purpose? Will our offspring someday admire Barbara Marx Hubbard of the Foundation for Conscious Evolution for her lifelong commitment to bringing hope to humanity, by making us aware of the true potential for our future, based on the view that our current global crisis is merely a birth and that we have the power to *consciously evolve* and co-create an entirely different world? How will future gurus tell the story of teachers like Louise L. Hay, Esther-Abraham Hicks and Wayne Dyer, who inspired a whole generation to take responsibility for their own reality, heal their lives using visualization and affirmations and teach their children about *conscious, deliberate creation* and the power of their thoughts?

And will the medical students of the future be taught that Dr Deepak Chopra was the 'Father of Quantum Medicine'? Will he be remembered as a man who inspired the transformation of Western medicine, by combining it with ancient Eastern wisdom, thus making many miracle cures possible for previously untreatable diseases? Will the scientists of the future prove that Dr Chopra was right all along, about the human body being controlled by a network of intelligence, grounded in quantum reality or a conscious Universe, and that we can in fact promote healing using the power of our minds? Will those medical students of the future also be instructed in the work of neuroscientist and pharma-cologist Dr Candace Pert, who proposes a biomolecular basis for our emotions, thus providing a bridge between the traditional concepts of mind and body? Will she possibly be honored as the person who discovered the scientific basis for 'gut feelings', or the pioneer who moved the focus of psychotherapy out of the brain's cortex and into the body?

Only time will tell.

There has always been that element within society that resists or scoffs at progressive new ideas and unusual concepts. Fortunately, there is balance in everything, and for every fanatical skeptic there is an ardent believer, or at least some adventurous, curious or courageous soul who is open to seriously consider something they are unfamiliar with. Were it not for such risk-takers, humanity would have made even more stupid decisions and unnecessary mistakes over the years.

Major blunders like World War I and II, the Holocaust, the atom bomb, pollution and global warming might not have been our only crowning glories, had it not been for some visionaries and rebels who had the courage of their convictions. For example, what would have happened had the computer industry taken seriously the opinion of Ken Olson, president of Digital Equipment Corporation, who in 1977 proclaimed that the idea of a personal computer made no sense because "there is no reason anyone would want a computer in their home". And the next time you encounter some skeptic engaging in scathing criticism of the latest quantum physics theory or parapsychology finding, remind yourself of Lord Kelvin who, when speaking to the British Association for the Advancement of Science in 1900 said, "there is nothing new to be discovered in physics now...all that remains is more and more precise measurement." Lord Kelvin also said in 1883 that "X-rays will prove to be a hoax" and in 1897 that "radio has no future". In similar fashion, Simon Newcomb, the Canadian-born American astronomer, stated in 1888, "We are probably nearing the limit of all we can know about astronomy". Pierre Pachet, British surgeon and Professor of Physiology at Toulouse, declared in 1872 that "Louis Pasteur's theory of germs is ridiculous fiction". And did you know that Columbus almost did not make it to the Americas, because the committee advising King

Ferdinand and Queen Isabella of Spain, regarding a proposal by Christopher Columbus in 1486, stated "so many centuries after the Creation it is unlikely that anyone could find hitherto unknown lands of any value."

In 1903 the president of the Michigan Savings Bank advised Henry Ford 's lawyer not to invest in the Ford Motor Company because, "the horse is here to stay but the automobile is only a novelty - a fad". He was not the only motoring skeptic, because the *Scientific American* reported on January 2, 1909 "that the automobile has practically reached the limit of its development... suggested by the fact that during the past year no improvements of a radical nature have been introduced".

Some of these cynical blunders were not necessarily made decades in advance, like T. Craven, FCC Commissioner in the USA who stated in 1961 that "there is practically no chance communications space satellites will be used to provide better telephone, telegraph, television, or radio service inside the United States". The first commercial communications satellite went into service four years later in 1965. Mary Somerville, pioneer of radio educational broadcasts stated in 1948 that "television won't last... it's a flash in the pan". She may have taken her cue from Darryl Zanuck, a movie producer at 20th Century Fox who exclaimed in 1946, "Television won't last because people will soon get tired of staring at a plywood box every night". A few years later, in 1955, *Variety* magazine predicted that rock 'n roll music "will be gone by June".

A Yale University professor assessed a college assignment in 1966 that proposed the business viability of a simple, yet reliable overnight delivery service. The professor was not impressed and wrote in his response, "the concept is interesting and well-formed, but in order to earn better than a 'C', the idea must be feasible". The assignment was by a student named Fred Smith, who would later go on to found Federal Express, now ranked as the largest company in terms of employee number in the world. Albert Einstein's teacher also made a blunder when he told the boy's father in 1895, "it doesn't matter what he does, he will never amount to anything". And the next time someone tells you something is impossible, think of Spencer Silver, the man who invented the unique adhesives for 3M *Post-It* notepads who said, "if I had thought about it, I wouldn't have done the experiment...the literature was full of examples that said 'you can't do this".

The Limitations of Newtonian Physicalism

What we need is a radical paradigm shift in how we observe, study and interpret our world. It is my belief that this long awaited new paradigm will have to be based on two fundamental premises: that we are *spiritual beings* having a physical experience, and secondly, that our material world or *reality* does not exist as most of us currently choose to perceive it. Life and the world as we know it, is more like a 3-D film, which all of us as co-creators collectively produce, direct and star in, on a daily basis.

To live a spiritually aware lifestyle in this day and age is not easy. We are consistently bombarded with fear-mongering, negativity and pessimism. To cultivate and maintain a meta-physical outlook on reality is a difficult mission, especially if you are constantly being confronted by a materialistic society that clings to a strictly physical understanding of what reality is. Academic institutions, churches and the mass media all contribute to upholding the status quo, and social prejudice prevents us from sharing our spiritual experiences or receiving support from family and friends.

The previous age was a period of intense research and discovery. It was a time of dismantling, disassociation and disinte-gration. We dissected flowers, frogs, chromosomes and the human brain. We separated all the elements into a periodic table, sorted all living things into categories and species, and divided people into blood groups, personality types and levels of intelligence. We split the atom, delved into the miniature world of micro-organisms and launched shuttles into deep space. We sent our scientists and explorers into the wide world and scoured every nook and cranny of our planet, for more and more things to take apart, study and classify.

In time most of the scientists and explorers have returned with all their knowledge, their discoveries, their theories and formulas, yet still there is so much about our Universe that we do not under-stand. Whatever remains to be discovered clearly will require a profound paradigm shift. This paradigm shift will have to be based on a new, or at least a different view of *consciousness* and the *spirit-mind-body* connection.

Over the past quarter of a century the 'deeper physics' has delved into the smallest components of the physical world on a subatomic level, and the deeper the scientists went the more they have been finding phenomena and anomalies that suggest that the Universe is not merely a collection of separate things, but that everything is connected to one, single field of consciousness.

What Is Consciousness?

We are all conscious as living beings, but we still do not know for sure how, or why. Only when we fully solve the mystery of our consciousness will we be able to fully unravel the remaining mysteries of the Universe. Since the time of the ancient Greek philosophers there has been controversy over what consciousness is and where it originates. Does consciousness come from inside of us, or does it have an external source? Is consciousness generated from within, by the brain and nervous system, or is there a part of consciousness that is located somewhere outside of us and we somehow access or tap into that? Simply put, is consciousness of physical, or non-physical origins?

The leading scientific paradigm of the previous four centuries is known as *Newtonian Physicalism*, and it is currently still dominating our worldview. Its different forms, such as Reductionism, Materialism, Behaviorism, Determinism and Functionalism, all propose that human nature can be explained by purely physical, logical and predictable means. From this perspective all aspects of our human consciousness and our perception of the world around us are explained through Neuroscience, namely that consciousness is generated by the inner working of the neurons in our brain and their communication with other neurons and organs through synaptic connections, much like the inner circuitry of a computer.

The Horizon Research Foundation reports that "most scientists have adopted a traditionally monist view of the mind-brain problem, arguing that the human mind, consciousness, and self are no more than by-products of electrochemical activity within the brain, notwithstanding the lack of any scientific evidence or even a plausible biological explanation as to how the brain would lead to the development of mind and consciousness."

This traditional scientific viewpoint has served us well and brought us far in our understanding of the functioning of the human brain and nervous system. However, we are now reaching a stage in our evolution where this paradigm is increasingly preventing us from further expanding our knowledge and insight, because its theories and terminology still fails to fully explain what consciousness really is and where it comes from. The inter-disciplinary fields of study that constitutes Neuroscience, such as Neurobiology, Chemistry, Computer Science, Engineering, Lingu-istics, Mathematics, Physics, and Psychology, all offer partial or limited explanations, but there is one essential question that remains unanswered. This is known as the *hard problem* of consciousness.

The Hard Problem

Neuroscience can currently provide physical explanations for how we are able to focus our attention on the fruit in a supermarket, when we are out shopping. It can also explain how we are able to discriminate between an apple and an orange; how we remember that apples and oranges are fruit that we can eat; how we can explain to each other that we prefer apples over oranges; and how we are able to control our body to place our selection of apples and oranges in our shopping basket. The philosopher David Chalmers calls these aspects of consciousness the *easy problems* of consciousness. They have all been explained by science.

However, the *hard problem* that neuroscience still faces is that it cannot provide an explanation for our *subjective experience* as conscious animals. It cannot clarify how we are able to have a *rich, inner life* as sentient beings and how we are able to have a *deeply personal experience* of tastes, flavors, colors, shapes, sounds, feelings and emotions.

These subjective conscious experiences are known as *qualia.* Qualia are basically how things 'seem' to us. How is it possible, for example, that we are able to experience the smoothness of an apple's skin and sense its color as being a refreshing, calming green? How can the smell of apples remind us of the taste of our granny's baked apple pie, while bringing to us a mixed feeling of both nostalgia and joy? And how do we imagine the textural sound quality and the juicy sensation of biting into a fresh apple? Or how do we hear in our mind the childhood jingle of "an apple a day keeps the doctor away", while we select our apples in the store? The notion that all of our consciousness is generated within the brain does not provide us with a satisfactory explanation for how we experience these forms of *subjective consciousness*.

If the brain is merely a 'bio-electro-chemical' generator of our consciousness we amount to nothing more than human computers, or zombies. Even the most conservative scientists know intuitively that this cannot be entirely true. If the human brain is really nothing more than a highly complex computer system, we would go through life merely *reacting* robotically to outside stimuli and therefore be utterly *predictable*. We also would not have the capacity for *free will*.

Non-Computable Consciousness

If we are human computers merely using some form of algorithmic computing, as proposed in the field of Artificial Intelligence, we would not be able to 'know' or 'sense' certain things *intuitively*. In his book *The Emperor's New Mind*, Roger Penrose suggests that human intuition and creativity is a *non-computable* function of our consciousness.

A recent breakthrough in medical research is an excellent example of the need for a new paradigm that accepts this 'non-computable' aspect of our consciousness. In September 2011 a group of online virtual reality gamers cracked a biological virus code that scientists have failed to do for decades. They did it by playing an online game that allows players to collaborate and compete in predicting the structure of protein molecules. Dr Firas Khatib of the University of Washington Department of Biochemistry challenged the gamers to produce an accurate model of an enzyme of an HIV-like virus, which had eluded medical researchers for more than a decade. The gamers successfully deciphered the structure of the enzyme in only three weeks. "We wanted to see if human intuition could succeed where automated methods had failed," Dr Khatib told the media.

The gamers were able to create such excellent virtual models that scientists were able to easily refine it to determine the enzyme's structure. It was even found that certain surfaces on the molecule stood out as potential targets for drugs that may be able to deactivate the enzyme, and therefore shut the virus down. In this instance the *creativity* and *intuition* of online gamers with no in-depth, scientific knowledge of enzymes, provided the breakthrough for further 'computing' by scientists.

The Subjectivity Elephant

Additionally, the one elephant in the room that no truly skeptical seeker or objective scientist can deny is the fact that all the scientific knowledge we have gathered until now is based on the 'frail' and 'fallible' human consciousness generated by the brains of scientists (as conventional science would have us believe). Charles H. Townes fittingly states that "we scientists believe in the existence of the external world and the validity of our logic. Nevertheless, these are acts of faith. We can't prove them." Townes is correct. Every research project, every new algorithm, and every new scientific theory or finding, have all been built one upon the other by applying our *subjective consciousness* and our *innate intuition*, not by mere 'zombie robot brains'.

As the French philosopher René Descartes pointed out almost 400 years ago, 'We think, therefore we are'. Our human consciousness created and tested all our past and current scientific theories from our internal, subjective experience of reality. Not only did we partly do this using our unexplained subjective experience of qualia, but we were also able to 'objectively' observe or perceive ourselves experiencing these qualia. We can in essence reflect on our own subjective experience of qualia. While standing in the fruit and vegetable section at the supermarket, we are not only able to imagine the textural sound quality and juicy sensation of biting into a fresh apple, but we can also *observe ourselves* biting into the apple from a *third person perspective!*

Admitting to any form of subjectivity in the current paradigm is generally viewed as scientific 'sacrilege', yet there is no denying the fact that we can never truly be objective in our research - not according to the current scientific paradigm. Science has never been able to show that man can experience the Universe from a purely external, objective perspective. If this is possible, it would defy the very fiber of traditional science. From the perspective of the conventional scientific paradigm, whatever we perceive or experience will always be from our own point-of view, because according to mainstream science there is no consciousness beyond the physical body, and we are therefore prisoners of the internal functioning of the human brain. All our science has therefore always been *subjective* in one way or another.

Furthermore, from a Quantum Physics perspective, it is possibly naïve to believe that science can ever be truly unbiased and objective. As described in the next chapter of this book, it may be not be possible for scientists to be truly unbiased and objective, because the outcome of research studies will always be determined or influenced by the researcher's expectation, intention, or observation. If what we think, feel and believe somehow creates our daily reality, then no scientist is immune to influencing the outcome and findings of his own work.

Additionally, it is difficult to trust mainstream scientific research in this day and age, as most of it is sponsored by multinational corporations and companies who have only one aim in mind and that is to somehow generate a larger profit from whatever research program they are funding. Holistic healing practices, for example, will not receive serious attention or consideration from mainstream science while medical research is being funded by the global pharmaceutical industry.

The Extra Ingredient

David Chalmers describes the gap in our current scientific approach in the study of consciousness as the need for an "extra ingredient".

We have seen that there are systematic reasons why the usual methods of cognitive science and neuroscience fail to account for conscious experience. These are simply the wrong sort of methods: nothing that they give to us can yield an explanation. To account for conscious experience, we need an extra ingredient in the explanation. This makes for a challenge to those who are serious about the hard problem of consciousness: What is your extra ingredient, and why should that account for conscious experience? There is no shortage of extra ingredients to be had. Some propose an injection of chaos and nonlinear dynamics. Some think that the key lies in non-algorithmic processing. Some appeal to future discoveries in neurophysiology. Some suppose that the key to the mystery will lie at the level of quantum mechanics. It is easy to see why all these suggestions are put forward. None of the old methods work, so the solution must lie with something new.

Could it be that this missing link or extra ingredient cannot be found in the physical after all? What if the brain and the conscious mind are two separate things? Could it be that the brain and nervous system is merely a processor or adapter for translating data from the collective unconscious, from the great 'unseen', from a grid of Universal Consciousness?

It may very well be that the brain is the processor for our physical *awareness* and *sensory perception*, such as the ability to see or hear, while our *consciousness* is *non-physical* and closely tied to what we understand to be the *soul* or *spirit*.

We already know that our awareness and perception is closely tied to the functioning of the body, much like a computer receives and processes objective data input. However, it does not explain the subjective experience of qualia. Neither does it justify our sense of self and our capacity for free will. Could it be that the reason we still do not understand consciousness is because we are ignoring the spirit, or the soul?

If spirit and consciousness are somehow connected, we will never be able to understand consciousness without also under-standing or at least acknowledging, our spiritual origins and meta-physical nature. Sri Aurobindo writes in *The Life Divine* that we will never be able to fully answer the question of the origins of our own consciousness and the existence of the Universe if we continue to study and interpret it from the old paradigm.

> *The intellect must consent to pass out of the bounds of a finite logic and accustom itself to the logic of the Infinite. On this condition alone, by this way of seeing and thinking, it ceases to be paradoxical or futile to speak of the inef-fable: but if we insist on applying a finite logic to the Infinite, the omnipresent reality will escape us and we shall grasp instead an abstract shadow, a dead form petrified into speech or a hard incisive graph which speaks of the Reality but does not express it. Our way of knowing must be appropriate to that which is to be known.*

It seems there may be only one solution to our existential dilem-ma, namely that we free ourselves from the confines of how we currently view consciousness. To get everyone on board, science will have to open up to the possibility that our consciousness exists beyond our inner awareness of it, and that there is an objective, conscious reality that may be invisible to us, whilst we are in the human condition. We would have to accept as a species that we may only be partially 'awake' and that there is much that we do not perceive or understand from our limited human state.

The 'extra ingredient' that we need for both science and society to progress lay in the non-physical, or the *meta-physical*. Just like we need in-depth knowledge and understanding of the human body, and its physical mechanisms, to explain how our senses are able to perceive, we need to develop an in-depth knowledge and understanding of the origins and nature of the soul or spirit, in order to grasp the true functioning of our subjective consciousness.

We may never be able to fully do this within the existing time-space reality using our limited level of human consciousness, but we are definitely capable of gaining a lot more scientific insight and understanding should we adopt a more metaphysical approach. A more spiritual approach in science and technology will also enable us to find new ways to interact with our environment and our planet and ensure our continued survival and evolution. It will enhance our quality of life, even if we never fully understand within this lifetime who we really are or where we really come from.

Intelligent Design

The need for an alternative approach to replace the current scientific status quo is also called for by the proponents of the concept of *intelligent design*. Intelligent design suggests that there is an underlying intelligence or creative design to the Universe, and to how it was created. According to the supporters of this alternative scientific model all of nature did not come about spontaneously, or by accident. The Universe is not the result of some undirected process, like the generally accepted natural selection concept associated with Darwin's evolution. Instead, life here on Earth came about through a complex and highly sophisticated 'cocktail' of elements that had to be 'just right' to ensure our survival.

According to Peter Ward's *Rare Earth* hypothesis the evolution of complex, multi-cellular life here on Earth required a highly unlikely combination of astrophysical and geological events and circumstances. Scientists know that the physical properties and laws of our Universe are both extremely *complex* and highly *specified,* to match the exact requirements that are needed for all life on Earth to be sustained. What this means is that the Universe contains the kind of highly complex-specified information (CSI) one would find in man-made things like modern day computers and machines. This implies that there must have been an Intelligent Design or Creative Force behind it in the first place. "The Universe has a plan; we are essential to that plan", says astronomer George Greenstein.

Language is another example of a system that has a high level of CSI. It is evident in this book you are reading right now, because its contents is made up of sequences of characters, both *complex* and *specified.* A simple, short English word in the dictionary is composed of only a few characters, which means it is specified, but not complex; and because it is simple it could have come about by chance. On the other hand, a very long, random sequence of letters and characters is complex, but not specified. The language you read in this book is however both complex and specific. The same is true for the underlying design of our Universe. The advocates of the *Intelligent Design* theory propose that there is enough scientific evidence to show that the Universe was indeed created by an unknown Intelligence, as Physicist Paul Davies explains.

> *The temptation to believe that the Universe is the product of some sort of design, a manifestation of subtle aesthetic and mathematical judgement, is overwhelming. The belief that there is 'something behind it all' is one that I personally share with, I suspect, a majority of physicists.*

Although this theory is not primarily meant to be a religious concept, it does represent a form of *Creationism* suggesting the existence of a God, or at least some form of Infinite Intelligence or a Creative Source. Intelligent design further proposes that the scientific status quo should adjust itself towards a more spiritual or metaphysical viewpoint. Unfortunately, the more scientific evidence emerges that supports this idea of a Creative Conscious Universe, the more it is seen as a source of controversy and a further cause for division between the fields of science and spirituality. The main reason for this may be that it tends to be exploited by some religious stakeholders to promote their own dogmatic agenda, which in turn could invite increased resistance from the conservative section of the scientific community.

God's Fondness For Beetles

Although there has been much debate over the idea of intelligent design, and although it is believed to be refuted scientifically, it still does pose some interesting questions which nobody has been able to answer thus far. For example, science today knows that there is so much more diversity in nature than Darwin could have known at the time he published his book, *The Origin of Species* in 1859. Rupert Sheldrake writes in *The Sense of Being Stared At* that there certainly appears to be more to creative evolution than mere natural selection, which is contrary to what Darwin's book suggests.

> *For me, it's an open question as to whether the intelligence that underlies the creativity in life is working in accordance with some fixed goal for the end of evolution. I don't get that impression. If you look at the diversity of life, several million species of beetles, for example, on this planet, you get the impression that there's a kind of creativity for its own sake, a proliferation of form and variety.*

Although science has been able to explain how all the different species of living beings have evolved over time, it remains unclear, for example, why there should be more than 350,000 kinds of beetles on Earth? Robert M. May estimates that there are even more beetles than that, and that they represent at least one million of the six million animal species found on our planet! Since there are only four thousand species of mammals, it means that there are about 1,500 types of beetles for each kind of mammal.

Someone once asked British geneticist J.B.S. Haldane what his lifelong study of life tells him about the nature of God. Haldane answered, "He seems to have an inordinate fondness for beetles."

In The Beginning

The mainstream view in astrophysics today is that the Universe is not infinite, because it must have had some kind of 'beginning'. The general consensus is that this beginning was due to a massive explosion, known as the Big Bang theory, which developed out of Einstein's theory of *relativity*. Einstein himself did not have an explanation for what he called "the necessity for a beginning" that his theory demanded. To work around it he invented a construct known as the *cosmological constant*, which he added to his equations, to make them less philosophical in nature and thus eliminate the need for him to explain of how the Universe began.

When the cosmological constant was disproved a few decades later, Einstein described it as the biggest "blunder" of his career. This statement was, however, an exaggeration, because new findings in 1998 indicated that the Universe is in fact accelerating, and generally speaking Einstein's "blunder" was therefore not entirely a mistake, since there does appear to be a mysterious force that may be keeping the Universe from collapsing.

Many astrophysicists today agree that the Universe must have had a beginning, and that it still continues to expand. But what caused this beginning remains a mystery. Theists, or spiritually inclined scientists, have an advantage here, because they are open to the possibility that the Universe may have been created by a God, or a Divine Force, or a Creative Source. Astrophysicist Hugh Ross writes *in New Astronomical Proofs for the Existence of God* that if there was "a beginning, then there must be a Beginner".

This of course leaves the next question: where did God come from in the first place? But at least the theist is one step closer to some kind of answer, compared to the non-theist who has simply no feasible explanation for how the Universe began, or what may be behind its intelligent design.

The Anthropic Principle

Another philosophical concept strongly associated with the idea of intelligent design, as well as the beginning of the Universe, is the *Anthropic Principle.* This paradigm proposes that there is abundant evidence in the sciences of Biology, Chemistry, Physics and Cosmology to show that life on Earth was *planned* or *designed*. It did not happen by accident.

Anthropic principles refer to scientific phenomena where the physical properties or parameters seem to be perfectly 'fine-tuned' to allow for life on Earth. Astrophysicist Hugh Ross likens the Anthropic Principle to tuning a radio into that specific frequency where the circuit has just the right resonance to lock onto a particular station. If certain physical and chemical properties in our world were just a small fraction outside their current parameters, you and I would not exist, and life here on Earth would have been impossible.

Conditions are therefore 'just right' for us to survive on this planet, a concept which has been dubbed the *Goldilocks principle*, in reference to the fairytale character who found her porridge to be 'just right'. The existence of these anthropic principles is well recognized in the scientific literature.

As humans we would not be able to survive without the ideal level of oxygen and carbon in our atmosphere. Ross explains "had the resonance level in the carbon been four percent lower, there would be essentially no carbon. Had that level in the oxygen been only half a percent higher, virtually all the carbon would have been converted to oxygen. Without that carbon abundance, neither you nor I would be here."

Another anthropic principle is the fact that water has some very unique and special properties without which life on Earth would have been impossible. Water, unlike similar substances, is more dense or heavy when it is liquid, compared to when it is in its solid form. Water also has a much higher boiling point than other substances.

Additionally, it appears that our solar system is also 'fine-tuned' for our needs, because the sun is just the right distance away from Earth. If the Sun was positioned closer or further away, it would make the surface of the Earth too hot or cold, and we would not have had liquid water to sustain life, because our oceans would either evaporate or become frozen. The Sun itself is also unique and very different from most other stars in our Milky Way. It appears that several of its characteristics are essential for life on Earth as we know it. It is further speculated that even the Moon is 'just right' for our evolutionary needs.

Astrophysicist Brandon Carter coined the term 'Anthropic Principle' in reaction to the well-known *Copernican Principle*, which states that humans do not occupy a privileged position in the Universe. Cater states that although our place as humans is not necessarily central or integral to the existence and functioning of the Universe, "it is inevitably *privileged* to some extent". The Anthropic Principle does imply that everything in the Universe somehow 'conspired' to create just the right kind of conditions for life on Earth. How this 'conspiracy' or unique set of circumstances came about remains a mystery. There are however several theories that offer an explanation.

The Creator Universe. The traditional theory is that the Universe was designed or planned by a Creator, or an Intelligent Designer, or a Creative Force, with the specific aim to make complex, intelligent life possible on Earth. The underlying intelligence, or complex-specificity found in the design of our Universe further also suggests that it was created especially just for us humans as a species. This theory is more commonly known as 'Creationism'.

The Multiverse. According to this theory there are a multitude of universes out there, with all possible variations and combinations of the characteristics, properties and laws found in our Universe. We are just lucky enough to find ourselves within this particular Universe, which allows for us to exist. In other words, we just happened to hit the 'winning jackpot' by being in the one Universe that happens to be just right for our survival. The odds of this happening is about as high as your chance would be of winning the national lottery, yet this is what somehow happened to our species by chance.

The Creator Universe and the Multiverse are probably the two most popular theories, but in his 2006 book, *The Goldilocks Enigma,* Paul Davies's offers additional explanations, which may serve as an alternative conclusion to the on-going debate on the anthropic principles.

The Absurd Universe. The Universe just happens to be this way; there is no method in its madness.

The Fake Universe. The whole Universe is an illusion or fantasy; we live inside a virtual reality simulation.

The Unique Universe. There is an unknown principle that unites all of Physics, and which makes it necessary for the Universe to be the way it is. One day some "Theory of Everything'" will emerge that will explain why all the various features of the Universe must have the exact values it has.

The Life Principle. There is an unknown principle that limits, or forces the Universe to evolve towards life and intelligence.

The Self-Explaining Universe. Only universes with a capacity for consciousness can exist. This is based on John A. Wheeler's *Participatory Anthropic Principle*, which proposes that intelligence or the mind can exist independently of matter, and that the mind can create its own physical environments out of the potentialities around it. From this perspective our Universe may also have been created by an intelligent or sentient Beings, Entities or Mental Forces.

The New Spirituality

In *Beyond the Postmodern Mind,* Huston Smith writes that "Rationalism and Newtonian science has lured us into dark woods, but a new metaphysics can rescue us". Mankind will never give up its quest to find spiritual meaning and purpose in this world. This quest is what has been driving both science and religion for centuries.

The Buddha said, "The teacher appears when the student is ready." The same principle applies to the human species as a collective. We have been exposed to new esoteric and scientific insights as we evolved - always when the time was right and the world was ready. Our prominent religions all over the world were all founded on esoteric wisdom and metaphysical insights delivered at various times throughout history by prophetic messengers. But as time passed and these religions expanded, they were contaminated by human bureaucracy, superstition, doctrine and dogma which distorted the original teachings.

Science developed out of this chaos, because dogmatic religion increasingly became unable to offer sensible explanations of the nature of reality and the Universe. In those early days the first scientists were in fact persecuted as godless heretics for questioning God and the church. Over the past century the pendulum swung back and the tables were turned, and we have been living in a world in recent times where scientific skepticism of all things esoteric or metaphysical has mostly been dominating the debate.

Both science and religion have however failed to produce all the answers we seek to the origins and meaning of our existence. Maybe the solution is to be found in religion and science coming together and combining its efforts. Albert Einstein said, "Science without religion is lame, religion without science is blind." Hopefully the divide between the two will someday soon be bridged, once and for all.

Today, as we venture deeper into the 21st century, the rising popularity of metaphysics, alternative spirituality and the 'new science' seems to indicate that the world is indeed ready for a fresh approach to delving into esoteric wisdom, supported by a paradigm shift in scientific exploration. Sir Arthur Eddington writes, "Life would be stunted and narrow if we could feel no significance in the world around us beyond that which can be weighed and measured with the tools of the physicist or described by the metrical symbols of the mathematician."

The time has come to reclaim our transcendental values - even if we are currently unable to prove them scientifically. Once we change our approach and begin to accept that there is more to our world than meets the eye, we will find new theories and new methods to find the scientific validations we have been looking for.

For example, should science begin to take seriously a metaphysical concept like 'Universal Consciousness', it might be able to ask all kinds of new questions about our reality and the Universe, and many new theories and concepts can grow from this new perspective. Science will not disappear or become obsolete. It will actually expand and grow, because it will have so many new frontiers and possibilities to explore, and new tools and words to do it with. Deepak Chopra writes in *War of the Worldviews* that "ordinary people aren't going to give up emotions and inspiration just because science sniffs at subjectivity. Science shouldn't be so edgy and defensive. Vandals aren't going to smash their way into laboratories and throw Bibles at the equipment."

People will keep searching and asking, because they will always wish to understand what it is that they are feeling and sensing, and more and more they will awaken spiritually. For it is inevitable that our intuition must at some point in our lives force us to admit that there may be more to our existence than what we see in the mirror.

Waiting For the Penny to Drop

We are on the brink of a new age in our development as a species. I believe we are set to either become spiritually aware or possibly face global calamity. This is our legacy and our only true destiny. Many emerging theories and scientific discoveries are increasingly challenging mainstream science and its outdated paradigm. Max Planck, the founder of Quantum Theory said "a new scientific truth does not triumph by convincing opponents and making them see the light, but rather because its opponents eventually die, and a new generation grows up that is familiar with it." There are currently many new pioneers who are championing the premise that our consciousness exists *beyond the physical functioning* of the brain.

The new *Consciousness Paradigm* will most likely view the brain and nervous system as a conductor or interpreter of consciousness, instead of being just a generator. While conventional science maintains its view that consciousness is something that came into existence at a certain point in our evolution, the 'new thinkers' have been adopting the view that consciousness is something that always existed and that we are able to actively access this consciousness more and more as we evolve. Some go further to propose that we are products or agents of a Universal Consciousness. This idea of a *Conscious Universe* is a familiar concept in many ancient religions and spiritual wisdom traditions.

Peter Russell writes in *A Singularity in Time* that the "global crisis we are now facing is, at its root, a crisis of consciousness - a crisis born of the fact that we have prodigious technological powers but still remain half awake. We need to awaken to who we are and what we really want." The problem is that our innate fear of the unknown and our inability to think out-of-the-box makes us cling to the past, and the familiar, and the predictable. We continuously recycle old ideas, conventional scientific theories and outdated commandments to solve our present day problems. We are still trying to apply the concepts of an outdated, mechanistic worldview to a reality which can no longer be understood in terms of newly emerging concepts.

The current Newtonian paradigm of physicalism is so limited that once we begin to seriously explore possibilities of a Conscious Universe, we would require a whole new set of terminology to describe all the 'weird and wonderful' theories that the global shift in our academic thinking will generate. A good example is the Princeton Engineering Anomalies Research (PEAR) which found, among other anomalies, that human consciousness has the ability to shape or influence physical reality.

> *Nearly three decades of intense experimentation leave little doubt that the anomalous physical phenomena appearing in the PEAR studies are valid, and are significantly correlated with such subjective variables as intention, meaning, resonance, and uncertainty. The stark inconsistencies of these results with established physical and psychological presumptions place extraordinary demands on the development of competent new theoretical models for constructive dialogue with the empirical data. But since the contemporary scientific approach leaves little room for such subjective correlates in its mechanistic representations of reality, it follows that science as we know it either must exclude itself from study of such phenomena, even when they precipitate objectively observable physical effects, or broaden its methodology and conceptual vocabulary to embrace subjective experience in some systematic way.*

After three decades of research the PEAR team further also came to the conclusion that their findings have profound *spiritual, moral* and *ethical implications,* beyond its obvious potential for technological application and its scientific impact.

> *Certainly, there is little doubt that integration of these changes in our understanding of ourselves can lead to a substantially superior human ethic, wherein the long-estranged siblings of science and spirit, of analysis and aesthetics, of intellect and intuition, and of many other subjective and objective aspects of human experience can be productively reunited.*

Many people all over the world have been experiencing a profound spiritual awakening in recent years, but until humanity achieves a significant critical mass in global spiritual awareness, the Divine Life we all deserve and hoped to experience in this lifetime will remain outside the reach of most. Instead, society at large will inevitably face continued chaos, physical hardship and psychological suffering on a road that seems to be going nowhere, and that may possibly end in calamity or even our complete extinction.

The way we have been doing things have brought many discoveries and advances in technology, and for the privileged our physical comfort is at an all-time high because of these advances. Yet, there are many aspects to how we have been doing things on this planet that are simply not working for us. We need a global attitude change.

There is much hope for us, and for the future of our children. The innate human desire for spiritual substance and purposeful living will increasingly inspire more and more academics, philosophers, scientists and leaders all over the world to adopt a new way of investigating and understanding the Universe, which will ultimately bring about enough critical mass for a new worldview or alternate scientific paradigm to be adopted. It will eventually no longer be a matter of choice.

But that day still seems very far away.

For you and I to wait for science and public opinion to catch up with some of the greatest thinkers and teachers of our age would be a mistake. History has shown that science tends to take its time when it comes to new concepts, or unusual, untested theories that challenge the status quo. Neither does it make sense to disregard or ignore tried-and-tested ancient wisdom and religious traditions that continue to transform lives, create miracles and provide a sensible explanation for human consciousness.

The greatest threat we face in our post-modern society is not pollution, global warming, famine, war, disease or poverty. Our greatest foe is our outdated worldview that continues to cloud public opinion and smother scientific exploration. If we are to change our worldview to embrace our innate spiritual origins, we will much sooner and more easily find solutions to many of the other issues and threats we currently face as a species.

In 1896 Leo Tolstoy made a political statement in *Patriotism and Christianity,* but he unknowingly also provided a prophecy for our current era of Divine Discontent, when he warned us of the threat of blindly following public opinion.

> *No feats of heroism are needed to achieve the greatest and most important changes in the existence of humanity; neither the armament of millions of soldiers, nor the construction of new roads and machines, nor the arrangement of exhibitions, nor the organization of workmen's unions, nor revolutions, nor barricades, nor explosions, nor the perfection of aerial navigation; but a change in public opinion. And to accomplish this change no exertions of the mind are needed, nor the refutation of anything in existence, nor the invention of any extraordinary novelty; it is only needful that we should not succumb to the erroneous, already defunct, public opinion of the past, which governments have induced artificially; it is only needful that each individual should say what he really feels or thinks, or at least that he should not say what he does not think.*

Our lives are moving forward at an increasingly faster pace and a global wave of spiritual awakening and elevated consciousness is steadily gaining momentum. Personally, I prefer to ride that wave, instead of being left behind to drown in the wake of a nihilistic worldview and skeptical public opinion, while clutching to the life buoy provided by the centuries old scientific paradigm of Newton and Copernicus. I do not require scientific justification for that which I already know to be true – that I am a spiritual being having a physical experience, and that I am indeed my brother's keeper. The reason why many people feel uncertain, confused or discontented with their modern lives is the fact that they continue to apply old solutions to new problems. They cling to outdated views and false beliefs, because it is what everybody else seems to think and believe. They believe that we are nothing more than highly evolved animals or 'badly behaved computers' and that we have no control over our reality or our future. It is public opinion. It is the dominant worldview. Consider the possibility that they may be wrong. Don't wait for public opinion and scientific paradigms to shift. You have the opportunity to create a different way of life for yourself right now. It is called a Divine Life.

12

THE CONSCIOUS UNIVERSE

Seeing is not necessarily believing. There has been increasing debate and speculation, since the beginning of the 20th century, about what 'reality' truly is, and whether we are somehow able to shape or influence our reality through our beliefs, thoughts and emotions. In 1899 the clairvoyance expert, Charles Webster Leadbeater, described our limited perception of the Universe very aptly when he wrote that our limited human perception is like "playing only a few select strings on an enormous infinite harp."

Many people who are spiritually awakened need no convincing of their inner knowing that our current time-space reality is not as simplistic and material as humanity perceives it. Many of us know from personal experiences that our reality is instead some form of *shared consciousness*, or *consensus perception*, or even a *collective illusion*. Many of us also know from our own successful results that we are able to *direct* and *control energy* to change our reality, manifest what we need and heal each other. We know from direct observation of the workings of the metaphysical and the paranormal in our daily lives, and from numerous first-hand 'supernatural' experiences that the world we see, hear, and feel around us does not exist in the way mainstream science still chooses to perceive it.

Several discoveries and developments in modern 'fringe' science, especially in the 'New Physics' or Quantum Mechanics, suggest that the current reductionist, materialistic and Newtonian view of reality and assessment of the nature of the Universe may need some serious renovation and refurbishment. Newton's scientific work was the foundation of a much-needed scientific revolution that occurred more than 300 years ago and enabled us to develop the incredible technology and expertise we have today.

But this does not mean that Newton's ideas cannot or should not be upgraded by a revolution in scientific thinking. Unfortunately, the status quo of Newton's 'physicalism' persists despite the fact that several breakthrough concepts in modern science now appear to be supporting the need for an alternative approach.

Since the beginning of the previous century there have been an increasing number of scientists, academics and theorists who support and affirm the belief that our shared reality is not just a Universe of matter, separated by time and space. Instead our reality may be something like a *Hologram of Consciousness* created by our collective projection of it, or it could be the product of an underlying, *Omnipresent Field of Consciousness*, which John Hagelin calls the Superstring Field or the Unified Field of Consciousness. An increasing number of scholars also maintain that we are somehow creating, or *generating reality* through our consciousness, or that we are at the very least able to *influence* or *shape* our shared reality.

Quantum Mysticism

These alternate theories about reality and conscious creation are collectively known as Quantum Mysticism. Skeptics and critics regard it as a pseudoscience, or a set of fringe theories, but they fail to acknowledge that Quantum Mechanics and Mysticism have always had a strong *inter-dependent relationship*. In fact, several of the founders of early Quantum Theory were very interested in the metaphysical and philosophical implications of their emerging field of Quantum Mechanics, and they used these ideas to debate and interpret their work.

Quantum Mechanics, or Quantum Physics, is a branch of science that studies the interactions of matter and energy at the subatomic level, i.e. smaller than atoms. Subatomic particles are basically the smaller units that make up all matter. The word *quantum* means 'discrete amount' or 'portion', and the units of energy that quantum researchers deal with are therefore known as 'quanta'. To better understand where Quantum Physics fits into science it is helpful to see where its subject matter fits into the *Hierarchy of Complex Systems*.

Biology ⇩	Ecosystems
	Organisms
	Organs
	Tissues
	Cells
Chemistry ⇩	Macro-molecules
	Molecules
	Atoms
Physics / Quantum Physics ⇩	Protons, Neutrons
	Quarks, Leptons
	Neutrinos

The field of Quantum Mysticism creates a bridge between science and spirituality, between Physics and Metaphysics, because it brings together Quantum Theory and Philosophy. Quantum Mysticism recognizes that several modern scientific developments appear to confirm some of the oldest beliefs found in many Eastern teachings, as well as ancient esoteric orders, indigenous traditions and in Western religions.

These beliefs include, among other, that we live in a world of *illusion*; that all perception is based on *energy,* and not physical matter; that *energy can become matter*; that there exists *other worlds or dimensions* beyond this reality; that we are all *inter-connected co-creators* of our reality; and that there exists a *Conscious Universe* or an underlying cosmic *Field of Consciousness* with an *Intelligent Design* from which all matter and living beings originate.

Since popular public opinion and mainstream science does not generally support the concepts of Quantum Mysticism, it is best to educate oneself as a layperson. As spiritual seekers we cannot afford to waste time waiting for the old scientific paradigm to embrace the new. Most of the memorable advances in science and civilization were made by courageous pioneers who chose not to adhere to the conventions of their time, but instead embraced new and innovative ideas. Our interpretation of the world around us is always based on what we have been taught, and how we have

357

been conditioned to think about life and reality. To free your Soul, you must first free your Mind.

To create a Divine Life it is necessary to know that what we have always perceived as reality may not be entirely accurate, and that our version of reality is a *subjective perception*. It also helps to know that we have *control* over our reality and that we can choose to perceive reality differently, or even create an entirely new reality through the *manipulation of energy*.

Being informed further enables us to interpret world events, consider public opinion and scrutinize existing belief systems from a more knowledgeable, open-minded and progressive perspective not prescribed by the mainstream academia and mass media. The best place to start your new science self-education for spiritual growth is in the field of Quantum Mysticism.

Matter Is Energy

We cannot think of our physical world as something that consists solely of 'matter'. None of the material, physical things you see around you exists only in the form that you perceive it. We have known since ancient times that all kinds of matter can be converted into *energy*. For example, we burn wood for heat, or convert the food we consume into physical activity.

Today we also know that the reverse is true, namely that energy can manifest as *matter.* Albert Einstein's famous formula $E = mc^2$ shows us that matter and energy are in fact *equivalent*. The following statement made by Einstein is from a 1948 film called *Atomic Physics.*

> *It followed from the special theory of relativity that mass and energy are both but different manifestations of the same thing - a somewhat unfamiliar conception for the average mind. Furthermore, the equation $E = mc^2$, in which energy is put equal to mass, multiplied by the square of the velocity of light, showed that very small amounts of mass may be converted into a very large amount of energy and vice versa. The mass and energy were in fact equivalent, according to the formula mentioned before.*

The theory that energy can be converted into matter has been proven. For example, scientists have observed highly charged photons of light known as 'cosmic rays' changing form and become matter. And when the waves of light, radio waves and X-rays are slowed down, they acquire mass and can be converted back to particles, while retaining some wave-like characteristics.

Matter Vibrates

According to the advances in Quantum Physics, the material things we see around us every day may actually be nothing more than a series of out-of-focus patterns that shift into focus in a certain way when we *observe* it, or when there is a certain expectation for it to manifest in a certain way.

Subatomic particles (electrons, protons, and neutrons) seem to be not made of energy, but simply is energy in its own right. This implies that matter actually consists of subatomic *patterns of vibration* within an organizing field that underlies a system's structure. From this perspective the human body, or any other living being or object, is a structure or a grid that consists of an organized *energy field* with several segments or patterns of *vibration.*

These findings about *vibrational frequencies* confirm the belief shared by many mystics and parapsychologists that each of our human senses is sensitive to a much broader range of frequencies than was previously believed. Even the cells in our bodies are sensitive to a broad range of frequencies. The fact that all these frequencies can be sorted, divided up, interpreted and constructed by the brain as different perceptions may be due to its *holographic nature.*

The world that we think exists as an objective reality may therefore just be a holographic blur of frequencies, from which the brain selects only a few frequencies to translate into sensory perceptions, which we then experience as our reality.

Matter Is Frozen Light

The measurement problem in Quantum Physics is another unusual phenomenon that has baffled experts for years. It was found that before matter manifests, it does not exist in a specific state, neither does it show up in a specific place, until it has been focused upon or observed. Only when a subatomic particle's behavior has been measured by *observing* it, can its actual state or future manifestation be predicted.

This strange behavior by particles was discovered in what is known as the 'double slit experiment', in which particles are fired at a wall through two vertical slits. It was found that when the particles are observed they behave more 'normally'. Like tennis balls they would either go through the left slit or the right slit before they hit the wall. But when they were not observed they sometimes went through *both slits at the same time*! That would be like a tennis ball splitting in two, or possibly turning into a paint ball or a water balloon, before it hit the wall, which would then enable the particle in question to be at two places at the same time in order to go through both the slits at the same time. The only way that this 'split' would be possible is if particles of matter *could also behave like waves* (similar to waves of light or sound). If you shone a light on the wall in the double slit experiment, it would shine through both slits at the same time.

This finding means that all types of matter, big and small, must be able to exhibit both *wave-like* qualities and *particle-like* qualities. In the past it was believed that electrons were particles existing at some point in space-time, but now we know that electrons are *not particles all of the time*, because they sometimes also behave like *waves*. This concept is known as the *wave-particle duality*. The most generally accepted explanation for the wave-particle duality is known as the Copenhagen interpretation, which states that all matter also exists as *waves of probability*. Although the physical world consists of the potential to be both particles and waves, it still functions as one interacting, integrated whole.

Until this dual nature of subatomic matter was discovered, it was unimaginable that particles could behave like waves, because it would in a sense mean that this book you are reading could also be something like a 'cloud of light', for example, instead of being a physical object (if it chose to behave in such a way). But you will not be able to observe it acting like a 'light cloud', because when you look at this book you expect it to be an actual, tangible book that you are physically able to hold and page through.

It is therefore possible that in your hands this book behaves as physical matter, and not as a 'light cloud', because you are observing it and expect it to behave as such. But according to Quantum

Mechanics it is perfectly possible that this book may at times turn into a 'light cloud' when you are not around to observe it!

The wave-particle duality further suggests that all matter may consist of various forms of light energy, for example. In *Vibrational Medicine*, physician Richard Gerber describes all matter as 'frozen light', because it is in essence light that has been slowed down and have thus become 'solid'. From the wave-particle duality perspective, the metaphysical concept that the Soul is a 'light body' manifesting as physical mat-ter therefore no longer seems all that far-fetched.

Matter Is Shaped By Observation

Quantum Physics shows us that our reality is somehow based on relationships, or tendencies, or correlations that have the potential to somehow manifest from a *complex set of potentials*. In other words, there may be no objective physical reality at all, only a *potential reality* that comes into being when it is observed or focused upon.

In the wave-particle duality we see, for example, that when we observe matter, the act of observing it somehow causes it to act in a more predictable or expected manner. But when we do not observe the particles, their behavior remains a 'cloud of probability' and they end up doing a little bit of everything. Sometimes particles go left, sometimes they go right and sometimes they act like waves and go both left and right at the same time.

One of the most interesting aspects of Quantum Physics is the role of the *external observer*, who not only brings matter into existence by observing it, but also influences how these particles and waves behave. It actually means that we may not be able to observe or think about anything without changing what we see. Several physics experiments have demonstrated that when a wave is observed it changes to a new state, and also that the *intention* or aim of an experiment will determine whether matter will behave like a wave, or a particle.

Subatomic particles are the basic building blocks of all matter. The fact that the double slit experiment has shown that these particles exist as both a wave and a particle at the same time suggests that the building blocks of every material object in our Universe has *no pre-existing state*. Matter exists as nothing and everything, all at once, until it is observed, until we focus on it, or pay attention to it, or think about it. Matter appears to remain mere *potential* until our consciousness manifests it in the physical world. The double slit experiment has shown that we not only shape the potential outcome through our observation, but that also our *expectation* of how the particles will behave determines the outcome.

The most compelling evidence that human consciousness plays an active role in the establishment of physical reality has come from thirty years of research conducted by The Princeton Engineering Anomalies Research (PEAR) program at the Princeton University's School of Engineering and Applied Science. The program studied "the interaction of human consciousness with sensitive physical devices, systems, and processes", and developed "complementary theoretical models to enable better understanding of the role of consciousness in the establishment of physical reality".

PEAR researchers Brenda Dunne and Robert Jahn conducted a series of experiments demonstrating that our thinking and our intentions can change or influence the outcome of events. Based on their findings, it appears that we do in fact create and shape our conscious reality, which is a universal truth known by the ancients and the mystics for millennia. According to the PEAR team the implications of these findings are far-reaching for our view of the world.

> *The evidence of an active role of consciousness in the establishment of physical reality holds profound implications for our view of ourselves, our relationships to others, and to the cosmos in which we exist. These, in turn, must inevitably impact our values, our priorities, our sense of responsibility, and our style of life.*

The implication of the PEAR findings and theoretical models, as well as phenomena like the double slit experiment, is that our thoughts and feelings become our reality, and that which we believe tend to *manifest in accordance with our expectation*, or how we perceive it. It further also implies that if all matter exists as a potential wave or a cloud of probability, then *anything that is possible could happen at any time*, and anything can manifest in our reality according to how we *choose to perceive* it.

Matter Exists In Many Places

A second explanation for the wave-particle duality, known as the *Many Worlds* theory, rejects the Copenhagen interpretation by suggesting that particles do not behave in one way or the other at a given moment, but that they actually behave in an infinite number of ways all at once, but *in different places.* This theory suggests that what we observe in our human reality is merely one of the probable behaviors of the particle, while that same particle may also be performing many other possible actions in *many other dimensions or universes.* To visualize this think of the stereotypical scenes in comedy films, where the actor believes he is looking at his own reflection in a mirror, but then discovers to his shock that his reflection is no longer mimicking his actions, but instead is performing its own actions!

The implication of this theory is that there are an infinite number of alternate or parallel universes beyond our known reality and that we may exist within all of them at the same time, but in different ways. In other words, while you are reading this book, you might also be somewhere else, in other parallel worlds or realities, busy dancing, cooking, climbing a mountain and sleeping in a hammock tied between two palm trees on an exotic island...all at the same time.

A number of modern scientific models propose that the Universe is in fact *multi-dimensional*, with at least six or more *hidden spatial dimensions* primarily composed of *non-physical matter*, also known as 'dark matter' and 'dark energy'. Could these hidden dimensions possibly include, among other possibilities, the Astral and the Etheric Planes we find in various metaphysical belief systems and esoteric traditions? These theories of a multi-dimensional Universe have far-reaching implications for the existence of an Afterlife, a Spiritual Realm or the concept of Heaven found in many world religions and spiritual traditions.

Matter Is Inter-Connected

There is another fascinating phenomenon to be found in Quantum Mechanics, known as the *theory of non-locality,* which suggests that nothing in the Universe is separate from anything else, that all points in time and space are the same. In other words, everything is *connected* to everything else, everything is *inter-related*, and the same consciousness is present in all things. However, this quantum theory has not yet been proven conclusively, but if all goes well it could soon be the one major breakthrough that may change Physics and modern science forever.

Until this concept of non-locality was discovered in Quantum Physics, Einstein's premise that matter cannot travel faster than the speed of light was a generally accepted principle. For something to travel faster than the speed of light it would have to break the time barrier. But quantum physicists discovered that under certain circumstances subatomic particles may be able to instantaneously communicate with each other, regardless of the distance separating them. Each particle always seems to know what the other is doing, whether they are a few feet or millions of miles apart. This phenomenon is a further consequence of the *wave-particle duality*, which allows for matter to manifest as particles or waves depending on how they are measured or observed.

In the article *The Wise Silence*, Robert Lanza says that according to the quantum mechanical view of reality "we are all the ephemeral forms of a consciousness greater than ourselves." He also states that the mind of each human being on Earth is instantaneously connected as "a part of every mind existing in space and time." This means that you and I are directly linked to each other consciously, as well as to all other minds in the past, present and future.

Matter Is Co-Conscious

Another quantum theory that strongly supports the idea that everything is inter-connected and co-conscious is the concept of *entanglement*. Research has shown that when subatomic matter, such as two electrons, are created together they remain forever entangled with each other. Scientists found that these two electrons behaved in a sense like 'psychic twins' who were somehow communicating telepathically. When the researchers changed the quantum spin in one electron, the other electron immediately also changed spin. Whatever happened to the one electron automatically and immediately happened to the other, even when they were miles apart in distance. Regardless of time and space these two electrons appeared to be permanently interwoven with each other.

In theory the two electrons could be separated by any amount of space – even the entire breadth of the Universe – yet they would still be connected to each other in such a way that the actions experienced by one would instantly affect the other. This means one of two things: either everything in the Universe 'touches' everything else and there is no time or space that separates things, or time travel is possible and information can be transmitted faster than the speed of light.

According to Big Bang theorists, every atom in the Universe was at some point in the past condensed into a singularity and the Universe may have expanded from a little orb of matter the size of a pea. From this theoretical perspective, time and space is merely an illusion created by our limited human perception. Beyond what we can see and feel there is an *inter-connected, co-conscious One-ness* that underlies everything and the Universe is like a hologram in which every little subcomponent contains the encoding or the 'DNA' of the larger whole.

There are several examples of entanglement that gives an unusual twist to the conventional view of reality. For instance, living heart muscle cells in a Petri dish will begin to beat together in a synchronized manner, although they are not touching each other. And when you set off a row of pendulum clocks at different times they will eventually begin to swing together in a perfectly coordinated rhythm.

Physicist Amit Goswami also conducted an experiment that showed how entanglement affects people. He had two people meditate together and then separated them into two rooms, so they couldn't see or hear each other. He then strobed a light over the eye of one person, which caused a measurable physiological response in the subject's brain. Amazingly, at the time this was done to the one person, the other person's brain also showed the same response in the other room, even though the second person was not exposed to the light at all. It appears therefore that we are somehow entangled with each other, something many of us have of course always known intuitively.

According to Bruce Lipton this study by Goswami demonstrates that "when two people become entangled, one person will conform to the energy of the other person". This there-fore confirms the humorous myth that life-long partners actually begin to look like each other after decades in a relationship, and it would also explain why some people seem to take on the appearance of their pets over time!

But our entanglement with everyone and everything around us also has much more serious implications for our health and happiness. Consider for a moment the potential effects your entanglement with negative people and unhealthy environments may have on your general well-being. "If your environment keeps draining your energy, it's like having a leaky bank account, where any money you're putting into the bank... keeps slipping out. You have to change your environment, including any harmful beliefs, before the energy can stay high," says Dr Lipton. From personal experience, I also recommend getting rid of poisonous people and toxic relationships.

The Holographic Universe

Several years ago Nobel Prize winning physicist David Bohm proposed a theory known as the *Holographic Universe*. Bohm states that objective reality does not really exist, that despite its apparent solidity the Universe is actually an intricate illusion, similar to a hologram with infinite layers, or segments, that each contains information about the entire whole. This view of reality is known as the *holographic paradigm*, and although many scientists have greeted it with skepticism, it has been welcomed by some. Please note that the intention of this theory is not to suggest that the Universe is an actual hologram. Instead it merely applies the concepts of holography to our understanding of the nature of reality. Viewing the Universe as a holograph provides a new insight and many potential answers to ancient questions about our consciousness and reality.

The term hologram is derived from the Greek words *holos* (whole) and *gramma* (message). A hologram is therefore a 'whole message', because each smaller piece of the hologram will always contain the information necessary to reconstruct the original, whole image. For example, when a photographic plate containing an actual holographic laser image is cut into two pieces and then illuminated by a laser, each half will still reflect the entire image of the original object. And when the halves are further divided, each quarter will once again contain a smaller, but complete version of the original. This process can be repeated an infinite number of times, and no matter how many smaller pieces the holograph is divided into, every little part of that hologram will contain a reflection of the whole.

It has been reported that a small, yet growing group of researchers believe that holography may be the most accurate model of reality science we have arrived at thus far. Furthermore, some believe it may solve some mysteries that have never before been explainable by science, and that it might even establish paranormal phenomena as a perfectly 'normal' aspect of nature. Numerous researchers, including David Bohm and his collaborator Karl Pribram, have noted that many parapsychological phenomena become much more understandable in terms of the holographic paradigm. It would, for example, readily explain how a mother and child is able to communicate telepathically while they are in different geographical locations, or how remote viewers are able to perceive tangible information about unknown targets thousands of miles away.

The Web Of Consciousness

Based on his holographic theory, David Bohm believes the reason subatomic particles in Quantum Physics are able to remain in contact with one another as seen in the *non-locality* phenomenon, regardless of the distance between them, is not because they are somehow breaking the time barrier to communicate with each other faster than the speed of light, but because the distance that separates them is an *illusion*. The particles are actually extensions of one thing, and not individual entities.

This concept brings new possibilities in our understanding of Eastern mysticism, psychic phenomena and even time travel. If the apparent separateness of subatomic particles is illusory, it means that at a deeper level of reality all things in the Universe are infinitely inter-connected and all of nature is ultimately one seamless *web of consciousness*. In a holographic universe, even time and space is an illusion and the past, present, and future all exist simultaneously.

Holography expert Frank DeFreitas states that, "It is therefore possible that the reason we could never record any transfer of energy between two subjects in telepathy was because there was no need to pass through the physical space in the first place. We were trying to detect and measure something that, through holographic principles, didn't exist. We were trying to measure fragmentation, not wholeness".

In the 1920s, brain researcher Karl Lashley found that no matter which portion of a rat's brain he removed, he was unable to destroy the animal's memory of how to perform complex tasks it had learned prior to surgery. This implied that memory is stored as a whole in every part of the brain, which does not make sense in terms of the generally accepted view that certain memories are stored in different areas of the brain.

Karl Pribram in turn described the brain as a hologram and used the concept of holography to explain this *memory storage phenomenon*. Holograms have an incredible capacity for information storage, so it also explains how the human brain can store so many memories in such a small space. By simply changing the angle at which two lasers strike a piece of photographic film, it is possible to record numerous different images on the same, small surface. Pribram's holographic model of the brain also explains how we are able to retrieve information so quickly from the billions of memories stored in our brain, and even more amazingly how it is possible that each and every bit of information seems to me instantly linked and cross-referenced with every other piece of related information, like the hyperlinks on a very complex and extremely fast website.

Interestingly, scientific validation for the concept of a Holographic Universe can be also found in Human Genetics and Microbiology, because every cell in the body contains the entire DNA needed to create or clone an entire person that is identical to the original.

Transpersonal Experiences

Stanislav Grof proposes that the holographic paradigm also offers a model for understanding many of the baffling paranormal and psychic phenomena people experience during *altered states of consciousness*. In the 1950s, Grof did many experiments involving the drug LSD, which revealed that when in an altered state of consciousness, subjects could provide startling details and accurate information about topics they had no former knowledge of. Grof's subjects appeared to tap into some sort of *collective unconscious*, which enabled people with little or no education to suddenly give detailed accounts of out-of-body experiences, precognition of future events, and regressions into past-life incarnations. The subjects' incredible stories were supported by in-depth, factually accurate descriptions of subjects like Hindu mythology or Zoroastrian funeral practices – topics they had no former knowledge of. In later research, Grof found the same range of phenomena manifested in therapy sessions which did not involve the use of drugs.

Because the common element in these experiences appeared to be the *transcending of an individual's consciousness* beyond the usual boundaries of Ego, as well as beyond the limitations of space and time, he called them *transpersonal experiences*. In the late 60's he contributed to the founding of a new branch of study called Transpersonal Psychology.

For years transpersonal researchers were unable to offer a mechanism for explaining the bizarre psychological phenomena they were observing, until the advent of the holographic paradigm. From this perspective the mind is actually part of a continuum, a labyrinth that is connected not only to every other mind that exists or has existed, but to every atom, organism, and region in the vastness of space and time itself. For centuries mystics have been very familiar with this *inter-connected, collective consciousness* of all that is, past, present and future. It is also known as the Book of Life or the Akashic Records, which can be described as an Omni-present, cosmic computer system or universal library containing recorded data of everything and everyone that ever was, is and will be.

Consciousness Creates The Brain

Keith Floyd, a psychologist at Virginia Intermont College, has pointed out that if the concreteness of reality is only a holographic illusion, it would no longer make sense to say the brain produces consciousness. Instead it is *consciousness that creates the brain*, as well as the body, and everything else around us that we interpret as physical.

Such a turnabout in the way we view biological structures has caused some more brave researchers to point out that medicine and our understanding of the healing process could also be transformed by the holographic paradigm. If the apparent physical structure of the body is but a holographic projection of our consciousness, it becomes clear that each of us is much more responsible for our health than current medical wisdom allows.

What we now view as 'miraculous' remissions of disease may actually be due to changes in consciousness, which in turn effect changes in the hologram of the person's body. Similarly, controversial new healing techniques such as *visualization* may work so well, because in the holographic domain of thought, these imagined images are ultimately as real as 'reality'. It has also been proven that daydreaming or fantasies are perceived by the subconscious mind as actual events and real experiences. Our subconscious mind cannot distinguish between that which is 'real' and that which is 'imagined'.

Consensus Reality

Although conventional scientific understanding is incapable of explaining the existence of spiritual manifestations, paranormal phenomena, extra sensory perception, energy healing and miracle cures, these experiences of many people all over the world become more tenable if 'reality' is actually a holographic projection. Perhaps what we perceive as 'reality' is just something 'we agree on', so that we all share the perception of what 'is there' or 'not there'.

This *consensus reality* that we choose to share is possibly formulated and consented to at the level of the *collective unconscious*, where all our minds are infinitely interconnected. If this is true, it is the most profound implication of the holographic paradigm of all, for it means that spiritual, metaphysical, psychic and paranormal experiences may currently not be commonplace for most people because we simply have not co-consciously programmed our minds with the beliefs that would make them more commonplace.

From the theoretical perspective of a holographic Universe there are therefore no limits to the extent to which we can *alter our reality*. What we perceive as reality is only a *field of potentially* waiting for us to mould it into the reality we desire. If the Universe is indeed a holograph, then nothing we used to believe about our reality would any longer make sense, and everything we perceive or experience as 'chance' or 'luck' or 'coincidence' or 'inexplicable' would suddenly make sense as *synchronicity* and an *underlying order* in the Conscious Universe. Even the most chaotic circumstances would reveal beneath its disorganized appearance an intricate network of graceful *harmony* and *symmetry*.

The New Worldview Of Consciousness

There are many parallels between modern physics and ancient Eastern philosophy, such as the Buddhist *Sutras*, the Chinese *Tao Te Ching* and the Indian *Upanishads*. The ancient wisdom traditions all agree that our reality and our Universe are beyond our complete human understanding, and therefore science will never be able to fully explain it. It seems inevitable that our scientific discoveries will continue to find possible new answers, but that these answers will only serve to raise more new questions. Our sciences are increasingly painting itself into a metaphysical corner.

All the progressive theories and concepts about *reality* and *consciousness* support what many sages, swamis and spiritual visionaries have known for millennia. They have been telling us for centuries that reality is not what it appears to be, that we have the power to shape and change reality, that we are all somehow interconnected, that there exists alternate realities or dimensions beyond our human perception and that the Universe is a conscious, expanding entity.

There will come a time in the future when many of these new scientific concepts will gain mainstream status as a part of the generally accepted *new worldview of consciousness*. Conventional science will ultimately have to embrace a new paradigm, born out of the new spirituality, which will be based on an acceptance of our capacity for *conscious evolution* of our species and *co-creation* of our reality.

The possibilities this offers us a global community would be incredible, like the reported results of the 'Maharishi Effect', through which so-ciety in general appears to receive benefits from only a small number of people participating in Transcendental Meditation (TM). It is believed that it can neutralize acute societal stress, in-cluding the ethnic, religious, and political tensions that typically lead to violence and conflict. The founder, Maharishi Mahesh Yogi, predicted that if only one percent of the population practiced Transcendental Meditation, the quality of life for the entire population would improve. Researchers with the Maharishi University of Management have shown that the Maharishi Effect was able to reduce crime and social violence, and improve positive trends throughout society. These research projects are however regarded with much disdain by the mainstream scientific community and once again described as a 'pseudoscience'.

To change this skeptical perspective, the new age of man will have to be defined by a reconnection of the secular and the spiritual, and the merging of the physical with the metaphysical. From this new paradigm we will need to integrate left and right brain thinking in our future efforts to expand our understanding of the Universe. We will also need to combine the forces of modern Western science with ancient Eastern wisdom. Our conscious and subconscious awareness must join forces, and we must fuse the natural with the supernatural.

The Story Of The Universe

According to cosmologist and geologian Thomas Berry the story of our shared Universe is the quintessence of reality.

> *We perceive the story. We put it in our language, the birds put it in theirs, and the trees put it in theirs. We can read the story of the universe in the trees. Everything tells the story of the universe. The winds tell the story, literally, not just imaginatively. The story has its imprint everywhere, and that is why it is so important to know the story. If you do not know the story, in a sense you do not know yourself.*

We will in time increasingly perceive our world in a more holistic manner and discover that everything in the Universe is actually interconnected, like a cosmic hologram in which each small component contains a reflection of the bigger whole. It makes no sense to continue to perceive the world as a collection of separate and unrelated parts that came into existence because of some random accident.

Critical Spiritual Mass

Physicist Basil Hiley writes that "we must be prepared to consider radically new views of reality". We are entering a new age where reductionism will ultimately be replaced by the *new holism*, and materialism will be supplanted by the *new spiritualism*. We really can choose to see our world in a different way and, most of all, we can begin to live differently *right now*, without the approval of the mainstream media, conventional science, public opinion or dogmatic religion. We do not have to wait for our metaphysical beliefs and values to be confirmed or proven beyond a shadow of a doubt by the scientific community.

We can continue on our quest towards greater spiritual connection and understanding. We can go ahead and share with each other, embrace our diversity, respect nature, protect the environment and cherish all living things. If we truly choose to stand together and take a collective evolutionary leap, we can ultimately even shift weather patterns and have a lasting influence on the global climate.

All that is needed is for you and me to make that choice to turn things around now; to make the decision to consciously push the evolution of humanity forward and make the world a better place. We are the masters of our own destiny, the creators of our own reality. You and I are Divine beings and we can choose to live a Divine Life.

Sadly, many of our fellow men remain sleeping deities, waiting to be aroused *en masse* to bring about the dawning of a golden age of greater harmony, peace and prosperity. If you are somewhat skeptical about the urgent need for us to consciously evolve and awaken spiritually at his point in our history, let me ask you this: If your life thus far has been so meaningful and remarkable, why are you feeling so restless or disillusioned? If having all this personal freedom in our modern world is so phenomenal, why are so many of us feeling so fearful, misplaced and jaded? If family, friends, romantic partners, or a Facebook profile are all we need to be happy, then why are we so disconnected and isolated. Why are many of us so lonely? And with all the advances we have made in science, technology and the arts, why are we still killing, starving and exploiting each other?

We have tried various philosophies, religions and systems of government, yet society remains a chaotic, unstable place with so many unhappy, searching people. What we need is a *spiritual revolution*, a soul awakening of immense magnitude, a global movement of man that will eventually reach critical mass. The sooner the better. It appears to be the only answer. As David Grinspoon states "the problem of survival is not fundamentally technological. It is spiritual and moral. It is evolutionary."

But how soon will we achieve this next evolutionary leap as a species? Will it become a reality in this generation, or at least the next? Will we achieved it on our own accord or will we be assisted by cosmic intervention? I have no doubt that we will ultimately evolve as a species to reach a new level of existence. We live in a continuously expanding Universe and I believe we do have much to look forward to. But what do we do in the meantime? Well, I for one plan to continue to develop my spiritual awareness and insight, and thus create a constantly improving reality for myself, together with a life of abundance and fulfillment. This is what I consider Divine Living.

Divine Living is the foundation of an increasingly conscious existence. It is the key to the mysteries of the human condition that has eluded mankind for centuries. The true meaning of your life can only be found in a Divine Life of conscious evolution and co-creation. All you need to do is reclaim the right to such a life, and it is easier than you may think.

To kick start your Divine lifestyle all you need to do is take the first step: simply acknowledge that we are more psychic than physical, more spiritual than secular. To do that you don't have to get togged up in saffron robes, or conduct pagan rituals. There is no need for any special process, religious conversion or mystical initiation. All it takes is a simple choice to accept that you alone are responsible for your own reality and that there is more out there than meets the eye.

Once you have made the decision to take control of your own destiny, instead of shaping your reality according to the limiting beliefs and outdated opinions of others, the door of your consciousness will swing wide open and set you free to reconnect with your Divine Self and your brand new Divine Life.

EPILOGUE

A New Kind Of Human Being

We are entering a new age of increased social and environmental responsibility, as well as unimaginable scientific and technological breakthroughs and currently inconceivable spiritual growth. For the first time in the history of our species we are now becoming more conscious of our Divine nature and our innate ability to shape our own evolution.

More and more of us are beginning to see that we do indeed create our own reality and that we are the masters of our destiny. More and more of us are beginning to gain access to formerly unseen realms that lie beyond the perception of our ordinary senses. More and more of us are waking up to our Divine origins and our place in the greater scheme of things. Once this new awareness has reached the point of critical mass we will collectively shift as a species into a much wider and more superior level of consciousness. Together we will be the architects of a New World and a New Way of Life for all.

An increasing number of people all over the world have been experiencing an acute spiritual transformation in recent years. This global awakening and shift in consciousness is the climactic culmination of a long process of spiritual evolution that began thousands of years ago. The early batch of pioneers in our previous stage of development included the Prophets, Messiahs and the Ascended Masters who were to set the scene for our next evolutionary leap. They began arriving on the planet as far back as 3000 years ago, and included among other Zoroaster, Abraham, Moses, Gautama Buddha, Lao Tzu, Confucius, Mahavira, Jesus Christ, and the Prophet Muhammad. The arrival of more teachers, gurus, saints, healers, sages and prophets followed. At first it was a tiny trickle that incrementally expanded over the centuries as we evolved and grew spiritually. With every new generation there came older souls with greater wisdom, insight and knowledge.

After World War II the next wave of evolved incarnations returned to the planet in increasing numbers. This group is today collectively known as the Lightworkers. They began to arrive as early as the 1940's and 1950's. The Lightworkers consist of a diverse group of souls who indentify with an array of spiritual paths and belief systems. They include among other the Indigo, Crystal and Rainbow children, as well as the Starseeds, Human Angels, Healers and other multi-dimensional and transpersonal incarnations. The Lightworkers are collectively acting as spiritual trend-setters and way-showers for all of humanity.

It is likely that you are also one of the first wave of 'new children' who arrived on our planet over the past century. We have been assigned several names and descriptions, as well as different theories about who we really are and why we came here at this time in history. Some believe that we are new kind of human being, others that we are the way-showers and pioneers to guide mankind through this period of rapid human evolution, while some hold the view that we are not at all from this planet - that we are representatives of an alien species.

It is all mere semantics to me. No matter what you choose to call yourself, I do believe that many of the people who are currently involved in the 'new spiritual revolution' are all part of an incredible group of very 'old' souls. I further share the belief that we have incarnated at this very special time in human history to guide humanity and serve the greater good. I guess you could say that we are the very first 'prototype' of a new kind of human being.

I hope you will join us on our collective mission to make the world a better place as we enter into a new age of conscious evolution. We really do need all hands on deck. May the energy of the Divine Self inspire you and the Light of the Soul direct you. Namaste.

REFERENCES

Agence France-Presse (AFP). *Online gamers crack AIDS enzyme puzzle.* September 18, 2011.

Borenstein, S. *Challenging Einstein usually a losing venture.* Associated Press, 2011.

Brooks, M. *13 things that do not make sen*se. New Scientist. Issue 2491. March, 2005. www.newscientist.com

Beck, M. *Thank You. No, Thank You. Grateful People Are Happier, Healthier Long After the Leftovers Are Gobbled Up* . The Wall Street Journal: Health Journal. November 23, 2010. www.online.wsj.com

Butler, S. *Inanna.* CG Jung Australia. www.zyworld.com

Cappon , D. *The Anatomy of Intuition.* Psychology Today. Volume: 26. Issue: 3. Sussex Publishers, Inc. 1993.

Choi, C. Top *10 Things that Make Humans Special.* August 22, 2011. www.livescience.com

Chopra, D. *The Seven Spiritual Laws of Success: A Practical Guide to the Fulfillment of Your Dreams.* New World Library / Amber-Allen Publishing, 1994.

Chown, M. *Anything Goes.* New Ṣcientist, June 1998, Vol. 158, No. 2137.

Comins N. *What If the Moon Didn't Exist? Voyages to Earths That Might Have Been.* HarperCollins, New York, 1993.

Counterbalance Foundation. *Counterbalance Interactive Library.*
www.counterbalance.org

Chromie, E. *Universal Answers in Static Electricity and a Swirling Magnetic Fields.* November 14, 2011. www.salem-news.com

Daniels, V. *Handout on Carl Gustav Jung.* Sonoma University.
www.sonoma.edu

Darnell, T. *The Hubble Deep Field: The Most Important Image Ever Taken.* www.deepastronomy.com

Davies, P. *The Christian perspective of a scientist.* Review of *The way the world is* by Polkinghorne. J. New Scientist, Vol. 98, No. 1354, June 1983.

Davids Landau, M. *Energy Healed Me -- Over the Phone! A Scientist Explains How.* October 19, 2011. www.huffingtonpost.com

DeFreitas, F. *Holomentation.* Holo-Gram Newsletter, Vol. 6, No. 2, 1988. www.holoworld.com

De Vries, M. *The Whole Elephant Revealed: Insights into Universal Laws and the Golden Ratio.* Ankh-Hermes, 2007.

De Waal, F. *The Age of Empathy: Nature's Lessons for a Kinder Society.* Crown Publishing Group, 2010.

Discover Earth. *Mass Exctinctions.* Discovery Communications, LLC. www.dsc.discovery.com

Eklund, D. *Divine Discontent.* Sunrise magazine, Dec 2005/Jan 2006. Theosophical University Press, 2005.

Ellermeier, F & Studt, M. *Cuneiform sign INANA*, Handbuch Assur 2003. www.wikipedia.org.

Emerson, R. *Self-Reliance.* Essays: First Series. 1841.

Emerson, R. *The Essential Writings of Ralph Waldo Emerson.* Modern Library, 2000.

Emmons, R & Kneezel, T. *Giving Gratitude: Spiritual and Religious Correlates of Gratitude*. Journal of Psychology and Christianity, 2005.

Ferlic, K. *True Freedom and True Creative Freedom.* Releasing Your Unlimited Creativity, 2007. www.ryuc.info.

Ford, A. *The Soulmate Secret: Manifest the Love of Your Life with the Law of Attraction*. HarperOne, 2008.

Frankl, V. *Man's Search for Meaning: An Introduction to Logotherapy.* Washington Square Press. New York, 1963.

Gagné, J. *Magical thinking: everything is about me.* www.jamesgagne.com.

Gonzalez, G. & Ross, H. 22. *Home Alone in the Universe*. First Things. www.firstthings.com

Greenstein, G. *The Symbiotic Universe: Life and Mind in the Cosmos.* William Morrow & Co, New York, 1988.

Grodzki, L. *Approaching A Theory of Emotion: An Interview With Candace Pert, Ph.D*. www.primal-page.com

Hicks, E. *The Secret* by Byrne, R. Prime Time Productions in association with Nine Network Australia. USA, March 2006.

Hicks, E & Hicks, J. *The Law of Attraction: The Basics of the Teachings of Abraham*. Hay House, 2006.

Hoggman, N. *Venus - What the Earth would have been like*. Space Daily. www.spacedaily.com

Horizon Research Foundation. *Death Bed Visions Study.* www.horizonresearch.org

Horizon Research Foundation. *Human Consciousness Project.* www.horizonresearch.org

Hutson, M. *Magical Thinking*. Psychology Today, March 2008. www.psychologytoday.com.

Inayatullah, S. *Eliminating Future Shock - The changing world of work and the organization*. September 12, 2006. www.futurist.com

Kuhn, T. *The Structure of Scientific Revolutions*. University of Chicago Press, 1962.

Lally, P., Van Jaarsveld, C. H. M., Potts, H., Wardle, J. *How are habits formed: Modelling habit formation in the real world*. European Journal of Social Psychology, 2010.

Lanza, R. *The Wise Science*. The Humanist Vol. 52, No. 6, 1992.

Lin, L. Back *From a Space Station Far, Far Away*. New America Media, Apr 19, 2008. news.newamericamedia.org

MacLean, K. *The Vibrational Universe (Spiritual Dimensions)*. The Big Picture, 2005.

Mann, F. *Wichita boy's garage-sale buy holds a treasure for his family*. The Wichita Eagle. May 25, 2012. www.kansas.com

Michalko, M. *Change the Way You Look at Things and the Things You Look at Change*. Creative Thinkering. August 29, 2011. www.psychologytoday.com

Miclaus, C. *The Golden Age of Mankind*. Buzzle.com. February 24, 2011.

Minow, N. *Interview: Tom Shadyac of 'I Am'*. Movie Mom, Beliefnet.com. March 30, 2011. blog.beliefnet.com/moviemom/

Moskowitz, C. *Is the New Physics Here? Atom Smashers Get an Antimatter Surprise*. November 17, 2011. www.livescience.com

National Opinion Research Center. *General Social Survey*. University of Chicago, 2006.

Norem, J. *The Positive Power of Negative Thinking: Using Defensive Pessimism to Manage Anxiety and Perform at Your Peak.* Basic Books, Cambridge, MA. 2001.

Packer, D. & Roman, S. *Contacting Your Divine Self.* Orindaben.com. LuminEssence Productions, 2011.

Parrott, W. *Emotions in Social Psychology*. Psychology Press, Philadelphia, 2001.

Pert, C. *Molecules Of Emotion: The Science Behind Mind-Body Medicine*. Simon & Schuster, 1999.

Polich, J. B. *Quantum Physics: Sensing Unbroken Wholeness.*

Poole, C, Miller, S & Booth Church, E. *Ages & Stages: How Children Use Magical Thinking.* http://www.scholastic.com

Princeton Engineering Anomalies Research (PEAR). *Scientific Study of Consciousness-Related Physical Phenomena* www.princeton.edu/~pear/

Reilly, T. *Moses.* The Catholic Encyclopedia. Robert Appleton Company, New York (1911). www.newadvent.org

Riedlinger, T. *Excerpts from Ralph Waldo Emerson's Harvard Divinity School Address.* Council on Spiritual Practices (CSP). www.csp.org

Roberts, J. *The Nature of Personal Reality*: a Seth book. Prentice-Hall, 1974.

Robinson, J.C. *Living the Myth of Inanna: A Descent into the Netherworld of Surgical Awareness.* Psychological Perspectives, Vol. 48, Issue 1, 2005.

Ross H. *Beyond the Cosmos.* NavPress Publishing Group, Colorado Springs, 1996.

Ross, H. *New Astronomical Proofs for the Existence of God.* http://www.reasons.org/resources/apologetics/newproofs.html

Russel, P. *The New Paradigm of Consciousness*. Evolutionary Theory Conference. November, 1999

Sample, I. *Kevin Nelson: 'Near-death experiences reveal how our brains work'*. The New Review, The Observer. March 13, 2011. www. guardian.co.uk.

Sample, I. *Living in the moment really does make people happier*. The Guardian. November 11, 2010. www.guardian.co.uk

Shepherd, P. *Transforming the Mind*. www.trans4mind.com

Smith, H. *Beyond the Postmodern Mind: The Place of Meaning in a Global Civilization*. The Theosophical Publishing House, Illinois, 2003.

Star Quotes. *Incorrect predictions Quotes*. www.quotesstar.com

Stenger, V. *The Myth of Quantum Consciousness*. The Humanist, May/June 1992, Vol. 53, Number 3.

Swaim, M. *5 Scientific Theories That Will Make Your Head Explode*. August 7, 2008. www.cracked.com

Telushkin, J. *Jewish Literacy: The Most Important Things to Know About the Jewish Religion, Its People and Its History*. William Morrow and Co., New York. 1991.

Than, K. *Particles Moved Faster Than Speed of Light?* National Geographic Daily News, September 23, 2011

The Center for Theology and the Natural Sciences. *Imago Dei ("image of God")* . www.counterbalance.org.

Timoshik, A. *Legless man climbs on top of the world*. Pravda.ru. May 17, 2006. www.english.pravda.ru

Todeschi, K. *Are Intuition and Psychic Ability the Same?* www.intuitive-connections.net. 2001

Trine, R. *In Tune With the Infinite*. 1910.

Van Loon, H. *The Story of Mankind*. Cosimo Classics, 2006.

Vastag, B. *2nd test affirms faster-than-light particles*. The Washington Post. November 18, 2011. www.cbsnews.com

Vaughn, S. *Global Ascension:* Evolution By Choice. April 30, 2011. www.seekingenlightenment.net

Ward, D.S. *Initiation - The Descent into Hades.* 1992. www.halexandria.org

Ward, P & Brownlee, D. *Rare Earth: Why Complex Life is Uncommon in the Universe.* Springer, 2000.

Weingarten, G. *Pearls Before Breakfast*. Washington Post. Sunday, April 8, 2007. www.washingtonpost.com

Wheeler J. *Law without law. In Quantum Theory and Measurement.* Princeton University Press, 1983.

Villanueva, J.C. *Wave Particle Duality*. July 22, 2009. www.universetoday.com.

Ware, B. *The Top Five Regrets of the Dying: A Life Transformed by the Dearly Departing*. Balboa Press Australia, 2011.

Wattles , W.D. *The Science of Getting Rich*. 1910.

Wikipedia. www.wikipedia.org. Various articles and subjects.

Zaki, J. *What, Me Care? Young Are Less Empathetic*. January 19, 2011. www.scientificamerican.com